THE CHANGE MANAGEMENT HANDBOOK

A Road Map to Corporate Transformation

THE CHANGE MANAGEMENT HANDBOOK
A Road Map to Corporate Transformation

Lance A. Berger

Martin J. Sikora

With

Dorothy R. Berger

IRWIN
Professional Publishing®
Chicago • London • Singapore

Sponsoring editor: Cynthia A. Zigmund
Project editor: Gladys True
Production manager: Laurie Kersch
Designer: Mercedes Santos
Cover designer: Tim Kange
Compositor: Publication Services, Inc.
Typeface: 10/12 Times Roman
Printer: Arcata Graphics/Kingsport

Library of Congress Cataloging-in-Publication Data

Berger, Lance A.
    The change management handbook: a road map to corporate
transformation / Lance A. Berger, Martin J. Sikora, with Dorothy R.
Berger.
       p. cm.
    Includes index.
    ISBN 1-55623-975-0
    1. Organizational change. I. Sikora, Martin, J. II. Berger,
    Dorothy R. III. Title
HD58.8.B472 1994
658.4'06—dc20   93–2663

Printed in the United States of America

6 7 8 9 0 AGK 0 9 8 7 6

Preface

The world is in a constant state of change as the 20th century winds down, and no business organization—in the United States or elsewhere—can escape the effects of operating on a continually evolving landscape. The forces of change are so great that the future success, indeed the very survival, of thousands of companies depends on how well they respond to change or, optimally, whether they can actually stay ahead of change.

That change exerts constant pressure—from such forces as industrial globalization, relentless technological advance, political upheaval, and opening of new markets—is widely acknowledged. But there is far less recognition of the need for individual companies of all sizes and types to shift their own gears in response to evolving developments in the world. And perhaps most disturbing is the poor batting average posted by companies that have sincerely dedicated themselves to change. Although a handful have scored seminal successes, the majority have failed to find the magic new mode or style that is needed in the volatile macroenvironment.

Identifying the primary reasons for this irksome difference and clearly delineating methods for aggressively combatting them are the primary purposes of *The Change Management Handbook*. Although the concept of a changing world has seemingly been explored to the most finite degree, *The Change Management Handbook* is the first work that spells out exactly how a company must execute its change actions—and promote a culture that places a premium on a comprehensive orientation toward continuous change.

Through firsthand experience and intensive research into cases of success and failure, the editors and authors have discovered that the winners have adhered to a concept of corporate alignment whereas the losers have let at least one key business element get out of their control. As *The Change Management Handbook* stresses, alignment comes at several levels, beginning with the alignment of the company to its market and the continual fine-tuning necessary to stay in step with customer needs and demands. Internally, alignment means ensuring continuous synchronization of four key business gears: a strategy that will develop a blueprint that attacks change, operations that are flexible and nimble enough to be quickly altered, a culture that encourages people to promote and work with change, and a compensation system that rewards people for buying into change and constantly seeking improvement.

The Change Management Handbook thus presents a road map for the actions needed to anticipate and execute change and simultaneously maintain alignment. It lists the specific actions that must be taken by senior business managers, by the people that they assign to implement change policies on line, and by the professional advisers they enlist to assist and monitor the change processes. The *Handbook* sketches the route that must be taken toward change and denotes the milestones, the turns, the stop signs, the red lights and yellow caution lights, and the sensing devices that keep people on the main road. But the *Handbook* does not set down rigid or generic approaches. In line with the *Handbook*'s dictum that companies must always be flexible and nimble, the approaches presented in the following pages stress the ways the basic format can be varied for firm- and market-specific situations.

The *Handbook*, then, is a practical, action-oriented document for use by change agents and managers. Its contents can be used to reference the entire process—from finding market changes to reaping the payoffs from the right responses—to determine how to fit two or more key elements together or to check out the change implications of just one facet.

The editors wish to thank our blue-ribbon group of authors who have crafted their array of skills both on the firing line and in the think tanks of change. They represent the leaders as well as the pioneers in the still-emerging discipline of change management, with its bedrock foundation of total alignment. They have contributed generously of their time and skills to *The Change Management Handbook* to provide excellent guidance for the business managers and their advisers who must live with change day in and day out.

We also are indebted to the nine change agents whose accounts, based on interviews with Lance Berger, of how they met the challenges of change have added a special dimension of practicality and experience to the *Handbook*. Some had the luxury of working their companies into a change environment; others were thrust into crises not of their making. But the remarkable way in which the concepts of alignment transcended all their experiences helped emphasize the key points.

The Change Management Handbook is dedicated to the families of the editors, who have been great sources of strength and support, notably Dorothy Berger, who has tirelessly assisted in editing, assembling, and processing our work, and Vivian Sikora, who has helped in editing and fact checking. The book is also dedicated to our parents, Henry Berger, Florence and Max Turk, and Anna Sikora; and our children, Adam, Craig, Cheryl, and Nancy Berger and Clifford S. Sikora, Esq., and his wife, Valerie. The *Handbook* is dedicated posthumously to Ruth Berger, who was a role model for women's rights and freedoms and who will be greatly missed.

The *Handbook* also is dedicated posthumously to Ralph Petersen, former Vice President of Human Resources at CPC International, a true professional and early change agent who was promoting the sound precepts of change long before most people even acknowledged that great change was a challenge. He is sadly missed but fondly remembered as a great mentor and a warm friend.

Contributors

Richard W. Beatty, Ph.D., Professor, Institute for Management and Labor Relations, Rutgers University, New Brunswick, NJ (Chapter 25)

Michael Beer, Ph.D., Professor of Business Administration, Harvard University, Cambridge, MA (Chapter 3)

Lance A. Berger, Chief Executive Officer, LBA Consulting Group, Bryn Mawr, PA (Chapters 1,30)

Terry L. Bowman, President, Global Concepts, Inc., Scottsdale, AZ (Chapter 26)

Jerrold R. Bratkovich, President, Business Issues Consulting, Opinion Research Corp., Princeton, NJ (Chapter 6)

Robert P. Breading, Senior Partner, H2L2 Architecture Design, Philadelphia, PA (Chapter 20)

Robin W. T. Buchanan, Managing Partner, Bain & Co., Inc., London, England (Chapter 10)

W. Warner Burke, Ph.D., President, W. Warner Burke Associates, Inc., Pelham, NY (Chapter 23)

Andrew Campbell, Director, Ashridge Strategic Management Centre, England (Chapter 10)

Alfred D. Chandler, Jr., Ph.D., Straus Professor of Business, Emeritus, Harvard University, Cambridge, MA (Chapter 2)

Daryl R. Conner, President, ODR, Atlanta, GA (Chapter 21)

Robert Cooke, Vice President, People Tech Consulting Inc., Toronto, Canada (Chapter 27)

Michael R. Cooper, Ph.D., Chairman and Chief Executive Officer, Opinion Research Corp., Princeton, NJ (Chapter 6)

William C. Copacino, Managing Partner, Strategic Services, Andersen Consulting, New York, NY (Chapter 16)

Keith T. Darcy, President, The Leadership Group, Inc., Pound Ridge, NY (Chapter 29)

Robert Davidow, Partner, Strategic Services, Andersen Consulting, New York, NY (Chapter 11)

Daniel M. Duncan, President, Management Structures & Systems, Inc., Louisville, KY (Chapter 14)

Randall G. Edmond, Ph.D., Senior Director, Opinion Research Corp., Princeton, NJ (Chapter 6)

Edward J. Giblin, Ph.D., Consultant, Ridgefield, CT (Chapter 32)

James W. Gouthro, Director of Consulting and Research, Baker, Rakich, Shipley & Politzer, Inc., Berwyn, PA (Chapter 5)

Judith R. Greener, Senior Director, Opinion Research Corp., Princeton, NJ (Chapter 6)

Thomas G. Gunn, President, Gunn Associates, Inc., Bryn Mawr, PA (Chapter 18)

Germaine Hall, Design Architect, H2L2 Architecture Design, Philadelphia, PA (Chapter 20)

Donald J. Kabat, Partner, Andersen Consulting, Florham Park, NJ (Chapter 19)

Robert L. Laud, Associate Partner, Andersen Consulting, Florham Park, NJ (Chapter 24)

Robert P. McNutt, Manager of New Compensation and Benefit Initiatives, E.I. du Pont de Nemours & Co., Wilmington, DE (Chapter 31)

Kenneth E. Mifflin, Associate Partner, Andersen Consulting, New York, NY (Chapters 9, 13)

Brian F. Morgan, Ph.D., Director, Opinion Research Corp., Princeton, NJ (Chapter 6)

Johannes M. Pennings, Ph.D., Professor of Management, Wharton School, University of Pennsylvania, Philadelphia, PA (Chapter 34)

Frederick F. Reichheld, Vice President, Bain & Company, Inc., Boston, MA (Chapter 8)

Anthony C. Rich, Managing Partner, Strategic Services, Andersen Consulting, Atlanta, GA (Chapters 9, 13)

Craig Eric Schneier, Ph.D., President, Craig Eric Schneier Associates, Princeton, NJ (Chapter 25)

James R. Sholder, Director of Corporate Planning, Baker, Rakich, Shipley & Politzer, Inc., Berwyn, PA (Chapter 5)

Martin J. Sikora, Editor of Mergers & Acquisitions, IDD Enterprises, Philadelphia, PA (Chapters 7, 12, 15)

Marti D. Smye, Ph.D., Chair, People Tech Consulting Inc., Toronto, Canada (Chapter 27)

Lyle M. Spencer, Jr., Ph.D., President, McBer & Co., Boston, MA (Chapter 22)

Bruce I. Spiegel, Principal, William M. Mercer, Inc., Philadelphia, PA (Chapter 31)

Dave Ulrich, Ph.D., School of Business, University of Michigan, Ann Arbor, MI (Chapter 28)

Michael Useem, Ph.D., Professor of Sociology and Management, University of Pennsylvania, Philadelphia, PA (Chapter 4)

Donald L. Weintraub, Senior Vice President, ODI, Burlington, MA (Chapter 17)

Martin G. Wolf, Ph.D., President, MAS Management Advisory Services, Inc., Philadelphia, PA (Chapter 33)

Introduction

The Change Management Handbook has been issued at a time when the stakes in successfully revamping a business are greater than ever. However, the *Handbook* and the concepts it encompasses have been evolving for decades.

The need to change a business so it meets the challenges of developing conditions in its marketplace is not new. It's been around perhaps as long as business and commerce themselves have been recognized forms of endeavor. But the rules have changed dramatically. The forces currently driving a business to change are more powerful than their predecessors and assert their potency far more frequently than in the past. Moreover, never before have so many "pile drivers" of change been in full force at the same time. The company of the 1990s and the early 21st century that is seriously interested in retuning itself must simultaneously deal with such issues as leapfrogging technology, globalization, political upheavals that have opened new markets, consolidation in major industries, environmental problems, dynamism in world population demographics, and alterations of legal systems.

As a result, the job confronting the change manager of the past was child's play compared with what his or her successors face today. And the realities that mark the road toward the 21st century demand an entirely new way of handling change. Companies no longer have the luxury of laid-back, trial-and-error, hit-or-miss approaches to change management that take huge amounts of time to implement. Tinkering has been replaced by decisiveness. Deliberation by speed. Halfway measures by total effort.

The company that gets in step with a ceaseless, systematic, companywide commitment to change management is the company that will be the winner after the smoke has cleared. That involves a total effort and nothing less. As we will blueprint in *The Change Management Handbook*, this commitment includes a process that starts with a formalized intelligence program to detect forces in the market place—or change triggers—that augur significant change for the business, changes that are powerful enough to destabilize the business. It is a process that has the company responding immediately to the trigger by taking actions to meet the competitive threats. It is a process that goes beyond the immediate responses to make sure that all primary elements of the company—under the umbrellas of strategy, operations, culture, and reward (compensation)—are totally in alignment and unified to get fully behind the new market responses. It is a process that will initiate major revisions in these four factors should any be found to be in conflict with the others. And it is a process with the goal of restabilizing the company so it can remain an effective competitor on a long-range basis—or at least until the next change trigger is spotted.

I have been fortunate enough to be in the business world during the past few decades as it moved from the era of inconsistent change and inconsistent response to the current era of rapid change and rapid response. That fact enables me to take stock of both periods, both to observe firsthand and to take part in change management efforts of various types and schools of thought. Most were well intentioned and, in general, timely. Yet I never ceased to wonder why some were striking successes and others were unceremonious duds. Why did some firmly stabilize the company, make it a stronger competitor, regain lost market share, or even prevent a threatened share erosion, with an actual gain in share? Why did others fall flat and perhaps force a company out of a changing market or even out of business? I concluded there were definite and definable reasons for the different outcomes. But what they were proved to be elusive. However, I was able to hone in closer on the "missing links" when I was given direct responsibility for assembling the strategic plan at the Hay Group, the Philadelphia-based worldwide management consulting firm. It was during this period that the concepts of *The Change Management Handbook* began to take shape. We were concerned that the rate of growth of our core practice—compensation, or the reward system employed by companies to provide incentives for its people—could slow down. At the same time, anecdotal reports from consultants suggested that clients were demanding higher value-added services. Exactly what was meant by higher valued-added services was not clear.

In retrospect, we realized our clients were telegraphing a change trigger that could damage the firm's alignment to its market. Although it was a little too early to fully recognize the concepts that are enunciated in the *Handbook*, we did know that there was enough evidence in hand to suggest that something had to be done.

I took an inventory of what we knew about the situation. Over the firm's 40-year life we, like our competitors, had transferred a great deal of our knowledge and technology to our clients. Basic compensation methodologies were becoming more well known to in-house practitioners. That reduced the market need for maintenance work by compensation consultants, such as follow-up consultations to ensure that programs were working well and to make adjustments if needed. These had been a traditional and major source of revenue for Hay and its competitors. But the impact of in-house expertise was even more far-reaching because the transfer of expertise could also affect our potential for new work assignments. What I would now call a change trigger was that the market no longer valued the services of compensation consultants as greatly as in the past simply because clients, through the instruction of my firm and its competitors, were now able to do much of the work at significant cost savings by themselves.

The prospect for destablization now existed, although none of us recognized it at the time. There was an intriguing ace in the hole, however. The request for value-added services—although we still didn't know what that meant—suggested that we had carved out enough of a reputation for quality and premium products, service, and delivery that the clients could be receptive to related offerings that we might present them.

So we started to review the results of a variety of analyses including the market research data that showed we had a preeminent position in slower-growing markets. The study was conducted by a multifunctional, multilevel global task force that confirmed our need to develop new services, particularly those that met clients' demands for higher value-added wares.

The next step was to get professionals from several practices together to shape an entirely new practice area that would reflect market requirements. Interestingly, and again this was something that wasn't quite defined at the time, we were actually ahead of the broad market's consciousness (although obviously not in front of the change trigger itself). We had, again without knowing it, sailed quickly and effortlessly through the zone of denial—the period immediately following the change trigger in which many firms try to sell themselves on the idea that either change is not imminent or they are so terrific that change will leave them untouched and unbloodied.

But being ahead of the market often is a two-edged sword. On the positive side, the firm in the vanguard starts out with a big lead over the competition. But there is the countervailing danger that the new and highly innovative offering is too far ahead, that the market is not ready for it. Market intelligence is required to determine if the new product's time has come or if the market requires conditioning prior to launch.

We had been conducting this intelligence through our market research and our multidisciplinary analysis. And we determined it was a bit early to move with our new product (practice). So we held back while preparing ourselves for a timely move through two key preliminaries. One was training our people in the discipline. The other was preparing to communicate with the market so that a broad segment of the management population would be receptive to our ideas. These actions evolved into important steps in the change management process that are discussed in this book.

Much like Milton L. Rock, the Hay managing partner and visionary, had done years before in his landmark *Handbook of Wage and Salary Administration,* we had to educate managers and executives about the implications and effects of the corporate reward system. In this respect, my goal was to work with my colleagues to transform our reward practice into a multidisciplinary service that spread it into even farther reaches of the business organization. What was the new practice? The discipline that we now call change management.

As a result, the market response that we had defined as a pressing need in our organization had actually become a metaphor for our clients' needs. Our work had determined that our clients lacked a unified approach to change management, were not nimble enough to change as quickly as the market demanded, and, when change was instituted, had no commitment to aligning the four key functions (strategy, operations, culture, and reward). Change was unsuccessful because a vital function needed to effect the change was in conflict with the other key elements and, therefore, change was being impeded. Our studies also affirmed how many companies shrug off the impact of change by bogging themselves down in the zone of self-deception and how, conversely, as in our case, many companies rush to market too soon with a response that the market is not yet ready to receive.

As the change management practice was coming together, I left Hay and veered off for a literary sabbatical that included working with Milt Rock on the grandchild of

Handbook of Wage and Salary Administration, The Compensation Handbook, and other endeavors. Three years later, I jumped back into the world of change management.

I must candidly admit, however, that the concept of change management is so new and so extensive that I could not handle the book on my own. My major function has been to tie often disparate pieces together—a process that has included designing and shaping the change management model, described in Chapter 1—to incorporate the major elements as operating parts, to format the book to reflect the components of the model and the change management process, to select the experts who could authoritatively comment on the individual elements, and to serve as a traffic cop to ensure that all of the contributors directed their best efforts to affirming the critical need for corporate alignment.

To turn the concept of change management into a book that lives and breathes as it prods people to action, I enlisted Martin Sikora as coeditor to add the literary touch. Marty is a colleague from my days at MLR Publishing, which followed my time at Hay. He has been fully prepared to facilitate the growth of the seedling that has been sprouting during all these years. Marty and I share many of the same beliefs about business concepts, and he has worked on various change management perceptions as editor of the premiere professional publication, *Mergers & Acquisitions,* and of several other successful business books. Marty brings the journalist's perspective of time and motion to change management, which adds an extra dimension to the book since it is at the heart of our change management ideas.

In other moves to nourish the seedling, we enlisted experts who have worked with me on change management or were my colleagues to write separate chapters. Collectively, these contributors constitute an outstanding collection of change management professionals. But more importantly, each author was distinguished by his or her willingness literally to push the envelope, to downplay traditional change management approaches and demonstrate how the bold and the ultrainnovative were the right ways to deal with change triggers that demand bold and ultrainnovative responses.

Finally, I am grateful to the senior executives that I interviewed because they shared with me their firing line experiences in successful change management. They all have done the job, and have done it well, acquiring invaluable skills and perspectives. We are pleased to have incorporated their views and experiences into our description of the Change Management Model in Chapter 1. These people include the following: Leonard Abramson, president of U.S. Healthcare; Jeff Boetticher, president and CEO of Black Box Corporation; Gary Fernandes, senior vice president of Electronic Data Systems; Paul Grunder, former president of CPC's Corn Products; James L. "Rocky" Johnson, chairman emeritus and retired CEO of GTE Corp.; Donald E. Meads, chairman of Carver Associates and former chairman/CEO of Certainteed Corporation; Joseph Neubauer, chairman/CEO of ARA Services; Stanley Silverman, executive vice president and COO of PQ Corporation; and Wayne Smith, former Airco Gases CEO.

Thus, *The Change Management Handbook* has been years in the formation and it has taken a team effort to produce it. But this underscores the pervasiveness of change management in both practice and impact. We have gathered the latest thoughts, the best talents, and the utmost in experience to size up the problems and demonstrate how they can be eliminated; and we have described firm courses of successful action that will allow change-minded companies to reach the goals that were set at the very beginning.

Change management is a big job and, yes, often a messy undertaking. But it is a task that can be done by committed people willing to work together. We hope *The Change Management Handbook* can help change-struck organizations accomplish their goals.

Lance A. Berger

CONTENTS

Chapter Twenty–Three
CRITICAL ELEMENTS OF ORGANIZATIONAL CULTURE CHANGE   285
W. Warner Burke

Chapter Twenty–Four
CULTURAL CHANGE AND CORPORATE STRATEGY   296
Robert L. Laud

I

THE CHANGE MANAGEMENT PROCESS

Structure of *The Change Management Handbook*

Section 3
The Gears of Change

3A Strategy
9. Game Plan for the Next Dynamic
10. The Strategic Connection: Mission, Strategy, and Values
11. Structuring the Change Initiative
12. Mergers and Restructurings: Aces in the Hole
13. Midcourse Corrections

3B Operations
14. A Bad Structure Can Be Fatal
15. An Introduction to Supply-Chain Management
16. Integrated Logistics and Supply-Chain Management
17. Only the Best: How Quality Systems Govern Change
18. Aligning Operations with Change Strategies: The Operations Blueprint
19. Information Technologies to Manage the Next Dynamic
20. The Change-Responsive Office

3C Culture
21. The Next Generation of Fire Walkers
22. The Right Stuff for the Next Dynamic
23. Critical Elements of Organizational Culture Change
24. Cultural Change and Corporate Strategy
25. Making Culture Change Happen
26. The People Factor
27. The Key to Corporate Survival: Change Begins and Ends with People
28. Human Resource Planning and Change
29. The Ethics of Change

3D Compensation
30. Aligning Business and Pay Strategy
31. Rewards for Executing Change
32. Compensation as a Change Stimulus
33. A Nimble Compensation System for Managing Change
34. Using Executive Compensation to Promote Change

Section 2
Market Change Triggers
5. Market Dynamics: Who's on Top?
6. Playing Off the Power Base: Importance of Market Positioning
7. Pile Drivers of Change
8. Measuring Change and Changing Measures

Section 1
The Change Management Process
1. Change Management
2. The History of Business Change
3. Managing Strategic Alignment
4. Driving Systemic Change

Chapter One

Change Management

Lance A. Berger

In 1989 Frederick Wang, chairman of Wang Laboratories, was outwardly optimistic about his company's prospects for working its way out of severe trouble. "We're a $3 billion company," he declared. "We're not just going to blow away." If Wang was assuming that size alone was a guarantee of survival, he was dead wrong. The company, which could not sustain its long reign as the leading supplier of computer-based workstations and other state-of-the-art office equipment, was unable to reverse its ill fortune. Within three years, Wang Laboratories' revenues had dropped nearly 50 percent, it had to file for court protection under Chapter 11 of the U.S. Bankruptcy Code, and major parts of the once-proud business were being sold piecemeal.

As starkly dramatic as the Wang story is, it is just one of many cases of one-time high flyers that have gone into tailspins during the 1990s. Many of the companies in trouble are much larger, such as IBM, Sears Roebuck, and General Motors. IBM, for decades the undisputed king of the hill in computers, is downsizing, forging technology alliances, and focusing more on clones and PCs. General Motors, also in a massive downsizing program, is considering the scrapping of several brands, retreating from the diversity strategy once regarded as a key strength. Sears, in an effort to refocus on its sagging core retail business, is cutting loose its highly profitable financial services operations.

All four companies are examples of reverse metamorphosis—turning from frog to tadpole. All were on top but couldn't stay there. They also share the same basic reason for faltering. They were unable to successfully manage the process of great change demanded by the changes in their markets that resulted from changing customer requirements, shifts in competitor strategies, or both. IBM kept pushing mainframe computers when technology dictated that customers move toward networks of smaller machines. GM failed to heed the market's shift toward higher quality cars and failed to streamline its manufacturing and part-sourcing processes to keep up with the times. Sears was hit hard by more cost-efficient and lower-priced discounters such as Wal-Mart and Kmart.

The parallels are alarming. The troubled companies were either slow to discern the changes or slow or reluctant to respond to them. Self-deception was a curse. The changes were regarded as passing fancies, or the companies perceived themselves as too big, too strong, or too good to worry about them. Wang's suggestion that size alone was an overpowering asset is a clear example. A deeper probe finds still more commonalities below the surface. Top management usually operated in isolation, unaware of the threats developing externally. There was typically an inability to align key organization processes with the market, too many people who were satisfied with the status quo and opposed change, a mismatch between the CEO and the business situation, a lack of honest self-examination, and weak or detached involvement by the board of directors.

Sadly, scores of other companies that have gotten in trouble and are trying to extricate themselves from potentially fatal difficulties followed the same route. In many cases, companies have given up on the abilities of incumbent managers to direct them out of danger—after all, they were the ones who got them into the jams in the first place—and have tapped retired executives, free of all baggage, to dispassionately direct the resurrections. Examples are John Smale (former CEO at Procter & Gamble who was named chairman at GM), Stanley Gault at Goodyear Tire & Rubber, Thomas Graham at Armco Inc., and Richard Clark at AKZO N.V. In each case, the CEO's style was considered inappropriate for dealing with the new business situation.

ARA Services president Joseph Neubauer thinks the best change manager CEO is one who has spent time at other companies before taking the helm. Neubauer, who helped remake the diversified service company by (among other things) turning managerial focus toward returns and profitability, says multicompany experience helps prevent a provincial outlook that impedes the nimbleness required for change.

Difficulties in managing and being receptive to change are not new, but they have become more problematic as the forces of change have grown both in frequency and in potency. However, many managements are oriented toward earlier times when things were done differently and conditions changed much less often.

Alfred Chandler, an economic historian at Harvard University, believes that the current problems can be traced to just after World War II, when major players in key industries began to find themselves in a vise of increasing competition and declining market share. Their response was to invest retained earnings into different businesses that had greater profit potential than their cores. Although this looked strategically and financially compelling, Chandler says, they began managing businesses they did not fully understand. As a result, Chandler adds, business decisions were driven more by financial considerations than by market or customer factors and measures. The process of market isolation began—after all, how could top management understand or touch base with several markets at the same time?—and the ability of multimarket companies to anticipate and respond to changes in the customer base began to erode. "Top management decisions were based on numbers rather than knowledge," Chandler observes.

It is incredible how well Chandler's description fits the primary examples of reverse metamorphosis, yet there are companies that have accepted change as a way of life and that structure their operations accordingly. They are the nimble and the quick. Although their methods differ, they are united in their dedication to their markets. Gillette operates through intense dedication to its core wet shaving business, with constant emphasis on technology and product upgrades that have the power to create change before a change is ready to take place. Motorola invests heavily in R&D and in a hard-driving quality control program to reduce product defects to a barely measurable minimum. Johnson & Johnson stresses entrepreneurship in developing new offerings for existing markets or actually creating new markets—even to the point of tolerating (within reason) project failures without penalizing the people involved.

In industries where change is much more common than stability, the best performers inject change detection into their management styles and sometimes try to create changes themselves.

Gary Fernandes of Electronic Data Systems telescopes the process to such a degree that a mere response, no matter how quick and how powerful, is not good enough. Fernandes prefers to deal from a position of strength—while things are still going well. "I would rather be in front of the power curve than behind it in terms of change," he says.

US Healthcare, the large and fast-growing HMO, has put itself ahead of the pack by setting medical quality standards for the healthcare providers it serves so that people are better able to make value-driven choices. From the change perspective, US Healthcare has taken a leadership position in an area where it can work the change controls itself.

From the successes and failures just enumerated, it is clear that any company that wants to succeed in the 1990s and beyond must have a systematic and well-oiled change management process in place. Given the frequency and potency of change, the system is no frill but a critical life-support network. Although approaches and mechanics may differ from company to company—indeed, an entirely generic approach is discouraged—the viable change management system shares these concepts and elements:

- The company must accept the fact that change is going to happen and recur frequently.

- A system must be put in place for early detection of *change triggers*—generally defined as the threats or opportunities that can destabilize an existing business situation. These triggers usually occur in the competitive market or the customer base, but can also be generated internally. In any event, they are so powerful that they necessitate a new way of doing things.

- The system must not allow the company to take an "it can't happen to us" attitude. This is what we call the *zone of self-deception* that can follow discovery of the change trigger. IBM, GM, Sears, and other companies spent too much time in the zone of self-deception and are paying the price.

- Once the triggers are spotted, the company must have a definite competitive program for combatting them or taking advantage of them—ultimately oriented toward the way customers are served.

- Whatever changes within the company are adopted, they must be executed so that four key levers—strategy, operations, culture, and compensation—are totally in alignment and the entire organization is aligned with the competitive market and customer base. A change in one primary internal element is always accompanied by changes in one or more of the others.

- Because change, whether good or bad, often is resisted in an organization, each company should have a sufficient number of critically placed people, known as *change agents*, who will spot the significant change and get the whole outfit to move on it.

- The board of directors must be actively involved in the change process. The chairman and the board's members must be considered change agents.

- The CEO must be a change agent in style, skill, and temperament, often taking the role of chief alignment officer. Only as chief alignment officer can the CEO significantly add value to his or her organization.

- As change management becomes more ingrained at more companies, U.S. firms should ultimately adopt the European governance style under which chairpeople of the boards are not chief executive officers because there is an inherent conflict of interest in the dual roles.

- None of the above measures will work unless the company has taken a blood oath—from the board on down—that the market and customer service rule the roost.

In the remainder of this chapter, I will explain the change management process in greater detail for use by the executives managing change. This chapter, in turn, is the gateway to the remainder of *The Change Management Handbook* in which this framework can be applied to a linked set of reference points that can expand the reader's understanding and ability to apply the change process.

WHAT IS CHANGE MANAGEMENT?

We define change management as the continuous process of aligning an organization with its marketplace and doing it more responsively and effectively than competitors. Alignment is the continuous synchronization of four key management levers—strategy, operations, culture, and reward. The reasons they must be in harmony will be discussed later, along with deeper analyses of what each lever symbolizes.

The concept of change management is grounded in the principle of continuous measurement and feedback on the people, processes, and systems within the organization, which is a play on the oft-quoted statement that people behave as they are measured. The corollary is that behavior will be sustained only if it is rewarded. No company can truly align itself to its market—which we describe as the customer base plus the situation surrounding the competitive jockeying for business—unless all its people are behaving as the market demands.

How Change Works

Figure 1–1 is the Change Management Model, which illustrates the flow of developments in a change situation. The inside circle represents the sequential execution of actions that begin with the detection of change triggers and run through steps leading to the decisive responses that culminate in restabilizing the company—at least until the next change trigger comes along.

The outside circle tracks the environment in the company that either stifles or encourages change. The most critical is the zone of self-deception, which invariably is mapped immediately after the change trigger is found. Staying in the zone too long can be fatal. It is a time of inaction when the competition and internal dysfunction may be increasing and the losses in the marketplace may become irretrievable. The sooner the company zooms through the zone of self-deception—or bypasses it altogether—and gets into the action phase, the better off it is and the more effective its response to change.

How Change Begins

The entire change process begins with a change trigger—actual and/or potential opportunities or threats that affect the company and destabilize it if not dealt with. Destabilization can manifest itself in such setbacks as loss of sales or customers, obsolescence or impairment of existing products, or reduced pricing and margins.

The trigger can begin in the company's market—either in the company's customer base or through an action taken by a competitor. IBM was destabilized because it stayed with massive mainframes at a time when technology was allowing construction of smaller computers with the same processing power. IBM was thus hit with a

FIGURE 1–1
The Change Management Model

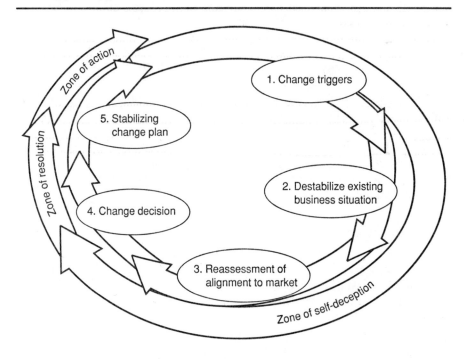

competitive assault on one flank and a customer backlash on the other. The newer styles of computers allowed companies to set up networks of smaller machines that would be more effective as they expanded their business locally and even globally.

The change trigger can also come in-house, through a need to change alignment in one or more of the four levers of company management. For example, utilities are used to operating as regulated monopolies and their cultures are oriented accordingly. As these markets become more competitive, the culture must change dramatically.

CPC International is a good example of a market leader rocked by change in the marketplace. The time was the 1970s when CPC's corn wet milling business, Corn Products, was stung by a combination of two new heavyweight competitors and the consolidation of key customers in industries including the paper, beverage, corrugated box, and textile industries. The initial response by Paul Grunder, the executive assigned to manage the change, was to shake up the culture by getting the message of trouble across and enlisting a series of younger, more nimble executives into the change program. Once that base was established, Grunder began to revamp the marketing and manufacturing processes needed to compete more effectively. Thus Grunder, before doing anything else, had to navigate Corn Products through the zone of self-deception quickly.

There is no limit to the origins of change triggers. Government policy, such as deregulation, can be a major source. Deregulation in the telephone industry, capped by the antitrust settlement that broke up the Bell system, was the change trigger that resulted in a great shake-up at GTE Corporation, according to former CEO Rocky Johnson. It forced the company to refocus on its telecommunications business (its cellular phone business is number two in a market growing at 30% annually) and discontinue its unrelated lighting and other industrial businesses. GTE now is attempting to marry its cellular business with its local phone service to create a seamless network that will allow customers to call almost anywhere with no difficulty.

In other instances, the thrust for change comes from within, or is of the company's own making. PQ Corporation's change was driven by its evolution from a small specialty chemical company to a $400-million multiproduct company in 20 years. PQ was a model of alignment in refitting the ship. The structural reorganization was keyed to deemphasizing small SBUs and creating three global businesses that were highly related and would maximize technology transfer between them. The culture was geared toward a participative, highly communicative mode that maximized commitment to PQ as a group. Compensation was harmonized with these other tenets to reward those who maximized profit best, strove for quality, achieved results in the face of tough times, and acted as team players.

As in the case of Airco, the trigger can be an external/internal combination. Former Airco chief executive Wayne Smith said the shifts resulted principally from a desire to get more out of a very large retail network in its merchant gases operation, which had been sharply expanded by 23 acquisitions. The management initiatives were difficult because this was basically a commodity industry where differentiation was uncommon. Smith hit upon a value-added approach—a marketing system in which Airco stores would sell not only products, but engineering and other services that showed customers how to reduce their consumption of industrial gases and lower operating costs.

Gary Fernandes at EDS regards nothing less than "success" and "failure" as the primary change triggers. Indeed, Fernandes thinks of "success" as the more important trigger of the two. "You have to reinvent yourself while you are not peaked out and you are still looking forward," he says. "Constant change is required to reinvent the corporation in order to sustain success. It's not the success itself but the sustaining of success that should be the change trigger. More often, however, the follow up to success is death and atrophy." Fernandes talks in terms of creating failure: constantly challenging his work force by having them seriously question whether even a successful accomplishment couldn't be done better. The change trigger with the most dire consequence is the threat of very real failure.

That's what faced Donald Meads when he took control of Certainteed Corporation in 1974 just as it seemed the building materials firm was about to go over the precipice because of a disastrous venture into real estate. Strategically, the initiative looked great—a form of vertical, forward integration in which Certainteed fiberglass insulation, roofing materials, piping, and other products would be used by its construction affiliate. Whipsawed by the mid-1970s recession, surging interest rates, and some dubious practices at the real estate unit, however, the whole idea went sour, leaving Certainteed with unsold properties, huge mortgage finance debts, and a real estate investment trust (REIT) that was quickly heading south. Compounding the financial problems was what Meads found in-house: management dysfunction at the top level that resulted in a cultural malaise. Meads had to start by reorganizing the top staff, replacing them with people who shared his vision, and then working things out with creditors. Within six months, real estate operations were folded up and the work force shrunk from 12,000 to 8,000. A drastic situation required drastic action. Certainteed moved into the black only a year later and subsequently became the flagship of its parent company's portfolio.

Jeff Boetticher of computer peripherals maker Black Box Corporation also was driven by a need for speed, but his job was complicated because he had to reverse the strategies of his heroic predecessor. Although the company had achieved 13 straight years of increasing sales and earnings, it had, as the CEO position shifted hands, run into a change trigger. Black Box's basic markets were eroding in the sour economy of the early 1990s and the firm's internal structures were impeding a quick response. Boetticher ultimately solved the problem by steps that included speeding up deliveries and rewarding the people who expedited service. Before moving, he had to educate the company that despite the successes of the past, the market had engineered a change trigger that demanded a new way of operating.

Regardless of where the trigger comes from, it must be recognized as an actual or potential destabilizing agent. The proof of destabilization usually is registered in phase 2, when the company starts to suffer, and forces even the well-managed company into phase 3, where it will reassess its alignment to market. Destabilization means that the four key elements of alignment are no longer synchronized with the market situation. Realignment isn't that easy, however, because change is often an unpleasant message that touches off self-deception and denial that change is needed, especially among managers who are smug from years of living off the fat of the land. As a result, every organization must have a corps of change agents who recognize the impact of a change trigger and champion the cause of change until the organization becomes aware of it and acts. Paul Grunder was a professional change agent at Corn Products.

Boetticher of Black Box was also a change agent, and he used communication to let the people know that a change was on the way. The emphasis was on the need for this change. Indeed, Boetticher determined that communication was his first job. He used action—in the form of the reward system initiatives—rather than words to make the necessary points. Boetticher dramatized the need for swifter deliveries by changing the bonus formula from one based on overall corporate success to one based on success of individual departments and business units. For example, 75% of bonus compensation was tied to meeting unit goals and objectives. The warehouse fulfillment teams, a pivotal element in the delivery apparatus, extended order-taking hours and got behind same-day shipments, with 99.4% accuracy. "Those employees earned 140% of their bonus, and nothing else suffered as a result," Boetticher said. Compensation became a measurement system—actual pay and bonus outlays formed the quantitative side—for changing employee behavior.

The right percentage of change agents is very important. An organization needs a certain number of people in key roles, and these people should have some level of protection so they can be effective. The exact percentage is related to the company's stage of development or growth; mature companies require more change agents and growing companies probably require fewer because growth itself is a state of change. And remember that too many cooks spoil the broth; however, too many change-oriented people can start to fix something that isn't yet broken by pressing for change when it is not needed.

THE BUSINESS SITUATION AND ALIGNMENT TO MARKET

A very important interim step before moving to the action phase is to determine the company's business situation. Different situations require different responses in both change management and alignment. Figure 1–2 combines much of the traditional thinking of General Electric Company and McKinsey & Company with some of the new concepts espoused by Reichheld (Chapter 8), Rich (Chapters 9 and 13), and Gouthro and Sholder (Chapter 5).

The framework links a company's market situation—the conditions in the market it serves—with the business situation, which is at least partially cued by the market situation. The market situation emerges in part from the type of customers in the marketplace, their aggregate demand, and their special requirements and demands. The second component is the competition—how many competitors are out there and the basis on which they compete: volume, market share, pricing, niche, profitability, and other factors. Grunder's job at Corn Products was highly complex because the corn wet milling business was hit from both sides at the same time.

Bear in mind, however, that the competition component also includes what is happening in adjoining markets where product and service substitutes may be developing to act as destabilizers, such as plastic components for metal parts in autos, or commercial finance companies as alternatives to banks for business lending.

FIGURE 1–2

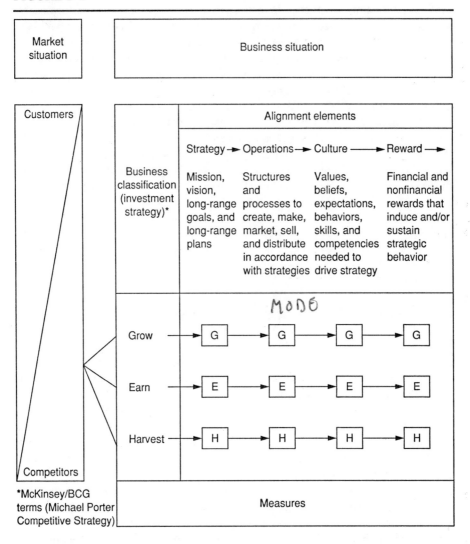

The market situation invariably influences the individual company's business situation as determined by its mode (grow, earn, or harvest). The company can be in a grow mode—invariably riveting on the top line—because the market is growing or there may not be much competition, or both. Earn-mode companies operate in markets of slower growth or virtually no growth, where emphasis may be on market share or cost cutting. In the harvest mode, the company's market is stagnant or in decline.

In each mode, the types of strategies, operations, culture, and reward systems are different, as are their alignment and the way they are aligned to the market. Change triggers can force change by affecting either the market situation or the business situation.

EDS has moved from a growth mode to a new and somewhat hybrid classification of quality growth: growth will continue to be important, but new business has to yield higher profit margins. GTE was able to move toward a growth mode through its big bet on cellular telephones. PQ, despite its sweeping change, had the clear aim of remaining in an earn mode. Airco is trying to change a potential harvest situation into an earn mode, and US Healthcare is structured to remain firmly within a growth mode. In the culture area, for example, US Healthcare discourages titles, allows no memos (which CEO Leonard Abramson calls "cover your ass" communiques), and bars meetings between 9 A.M. and 4 P.M. Abramson regards all of these artifacts as anathema to the entrepreneurial growth mode he stresses and prefers that his "tigers" go to each other in person when they want to talk and make a quick decision.

Interestingly, both of the growth companies have strong ideas about whom they will recruit for key jobs. Management candidates come from working-class backgrounds; and people who attended state universities, rather than Ivy League institutions and their peer schools, are preferred. The secret ingredients: hunger and willingness to change.

Regardless of the mode and some differences in the way culture is executed, there is a shared belief among change-minded companies that looser is better. The fewer the bureaucratic layers and the easier it is for various levels of managers and employees to mix and communicate, the more in touch with the market and the more adaptive to change the company will be. Gary Fernandes of EDS prefers individual efforts to team approaches in certain situations, saying that teams cannot "look around corners, but individuals can," whereas PQ encourages "team players" and even has that as a criterion in its reward package. CEO Leonard Abramson of US Healthcare abhors meetings as impediments to getting things done, but PQ thinks meetings can be valuable forums for communicating, especially if a member of top management sits in.

ARA's Joe Neubauer sums up the idea when he says that the CEO, as a change manager, ought to be in touch with the entire organization to create trust, detect trouble spots such as disharmony, and develop the channels for a free flow of information in all directions. Clearly that is what Boetticher of Black Box had in mind when, saddled with 36 reporting managers, he quickly took steps to streamline the process. In a move to "start empowering my managers"—thus driving decision-making closer to the market—Boetticher distributed responsibilities downstream. This also gave him more time to deal with broader and long-range issues and to spend additional time with the eight people who continued to report to him.

THE MARKET SITUATION

In Figure 1–3, we have developed a variation of the Company Position Industry Attractiveness Screen described by Harvard University strategist Michael Porter.[1] Our version emphasizes the role of the customer base as a greater determinant of business classification or investment strategy. It is this classification that drives the various alignment sequences outlined in the illustrative chart in Figure 1–4.

Each business classification has a unique alignment pattern. When a business classification changes vertically, so must the alignment sequence. The early detection and plan for rapid realignment (managing through the zone of self-deception) become essential ingredients for successful change management. The reassessment of the market situation leads to a reassessment of alignment.

Reassessment of Alignment

Once an organization recognizes actual or potential destabilization prospects, it must begin the reassessment of its alignment to market (phase 3). This inverse process consists of the following steps:

Establishing the current and projected business classification (grow, earn, or harvest).

Creating an ideal alignment model to describe the set of relationships between strategy, operations, culture, and reward required by the market situation.

Ensuring that the organizational readiness in each dimension corresponds to a new or existing alignment model.

This process can take place only through the implementation of a well-designed process driven by a group of change agents and change managers (including members of the board) who will perform the assessments and make the final decision on whether a business classification change is demanded or whether the existing classification will continue.

Change Decision

Once the analysis of market and internal alignment is complete, an organization must make one of three decisions:

Do nothing or make minor adjustments.

Create a set of major vertical alignment adjustments to ensure continuation within a given classification.

Create a major set of horizontal adjustments (paradigm shift).

Phase 4 begins the *zone of resolution,* which is signified by the issuance of an alignment blueprint (Figure 1–5) that describes a realistic representation based on

FIGURE 1–3
Business Classification ✓

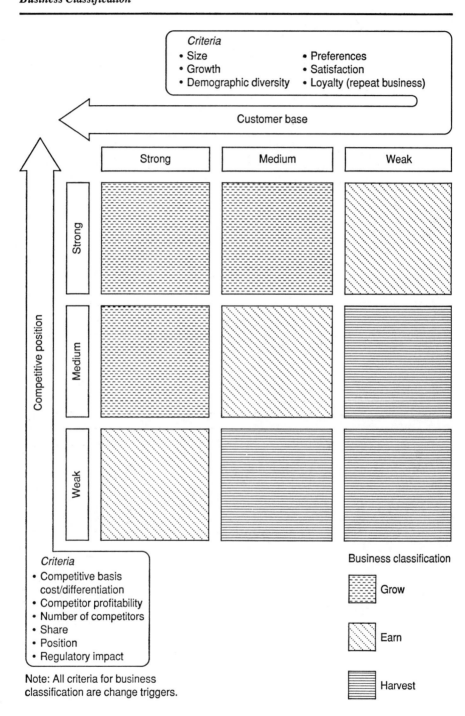

Criteria
- Size
- Growth
- Demographic diversity
- Preferences
- Satisfaction
- Loyalty (repeat business)

Customer base

Competitive position

| Strong | Medium | Weak |

Strong

Medium

Weak

Criteria
- Competitive basis cost/differentiation
- Competitor profitability
- Number of competitors
- Share
- Position
- Regulatory impact

Note: All criteria for business classification are change triggers.

Business classification

Grow

Earn

Harvest

FIGURE 1–4
Alignment Model

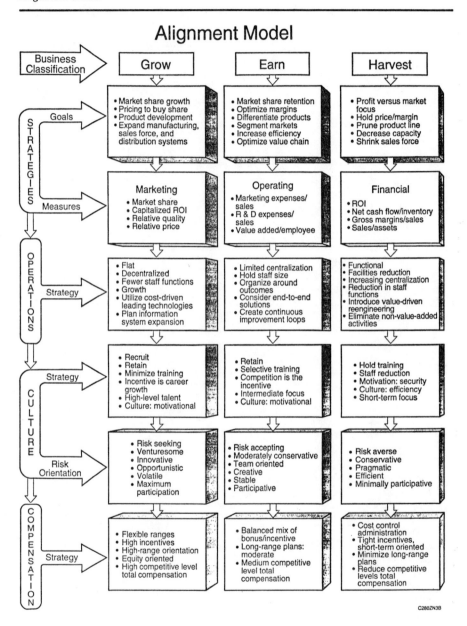

Alignment Model

Business Classification → **Grow** | **Earn** | **Harvest**

STRATEGIES

Goals

Grow:
- Market share growth
- Pricing to buy share
- Product development
- Expand manufacturing, sales force, and distribution systems

Earn:
- Market share retention
- Optimize margins
- Differentiate products
- Segment markets
- Increase efficiency
- Optimize value chain

Harvest:
- Profit versus market focus
- Hold price/margin
- Prune product line
- Decrease capacity
- Shrink sales force

Measures

Marketing
- Market share
- Capitalized ROI
- Relative quality
- Relative price

Operating
- Marketing expenses/ sales
- R & D expenses/ sales
- Value added/employee

Financial
- ROI
- Net cash flow/inventory
- Gross margins/sales
- Sales/assets

OPERATIONS

Strategy

Grow:
- Flat
- Decentralized
- Fewer staff functions
- Growth
- Utilize cost-driven leading technologies
- Plan information system expansion

Earn:
- Limited centralization
- Hold staff size
- Organize around outcomes
- Consider end-to-end solutions
- Create continuous improvement loops

Harvest:
- Functional
- Facilities reduction
- Increasing centralization
- Reduction in staff functions
- Introduce value-driven reengineering
- Eliminate non-value-added activities

CULTURE

Strategy

Grow:
- Recruit
- Retain
- Minimize training
- Incentive is career growth
- High-level talent
- Culture: motivational

Earn:
- Retain
- Selective training
- Competition is the incentive
- Intermediate focus
- Culture: motivational

Harvest:
- Hold training
- Staff reduction
- Motivation: security
- Culture: efficiency
- Short-term focus

Risk Orientation

Grow:
- Risk seeking
- Venturesome
- Innovative
- Opportunistic
- Volatile
- Maximum participation

Earn:
- Risk accepting
- Moderately conservative
- Team oriented
- Creative
- Stable
- Participative

Harvest:
- Risk averse
- Conservative
- Pragmatic
- Efficient
- Minimally participative

COMPENSATION

Strategy

Grow:
- Flexible ranges
- High incentives
- High-range orientation
- Equity oriented
- High competitive level total compensation

Earn:
- Balanced mix of bonus/incentive
- Long-range plans: moderate
- Medium competitive level total compensation

Harvest:
- Cost control administration
- Tight incentives, short-term oriented
- Minimize long-range plans
- Reduce competitive levels total compensation

C280ZN3B

FIGURE 1–5

The ABC Company Alignment Blueprint (Business Classification = Growth)

Mission	Financial Goals
To have a major impact on the global electronics products industry by providing customized and computer standardized software solutions to end users and third parties	To provide superior growth and return to investors when compared with competitors + 20 percent revenue per year + 8 percent ROI

Market Distinctiveness	Market Goals/Measures
• Depth and breadth of industry expertise • Premium products • Large contact network • Customization capacity • Customer relations systems	No. 1 market share in chosen market No. 1 in ROI in chosen market Grow at 5 percent more than market (25 percent for this industry niche)

Operations	Business Strategies
• Centralized R & D • Centralized manufacturing • Four levels of structure is maximum • Limited staff functions	Identify and introduce new products before competitors Emphasize premium pricing for new products and customer service Reduce pricing—aim for volume—with mature products Create and implement a globalization plan using five design criteria: service definition, defined target market, recognized customer service, early product introduction

Core Competencies	Compensation Stategies
• Software design quality • Direct sales • Knowledge of decision makers and their processes	Equity orientation (ESOPs) Broad salary ranges Moderate base salary target (High total compensation target) Combination individual/group incentive

Key ABC Values	
Customer focused	Respect for customer/each other
Creativity	Quality focused
Leadership orientation	Support of individual differences
Teamwork/cooperation	Honesty
Well managed	Integrity
Innovative	Risk accepting
Willingness to experiment	Respect for local communities

"the art of the possible." This alignment blueprint creates the framework for the change plan.

Four types of change are most likely to emerge from the change decision. Each type describes the degree of gradation in the change, although in each case the change is significant. The four types are as follows:

Linear change   Generally, this is a major move within the same market, product line, or business, but the move is into an area not previously penetrated. IBM's late move into PCs is an example.

Geometric change   The change an individual company must make is part of a very significant change trend within an industry or market. Consolidation within the airline industry, with the plethora of 1980s mergers resulting from deregulation manifesting the trend, is an example of geometric change. The consolidation in the defense industry (mergers, firms giving up their military operations, and other consolidations) resulting from federal budget cutbacks in defense is another example.

Quantum change   This term refers to a move by a company into a related market or technology to support or extend its core business. AT&T's acquisition of NCR Corporation to build a world-class computer capability it could not quickly develop on its own is an example. The deal gives AT&T an edge in the convergence of telecommunications and computer technologies.

Metamorphosis   The company totally remakes itself, invariably by leaving the industry in which it was born. Greyhound Corporation (now called Dial Corporation) sold its bus business to concentrate on consumer products. Allied Corporation, now known as Allied-Signal, turned itself into a high-tech firm from an old line maker of commodity chemicals.

The Change Plan

As the organization passes through the zone of resolution, it moves into the zone of action. The organization is now ready to restabilize itself against the change triggers. An illustrative change plan is outlined below.

The Berger Company Change Plan

1. Formally communicate your new alignment blueprint to all stakeholders in ways appropriate to each group.

2. Make a visible symbolic change in the organization to signify the enhancement or change in a business classification and the basis for the resulting alignment model. These changes could involve replacement of key executives and/or organization structure change—the crisis factor.

3. Introduce a new performance management system (the main change driver) focusing on goals, measures, and rewards necessary for the realignment of the organization to its market situation. Use cascading goals, measurements, and rewards to drive the company objectives to the lowest levels of the organization while creating training programs to introduce new skills and competencies; initiate technology, process, and facilities restructuring and team development.

4. Create a *vision group* (a multifunctional, multilevel unit) made up of change agents and change managers around key customer, competitive, or internal alignment issues. These people will take scanned information and drive it through the organization in the form of proposed action plans. According to Michael Beers, this process must incorporate the capability "to discuss the undiscussable." Be sure that the change agents and managers have CEO/COO sponsorship.

5. Gain control of the *gatekeepers* (recruitment, promotion, and termination processes) and immediately link them to the requirements of the alignment blueprint. Make sure the correct culture mix is being developed to meet business requirements. Install a mandatory time job movement program encompassing all jobs, including that of the CEO. Such a program would include promotions, rotation, and skills enhancement. Planned movement will embed the change process into the infrastructure.

6. Train people in self-discipline and the process of managing change. People must see the benefit of managing change or they will resist it. Michael Beers says that "compliance without commitment will not lead to real change." The recent failures of total quality programs and the reduction in applications for Baldrige quality achievement awards support this hypothesis.

7. Make sure you have the correct distribution and positioning of change agents, change managers, facilitators, buffers, and resistors for your business classification. This will ensure that the change will be introduced and managed in an orderly way (Figure 1–6).

8. Establish and promote a core set of business ethics (change stabilizers). This code must survive any change in alignment.

9. Continually communicate the status of the company's market and internal alignment in an open and constructive way.

10. Codify the trigger scanning process to continually assess opportunities and threats to the customer base, competitive position, and internal alignment. Empower the scanners and make sure that the board is part of the scanning process. There must be continual assessment of the market and internal alignment as well as assessment of readiness to change.

FIGURE 1–6

Illustrative Distribution of Change Types

Business Classification	Change-Types				
	Agents	*Managers*	*Facilitators*	*Buffers*	*Resistors*
Grow	H	L	H	L	N/A
Earn	M	M	M	M	N/A
Harvest	L	H	L	H	N/A

H = High   M = Medium   N/A = Not applicable

11. Don't be afraid to experiment with change. Some changes will be linear, others geometric, others quantum, and still others will be metamorphoses.

12. Remember the underlying principles of alignment to market: continual and pervasive measurement, reward for achievement, and continual cultural adaptation.

Before this plan can begin, however, the board must reevaluate the CEO and COO to determine whether their current competencies and style fit that of the projected business classification. Daryl Conner's chapter (Chapter 21) presents the generic profile of a change-oriented CEO. For example, a grow CEO should not automatically direct a paradigm shift to an earn mode or vice versa. Similarly, no CEO should hold the position if he or she is viewed as an organization custodian. Once annointed, the CEO change manager should be ready to implement realignment.

Culture Mix

Each company culture's readiness for change can be expressed in terms of its distribution of change types. Without the proper mix of these change types, a company will probably not be able to make the required adjustments to continually align itself with its market. No CEO or COO will succeed without managing the mix through recruitment, promotion, and termination.

Five profiles of change types are broadly defined below:

• *Change Agents* These are people who have recognized a change trigger and its impact and who have a passion to force an organizational response. Successful change agents all have organizational sponsors, and well-managed companies such as Motorola and Apple have legitimized the role. The board of directors should also include some change agents. Frequently, change agents are ostracized from an organization because their message is not welcome. To ensure their safety, each must have a well-positioned sponsor.

• *Change Managers* Sometimes change agents can become change managers, but most likely they will not. Change managers go beyond the old concept of leadership because they incorporate authority conferred from above and respect from below with a capacity to plan, organize, and implement change plans quickly and decisively. They are the nimble managers described by Daryl Conner. Unlike change agents, they are able to develop flexible processes for change and tend to rely heavily on others rather than solely on themselves. They are capable of using the system to gain results.

• *Change Facilitators* All individuals who actively support change managers are change facilitators. They can be located at any organizational level and any function. They commit to, rather than comply with, the change plan and thereby ensure its success. The majority of people in any organization must be change facilitators.

• *Change Buffers* People who passively resist change or comply without commitment are change buffers. They typically deny the need for change, and when change programs are implemented, they feel that they've "been through this before." This behavior was most likely seen in General Motors' and IBM's attempts to generate a more responsive organization—executive change buffers never saw the benefit of change. Change buffers can serve a legitimate role in forcing the organization to consider all options before actions are taken, however.

• *Change Resistors* These are people who campaign against change because of their perceptions that change will have a severe negative impact on them personally. They are strong agents of the NIH (not invented here) syndrome and are the least likely to make an adaptation. Change resistors can and do destabilize existing organizations. No organization can tolerate change resistors. They are the organizational equivalent of internal terrorists.

Each business classification suggests a different change-type distribution. An organization must close the gap between its existing organizational culture and the types required to implement the change plan. The only way to manage this cultural change is by gaining control of the gatekeepers.

Gatekeepers of Change

Equal only to goal-setting and measurement in driving change are the gatekeepers (those processes involved in recruitment, promotion, and termination). Few organizations adequately address management of gatekeepers. These are the entrances, elevators, and exits to the institution. The tenets of the alignment blueprint must be embedded in gatekeeper processes and all managers must be thoroughly trained in their execution. A key role of the board is to ensure that the organization, beginning with the CEO selection, is managing its gatekeepers. Wayne Smith, formerly of Airco, speaks extensively of building organization values into performance appraisal and selection processes.

FIGURE 1-7

Integration

Phase	Description	Impact	Functions	Agents
1	Change trigger	Destabilize	Board/CEO/Top management/Vision groups/Scanners	Change agents
2	Existing business situation	Creation of opportunity or threat	CEO/Top management/Planning/Business units	Change agents/Managers
3	Alignment to market	Reassess	Chairperson/CEO/President	Change managers/Facilitators/Buffers
4	Change decision	Hold, modify, or change business classification	Board/CEO/Top management/All Functions	Change managers/Facilitators/Buffers
5	Change plan	Stabilize	All staff/Customers/Suppliers	Managers/Facilitators/Buffers

Figure 1-7 summarizes the key aspects of the change management process described in this session.

This chapter captures the essence of a change management system required to survive and to thrive in the 1990s and into the next century. It is specific enough to light the way through the rough waters of change, yet flexible enough to allow individual companies to take the initiatives that suit them best. Ultimately, a common thread links all companies trying to make it these days. They must recognize that change is never-ending and they must recognize that managing change is no longer for amateurs.

We must develop a cadre of change agents and managers at each company, led by the CEO and actively promoted and monitored by the board of directors. That calls for nothing less than the emergence of change management as a new management discipline and, most likely, a new profession.

The impact on corporate governance, as the change management profession and orientation takes hold, should be great. It calls for a split function at the very top. The CEO should become the primary change manager and the chief alignment officer. If the system is to work, the CEO needs a strong board of directors to keep watch on his or her change efforts. In that setup, the CEO must be separate from his or her role as board chairperson and give this job to an independent outside board member who can operate more freely as an independent change agent. This dynamic will enable companies to successfully and continuously align themselves with their markets.

NOTE

1. Porter, M. E. *Competitive Strategy: Techniques for Analyzing Industries and Competitors.* New York: The Free Press, 1980.

Chapter Two

The History of Business Change

Alfred D. Chandler, Jr.

T he challenge of change management in the 1990s can be better understood if it is viewed in the context of corporate expansion, contraction, and restructuring during the recent past. The issues and challenges for today's managers, particularly those heading large industrial enterprises that are the core of any competitive modern economy, are the outcomes of strategies taken and structures shaped during the 1960s, 1970s, and 1980s. This chapter reviews the history of this cycle of expansion, contraction, and restructuring, relating it to rapidly changing technology, intensified competition, and turbulent markets during those years.

The economic and technological trends driving corporate change in the 1990s actually began to take shape a decade before. And a primary legacy of the 1980s is the bundle of methodologies and techniques that were developed or refined during that 10-year period to manage change and capitalize on the opportunities it offers.

COMPETITIVE, TECHNOLOGICAL, AND FINANCIAL BACKGROUND

Intensified competition and new production technologies set off the current cycle of expansion, contraction, and restructuring. After World War II, American industrial enterprises dominated both global and domestic markets. But by the mid-1960s, the European economies and their industrial companies had regained their prewar strength. By then, Japan, after a massive transfer of technology, largely from the United States, was preparing to enter global markets. By the mid-1960s, foreign competition was becoming intense.

At the same time, major new technologies were demanding increased expenditures in production facilities and in research and development. Their emergence intensified product and process competition, not only between companies in the same industry but also with firms in related industries. For example, by the 1970s chemical companies were competing with oil, glass, metals, food, paper, textile, and drug companies in the markets created by the commercialization of new manufactured materials. At the same time, new electronic devices (most importantly the computer, which stimulated a sweeping information revolution) demanded increased investment in new and improved facilities and the development of new technical skills.

Many American companies responded to the competitive and technological challenges in the same way their predecessors had, by investing retained earnings into improvement of their existing capabilities. The chemical companies provide a good example. But others searched for investment opportunities in industries that appeared to show greater profit potential than their own, even though operations in these industries called for organizational capabilities very different from those their firms traditionally employed. For the first time in American industrial history many firms began to grow by entering businesses in which their enterprises had little distinctive competitive advantage. Because they lacked knowledge of the operations of the target industries, they had to obtain facilities and personnel through merger or acquisition. This unprecedented strategy of growth into industries whose operations required capabilities that were only distantly related or totally unrelated to those of the acquiring firm raised unprecedented problems of management and altered relationships between the managers of these enterprises and the financial community.

By 1969, the drive to grow through merger and acquisition had become almost a mania. In 1965, the number of sizable mergers and acquisitions was just over 2,000. It rose to 4,500 in 1968 and to more than 6,000 in 1969. Then the mania waned as the economy softened, interest rates rose, and inflation jumped amid an energy crisis. By 1974 the number of mergers had dropped to 2,861. During the period 1963–72, close to three fourths of the assets acquired were for product diversification. One half of these were in unrelated product lines. In the years 1973–77, one half of all of the assets obtained through merger and acquisition were from industries unrelated to the buyer's core business.

Such unprecedented diversification led to another phenomenon unprecedented in American business. That was the separation between top managers at the corporate office—the executives responsible for coordinating, managing, planning, and allocating resources for the enterprise as a whole—and the middle managers responsible for maintaining the competitive capabilities of the operating divisions in the battle for market share and profits.

Massive diversification led to a separation for two reasons. First, the top managers often had little specific knowledge of or experience with the production processes and markets of many of the businesses they had acquired. Second, the large number of different businesses in the corporate portfolio created an extraordinary overload in decision making at the corporate office. Before World War II the corporate office of large, diversified, international enterprises rarely managed more than 10 divisions, and only the largest as many as 25. By 1969, numerous companies were operating 40 to 70 divisions and a few owned even more.

Because most senior executives had neither the training nor the experience necessary to evaluate the proposals and monitor the performance of so many divisions in so many different activities, they had to rely increasingly on impersonal statistics to set policy and reach decisions. But, as Thomas Johnson and Robert Kaplan point out in their *Relevance Lost: The Rise and Fall of Managerial Accounting,* such data were losing relevance in devising realistic cost controls and understanding the complexities of competitive battles.

Even so, the problem lay less in the data than in their use. The rapid growth of firms meant an increase not only in the number of divisions but also in their size. Many divisions themselves had become multiproduct and multiregional. So the coordination of product flow and the responsibilities for performance in terms of profit and market share were assigned to profit centers within divisions. In the 1960s, for example, General Electric Company and ITT Corporation each operated more than 150 such profit centers. This meant that the statistical return on investment (ROI) data, as they applied to performance, profit, and long-term plans, were no longer the bases for discussion between corporate and operating management. Instead ROI became a reality in itself—a target sent down from the corporate office for division managers to meet. Since the compensation and promotion prospects of managers depended on their ability to meet these goals, middle managers had a strong incentive to adjust their data accordingly.

In the postwar years, capital budgeting, like the monitoring of performance, became more statistically based. In the late 1950s, a capital budgeting model was introduced to determine long-term ROI of proposed capital projects. The new concept was a more precise determination of the earning rate required to make a project profitable. The model was used to determine the cost of time and to incorporate risk—the longer the time, the greater the risk, the larger the rate. Such seemingly precise estimates of anticipated project costs, if taken literally, could shorten managers' investment time horizons.

Moreover, these capital budgeting exercises, as well as strategic review processes, often failed to incorporate complex nonquantifiable data related to the nature of specific product markets, factory methods, competitor's activities, and organizational settings. The same was true of ROI figures used to evaluate the performance of profit centers and divisions. Top management decisions increasingly were based on numbers rather than on knowledge.

Managerial weaknesses resulting from the separation of the executive suite and operating management quickly led to another phenomenon—the selling off of operating units in unprecedented numbers. Before the mid-1960s, divestitures were rare. By the early 1970s, they had become unexceptional. In 1965 there was only one divestiture for every 11 mergers. In 1969, at the height of the 1960s merger wave, the ratio was 1 to 8. By 1970, it was 1 to 2.4, and for the four-year period of 1974 to 1977 the ratio was close to or even less than 1 to 2.

The unprecedented number of mergers and acquisitions, followed quickly by an unprecedented number of divestitures, helped to generate still another phenomenon—

the buying and selling of corporations as an established business, and a most lucrative one at that. Although industrialists pioneered in this business, the financial community prospered from it. This new activity changed the role of investment banks from assisting their clients in marketing securities to financing long-term capital investments to profiting from the buying and selling of corporate entities themselves.

This new business was further stimulated by the rapid growth of a relatively new type of financial institution: the mutual and pension fund administered by professional managers. Before World War II the majority of corporate securities were held by relatively wealthy individuals and families. Even as late as 1952, only 4.2 percent of the U.S. population (including owners of mutual funds) held corporate securities. After World War II, increasingly large numbers of the voting shares of American industrial enterprises entered the portfolios of pension and mutual funds.

The funds began in the 1920s and suffered severely during the Depression years of the 1930s but started to come into their own in the 1960s. The success of the fund managers was measured by their ability to have the value (dividends and appreciation) of their portfolios outperform the Standard & Poor's 500 Index. To meet their portfolio objectives, they constantly had to buy and sell securities—transactions based far more on short-term corporate performance than a long-term potential. Eventually these portfolio managers—as the new owners of American industry—increasingly traded securities in large blocks of 10,000 shares or more. Block trading accounted for only 3.1 percent of total volume on the New York Stock Exchange in 1965. By 1985 it accounted for 51 percent of share turnover. During the same period, the volume of total transactions on the Exchange surged from close to 1.5 billion shares annually in the early 1950s to 3 billion at the end of that decade to 27.5 billion by 1985.

The great increase in the total volume, the rise in the turnover rate, and the growth of block sales led to still another phenomenon—the institutionalized market for corporate control. For the first time individuals, groups, or companies could obtain control of well-established enterprises in industries in which the buyers had no previous connections simply by purchasing their shares on the stock exchange. Large blocks of stock were being traded regularly; and buyers had little difficulty in raising funds for control purchases from financial institutions and financiers.

The full impact of the market for corporate control was felt only in the 1980s. As the figures on divestitures indicate, corporations began in the 1970s to realign their lines of business. In many cases, the reshaping was carried out in an unplanned manner. Often the acquisitions simply were not performing as expected. But in many companies, senior executives began to carry out more systemically the realignment of their business portfolios. Such long-term competitive strategies in some cases led to unfriendly takeovers. Unfriendly or not, the acquisitions and mergers of the 1970s were investment oriented. That is, their purpose was to help ensure long-term profitability of the acquiring companies.

But in the 1980s, the predominance of hostile takeover activity shifted from the strategic deal to the transactional merger and acquisition, essentially a deal driven purely for financial purposes. They were initiated and carried out by investment bankers, financial entrepreneurs, and wealthy individuals, as well as in a few cases corporate managers, primarily for the short-term profits to be made from the transaction itself. The 1980s were the glory years of corporate raiders, "bust-up" takeovers, junk bonds, and leveraged buyouts (LBOs). Transaction-oriented deals weakened the long-term productive and competitive strengths of their targets. They hastened the advance of foreign competitors into global and U.S. markets, particularly competitors from continental Europe and Japan. In those countries investment banking houses and other financial institutions still concentrated on working closely with their corporate clients to maintain long-term profitability.

Nevertheless, for all its turbulence, the 1980s was the decade when senior managers of U.S. industrial enterprises focused successfully on realigning their product line portfolios to make the fullest use of the organizational capabilities their firms had developed. At the same time they adjusted internal structures and accounting systems to manage their core businesses more effectively. By 1990 most major U.S. companies were well on the way to completing this painful restructuring process.

CORPORATE RESTRUCTURING IN THE CHEMICAL, FOOD, AND MACHINERY INDUSTRIES

The results of the process of corporate expansion, contraction, and restructuring can be illustrated by the experiences of three different types of industries—chemical, food, and machinery.

The chemical industry typifies the high-tech industry in which continuing development of new products and processes has been essential to maintain competitive strength. In machinery, where the product has remained much the same over the years, competitive strength rests primarily on product design, on maintaining the best practices, and on low-cost techniques of production. In food, where truly new products were even more rare than in machinery, competitive success has been based more on effectiveness in marketing and distribution than on product design and process improvement.

Chemical

In chemicals, some firms overdiversified through acquisition in the 1960s and pulled back in the 1970s and 1980s. But the industry's fundamental post–World War II challenge was to exploit the opportunities of a new technology. During and after the war the science of polymer chemistry created vast new markets for synthetic materials that replaced existing products made from natural fibers, wood, and metal. By 1970, synthetics accounted for more than 70 percent of the fibers produced in the United States. New plastic materials, themselves constituting a major U.S. industry by 1970, new pharmaceuticals, and new biological and agricultural chemicals also reached the market. All of these products in turn were produced from a number of new commodity polymer chemicals such as those identified by the initials PP, PS, PVC, LDPE, and HDPE.

Between 1959 and 1970 the overall chemical market grew at an annual rate of about 2.5 times the growth rate of GNP. By 1970 the chemical industry was making the largest annual capital expenditures for production facilities of any major U.S. industry. Only the electronics and aircraft and aerospace industries (heavily government funded) recorded larger expenditures for R&D than chemicals.

During the growth years, some industry leaders, such as DuPont, Monsanto, and Rohm & Haas, concentrated on end products whereas others, including Dow, Union Carbide, and Hercules, focused on production of commodity polymer chemicals. Simultaneously all of them continued to produce nonpolymer products as well. The firms concentrating on commodity chemicals integrated backward, acquiring oil refineries and even oil fields. The same concern for assured supplies also prompted the firms focused on specialty products to maintain their production of commodity chemicals.

Competition quickly intensified. Foreign firms moved into the production of polymer chemicals as did companies in related industries such as oil. Overcapacity soon reigned. Unit costs rose as new plants operated well below a minimum efficiency scale. The oil shocks of the 1970s exacerbated the problem. Oil, which had sold at $1.80 a barrel in 1970, was at $34.00 a barrel by 1979.

The response to the fierce competition, increased production costs, and the sharp rise in raw material costs led to one of the most significant industrywide restructurings that occurred in the United States during the 1980s. The chemical companies, whose organizational capabilities had been shaped by commercializing new products and processes, sold off their commodity chemicals to oil companies, whose capabilities rested on exploitation of the scale economies inherent in massive continuous process production. By the end of the decade, the oil companies dominated commodity chemicals, and the chemical companies were moving ahead in specialty intermediates and in such end products as additives for gasoline and food, industrial coatings, enzymes, new fibers, fiber and metal composites, new engineering plastics, ceramics, imaging equipment, electronic materials, biological chemicals, and pharmaceuticals.

This realignment process was carried out almost totally by senior executives of the companies involved. Investment banks and financial institutions played their traditional role in facilitating investment-oriented mergers and acquisitions. Only a few damaging transaction-oriented mergers occurred. Samuel Heyman's hostile acquisition all but eliminated GAF Corporation as a major chemical firm, whereas his unsuccessful raid on Union Carbide seriously crippled its restructuring efforts. Under Edward Hennessey, who took office as CEO in 1979, Allied Chemical became a conglomerate and changed its name to Allied Corporation. Hennessey was more interested in profiting from the buying and selling of companies than from the making of products. After Allied merged in 1985 with Signal, another conglomerate headed by Dr. Michael Dingman, the resultant consolidated company, Allied-Signal, had only a quarter of its sales remaining in chemically related products. But with these few exceptions the restructuring in the chemical industry provides an outstanding model of successful corporate reshaping during the 1980s.

Food

Food and also tobacco companies differ from chemical firms not only because R&D investment is much smaller—1982 R&D investment in food was $917 million compared with more than $4 billion in chemicals (Hall 1990)—and production processes are less technologically complex but also because competition has been much less intensive. Only a few foreign food firms have moved into the U.S. markets. Japanese and German foodstuffs are still rare on supermarket shelves. Nor have many companies from other industries added food products to their lines. A number of sensational transaction-oriented mergers and acquisitions occurred, RJR Nabisco and Beatrice being among those that received much notoriety. But such transaction-oriented deals were atypical. As one study documents, during the period of 1978–87 companies with substantial shifts in debt-equity ratios (a useful indicator of transaction-oriented mergers and acquisitions) employed only 1.6 percent of the food industry's workers (Hall, 1990).

In the 1960s and 1970s, major food companies including Borden, Campbell Soup, Quaker Oats, Heinz, Ralston Purina, CPC International, Pillsbury, and General Mills—all long-established enterprises—diversified into markets where they had little competitive advantage in the hope of getting wider profit margins and faster growth. But by the 1980s, they pulled back to lines that fitted their core capabilities.

General Mills provides a well-documented example (Donaldson, 1990). In the late 1960s, General Mills began to move from its food processing core into crafts, games and toys, apparel, jewelry, specialty retailing, restaurants, and specialty chemicals. In 1968, 89.5 percent of its sales were in food processing. By 1976, the food processing sales dropped to 61.8 percent.

But in the late 1970s, with the arrival of a new CEO, restructuring and reemphasis on food began. Specialty chemicals went first; then toys and fashions. By 1988, 72 percent of General Mills' sales and 82 percent of profits came from consumer food products. The funds from the divestitures were reinvested in facilities, in building the marketing force, and in purchasing blocks of the company's stock. Other food companies carried out comparable moves. As at General Mills, these investment-oriented strategic moves were determined and implemented by senior corporate managers. Food companies thus provide a useful model of expansion and restructuring in industries where expenditures for production and facilities and R&D are relatively low and where international and interindustry competition is not intense.

Machinery

The experience of the machinery and transportation equipment industries differed sharply from that of the high-tech chemicals and low-tech food. In these industries the products themselves—sewing, agricultural, construction, and mining machinery, and trucks, buses, and automobiles—remained much the same. But continuing long-term investment in production facilities and R&D was essential to meet increasingly fierce international and interindustry competition. Transaction-oriented mergers and acquisitions of the 1980s were the most numerous in machinery and transportation equipment and the most damaging to the competitive strength of any U.S. industry. More than in any other industry increases in debt, particularly those made to fend off hostile takeovers, resulted in a sharply reduced investment in R&D and capital facilities. The cutbacks came at the exact time that investment in new materials and improved production processes were needed the most, because in the 1980s, Japanese, German, Swiss, and Swedish firms that had adopted the new computer technology (CAD/CAM) and computer numerically controlled machines were driving forcefully into the United States as well as into global markets. At the same time, U.S. machinery and commercial vehicle firms were moving into each other's market. Providing funds for essential facilities and R&D activities required either a cut in dividends or external financing by increased debt or equity. Either move too often brought a drop in the price of shares, which, in turn, attracted the attention of transaction-oriented financiers.

Even without the intervention of Wall Street, intensified competition and the cost of new facilities and equipment brought down such major American companies as International Harvester, Allis-Chalmers, White Motor, and Studebaker-Worthington. On the other hand, John Deere, Caterpillar, Eaton, Paccar, and Cummins Engine (despite fighting off two takeover threats) were able to make the necessary investments in R&D and in new equipment to maintain strong dealer organizations and to negotiate successfully with labor unions. So, too, did firms with a focused strategy of related diversification, such as Ingersoll-Rand, Dresser Industries, McDermott, Cooper Industries, and FMC. They successfully realigned their product portfolios, selling off some lines and buying others that offered a better fit. They did so in much the same way that the chemical and oil companies realigned their product portfolios at the same time.

But other major machinery and equipment firms were severely crippled and in some cases destroyed by financial entrepreneurs working with investment banking houses. Thus, Paul A. Bilzerian, financed by Shearson and T. Boone Pickens, obtained control of Singer Co. after the October 1987 stock market crash. He had sold off eight of Singer's 12 divisions before he was indicted in May 1989 on charges unrelated to the takeover and later convicted, sentenced to jail, and fined $30 million. Transaction-oriented mergers and acquisitions seriously damaged Borg-Warner (raided by Samuel Heyman), Fruehauf (raided by Asher Edelman) and Clark Equipment (raided by Hollywood producer Bert Sugarman). The resulting costly, highly leveraged financial organizations brought down Fruehauf and deprived Borg-Warner and Clark Equipment of funds for R&D and equipment essential to their competitive strength.

Nevertheless, most of the restructuring of American machinery companies during the 1980s was executed successfully by senior corporate managers in the manner of the chemical and food companies. The large majority of mergers and acquisitions was carried out to implement long-term investment strategies. Even the transaction-oriented deals became integrated into these strategic restructurings. As a recent study of major hostile takeovers in the 1980s has shown, 72 percent of the assets of target companies ended up in the hands of firms managing similar assets. Only 4.5 percent of the assets wound up managed by unrelated acquirerers (Schleifer and Vishny, 1991).

*****

But all of this is history—an institutional transformation to be analyzed ultimately by historians and economists. The raiders all but disappeared in the early 1990s. The financial community seems chastened. In the 1990s, financial intermediaries should be more concerned with maintaining and enhancing the competitive strength of American companies rather than profiting from crippling it. But the underlying challenges remain. Rapid technological change continues. As markets become more global, international and interindustry competition is becoming even more intensive.

American managers have learned the lessons of overdiversification. They have become knowledgeable in the ways of restructuring. They are aware that the specifics of these technological and competitive challenges differ from industry to industry, as must the organizational responses to them. And as the experience of the 1980s so forcefully demonstrates, continuing organizational alignment must rest on an acute awareness of an organization's specific competitive skills and capabilities.

REFERENCES

Unless indicated below, the factual information in this chapter came from my *Scale and Scope: The Dynamics of Industrial Capitalism,* Belknap/Harvard, Cambridge, MA, 1990, and my ongoing research on post–World War II developments of U.S. industrial enterprises. The references cited are:

Donaldson, G. "Voluntary Restructuring Program, The Case of General Mills." *The Journal of Financial Economics* 27, no. 1 (September 1990), pp. 117–41.

Hall, B. H. "The Impact of Corporate Structuring in Industrial Research and Development." *Brookings Papers on Economic Activity: Microeconomics, 1990.* Washington, DC; Brookings Institution, 1990.

Schleifer, A. and R. W. Vishny, "Takeovers in the 60s and the 80s: Evidence and Implications." *Strategic Management Journal* 12, special issue (Winter 1991), pp. 51–59.

Chapter Three

Managing Strategic Alignment

Michael Beer

I n the mid-1980s, the new CEO of a major international bank—call it U.S. Financial—announced a companywide change effort. Deregulation was posing serious
competitive challenges—to which the bank's traditional hierarchical organization was
ill suited to respond. The only solution was to change fundamentally how the company operated. And the place to begin was at the top.

*The CEO held a retreat with his top 15 executives where they painstakingly reviewed the
bank's purpose and culture. He published a mission statement and hired a new vice president of human resources from a company well-known for its excellence in managing people. And in a quick succession of moves, he established a series of companywide programs to push change down through the organization:*

- *A new organizational structure,*

- *A performance appraisal system,*

- *A pay-for-performance compensation plan,*

- *Training programs to turn managers into "change agents," and*

- *Quarterly attitude surveys to chart the progress of the change effort.*[1]

As much as these steps sound like a textbook case of realigning an organization to
compete in a new environment there was one big problem. Two years after the CEO
launched the change program virtually nothing in the way of change had occurred in
how managers actually managed. What had gone wrong?

The answer lies in the CEO's assumptions about managing strategic change. He
assumed that the whole corporation should be changed at once, that change should
start at the top, and that changes in structure, systems, and human resource policies
and practices can produce changes in people's attitudes and behavior, the ultimate
target of any strategic change effort. These assumptions, research has shown, are
flawed.

THE DEMANDS OF THE COMPETITIVE
ENVIRONMENT

U.S. Financial's story is not unusual. Many corporations around the globe are struggling with managing the same kind of strategic change demanded of U.S. Financial. Global competition, advances in information technology, and rapid changes in markets as well as product technology demand that companies reformulate their strategies. In this environment companies must compete on quality, cost, and innovation. Japanese competitors have shown that excelling in one or even two of these competitive factors is no longer sufficient. Consider developments in the automobile industry where the position once held exclusively by Mercedes-Benz in the high end of the market is being challenged by lower-cost, high-end cars such as Lexus with more innovative features and higher quality. The Japanese, who are responsible for the new upscale entrants, have shown that quality, innovation, and lower cost are not mutually incompatible.

But redefinition of strategy is only the beginning. Companies also must develop an organization capable of implementing strategies and of reformulating them based on what they learn from their experience in implementation. These experiences may reveal unanticipated market conditions and/or organizational and human resource strengths and weaknesses that call for modification.

Increasingly, we are learning that approaches to organizing and managing people that worked in a stable environment do not work when focus, rapid response, and flexibility are called for—when an organization must be capable of aligning and realigning itself often within a rapidly changing environment.

Recent research that I conducted with associates has shown that companies like U.S. Financial are moving away from the command and control structure to the *task-driven* organization.[2] These organizations differ from the traditional hierarchical and functional structure characterized by decision making at the top, division of labor, and procedures and rules as the means of control. Instead, the task-driven organization seeks to channel energy toward business goals by forming teams that cut across functions, divisional boundaries, and national borders, sharing information widely, and delegating responsibility and accountability far down the hierarchy. Constant improvement is encouraged by a culture that places more emphasis on the hierarchy of ideas than the hierarchy of position. Because Japanese automobile companies like Nissan and Toyota long ago put these organizing and managing principles into practice, they are able to produce innovative high-quality automobiles at lower cost than Mercedes-Benz.

The problem faced by U.S. Financial's CEO and others like him is how to realign the corporation so it is capable of implementing the new strategy, while at the same time developing the capacity of managers and workers to change and adapt continuously to new circumstances. To develop this capacity—what some have called the learning organization—three key organizational capabilities must be developed by the change process:

1. *Coordination* and teamwork around key tasks and processes must be enhanced. Unless coordination across functions, businesses, and national borders is improved, the company is doomed to rely on the traditional and slower hierarchy.

2. *Commitment* to the firm's purpose and strategy must be substantially improved in the realigned and adaptive corporation. Teamwork between groups and individuals who do not report to a common boss is impossible unless individuals and groups are willing and able to work beyond narrow career and/or functional interests.

3. *Competence* in managing, leading, and negotiating must exist at all levels and in all parts of the organization if teams of committed employees are to be effective in improving business processes. These competencies are in short supply because the command and control structure did not demand or develop them.

Why did U.S. Financial fail to make significant improvements in coordination, commitment, and competence despite major changes in organization structure, the mission statement, the performance appraisal system, the compensation system, and significant training and communication efforts to spread the word? We now turn to this question.

THE FALLACY OF PROGRAMMATIC CHANGE

Although senior executives understand the necessity for change so as to cope with new competitive realities, they often misunderstand what it takes to bring real change about. They tend to share two assumptions with the CEO of U.S. Financial:

1. Change must start at the top of the corporation with a flurry of programs designed to change individual attitudes and knowledge.

2. Employee behavior is best altered by changing corporate structure and systems. Recent research suggests the opposite. The greatest obstacles to changing the way people actually behave show up in companywide programs typically sponsored by the CEO and implemented in his or her name by a corporate staff group such as human resources.[3]

Consider a company with $10 billion in revenue that implemented a quality circle program in the early 1980s. A *quality circle* is a group of employees engaged in identifying and solving production problems. Top management demonstrated its commitment to this change by holding general managers accountable for introducing working quality circles. These managers complained, however, that the program took their attention and energy away from the issues they thought were most important for the survival of their businesses. They did not argue that quality circles were a bad idea. They pointed out, however, that in many cases quality circles were not the solution to their most important business problems. Efforts to introduce quality circles met with compliance but little commitment. Moreover, precious time and focus were taken away from the problems that the general managers had identified as the most important in their units.

The CEO of a large global company used reorganization in the form of structural change to consolidate domestic and international marketing and advertising. The objective, probably valid for some products and some geographical locations, was to develop a worldwide marketing and advertising strategy. Although the reorganization brought together two groups that needed to coordinate their efforts, it left managers in international marketing demoralized, cynical, and uncommitted to the change. Interviews revealed that they had been making their own informal efforts to coordinate advertising and marketing strategy with domestic executives. The reorganization from the top, they feared, would cause all products to be marketed and advertised in the same way across the entire world, an approach they were sure was not valid. "If that is the way they want it, we'll do it their way, but to hell with them," said one executive. An effort to improve coordination through reorganization from the top had resulted in low commitment and a questionable organizational solution. Moreover, it left managers less willing to take initiatives on their own and more inclined to wait for top management to tell them what to do and when to do it.

Yet another example of programmatic change can be found in a companywide education program for middle and top managers at a large manufacturing company. Sponsored by an executive vice president who was later to become the CEO, the program was regarded by its participants as highly relevant to the company's needs. But it failed to change the company, according to interviews five years after the program began, despite enthusiasm of participants during and immediately after the program. Many found it difficult to transfer the knowledge and enthusiasm developed by the program into action. Commitment quickly waned as participants reentered their traditional work environments where attitudes, systems, policies, and procedures remained unchanged despite top management's participation in the program and support for it.

Pay-for-performance systems, culture programs, mission statements, and other top-down initiatives met similar ends. Cynicism was the most frequent outcome. It inoculated companies against change as employees found it difficult to believe that wave after wave of programs would make a difference. Many of the people interviewed said of the latest program, "It too will pass."

Why do such programs typically fail? The reason lies in the nature of organizational change. It is typically assumed that changing attitudes and knowledge of employees will produce changes in behavior, particularly the coordination and teamwork so critical to competitiveness. In reality organizational change follows a different sequence. When changes in behavior are *voluntary*, they produce changes in attitudes, and these in turn lead to the motivation to learn new skills. In effect, revised patterns of coordination in the process of doing work—such as creating process improvement teams, product development teams, or worldwide strategy teams with goals and accountabilities—place individuals in a new organizational context that demands that they act and think differently. The process of interacting with others in solving important problems can motivate all but the most cynical and alienated employees.

How can an organization bring about a new pattern of managing and interacting without resorting to top-down reorganizations and programs that alienate and demotivate? How can employees become committed to a new organizational context that *forces* new patterns of behavior? This is the difficult conundrum facing managers engaged in strategic change.

A NEW ROLE FOR THE CEO: ENABLE A PROCESS OF STRATEGIC ALIGNMENT AT THE UNIT LEVEL

Corporations that succeed in managing strategic change have recognized that change must occur plant by plant and business unit by business unit. Often this process starts at the periphery or the bottom of the corporation and then spreads inward and upward until the total corporation adopts new patterns of management modeled by innovative units. The CEO's role is to encourage and monitor a unit-by-unit change process, not to launch a program aimed at introducing top management's solution to the competitive challenge.

In effect, corporate change is a learning process in which top management motivates unit general managers to engage in a change process. They do this by articulating why and how the external environment is demanding change and by allowing, or even demanding, that general managers begin self-directed improvement processes in their units. Research has shown that the top management of companies that experienced relative success in moving change along began to attend to innovations in organizing and managing initiated in lower-level units when they realized that these innovations held answers to competitive problems faced by the company as a whole With a growing conviction, they encouraged other general managers to undertake change processes that would cause them to revitalize their own units.

In this first phase of corporate change, the role of the CEO is that of orchestrator. The CEO comes to understand the value of innovations in organizing and managing and encourages their spread throughout the company. Top management members do not, however, always incorporate what they learn at lower levels into their own behaviors. For instance, one CEO who led a relatively successful corporate change effort was seen by many in the company, our research showed, as espousing changes that were inconsistent with his own management practices.

As change began to spread from unit to unit, however, the experience was that the top management unit—the CEO and key line and staff executives—began to feel pressure to change. Unit general managers complained about staff groups and corporate policies that did not support what they were trying to do. Teamwork in their units was not replicated in their dealings with other units across the company. Sustaining corporate change in this second phase of a corporate transformation depends on the CEO's willingness and skill to lead the top management unit through a change process that examines how the company as a whole is organized and managed.

Though corporate change could, and probably should, start with a CEO-led process applied to the organization and management of the company at the top, this did not happen in any of the companies we studied. Perhaps organizational barriers to performance in factories, branch sales offices, and business units are more visible than in the top executive suite. Perhaps younger general managers in units far from headquarters feel less constrained to innovate. Perhaps the position of power of top management makes obtaining valid information about barriers to effectiveness in its own rarefied ranks more difficult. Whatever the reason, change at the top seems to be a response to a continually growing circle of lower-level units that have successfully reinvented themselves into new management practices.

Because corporate transformation is a function of successful change in an increasing number of subunits, it becomes important to understand how to manage such a change process. Not all unit change efforts we studied were equally successful. In a few instances failures at the unit level retarded the transformation of the company as a whole.

General managers succeeded in managing change when they focused their organizations on the most important business problems facing them. We have come to call this nonprogrammatic change process *strategic alignment*. Focusing on the unit's key strategy or task energizes the particular organization to change. In most organizational units, everyone—workers, managers, and union leaders—became committed to participating in a change process when a consensus was forged that the competitive environment demanded change. Business imperatives, in other words, motivated a cooperative search for a better way to manage.

STRATEGIC ALIGNMENT

Consider the following example of a strategically aligned change process in a manufacturing plant that had been performing poorly under a financially oriented manager.[4] After taking over, a new plant manager discovered that quality problems caused the facility's market share erosion and poor profitability. He could have responded by giving a speech on quality, introducing training in total quality for all employees, changing the reward system of managers and workers to provide an incentive for quality improvement, or breaking down the functional barriers to quality improvement by reorganizing. He did none of these things.

Instead the new factory manager formed a quality committee composed of people who reported directly to him and of several other key personnel associated with the quality problem. After collecting data about quality problems from customers and sales and marketing personnel, the committee developed a list of 30 quality problems and ranked them in importance. At the same time, the quality committee asked employees in the plant to respond to a survey about barriers to effectiveness. The results pointed to interfunctional conflict as the probable cause of the quality problem.

The process of collecting data from customers validated the plant manager's assessment that quality was the most important problem. The views of employees about barriers to effectiveness disclosed information about poor interfunctional coordination, low commitment, and deficiencies in management skills that were known to many but could not be openly discussed. The committee, with leadership from the plant manager, quickly developed mechanisms for cross-functional coordination to gain control of the manufacturing process.

After two years, the plant succeeded in making significant improvements in quality and financial performance. Why did this plant manager succeed where the other had failed?

The change effort focused on improving quality, a task that all agreed after discussion and analysis was the key to the survival of the plant. Employees at lower levels who knew why the plant was experiencing performance problems were involved in identifying barriers to achieving higher quality. The top team developed a conceptual model of how the plant should be organized and managed to eliminate these barriers. The organization they envisioned *forced* functional departments to coordinate their efforts in order to gain control of a manufacturing process that flowed through their respective departments.

The change was not motivated by a program directed by the CEO or the plant manager. It was the result of a collaborative process of problem definition, diagnosis, organizational reinvention, and action planning.

The effect that the collaborative process had on the top team is the most important reason for the successful change in the plant. Working together on the quality problem spurred the plant manager and her staff to develop a commitment to teamwork and to learn how to work as a team. In short, they learned from their own experience. As they struggled with defining the quality problem, they became aware of how serious the problem was in a way that speeches and training programs could not accomplish. Open discussions of organizational barriers to improved quality caused functional managers to learn how their own parochial behavior had created the quality crisis to begin with.

As illustrated in Figure 3–1, what occurred at the plant was a mutually reinforcing process of change in commitment (motivation), coordination (behavior), and competence (skills). As the quality problem came into view, commitment to change increased. As the top team members began to work together to define the quality problem and the barriers to effectiveness, coordination and teamwork improved at the top. As they grappled successfully with problems, the top team began to feel it was mak-

FIGURE 3–1

A Mutually Reinforcing Cycle of Change

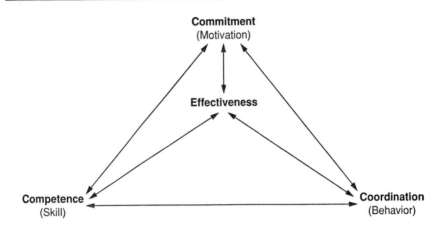

ing a difference, that its members were effective. Every individual as well as the group as a whole was motivated to learn new interpersonal and communication skills. This cycle of behavior and performance improvement is the same one that successful sports teams experience. It is essential if fundamental and sustained change is to occur.

The fact that the top team worked cohesively was the key to similar initiatives at lower levels. Assigned to teams with goals, managers and workers were drawn into the same mutually reinforcing developmental cycle the top team had experienced. Moreover, because management "walked the way they talked," they provided a model to imitate. An education program or a quality circle program introduced at lower levels would have been short-lived. Attitude and skill changes would not have been reinforced by a heightened sense of efficacy that comes from solving cross-functional problems as a team.

The pattern of change just described was repeated in other successfully transformed business units and manufacturing plants that we observed.[5] In almost all cases the change process was triggered by a competitive crisis, however.

The high cost of crisis-driven change led Becton Dickinson Co., a global medical technology company, to develop a strategic alignment and change process called strategic human resource management. It is intended to mobilize a continuous realignment process in business units, company sectors, and at the corporate level.[6] It specifies a means for diagnosis, vision development, and change that any business unit manager or CEO who wants to manage strategic change can undertake. Consistent with research findings already discussed, the role of the CEO is to motivate managers to utilize the strategic change process and to hold them accountable for implementing it effectively, but not to initiate change programs.

HOW TO MANAGE STRATEGIC CHANGE WITHOUT CRISIS

The research just discussed indicated that an imperative must be found to unleash energy for change and it must be the organization's most important problem or opportunity. A strategic change effort without a crisis must, therefore, start with an analysis of the competitive environment and customer needs. The strategic task becomes the rallying point for change and adaptation. A general manager and his or her top team can use the following steps to mobilize energy for change and begin the transformation process.

Define Strategic Tasks as a Group

An analysis of the competitive environment, if done jointly by the top team in collaboration with other members of the organization, can produce understanding of and commitment to the *strategic tasks* of the organization. Strategic tasks such as rapid development of product extensions, improved product quality, reduced cost, provision of the best service, or introduction of new products are the means by which the business will compete. These strategic tasks can become the basis for defining and developing the organizational capabilities required to compete. When produced by the top team, as opposed to external consultants, for example, the process develops understanding and commitment to a direction. That commitment is essential if the top team is to reinvent itself into the pattern of organizing and managing needed to implement the strategy successfully.

Collect Data about Undiscussable Organizational Barriers

Ineffective work processes at the operating or management level can pose barriers to strategy implementation. They are typically functions of poor coordination and information sharing. Because ineffective coordination and information sharing point to power differentials, lack of cooperation, and the inability of managers to lead, they are usually undiscussable.

Strategic change, therefore, requires a means for disclosing, discussing, and diagnosing the undiscussable and then using the data to reinvent the organization. As the research already discussed suggests, this should be done by members of the organization if commitment and learning are the goals of organization change. Whereas management consultants are typically used to ferret out undiscussable problems and recommend organization changes, the use of outsiders does not necessarily ensure effective implementation of change recommendations.

Consider a company that is falling behind in meeting its financial goals. The CEO engages a consulting firm to redesign the organization completely based on its analysis of the competitive environment and diagnosis of the organizational barriers to competitiveness. Although the expertise of consultants can produce superior organizational solutions, managers may not have the commitment or competence to implement the new organization. Nor will they have learned how to bring to light undiscussable data, analyze them, and reinvent the organization, all of which must be learned if the organization is to be adaptive.

It is more effective to involve managers and workers in the process. Becton Dickinson found that a task force can be appointed to interview employees within the organization and also interview interdependent units, customers, and suppliers. Asking about barriers to implementing strategic tasks reveals problems in coordination, commitment, and competence. Usually many people in the organization knew about these problems before the task force began its data collection, but there was no way to discuss them and craft solutions.[7]

Receive Feedback and Perform a Diagnosis

A forum for an unhurried, open, and contemplative discussion of task force findings must be created. Holding a meeting away from day-to-day business pressures can help create the environment needed. A third-party consultant who can promote an open and honest discussion of task force findings is essential. If the consultant knows about organizational effectiveness and change and has skills in leading a group through a diagnosis, he or she can help the management team understand the root cause of organizational barriers.

Becton, Dickinson found that an employee task force can deliver richer and more open feedback by using a *fishbowl* method. The task force sits in the middle of the room discussing what their interviews with employees revealed, while the general manager and his or her team sit in an outside circle and listen. This method allows task force members to convey deep-rooted attitudes and behaviors that would never surface in an ordinary presentation. Some fishbowl discussions have lasted up to six hours, and they never fail to move the top management team emotionally. In effect, the general manager and his or her staff receive a report card of their effectiveness as managers from high-potential employees they selected. That they selected these well-regarded employees makes it hard to deny the feedback and its implications.

Feedback must be followed by a diagnosis. But before diagnosis can proceed, motivation to change must be established. The research already discussed showed that motivation to change developed when an organization unit identified its most important business problem and used it to rally support for change.

Using these findings as a guide, Becton Dickinson designed a strategic change process it is now attempting to institutionalize. It asks its general managers to start the process by determining if the organizational and management issues identified by the task force have had a negative impact on the performance of the business, or if they are likely to block implementation of the business unit's key strategic tasks in the future. Only if the top management team can link the issues raised by the task force to performance and/or strategy implementation can motivation for change be developed without a crisis. Now the top team is ready to search for root causes with commitment and honesty.

FIGURE 3–2

A Systems Framework for Organizational Diagnosis

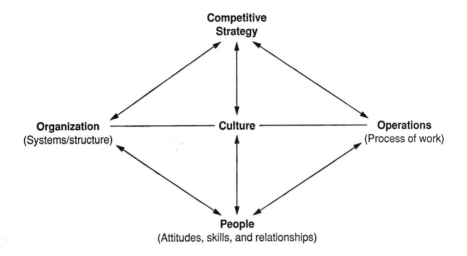

    The diagnosis should be made within a systems framework for organizational func-
tioning. Such a framework can guide managers to ask questions at four different but
interconnected levels of analysis, strategy, organization, operations, and people (see
Figure 3–2).
    Having identified key strategic tasks at the beginning of the change process, man-
agement now must examine how well the remaining three elements are aligned. How
do the processes for operating the business block strategy implementation? How do
organization structure and systems cause the process problems that were identified?
How do attitudes and relationships of individuals and groups cause ineffective
processes? Without such a systemic framework, the multiple factors that typically
cause low coordination, commitment, and competence cannot be identified and managers would not be prompted to examine their own management behavior. Unless the
diagnosis examines multiple factors and touches on personal behavior of managers,
the organizational culture that shapes behavior will not be confronted.

Reinvent the Organization

A candid diagnosis leads to deep understanding of the organizational and human
capabilities that are lacking in order to implement strategy effectively. That understanding must be translated into a vision of the kind of organization and human capability that are needed. Organizational units that succeed in accomplishing radical
change are able to develop a strategically aligned vision of how they should organize

and manage to remain competitive.[8] Sometimes vision development is aided by visits to other companies where innovative practices are used. Whatever the means, the general manager and the manager's team must be able to define how the organization will operate differently. Also they must show how this difference will address the fundamental barriers to strategy implementation that were identified by the diagnosis.

The vision is like an architectural drawing for a new house. It specifies in some detail the structure, systems, staff, skills, style, and shared values that the organization must adopt to compete.[9] Such a systemic definition of the future state points to how the organization and its managers must change their own attitudes and behavior. It is the personal change called for by the vision that is most difficult for managers to accept and implement, but accept them they must if change is to occur.

The vision development process should involve people from various levels and parts of the organization. Committees and task forces may be assigned to invent elements of the new vision, such as a new reward system, a new structure, a new procedure for product development, or a new budgeting and resource allocation process. But the process starts with the top team's definition of the overall pattern of organization and management that is needed to compete.

Moving Change Along

Strategic change that alters fundamental patterns of behavior is a process that evolves over time. Managers and workers must learn to work in a new way. That new way leads to learning about what the new organizational invention really means and what it demands in attitudes, behavior, and skills.

Change starts with a communication to employees about how the organization will operate differently. Because competing in the global economy requires a paradigm shift in organizing and managing—from a hierarchical organization to a task-driven team-based organization—the new organizational vision will require a radical change in behavior.

Not until people start operating within the newly invented organization, however, does real learning take place. From the successes and failures of individuals in adapting to the new organization, general managers discover who is capable of learning and who is not. Replacement of those who cannot adapt must take place if change is to move forward. As change progresses, general managers also form a much more concrete understanding of the types of people the new organization should recruit and promote. Armed with this knowledge, they can develop recruiting and succession plans that fit the new strategically aligned vision.

TAKING THREE STEPS FORWARD AND TWO STEPS BACK

No strategic change process is linear or smooth. New problems are created by change and old problems are redefined. As discussed before, the skills and competence of managers to learn are challenged and their inability to meet these challenges produces difficult problems that must be confronted. External forces, business cycles, demands for cost reduction, changes in key executives, and corporate demands all affect the process of change. The persistence of the general manager in anticipating setbacks and the manner in which he or she handles them make the difference between success and failure.

The top management team must, therefore, continuously monitor the progress of the organization in moving toward the vision and it must respond to slippage. The challenge is to respond with the same high-involvement process that produced the new strategically aligned organization in the first place. Deviating from this process inevitably leads the organization into top-down programmatic change and blocks the mutually reinforcing cycle of improvement in the coordination, commitment, and competence needed for fundamental strategic change.

So as to sustain commitment to a high-involvement process of strategic change, a partnership between employees, unions, and management must be developed. Saturn Corp., the small car subsidiary of General Motors Corp., has involved workers, managers, and unions in the invention and reinvention of the organization for almost a decade and reaped a good deal of success. At Honeywell Inc.'s Commercial Aviation Division, the general manager created a change management team composed of managers, union officials, and employees from different functions and levels to monitor change and participate in developing new strategies. At Becton Dickinson, some general managers have made the employee task forces that provided initial feedback a permanent partner in managing change. The task force gathers employees' reactions to change initiatives, informs top management of barriers to change posed by procedures or people, and when needed confronts top management with how their own leadership practices are blocking change.

STRATEGIC CHANGE REQUIRES LEADERSHIP

The preceding strategic change process requires general managers to possess skills that are in scarce supply in many corporations. To lead a top team through the process demands a unique combination of confidence, business knowledge, results orientation skills as an organizational architect, and interpersonal and communication skills. It requires the capacity to manage soft aspects of management in a hard way, to be vulnerable yet tough, and to be both directive and nondirective depending on the situation and the issue.

The characteristics of effective leadership received much attention in the 1980s.[10] This occurred in large part because companies facing competitive crises found their managers unable to mobilize the commitment of employees to change. Despite much research, the characteristics and skills of leaders able to manage change remain elusive and cannot be identified with any degree of certainty. This presents the top management of a corporation with a difficult dilemma. How can the highest level of executives have confidence that their general managers know how to lead change, or that the managers are applying necessary knowledge and skill in their business units?

How can they ensure the development of leadership skills among their present and prospective general managers? The answers to these questions lie in the institutionalization of the strategic change process.

INSTITUTIONALIZATION OF STRATEGIC CHANGE AND RENEWAL

Rapid change in markets, society, and technology requires that the process of strategic change become part of the management process at all levels. Managing organizational renewal and learning will have to become the norm.[11] Given the difficulties in identifying change leaders and developing their skills, how can this be done? The answer is to develop an institutionalized process of change that guides managers through the process, helps them learn from their experience, and targets for promotion those who can lead change.

It is essential that top management require its line managers to use a process of strategic change routinely that adheres to the specifications outlined in this chapter, just as they now require their general managers to develop and reassess business strategy. By requiring managers to follow a standardized process that is based on research findings, the corporation sets a standard for leading change against which they can judge the efficacy of their managers. This process can be done, however, only if the company requires general managers to report diagnoses of their organizations to higher management. The report should include how their own management contributed to identified problems, the visions they have crafted, and the progress of change toward the visions as perceived by various constituencies in the organization. Knowing how managers respond to feedback, how effective they are as organizational architects, how well they involve different stakeholders in developing consensus for a strategically aligned vision, and how well they confront individuals and groups whose behavior must change, enables the top management to assess a general manager's skills in managing strategic change.

The key to the institutionalized process proposed here is transparency about organizational problems and progress in managing change. Transparency is not easy to develop. It can be encouraged only if top management takes an analytical and developmental stance, rather than a judgmental position on revelations about organizational and management problems at lower levels.[12]

The development of a standardized process of change, based on latest knowledge, still is not sufficient for the company to develop change leaders. Corporations must provide internal consulting resources to help general managers learn how to lead change, and they must hold these managers accountable for effective change within organizational units. Over time, managers who develop change management skills and make significant improvements in their organizations' effectiveness should be promoted. Those that prove unable to lead change must be demoted. That is the only way a company can increase its capability to manage strategic change.

General Electric Co. has institutionalized a change process it calls "Workout." It is a standardized process that requires managers to involve employees in identifying barriers to effectiveness and to respond with a change plan. To ensure that General Electric has a supply of effective change leaders, CEO Jack Welch holds that the only managers who will be promoted are those whose divisions meet performance goals *and* whose management practices are aligned with GE's values. Presumably, Welch considers a manager's effectiveness in leading the Workout process to be an indicator of whether he or she possesses the values and skills General Electric believes are important.

The strategic change process outlined in this chapter has been applied at Becton Dickinson for the last five years with some success, although research is still underway. Although the approach is still voluntary, the ultimate goal is to require general managers to use the change process periodically. Managers already have come to realize that use of the change process is valued in the company, and they thus are using it with increasing frequency. Managers are required to report the results of their diagnoses and progress in managing change to the next level. This has provided upper management with knowledge about organizational capability and leadership skills in business units that they previously did not have. If used to coach managers and to inform management succession plans, an institutionalized process promises to improve competence for leading change in the company. For a medical technology company in a global business this capability is essential.

CONCLUSION

Strategic change requires simultaneous change in coordination, commitment, and competence. These can change only when people in the organization are committed to changing the organizational arrangements that have shaped past attitudes and behavior. Programmatic change from the top of a company cannot achieve this. Only a self-directed process by each business unit can hope to develop the commitment needed for fundamental change.

A high-involvement, general-manager-led process of defining strategic tasks, collecting information about barriers, developing a vision of the future state, and managing change over time can develop an organization capable of implementing strategy and reformulating it. But only if managers are required to make the results of the process transparent can they be coached to improve the change management skills that are scarce but vital to a company's capacity to survive and prosper in a competitive environment. Transparency makes it possible for top management to hold managers accountable for improving organizational capability and promote those who are skilled in leading change. Because people whose skills are well developed in leading strategic change are key to a corporation's capacity to renew itself, institutionalizing a process of strategic change will become the norm for companies in the 21st century.

REFERENCES

1. M. Beer, R.A. Eisenstat, and B. Spector, "Why Change Programs Don't Produce Change," *Harvard Business Review,* November/December 1990, pp. 158–166.

2. M. Beer, R.A. Eisenstat, and B. Spector, *The Critical Path to Corporate Renewal* (Boston, MA: Harvard Business School Press, 1990).

3. Ibid.; R. Schaffer, *The Breakthrough Strategy* (Cambridge, MA: Ballinger, 1988).

4. Beer, Eisenstat, and Spector, pp. 47–50.

5. Ibid.

6. M. Beer, R.A. Eisenstat, and R. Biggadike, "Developing an Organization Capable of Implementing and Reformulating Strategy," Working Paper, Harvard Business School, 1990.

7. Ibid.

8. R. Walton, "Vision Led Change, Organizational Dynamics," 1986. M. Beer, R.A. Eisenstat, and B. Spector, *The Critical Path to Corporate Renewal* (Boston, MA: Harvard Business School Press, 1990); R. Howard, "The CEO as Organizational Architect: An Interview with Xerox's Paul Allair," *Harvard Business Review,* September/October 1992

9. R. Waterman, T. Peters, and R. Phillips, "Structure is Not Organization," *Business Horizons,* 1980.

10. J. Kotter, *The Leadership Factor* (New York: The Free Press, 1988); J. Kotter, *A Force for Change* (New York: The Free Press, 1990); R. Howard, "The CEO as Organizational Architect: An Interview with Paul Allair," *Harvard Business Review,* September/October 1992.

11. P. Drucker, "The New Society of Organizations," *Harvard Business Review,* September/October 1992.

12. M. Beer, Note on Performance Appraisal, *Harvard Business School,* Boston, MA, 1977.

Chapter Four

Driving Systemic Change

Michael Useem

T hough change may seem ubiquitous, it is an unnatural condition for most organizations. It tends to come in fits and starts when it comes at all. Worse yet,
piecemeal fixes can make the organization less effective than before, and adverse
unanticipated side effects often sabotage the best-intended efforts. Thus, the most
effective reorganizations are pursued broadly, conducted on a systematic basis, and
executed by making simultaneous and related changes in a number of organization
components that will be simultaneously impacted.

The dictum of "leaving well enough alone" finds daily application for good reason.
Organizations are built on the routinized mobilization of human and capital resources.
Without continuity in reporting relations, stability in manufacturing methods, and,
above all, consistency in purpose, even the most mundane tasks become prohibitively
burdensome. Analysts Richard Nelson and Sidney Winter argue that all organizations
develop these routines to work effectively.[1] Stable cultures protect the company from
fickle demands; consistent strategies give direction to the work of all people and units
within the corporate organization.

Once embedded in the organization, most of the created routines are no longer
even perceived as such by those who practice them. Rather, they are taken for
granted—the natural way for doing business. As such, they provide automatic tem-
plates for managing the continuous flow of decisions and tasks that constitute organizational life. Yet the enormous inertial guidance created by routinization is also a
seed of ultimate instability. As markets and technologies change, a company's failure
to transcend its own inertial forces is a sure prescription for eventual decline. The
stabilizing tendencies built into any organization are a source of daily strength, but
they can also become a cause of ultimate failure.

Stability's downside burden is evident in industries ranging from auto manufacturing to retail services. One experience with technological innovation in the computer
industry illustrates the fate that can befall those unable to redirect their inertial
momentum. Between 1962 and 1986, five distinct technologies successively emerged
for the manufacture of computer chips, each superior to its predecessor. Yet the

company that became the market leader with the first generation of technology was unable to change itself fast enough to succeed with the next. A new market leader dominated the second generation of technology, but this company failed to succeed with the third generation. Another company became dominant, only to find its own position eclipsed by still another upstart when the fourth-generation technology took hold. The cycle was repeated when the fifth generation emerged as well.[2] All of the leadership companies were forced from a market each had dominated because technological change simply outstripped their capacities for organizational change.

The art of management, then, is a matter of not only preserving the status quo but also—on required occasions—breaking it. Executing a needed shift, however, is a formidable task. Because an organization's many components generally are designed to facilitate routinized operation, moving beyond the status quo can require an integrated transformation of all the components. Change management thus faces a systemic problem: All facets require simultaneous and integrated redesign. This in turn leads to two practical problems for management. Because simultaneous change of the many organizational components exceeds what most managements have the capacity to engineer, identifying specific means for management intervention becomes critical. And since the most effective thrust for the systemic change varies with both the organization and the era, identifying the appropriate direction of the change becomes a critical concern for management as well. In what follows, we focus on the need for systemic change and these two practical problems in managing it.

MAKING SYSTEMIC CHANGE

An organization's major components can be classified in several ways, but leading any list are an organization's goals and strategies, production technologies and information systems, formal and informal groupings and boundaries, human resource systems, and culture and values. Organizational design is concerned with how these categories should be best developed and fit together. Systemic organizational change is concerned with how they should best be jointly redeveloped and refit.[3]

An organization's components are generally too interrelated to permit effective tinkering in one without the others. Adjustments in single areas are, of course, made all the time, as illustrated by the periodic introductions of new machinery on the shop floor, new products into the consumer market, and changes in employee benefits provisions. Yet these moves are typically little more than spot changes, responses to momentary opportunities or limited needs.

Often, however, single components are changed in anticipation of major improvements in the organization. New information systems sometimes are heralded as transformative. So too, at times, are the automation of manufacturing lines, the introduction of quality circles, and the diversification of governing boards. Research studies generally show, however, that changes in single components without parallel changes in other components often leave the intended effects stillborn. This can be seen in the results of studies in four areas of corporate innovation.

1. *The introduction of new information systems.* During the 1980s, new computer-based information systems often were regarded as powerful tools for enhancing efficiency. Advocates offered compelling forecasts of productivity gains and cost reductions. Yet studies by Edgar Schein, Michael Scott Morton, and Shoshana Zuboff reveal little positive impact unless other changes are introduced in tandem with the information system. They include empowerment of the work force to use the information, enhanced flexibility in the design of teams and tasks, and top management commitment to utilize and support the new information systems.[4]

2. *The introduction of lean manufacturing technologies.* Japanese manufacturing technologies often have been heralded as models on which U.S. organizations would do well to draw. In their study of "lean" production methods pioneered by the Japanese automobile industry, for instance, John Womack, Daniel Jones, and Daniel Roos offer a compelling portrait of a world of manufacturing that requires half of what was needed in traditional mass production methods: half the space, half the tools, half the engineering time, and half the human effort.[5] Yet associated researchers John Paul MacDuffie and John Krafcik also found that the introduction of lean production only works well if accompanied by related changes. The organization's human resource policies must simultaneously enhance employee skills, motivation, and flexibility, and its decision-making process must stress continuous problem solving and improvement.[6]

3. *The introduction of employee stock ownership plans.* Employee stock ownership long has been viewed as a foundation for improved worker commitment. Few better ways can be found, it has been argued, to align the interests of employees and their organizations, reduce turnover, absenteeism, and sabotage, and, in the end, enhance work motivation, product quality, and company productivity. With this in mind, many companies have introduced employee stock ownership plans, but the impact on productivity often has proven disappointing. Careful study of numerous stock ownership plans by Michael Conte and Jan Svejnar shows why. Unless coupled with other changes intended to give employees greater voice in organizational decision making, stock ownership plans fall flat.[7]

4. *The introduction of governance reforms.* During the late 1980s and early 1990s, the governance of publicly traded firms came under attack by institutional investors, shareholder groups, and even some senior managers. Urged on by these parties, the Securities and Exchange Commission altered its rules on several matters, including company reporting of executive compensation and the formation of investor coalitions for pressuring firms. Companies quietly changed many of their own practices as well, moving, for example, to exclude inside directors from compensation and nominating committees of their boards. Yet in the governance area as well, careful study suggests that piecemeal reform may accomplish little. Drawing on the work of a team of scholars, Michael Porter concluded that only wholesale overhaul would achieve the ends sought. His summary lines could equally well have served the foregoing studies: "Reform of the U.S. system must recognize that it is an internally consistent system

involving many parts.... Altering one aspect of the system without simultaneously altering others may well lead to counterproductive consequences."[8]

Whether targeting information, production, ownership, or governance, research studies thus confirm that reengineering efforts taken in isolation tend to yield little gain. A new production technology *or* human resource system *or* governance structure may be put in place, but the impact on productivity and performance, the ultimate objectives of most such efforts, may be close to negligible. By contrast, when a new production technology *and* human resource system *and* governance structure are simultaneously put in place in integrated fashion, their mutual reinforcement and implementation move the organization toward the intended impact.

DRIVING SYSTEMIC CHANGE

Although wholesale change may be essential, managerial pessimism about achieving it should come as no surprise. If the entire organization must be transformed, the scope of the time and investment required is likely to be well beyond what most managers believe is theirs to give. To say the entire system must be changed is for some to say it cannot be changed. Yet, since cases of organizational revitalization and turnarounds abound, we know it can be done. At the same time, many cases of prolonged failure also abound, telling us it cannot necessarily be done.[9] Comparing the latter with the former often reveals that a principal lever to make it happen is a class of devices usefully grouped together under the rubric of *change drivers*.

Change drivers are management tools that are used to lead the process of organizational change. They are used to align an organization with its new strategy. Although they are targeted to change specific features of the organization, they also have the potential for simultaneously inducing change in other features of the organization. Change drivers provide a concrete means for managers to analyze change throughout their unit or enterprise.

Change drivers may come in the form of contingent compensation systems that more closely link personal and organizational fortunes, employee workshops that disseminate company value and vision, and special programs that provide generic guidelines for improving efficiency. Whatever the particular form, change-driver actions require four main qualities to be effective:

1. *Visibility*. Visibility means that the actions and their impacts are evident and tangible. A change driver must have an intense, immediate, and identifiable character. Programs for total quality management often exhibit this quality.[10]

2. *Incentive*. Incentive means that the actions bring specific and immediate benefits to those who take them and that the benefits are in some way proportional to the contributions. Because organizations depend on high performance by individuals and units, both personal and collective incentives are important. Some performance-based contingent compensation systems display this quality.[11]

3. *Linkage.* Linkage means that the actions are tightly coupled to other organizational components. Once actions are implemented in one area, the continuing search for internal consistency leads to changes in other areas. Educational programs that introduce all employees to a company's "way" frequently illustrate this quality.[12]

4. *Alignment.* Alignment means that the actions' thrust is closely tied to the organization's objectives. Whether large or small, the actions should be clearly seen as furthering the goals of the organization. Strategic planning in which projects and programs are carefully scrutinized for their benefits to a publicly traded firm's "shareholder value" often show this quality.[13]

Though it is tempting to search for a "best practice" among a repertoire of potential change drivers developed elsewhere, it appears that each organization is best at adapting and customizing its own distinctive blend. What works well for some may not be effective for others. This is demonstrated by a study of why some companies successfully revitalized their cultures and operations and others failed. Michael Beer, Russell Eisenstat, and Bert Spector compared a small set of companies that had achieved "corporate renewal" with a matched set of companies that had not. The differing courses could not be explained merely by the initiation of quality circles, management education, and other drivers that were expected to make a difference. Both the revitalized companies and the comparison group had implemented many such efforts. What instead distinguished success and failure was the practice of what these analysts termed "task alignment." This entailed a sharpening of employee understanding of company objectives, a focusing of company resources around these objectives, and a tightening of organizational support, such as linking performance appraisal and compensation systems more explicitly to the objectives. The successfully revitalized firms had reconfigured work responsibilities and job designs to focus work tasks more precisely on achieving the objectives of the business unit and company.[14] The failures made changes without such focus and coordinated alignment.

In judging alternative change drivers, it is useful to examine their prior applications by other organizations. Yet, wholesale borrowing rarely works well, and effective local adaptation or fresh invention depends on the extent to which the chosen drivers exhibit visibility, incentives, linkages, and alignment within the particular organization. It also can require considerable experimentation before these qualities become fully evident. Employee education may work especially well in one setting, whereas using compensation to provide incentives may prove more effective in another. Only through trial-and-error testing will their relative powers become evident.

The importance of experimentation was revealed in a large-scale effort by the Government of Indonesia and several international agencies to reduce the use of pesticides in rice agriculture, the mainstay of the Indonesian economy. Massive pesticide applications throughout the country created a host of environmental and biological problems, but the risks facing individual farmers if they dispensed with pesticides were too high for most to bear. Despite widespread resistance to any change in pesticide applications, a national organization nonetheless was created to achieve reduction or elimination in their use.

Building on the successes and failures of a number of earlier efforts to transform rural agriculture in the Asian region, the Indonesia group developed an exceptionally powerful change driver around two main elements. The first was a massive training capacity, reaching more than 50,000 farmers per cycle. The objective was to build a well-informed and flexible populace with the managerial skills required to protect a rice field through ecological rather than chemical methods. This was coupled with a set of individual and collective incentives that placed more cash but no less rice in the hands of those who adopted the natural methods. The change drivers worked. Pesticide applications dropped by more than 50 percent, creating massive change in an area where pessimism about sustaining any change long had prevailed. But it was only through prolonged experimentation that the right combination of organizational change drivers for this setting was discovered.[15]

DIRECTING SYSTEMIC CHANGE

With the need for systemic change confirmed and the change drivers identified, the directional question remains: What design should emerge from the change process? That of course depends to a great degree on the problems confronting the organization. Thus, there is rarely a single best method or preferred path.

Still, a distinctive thrust to much systemic change, often grouped under the rubric of corporate restructuring, emerged during the past decade. It addressed key problems faced by many organizations. The thrust was especially evident among large publicly traded firms, but other organizations, ranging from small companies to non-profit agencies, moved in much the same direction.

The dominant forms of restructuring have varied with the era. The multidivisional firm arose from business turbulence around the turn of the 20th century, and the diversified multinational firm took form during the post–World War II era.[16] In recent years, a still different organizational cast arose from these foundations.

In decades past, there had been a gradual but seemingly inexorable shift of control of large corporations from founding owners and shareholders to nonowner professional managers. This was the "managerial revolution" identified by Adolph Berle and Gardiner Means in their 1932 landmark study of corporate governance.[17] Dissatisfied shareholders were left with the sole option of selling. The "Wall Street Rule" of disinvesting ownership rather than challenging management had become a norm of necessity.

Later analysis confirmed what Berle and Means were then witnessing. In 1900, only a fifth of the nation's largest companies were management controlled; by 1970, only a fifth were still controlled by principal owners. True, top management retained large numbers of shares, but its ownership stake had been reduced to a tiny fraction of the total. By the mid-1970s, the CEO of a large firm and the CEO's family typically held a mere 0.05 percent of the CEO's company's stock.[18]

Events of the past decade, however, began to stand this managerial revolution on its head. At root was a historic reconcentration of share ownership in far fewer hands. Institutional shareholding soared as money poured into pension funds, insurance companies, bank trusts, and mutual funds. Institutions held less than a third of the value of all company equities in 1980; by the decade's end they owned nearly half the value of public shares. The ten largest private and public pension funds, led by the California public employees fund (commonly known as Calpers), managed well over $500 billion of assets. Of the 1,000 largest publicly traded companies, average institutional shareholding stood at better than 50 percent, and among some firms, institutional stakes reached 80 percent or more.[19]

The concentration of shareholdings made the Wall Street rule less practical, leading discontented investors to construct a new rule. Impatient with results but unable to trade their large holding, Calpers and other funds pressed for changes in company policies instead of their own portfolios. Other investors quietly threw their voting weight behind the charge. Through early support for buyout funds, hostile tender offers, and, later, shareholder resolutions and proxy battles, large investors created the "institutional investor rule": If an investor company lags its industry, press for changes in policy; failing that, press for changes in governance, compensation, or even management.

Between 1985 and 1990, the number of dissident shareholder resolutions, primarily targeted at rescinding poison pills and creating confidential voting for directors, expanded tenfold. By the 1990s, dissidence had grown from petty annoyance to serious challenge. Poison pill rescission proposals were on average attracting better than 40 percent of the shares voted. At the same time many large firms took the offensive through creative defenses. A host of governance measures were introduced to ward off unwanted takeovers and undue shareholder pressures. The number of Fortune 500 firms with a poison pill doubled between 1985 and 1990, from a third of the list to nearly two thirds. Threatened firms pressed for—and readily obtained—antitakeover statues from their home states. Between 1982 and 1987, only five states passed antitakeover legislation to protect an in-state company from an unwanted acquisition. By 1991, 41 states had adopted some form of antitakeover legislation.

The newly erected corporate defenses provided an invaluable umbrella. With hostile raiders held at bay, senior managements turned to recrafting the firm within. Quietly implemented, the transformations ushered far-reaching changes into the culture and organization of the company. Though rarely taken in explicit response to shareholder pressures, the changes nonetheless were often intended to bring company actions into accord with stockholder concerns.

The intensified focus on shareholder value led to a stress on consistent, integrated linkages among major elements of company organization. Some firms tightened their focus on core businesses, shedding marginal divisions. Others disposed of office perquisites, extolling the virtues of a lean operation. Still others pushed more authority into the hands of those responsible for key operations. Although the specific strategies for restructuring varied from firm to firm, an underlying objective was enhancement of the company's worth to its owners. Eight common features of the reorganizations conducted by a set of large companies that I have intensively studied are shown below:

1. *Devolved authority.* Authority to succeed and fail was pushed lower in the organization, giving managers and operating units greater operating autonomy.

2. *Dispersed information.* Information was more widely distributed among managers and more focused on ownership issues.

3. *Contracted headquarters.* Central offices were scaled back, in some cases to a fraction of the original sizes.

4. *Decisions more focused on shareholder value.* Managerial decisions were more explicitly judged on the basis of the anticipated worth to stockholders.

5. *Better managed managers.* Top management invested greater time in managing and developing their successors.

6. *Tightened promotions.* More stringent selection criteria were used in filling management positions and elevating executive personnel.

7. *More incentives for good performance.* Management compensation was made more contingent on performance, and performance measures were more tightly linked to shareholder value.

8. *Enhanced internal ownership.* Incentive and decision-making systems were designed to make senior managers into de facto owners.

The changes in each of these areas were pronounced. The magnitude can be illustrated with the changing composition of senior management compensation. Between 1982 and 1990, base salaries declined from 44 to 34 percent of total compensation, whereas long-term incentives rose from 16 to 33 percent. Moreover, the incentives were increasingly tied to enhanced dividends and share price.

Companies promoted changes in most of these areas simultaneously, though not all with the same vigor or success. Several were viewed as change drivers, others as change reactors. Some firms used management compensation as the primary vehicle for promoting companywide transformation, others utilized management succession as the leading edge, and still others used education programs to foster the process. But the eight features were generally seen as a package, each requiring the seven others to be implemented in conjunction for effective reinforcement.

Like developing countries, change among these firms often followed an uneven course, with redesign of some features leading and others lagging. Although changes in the distribution of authority and performance compensation were relatively well advanced, for instance, changes in the governing board remained relatively underdeveloped. Major investors in many cases had called for company directors to be less dependent on management and more independent in thought. But despite a host of proposals to provide incentives to directors and enhance their autonomy and power, change was relatively slow in coming to the board.

Still, the relative tardiness of governance changes was likely to be a momentary condition. Systemic organizational change carries a logic of consistency. As managerial work becomes increasingly based on incentives and managers acquire more power to do their work, similar developments can be expected for the corporate directors as well. Change drivers do their initial work in targeted areas. But if they are effective system changers, they will be felt eventually in all parts of the organization.

CONCLUSION

Organizational effectiveness depends on consistency among its components. This is one of the foundations of modern organizational theory. Richard Cyert and James March warn that individuals and units tend to pursue a range of personal and local goals, goals often at odds with the firm's objectives. A central task of any organization, they argue, is to bring these individual and unit goals into consistency with its overarching objectives, an "aligning" of the organization's many parts. Similarly, David Nadler and Michael Tushman emphasize the importance of what they term "congruency" for constructive integration of an organization's parts. And Andrew Pettigrew and Richard Whipp emphasize the need for "coherence" and "consistency" between a company's strategy and internal structure.[20]

If alignment is a critical feature of organizational effectiveness, information, technology, culture, strategy, and human resource practices must be altered together. Moreover, relations among these organizational components must be altered as well. Rebecca Henderson and Kim Clark have developed the concept of "architectural innovation" to refer to change in the engineering *relations* among the components of a technological product, not just the components themselves. Architectural change is an apt concept for thinking about realigning relations among the organization's components as well.[21]

As managers look at transforming an organization they long have helped build, the task is sure to appear formidable. The routines they created to permit stable growth can feel like an enormous flywheel. Yet examples abound of wholesale change, and it is often instigated by those who are products of the system, not just outsiders brought in to restructure it. We know from research evidence that senior managers are not necessarily trapped by an organizational "iron-cage."[22] Though organizations are built on stability, they can also be restabilized with radically different architectures. The crux of initiating the redirection is to develop and apply effective change drivers. With appropriate degrees of visibility, incentives, linkages, and alignment, drivers offer managers a lever for leading the change, with other features to follow.

Organizations face distinct problems in different epochs. If divisionalization and diversification were the problems of earlier periods in U.S. business history, the devolution and incentivizing of authority were among the leading problems of the past decade. As a result, much of the organizational restructuring of recent years has been in the direction of increased alignment of the organization's components around its main goals, improved incentives for achieving the goals, and wider distribution of authority for doing so.

The present era of corporate restructuring has yet to run its full course. The period's performance problems are widespread and far from resolved. Organizations large and small, both for profit and nonprofit, are thus likely to move further in these directions in years to come. Enhanced appreciation for the special problems of systemic change and the special value of drivers for change should hasten the process.[23]

NOTES

1. R. Nelson and S. Winter, *An Evolutionary Theory of Economic Change* (Cambridge, MA: Harvard University Press, 1982).

2. R. M. Henderson and K. B. Clark, "Architectural Innovation: The Reconfiguration of Existing Product Technologies and the Failure of Established Firms," *Administrative Science Quarterly* 35 (March 1990), pp. 9–30.

3. M. L. Tushman, W. H. Newman, and E. Romanelli, "Managing the Unsteady Pace of Organizational Evolution," *California Management Review* 29 (Fall 1986), pp. 29–44.

4. E. H. Schein, "The Role of the CEO in the Management of Change: The Case of Information Technology," in *Transforming Organizations,* ed. T. A. Kochan and M. Useem (New York: Oxford University Press, 1992), pp. 80–95; M. S. Scott Morton, editor, *The Corporation of the 1990s* (New York: Oxford University Press, 1991), S. Zuboff, *In the Age of the Smart Machine: The Future of Work and Power* (New York: Basic Books, 1988).

5. J. Womack, D. T. Jones, and D. Roos, *The Machine that Changed the World: The Story of Lean Production* (New York: HarperCollins, 1990).

6. J. P. MacDuffie and J. Krafcik, "Integrating Technology and Human Resources for High Performance Manufacturing: Evidence from the International Auto Industry," in *Transforming Organizations,* ed. T. Kochan and M. Useem (New York: Oxford University Press, 1992), pp. 209–225.

7. M. A. Conte and J. Svejnar, "The Performance Effects of Employee Ownership Plans," in *Paying for Productivity: A Look at the Evidence,* ed. A. S. Blinder (Washington, DC: The Brookings Institution, 1990), pp. 143–172.

8. M. Porter, *Capital Choices: Changing the Way America Invests in Industry* (Washington, DC: Council on Competitiveness, 1992).

9. M. W. Meyer and L. G. Zucker, *Permanently Failing Organizations* (Newbury Park, CA: Sage Publications, 1989).

10. A. Israel, *Institutional Development: Incentives to Performance* (Baltimore: Johns Hopkins University Press, 1987), pp. 47–69.

11. M. L. Rock and L. A. Berger, eds., *The Compensation Handbook* (New York: McGraw-Hill, 1991, 3rd ed.).

12. D. A. Nadler and M. L. Tushman, *Strategic Organization Design: Concepts, Tools, and Processes* (Glenview, IL: Scott, Foresman, 1988).

13. L. Berger, F. J. Gouillart, W. C. King, and M. Useem, "The Age of Alignment," *Directors & Boards* 16 (Fall 1991), pp. 13–15, 18.

14. M. Beer, R. A. Eisenstat, and B. Spector, *The Critical Path to Corporate Renewal* (Boston: Harvard Business School Press, 1990).

15. M. Useem, L. Setti, and J. Pincus, "The Science of Javanese Management: Organizational Alignments in an Indonesian Development Program," *Public Administration and Development* 12 (December, 1992), pp. 447–471.

16. A. D. Chandler, Jr., *The Visible Hand: The Managerial Revolution in American Business* (Cambridge, MA: Harvard University Press, 1977); N. Fligstein, *Transformation of Corporate Control* (Cambridge, MA: Harvard University Press, 1990).

17. A. Berle, Jr., and G. C. Means, *The Modern Corporation and Private Property* (New York: Harcourt, Brace and World, 1967, reprint edition).

18. E. S. Herman, *Corporate Control, Corporate Power* (New York: Cambridge University Press, 1981); M. C. Jensen and K. J. Murphy. "CEO Incentives—It's Not How Much You Pay, But How," *Harvard Business Review* (May-June, 1990), pp. 138–153.

19. Much of the following discussion is drawn from sources and information reported by M. Useem in *Executive Defenses: Shareholder Power and Corporate Reorganization* (Cambridge, MA: Harvard University Press, 1993).

20. R. M. Cyert and J. G. March, *A Behavioral Theory of the Firm* (Englewood Cliffs, NJ: Prentice-Hall, 1963); Nadler and Tushman, 1988, cited in note 12; A. Pettigrew and R. Whipp, *Managing Change for Competitive Success* (Oxford, England: Blackwell Publishers Ltd., 1991).

21. Henderson and Clark, 1990, cited in note 2.

22. D. C. Hambrick, *The Executive Effect: Concepts and Methods for Studying Top Managers* (Greenwich, CT: JAI Press, 1988).

23. Related commentary on managing organizational change can be found in L. Hirschorn, *Managing in the New Team Environment: Skills, Tools, and Methods* (Reading, MA: Addison-Wesley, 1991); R. M. Kanter, *The Change Masters: Innovation for Productivity in the American Corporation* (New York: Simon and Schuster, 1983); R. M. Kanter, *The Challenge of Organizational Change: How Companies Experience It and Leaders Guide It* (New York: Free Press, 1992); T. A. Kochan, H. C. Katz, and R. B. McKersie, *The Transformation of American Industrial Relations* (New York: Basic Books, 1988); and A. M. Mohrman, Jr., S. A. Mohrman, G. E. Ledford, Jr., T. G. Cummings, and E. E. Lawler, III. *Large-Scale Organizational Change* (San Francisco: Jossey-Bass Publishers, 1991).

II

MARKET CHANGE TRIGGERS

T he cornerstone of a good change management program is a continual focus on the marketplace. The external view should be supported by active intelligence and market research programs to generate the critical information the firm needs in executing intelligent change decisions. By consistently looking outward, a company keeps in touch with its customers, has a good idea of what its competitors are doing, finds a large number of the change triggers that impel internal change, and determines how its own initiatives—which have the potential to become change triggers themselves—will be received by the market, both customers and competitors.

Getting all of this information means nothing unless it is put to use. Executing change is the best way of activating it. But how good is the execution? How much value is being created by the change? Is the change program achieving its goal, sustaining alignment, and forming a stronger competitor? All of these questions have to be monitored and the improvements forged by the change program have to be monitored and measured (Reichheld, Chapter 8). For the change managers seeking answers there are proven ways of tracking the progress of change.

Structure of *The Change Management Handbook*

Section 1
The Change Management Process

1. Change Management
2. The History of Business Change
3. Managing Strategic Alignment
4. Driving Systemic Change

Section 2
Market Change Triggers

5. Market Dynamics: Who's on Top?
6. Playing Off the Power Base: Importance of Market Positioning
7. Pile Drivers of Change
8. Measuring Change and Changing Measures

Section 3
The Gears of Change

3A Strategy
9. Game Plan for the Next Dynamic
10. The Strategic Connection: Mission, Strategy, and Values
11. Structuring the Change Initiative
12. Mergers and Restructurings: Aces in the Hole
13. Midcourse Corrections

3B Operations
14. A Bad Structure Can Be Fatal
15. An Introduction to Supply-Chain Management
16. Integrated Logistics and Supply-Chain Management
17. Only the Best: How Quality Systems Govern Change
18. Aligning Operations with Change Strategies: The Operations Blueprint
19. Information Technologies to Manage the Next Dynamic
20. The Change-Responsive Office

3C Culture
21. The Next Generation of Fire Walkers
22. The Right Stuff for the Next Dynamic
23. Critical Elements of Organizational Culture Change
24. Cultural Change and Corporate Strategy
25. Making Culture Change Happen
26. The People Factor
27. The Key to Corporate Survival: Change Begins and Ends with People
28. Human Resource Planning and Change
29. The Ethics of Change

3D Compensation
30. Aligning Business and Pay Strategy
31. Rewards for Executing Change
32. Compensation as a Change Stimulus
33. A Nimble Compensation System for Managing Change
34. Using Executive Compensation to Promote Change

Chapter Five

Market Dynamics: Who's on Top?

James W. Gouthro and James R. Sholder

O ne of the most powerful forces signaling the necessity to realign your company—its strategy, organization, culture, and compensation systems—is a change in market dynamics. By market dynamics, we mean changes in industry structure, within and between your business and neighboring industries (see Figure 5–1). Companies tend to focus their assessment of competitive standing on traditional competitors within the industry. But often they are blindsided by moves from new competitors in neighboring industries. Only senior management can make realignment decisions, and it is senior management that must pay greatest attention to the threats and opportunities posed by significant changes in industry structure.

All industries face change, but the pace of change varies widely. It ranges from the relatively slow rate of industries such as electric utilities, which enjoy regulated monopolies, to the very rapid one that typifies technology firms such as computer chip manufacturers, whose businesses and competitive positions are reinvented annually or sometimes faster.

Most larger companies probably fall somewhere in the middle of the change continuum. Competitor assessment will let you know where your company and its industry may need realignment, by providing important insights to the following:

- Gain advantage in the marketplace (strategies)
- Identify new ideas and/or better approaches (benchmarking)
- Measure yourself (set standards)
- Discern major structural change in the industry (new paradigms)

Let us consider some specific cases involving changing industry structures.

FIGURE 5-1
Industry Structure

"Industry structure" includes these features:

1. Definition of the industry, including what benefits you bring to your customers, by market and market segment, and the portion(s) of the value chain in which you operate

2. Boundaries of the industry, which determine who your present and potential competitors are

3. Degree of concentration in the industry, along with levels of profitability this makes possible for the leaders, threshold companies, and followers

4. Pace of change in the industry, including the dynamics of movement in competitors' market shares due to innovation in products, marketing, distribution, and use of technology

---

CASES IN CHANGING INDUSTRY STRUCTURES

Structure in the Making

The convergence of the telephone, computer, television, and information industries is still in flux, and the eventual leaders are still to be determined. In that context, the Bell Operating Companies provide a switched, wired network for voice, data, and fax, with video communication to be added soon. How do they compete in today's world, given regulatory restraints, the entry of new competitors in the local loop, and the onrush of wireless alternatives? This is a multibillion-dollar question for companies that grew up with cultures appropriate to a monopoly position.

Structure Almost Closed

The beer business in the last 30 years has cast off a fragmented industry structure that had been in place since the end of Prohibition. It used to be structured around the transportation cost advantages of local and regional brands. Now consolidation is nearly completed, with Anheuser-Busch Cos. capturing close to half of the total market. With Miller's share points, the top two brewers have about two thirds of the market. If you are a threshold company or a follower in this industry, what strategy do you use to compete?

FINDING PROFITABLE NICHES IN THE STRUCTURE

At the macro level, the property-casualty insurance industry is a textbook case of low market shares, commodity products, and price taking. There are segment pockets, however, and exceptions to the general rules of this industry structure.

FIGURE 5–2

Competitor Assessment Process

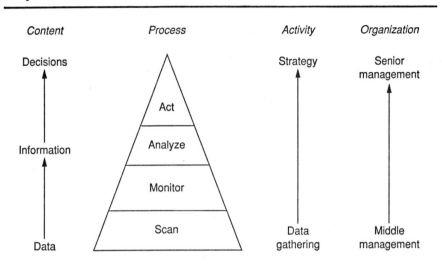

The industry is driven by an underwriting cycle of supply and demand for risk bearing and risk management services covering every industry, all sizes of companies, and most households. Niche positions are possible as a result, even specialized positions of considerable size. For example, AIG is the most profitable financial services company of all, building on disciplined underwriting of jumbo risks for multinationals. Progressive, on the other hand, specializes in substandard, personal lines of automobile insurance. Its risk selection permits the company to avoid price taking. Progressive compensates for higher risks through critical mass of pricing and claims experience by market.

TOOLS FOR SENIOR MANAGEMENT

The total competitor assessment process is graphically illustrated in Figure 5–2 as a hierarchical pyramid. Both activities and organization require an increase in the level of experience and decision-making capability as the assessment process moves up toward the top of the pyramid.

Furthermore, each stage in the assessment pyramid indicates the relative amount of data that must be processed. For example, the scanning phase absorbs much higher volumes of data than subsequent stages. Thus, a weeding out of information and a development of focus occur as the process moves to higher levels.

Although senior management will not be directly involved in the scanning, monitoring, and much of the analyzing, it must provide direction for the entire organization, and, thus, some understanding of tools and techniques will be beneficial.

Practical competitive assessment and resultant strategy selection will involve at least five key steps:

How Much Resource Is Needed and How Will It Be Organized?

The answer comes back to where you fall on the aforementioned continuum of change. That, in turn, depends on whether you primarily face risk or uncertainty in your business. Risk is defined as variation around a known trend line. Uncertainty is not knowing where the trend line is or where it is moving.

The following scheme comes out of the aerospace industry but it has universal applicability. It illustrates the differences between risk and uncertainty.

Known Knowns—knowing the skills you have to have to meet the market's performance requirements and knowing how to deliver them

Known Unknowns—knowing the skills required, knowing you do not have them, but betting you can acquire them in sufficient time

Unknown Unknowns ("Unk Unks")—not knowing that a skill is needed, nor how to get it in the relevant time frame

The more uncertainty you face ("Unk Unks"), the greater should be the resource allocation for competitor scanning and monitoring, and the higher their organizational placement. Competitor scanning in this instance has to be done through a specialized approach to avoid the problem of "the blind leading the blind." The problem with the Unk Unk is that there won't be much, if any, knowledge about the problem anywhere—and at any level—in this organization. Thus, bucking the problem up the line—or down the line closer to the market—could be the wrong approach, especially if there is an unfounded assumption that someone in either direction has a handle on it. The special approach may have to involve solid new investigation by a team of people with various skills, disciplines, and insights from a number of levels. If neither you nor your competitors know where the industry is moving, conventional assessment adds no insight (see "Paradigm Shifts").

In contrast, the more you face well-defined risks (Known Knowns), the less the resource allocation and the closer the competitor monitoring should be placed to business units making daily decisions in the marketplace.

Ultimately, only senior management can decide the importance of the information and what it means for the future of the firm. Organizational structure should suit the process, with a broad audience scanning for trends, lower-level analysts providing preliminary analysis based on specified guidelines, and higher levels of management deciding on the strategic importance of the information.

Who Should Be Scanned and Monitored?

A company needs to scan and monitor market trends continually for new customer expectations and changes in the customer's preferred source of supply. Increasingly, the customer may be the preferred source of this information. Consider these examples:

- Today, companies across industries self-insure their health benefits as a way of containing health care cost. In life insurance, fitness practices and longer life spans translate into lower premiums for individuals' mortality protection, and policies are being focused on a greater need to accumulate savings for retirement.

- Major companies have bypassed the credit functions of banks and go directly to financial markets with commercial paper.

- In telecommunications, large corporate users have purchased dedicated lines and seek bypasses around regulated utilities.

Important point. Companies often misunderstand these dynamics and track the wrong things under the heading of *customer satisfaction* and *quality*. What they may be picking up in these measurements is resignation to the choices available, rather than genuine satisfaction.

Consumers, whether corporate or individual, are gaining increasing options. Economists in fact define the boundaries of an industry by "cross-elasticity" of demand, that is, a movement from one industry to its neighbor (for example, an alternative product or service can fulfill the same function) when there is a significant change in comparative prices.

This means scanning and monitoring must reexamine the *customer's own behavior* in addition to how traditional competitors behave. For instance, the usual choice that manufacturing companies have of making versus buying components is more complex in today's world, given downsizing, "core staffing," and new alliances with suppliers. It also means that neighboring industries have to be examined. They often can deliver similar benefits to your customer but may have advantages over you in areas such as the use of technology, regulatory requirements, capital costs, or distribution.

A primary example would be the shifts in fuel usage engineered by electric utilities during the energy crunch of the 1970s. As oil became scarce and its prices spiraled to record levels, the utilities quickly moved to the more abundant and cheaper-priced coal to run their generating plants. Ironically—and this often happens when there are price-driven shifts to alternative products—the price of coal went up because of rising demand. However, the relative price differential between coal and oil held, and coal continued to maintain the economic edge until oil prices sagged and supplies became more plentiful in the late 1970s.

FIGURE 5–3

Comparison of Scanning and Monitoring

	Activity	Data	Organization Level	Results
Scanning	Broad brush; identify emerging trends	Raw; voluminous	All levels	Input for monitoring
Monitoring	Focus on specifics	Organized	Researcher/ analyst	Competitors' situation analysis

What is scanning versus monitoring?   *Scanning* is a process that involves a broad gathering of data on peers, other sources of competition, and potential replacements or alternatives for your product or service. Some management-level expertise may be necessary for pattern recognition—to understand the meaning of anomalies versus trends, but in general the gathering and sifting of information should be broadly based.

Monitoring has more focus on the specific issues and companies that are identified through scanning efforts. The monitoring process begins to move away from trend recognition and adds another element of analysis. *At a minimum,* monitoring looks at known peer competitors—those that senior management already knows as the competition.

The basic differences between scanning and monitoring are illustrated in Figure 5–3.

As part of a regular monitoring process, the same set of information on your firm should be gathered and compared with the competition; this will be useful for setting standards or performance measurements.

Paradigm Shifts

In the process of scanning and monitoring your competitive environment, a very difficult issue to identify or predict before it happens is a change in the paradigm under which your industry operates. By paradigm, we mean the accepted belief system that, in effect, sets your constraints or determines what you believe is practical or realistic to implement.

What is an example of a paradigm shift? For many years, no one ran a mile in less than four minutes, and many believed no person could. After Roger Bannister broke through the four-minute barrier, a paradigm shift occurred. The belief system was forcibly altered—and sub-four-minute miles are now almost regular occurrences.

One problem in identifying changes in paradigms is that often your belief system can also be your blinders. It is difficult at the beginning of a new trend to see something happening when you do not believe it is possible. Another problem is that quite often paradigm shifts will be caused by some entity outside of the normal industry environment and therefore not constrained by your industry's accepted belief system.

There is no simple answer to the problem of identifying these changes, but the potential impact on the future of your industry and organization is so great that some attention should be given to discovering paradigm shifts while they are happening. There are two approaches that may be useful:

1. Look for anomalies in the behavior of competitors. When unusual behavior is identified, investigate to see if the competitor's assumptions and beliefs have changed.

2. Be alert to any encroachment on your market and customers from outside of your normal competitive spheres. This bears close watching to see whether it is more of the same or a radical alteration of beliefs about the environment.

Analyzing

Within the competitive arena, the analysis phase can be viewed from several contexts:

Industry structure

What is the structure of your industry, and how is it expected to change over time?

What is your firm's alignment within the industry?

What are the critical success factors within your industry, and how do you and your competitors measure up against those characteristics?

What are the options available to establish competitive advantage?

Specific competitors

Examine strategic clues to clarify *intentions* versus *resources*. Strategic clues may be found in the following:

- Management actions and statements
- Spending emphasis
- Positioning
- Market forces
- Capabilities

Further clarify competitor intention by examining quantitative measures of the firm's behavior and trends.

FIGURE 5–4
Competition within an Industry

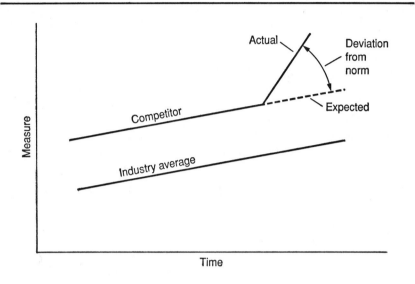

Competitors' *resources* are tougher to assess, particularly the organizational will and ability to use these resources.

Organization is often overlooked as a source of competitive advantage and offers its own kind of special competency. Managements' belief systems—yours and competitors'—are at the core of that competency and ultimately dictate how resources are deployed and whether vested interests act as an internal barrier to change.

What needs to be scanned and monitored.

- Who has the resources and organizational will to meet customers' needs, inside or outside the presently defined industry?

- Where is there a performance differential, positive or negative, between your company and your competitors in satisfying that need?

- What is the source of that performance differential, and how can it be strengthened or offset, depending on where your company stands in the comparison?

Activity measures versus results measures. Not all numbers are alike. We distinguish between activity measures and results measures. *Activity measures* usually represent a deliberate decision on the part of management to spend, invest, or realign. *Results measures* provide an indicator of performance, but they represent the results of changes in activity and usually are controlled by alterations in the activity.

It is our belief that activity measures provide earlier and more accurate insight into a company's strategies. Activity measures would include marketing expenses; investments; changes in pricing, advertising, capacity, research spending, and product mix; and acquisitions. Results measures would include profit margins, market share, sales growth, and productivity.

Competitors relative to industry.   Within an industry, a company tends to maintain the same relative position over time on key financial and marketing measures. A significant deviation from a competitor's norm may indicate a recent strategic decision or signal a future strategic correction. Within the context of competitor analysis, it provides another strong strategic clue (see Figure 5–4).

When to Act and When to Realign

The final stage in the process requires senior management's decision for change. Analysis of the evidence, tempered by management beliefs and expertise, will identify windows of opportunity. This leads to development of strategy that will become the corporation's call to action. That action may include realigning the company—its strategy, operations, culture, and compensation system. Generally, all have to be changed in unison so they remain compatible with each other.

Chapter Six

Playing Off the Power Base: The Importance of Market Positioning and Organizational Delivery

Michael R. Cooper, Brian S. Morgan, Randall G. Edmond,
Judith R. Greener, Jerrold R. Bratkovich

T he well-managed firm is the well-informed firm. The strongest competitor is the firm that constantly monitors the market it serves to determine what is really taking place in its customer base. The best performer is the firm that reaches its decisions on in-depth, hard, and accurate information that it has developed firsthand from the market.

Facts are critical to smooth, efficient, highly profitable, and value-creating operations. And the premium on good information is growing larger in the age of information and its close cousin—the age of managing change. It is the well-informed firm that is best able to spot change, to realize what it is, and to respond speedily with the steps needed to restabilize and realign the firm.

The stakes in the age of constant change are putting increased pressures on companies to maintain continuing market intelligence or market surveillance efforts. This information-gathering system should be in constant use and should guide decisions on a day-to-day basis at a time when already fierce competition is intensifying. But its value can be the highest when it zeroes in on a change trigger within the firm's market and sends back timely signals of the market's reconfiguration to the company's management.

Clearly, the firm with the right intelligence network has an edge on the rest of the field. Its effort becomes the business equivalent of a DEW line that draws a bead not only on the timing of the change but also on the breadth and depth of its significance. Good intelligence is the prime requisite for decisive and effective action.

Frankly, the firm that soft-pedals good intelligence—that flies blind, keeps a wet finger in the air, or operates by intuition—is going to be a loser in this day and age. It's never really going to get the idea of change management—from detecting the change trigger to realizing the trigger's impact on the market to taking the proper steps that will respond to the trigger and realign all key facets of the organization. This is the kind of company that—by not relying on intelligence—is in effect saying it doesn't want to be bothered by the facts. And that kind of company, even if it gets some inkling of the change by some manner, is going to stay too long in the zone of self-denial.

That's a scary prospect because, once enmeshed in the zone, the naive company can get battered by competitors who have picked up the change trigger and are beating its brains out. And it may never get out. Or at best, it has to play catch-up.

Thus, a continuous flow of quality information can be assigned a shock value. But there is some irony in the impact. The well-informed firm routinely operating a high-powered intelligence system will recognize the shock value of a change trigger. But it won't be shocked because it has accustomed itself to deal with shock. Instead, it will proceed to response and realignment without a hitch. But the inured company, which should be shocked the most, probably will react by denying that what is happening really is happening.

Now a market intelligence system does not require constant surveys or investigations of the market or the customer base, although they are appropriate at frequent intervals. One such time is when a change trigger has been picked up and more information is needed to verify it or get a handle on its significance. Rather, the good intelligence system means continually listening to the market, more specifically the customers. In that regard the sales force can act as an intelligence-gathering network from day to day and periodic discussions between executives and customers can be quite helpful. What is most important is an orientation to focus outwardly on the market and to keep eyes and ears open for meaningful information and trends.

Basically, the properly functioning firm is most concerned with its market position. And its intelligence gathering should be concerned with whether there are any actual or threatened changes in the market that could impact that position negatively or positively. If the impact is negative, the company must move to protect its position by countering the adverse forces. A positive impact can open opportunities for profitable expansion of sales or variations on existing offerings that might have been missed had the intelligence system not been working. So regardless of the direction of the trends, the firm can be caught in a painful squeeze by failing to pick up a change trigger.

To a large degree, market position depends first on the values that the customers of a company ascribe to its products or services. In other words, what qualities about the product or service prompt the buyer to purchase the firm's offerings over those of competitors? Second, market position can be determined by the reputation of the firm—or what the buyers think of it as an organization. This can be probed with solid intelligence programs, and it can consist of key areas in which change triggers may be embedded as buyers' values change or the firm's image changes.

Good market intelligence is critical for organizational alignment in response to a change trigger. The keys to alignment are *market positioning* and *organizational delivery*.

Market positioning involves understanding the current and future values of the firm's customers and then determining how buyer values position the company in its market. Do these values sufficiently differentiate the product from competing wares, and have they made enough of an impression—have they captured a share of the customers' minds—with buyers to be classified as a preferred product? Organizational delivery links that knowledge of the external market with the firm's internal system for delivering the products so that delivery helps achieve the promise of the market position.

Thus aligning market position and delivery systems is an initial—and a continuous—facet of alignment. An effective intelligence system is essential to maintaining alignment. Unfortunately, many companies do not integrate market positioning and organizational delivery but operate them in isolation. The value of integration, however, usually is realized best by firms that emphasize the need for up-to-date information. And it is these firms that appreciate (1) the early signals of change and (2) the need to realign the company to cope with change.

We now can discuss the integration of the market positioning process. Positioning can be regarded as an organized system for finding a window in the minds of current and potential customers.[1] It is a process of building and managing a set of expectations and beliefs about what a brand represents. The key strategic decision is how the company can differentiate itself in a constantly changing and highly competitive arena.

Ultimately, market position is determined externally—by the customers that the company serves and by the firms that it competes against. Changes in the market may be observed by intelligence and may take place in these very areas. In other words, they are primary sources of change triggers. Changes in buyer values, dictated by their technological needs, costs, or preferences; entrance of a new competitor; or introduction of a significant new product that changes the market's landscape all are important change triggers.

On an ongoing basis, however, the organization is constantly challenged to shape its offerings and its delivery so they are consistent with buyer values and capture a share of customers' minds. The position is shaped by communications to the marketplace, quality of goods and services, and the timeliness and efficiency of delivery.

Constantly monitoring the firm's market position is among the most important functions of intelligence. Any change in position is a change trigger.

A key reason that there is no substitute for a firm's own intelligence in order to define and detect market position is that the positioning process is not purely rational. Market communications, for example, can play to emotions and perceptions that may be entirely different from the tangible performance aspects of products and services. As a result, intelligence is needed to understand both the emotional and the fact-based drivers of market position and to allow the firm to react appropriately.

Although market position is defined externally, it is *managed* internally by management and employees. Internal organizational culture, structures, and processes shape the capacity of the organization to deliver as well as its delivery style. The effectiveness of management in communicating to the market and organizing to deliver goods and services provides the criteria that the market will use to define the position. Thus, position is a result of the interplay of market and organizational forces.

In this era it is extremely difficult for firms to differentiate on product or service alone. With the exception of a few breakthroughs, most new product and service offerings are refinements of existing lines. Even innovative products are easily emulated, so that most breakthroughs do not provide a sustained advantage. At the same time, image alone is not a differentiator. Without substance in goods or services, cachet is short-lived. With differentiation based on product or image difficult, positioning has become a way for a company to define its uniqueness.

THE POSITIONING PROCESS

To develop and execute an effective market positioning strategy, the firm must constantly measure buyer values, examine its own reputation, and determine its competitive position in the marketplace. Market intelligence provides the information for carrying out this chain of action. In turn, intelligence can provide important insight into the future—possibly allowing one's firm to get in front of a change trigger. If the information-gathering system finds that future buyer values—that is, anticipated values—will change, it can have a leg up on the competition in making and delivering the wares that will keep and enhance position. But when current values of customers change, that is enough of a signal that a change trigger is underway and that a restabilization must be accomplished.

Assessing Buyer Values and Understanding Their Impact on Company Products and Services

To position products and services effectively, one must understand buyer values. Buyer values are clusters of attitudes toward products and services held by potential purchasers. Buyers will be more likely to purchase the goods and services that, in their view, offer the characteristics they value most. A typical set of buyer values emerging from a study of business purchasers of services might include the following:

- *Industry Expertise*—the supplier's knowledge of the industry, actual experience in the industry, and acceptance of the service by other buyers in the industry.

- *Business Relationship*—the service provider's track record and familiarity with the buyer's company and its management.

- *Service Delivery*—the provider's reputation and past performance in delivering high-quality services as promised, on time, and at the agreed-upon price.

- *Innovation*—the provider's ability to deliver state-of-the-art, leading-edge solutions tailored to the buyer's concerns.
- *Technical Expertise*—the knowledge and technical resources of the provider in its service area.
- *Value for Price*—the provider's image as a high- or low-cost provider, and the provider's ability to deliver added value.

Each value represents the synthesis of a set of specific attributes, elements, and feelings. For example, in the mind of the buyer the value labeled *Service Delivery* can be made up of feelings about the importance of the overall trustworthiness of an organization and its ability to deliver on time, to deliver what is promised, and to hold to the promised price.

Understanding these elements is important to effective operation of the intelligence system. The identification of the values gives the system a number of specific points on which to focus to determine if and where changes are taking place. Therefore, the values are subsets of the market position that can lead to, or themselves become, change triggers. In addition, the values keep the firm's information-gathering riveted on the market and the customer base. If changes in values do occur, the firm will know about them and be in position to respond with actions that include realignment and are aimed at restabilization.

When buyers assess an individual organization in terms of their values, their impression is based on a combination of facts, feelings, experiences, and illusions. An organization's ability to change these attitudes requires attention to both the actual positioning elements and the overall image of the organization.

Buyer value assessment involves direct interviews with a carefully selected cross section of bona fide purchasers of the goods or services provided by the company and its competitors. The result of the assessment should be a definition of a set of buyer values and an identification of the relative importance of each value in determining customer purchase decisions. No single set of buyer values applies across industries and markets. So a custom-tailored set of values and value attributes must be developed for each.

In addition, buyer values within a given market can change over time, although these changes usually are not fast enough to serve as change triggers. But it is important to track buyer values over time after getting a thorough baseline measure. Early identification of an emerging buyer value can provide a strategic edge in market communications. Consider the issue of concern for the environment. Until recently, business purchasers were not particularly sensitive to this issue. However, as we see in Figure 6–1, this aspect of reputation suddenly moved from having little relationship to the bottom line in 1991 to having a significant relationship with the price/earnings ratio in 1992. These data are collapsed across industries. In sectors such as Chemicals and Forest Products, where environmental issues are most salient, the firms committed to tracking buyer values could be among the first to profit from a new positioning opportunity.

FIGURE 6–1
Corporate Reputation, Price/Earnings Ratio, and Emerging Buyer Values

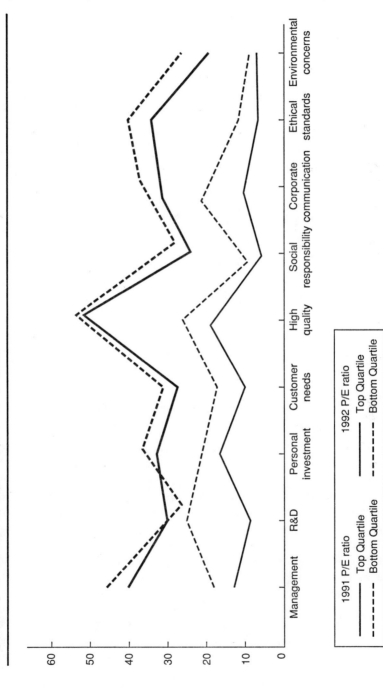

FIGURE 6–2
Positioning Map

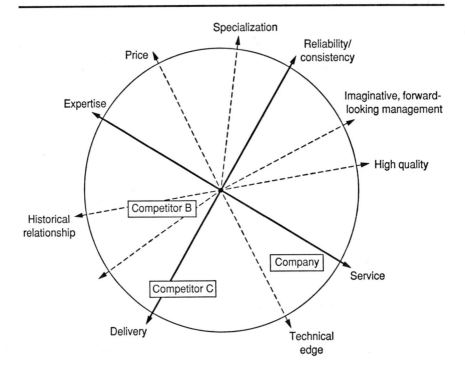

Assessing Reputation and Competitive Position in the Marketplace

Armed with an understanding of buyer values, the company can move on to examine its competitive positioning. In this phase the buyer rates the company's market position against those of its competitors—by share, pricing power, dominance in a niche, and so on. This phase of the intelligence/analysis is important since it can identify one of the most crucial change triggers—when your position gets stronger or weaker vis-à-vis key competitors by whatever characteristics of good market position the firm wants.

In the buyer assessment, the firm moves from an identification of important customer values to what the customers think of how the competing firms deliver on those values. Then the company can compare its position to those of competitors by mapping where they stand on buyer values. The mapping in effect allows the firm to benchmark itself against competitors. Mapping shows where the firm must change in order to get more in step with buyer values, it influences change in behavior that may be a needed response to a change trigger, and it also underscores the competitive mind-set that the firm is in so any changes are done with appropriate alignments in mind.

A sample positioning map is displayed in Figure 6–2. The questions addressed in a mapping exercise include the following:

- What buyer values are most closely associated with the company? With its key competitors?
- What are the company's strengths in delivering on buyer values? Where are the largest gaps?
- Is the company's position clearly differentiated?
- Is the company's position what management wants it to be?
- Which gaps are most important to close?
- Are there buyer values not addressed by any competitor that represent opportunities to differentiate?

The matrix displayed in Figure 6–3 shows how the results of a buyer value and competitive assessment can be configured to guide decision making. The axes represent a company's performance in delivering on buyer values and the importance of the values in guiding buyer behavior. Four clusters of values and four related sets of actions are identified. Defined by the action to be taken, these clusters are as follows:

1. *Strengths to defend.* These key drivers of consideration are unique to the company or its brands and should be emphasized in market communications. For example, a company that finds it is considered the leading-edge player in a market that values innovation would want to promote its advantage heavily. Also included in this cluster are aspects of value that represent the price of entry for all brands. These must be maintained, but because they are not differentiators, they should not be primarily emphasized in communications. For example, a company might find that its buyers value technical expertise but that all key competitors are perceived as able to deliver on technical requirements of programs. There is no differentiation between the company and its competitors.

2. *Opportunities to improve.* These are drivers of purchase intention in which the company is deficient. They represent priority areas for improvement, and they are keys to market expansion. For example, buyers may place a premium on delivering on time. If a company was perceived as deficient in this area, that would be a primary area for improvement in performance and communication to the market.

3. *Areas to maintain.* These are areas that are not key drivers of purchase decisions and not areas of major focus by the company. They do not require attention, but in dynamic markets they require monitoring since they could become more prominent in the minds of buyers. Responsiveness to environmental concerns, which were described earlier, is a good example of a factor moving up from this category to become a candidate for improvement.

4. *Candidate for reallocation.* These areas, although closely associated with a brand, are not critical determinants of choice. An example could be information

FIGURE 6–3

Buyer Value Importance and Performance

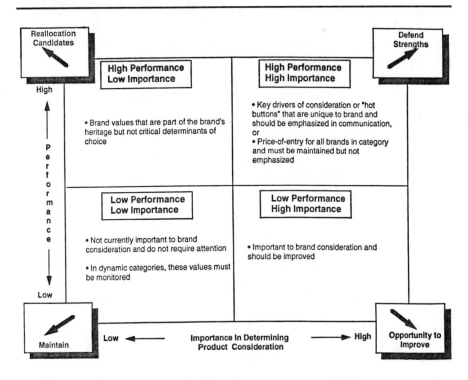

companies that invest in maintaining an edge in mainframe computing in the face of increased market desire for personal computer-based solutions. This is an example of self-deception. Mainframe expertise may be part of a company's heritage, so it may be culturally difficult to deemphasize it. Nevertheless, areas like this one may represent overinvestment of valuable resources and a diversion from change triggers and the need to respond to them.

Development of Positioning Strategy

Working with knowledge of buyer values and the resulting competitive assessment, an organization moves to develop a positioning strategy. The primary objective of this process is to identify areas to which resources should be devoted to best gain competitive advantage. Questions to be addressed at this stage include the following:

- How much market growth is the company likely to gain over time?
- What does the company have to do to achieve this market growth?

- What is the cost of the selected strategy? What is the financial return?
- How should the company position itself to gain sustained competitive advantage?
- What long-term strategy is required to develop the company into a market leader?

As a company addresses these issues, it can employ buyer value and competitive positioning data to address three key issues:

1. Examining emerging values.
2. Identifying excitement attributes.
3. Selecting a target positioning and a unique high ground.

Emerging values.   Emerging values, as noted earlier, are buyer values of growing importance. Early identification of these values allows a company to mount a communication campaign to give it an edge in the market of the future and to beat competitors to an advantageous position. Emerging values can be very significant triggers and the company's responses represent sound management of change.

Excitement variable.   Among the drivers of purchase consideration are several classes of attributes. These include threshold, performance, and excitement variables. Threshold variables are "price of entry" attributes for all competitors in a category. Technical expertise is an example. Performance variables are key purchase attributes that are expected of the leaders in a product or service category. In a crowded market, industry expertise might be such a variable. It is highly valued and it weighs heavily in purchase decisions. But industry expertise is enjoyed by most leading competitors in a market. Excitement variables are those components of buyer value that have strong, often emotional appeal. For example, cash rebates by Discover Card on purchases offer something unique to the buyer that sets it apart from other credit cards.

If associating a brand with threshold and performance variables provides an even footing for competition, then identifying an excitement variable and associating it with a brand can provide a strong competitive advantage. Figure 6–4 illustrates the potential impact of an excitement variable. The lack of an excitement variable forces a company to compete on price. This will erode profit margins unless the company can find ways to become a low-cost producer, in which case low price may become an excitement variable.

Target positioning and high ground.   A unique high ground is a desirable market position that is held by only one company. It can go hand in hand with market power. The high ground is based on a combination of the company's perceived

FIGURE 6–4
Impact of Excitement Variables

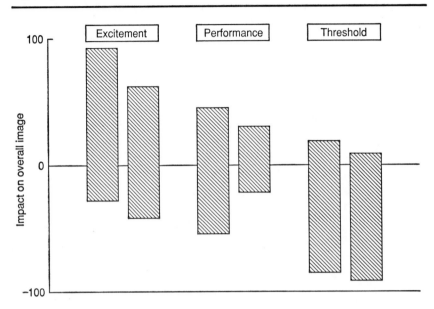

strengths and the most important buyer values expressed by customers. Examples of companies that own a unique market position include the following:

- Johnson & Johnson, with its reputation as a good corporate citizen.
- Merck, known as the company that attracts and retains scientists with world-class reputations.
- Rubbermaid, perceived as the company with an unwavering commitment to quality.
- 3M, considered the innovative company, committed to aggressive research and development.

Knowledge of the key positioning elements is the starting point. Then, the company has to use this information to develop a set of targeted messages through a focused communication strategy (the steps involved in this process are not addressed in this article). The overall aim is ownership of a market position.

ORGANIZATIONAL DELIVERY

Ultimately, an organization's competitive position is shaped by interaction between the organization and its buyers. A communication program addressed to key buyer values can attract buyer interest. But developing and sustaining a relationship between the organization and its buyers must depend on the quality of goods and services and the way they are delivered. Deliverables and processes must be grounded in a clear understanding of what buyers value and what the company's market positioning promises. Then, the organizational delivery must be aligned with the market positioning.

Such an alignment process has two key components:

1. *Market management,* or building knowledge of the market into company operations and processes.

2. *Customer orientation,* or building knowledge of the customer into the minds of employees, and organizing to place the highest priority on delivering on customer needs and expectations.

Market Management

Market management is the process of building bridges between external market measurement and performance levels on the one hand and internal processes and reward systems on the other. It involves shaping operations and management processes that focus on customer retention and relationship extension. The value of customer retention has been well documented: It is far more cost effective to keep an existing customer than it is to secure a new one. Note how these alignments resemble those desired in the change management process.

To achieve this objective, companies must actively use market information to guide day-to-day management. A recent benchmarking study by Opinion Research Corporation (ORC) of Princeton, NJ, documents that some companies are not doing a particularly effective job in this area and therefore are not set up to monitor shock waves from a change trigger. Although most companies have systems for recording customer complaints and for surveying customer opinion, the data in Figure 6–5 indicate that just half of those studied use the data as part of an active program to help individuals and teams improve quality, and less than half use the information to track quality improvement and to establish strategic quality goals. Even fewer companies use external customer data to determine incentives and salary increases. However, companies that are quality leaders are far more likely than others to use feedback from customers for these purposes. Effective performance in these areas helps an organization gain a competitive edge.

Often a substantial communications gap exists between marketing and human resources management. Customer information usually is gathered and consumed in one department and not shared with others. Even if the market data are of high quality, they seldom include knowledge of customers added by the efforts of sales and customer service employees. Whether the newcomers have the same or different buyer values, the information can fall through the cracks. Although the company already has important information in-house, it is not being supplied to or incorporated in the knowledge base being used by the marketing people to organize the delivery to

FIGURE 6–5
How Companies Use Data from External Customers

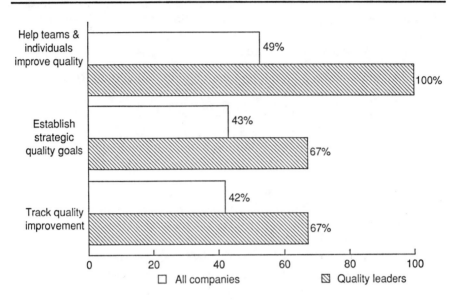

market. The project could very well fail or opportunities could be lost especially if new customers came aboard as a result of new buyer-values.

Customer Orientation

Customer orientation is the process of aligning the entire organization in an integrated manner to deliver on buyer values and enhance customer relationships. It requires a focus on customer relationship management. Given the current weak linkages between market data and internal management practices in many organizations, effective organizational alignment represents an opportunity to build substantial competitive advantage.

The integration process includes the following steps:

- *Ensuring that employees understand company objectives and customer needs and expectations.* Communications professionals who use buyer-value data to construct messages to the marketplace must recognize the strategic value of the information for internal functioning and focus on delivering the information to the company's own work force as well as the market.

- *Understanding employee work values and linking valued rewards to delivery on company objectives and customer needs and expectations.* Sharing information is a starting point. Directing employee effort toward delivery on buyer values requires that this information be used to help structure reward systems. As noted earlier, this represents a major opportunity to differentiate, as few organizations are doing an effective job in this area.

- *Developing the commitment levels required to translate objectives into action.* Achieving acceptance is too often neglected in an era of declining loyalty of companies to employees and vice versa. However, absence of employee commitment can leave a company vulnerable to a front-line work force that delivers perfunctorily and without the enthusiasm for products and services needed to build and sustain relationships.

- *Creating the requisite human capacity for delivery.* In ORC's experience, crucial components of ability to deliver often have been compromised or even gutted in restructuring efforts. Effective direction of scarce resources requires an in-depth look at staffing levels and training initiatives dedicated to service delivery.

- *Giving employees both the power to deliver and the accountability for delivery.* The ORC benchmarking study cited earlier reveals that companies are increasing employee empowerment, but this is a gradual process, even among leaders. Both accountability to deliver and resources for delivery must be monitored and allocated effectively.

- *Integrating internal functions to provide effective service, build customer relationships, and reinforce positioning.* This is an area of glaring deficiency for most organizations. Departments and divisions become even more self-protective and self-interested in difficult times. Teamwork is a strength in very few organizations: The ORC employee attitude data base reveals that just 30 percent of employees in U.S. companies say teamwork is good or very good. The example of the compartmentalized use of market information discussed earlier in this section is a good example of what happens when teamwork is absent. The company moves forward but on few cylinders, and it can't mobilize all of its power to deliver effectively. What results is waste and poor performance.

Case Study

Several of these issues came together in the case of a direct mail marketing organization, where results of a buyer value and competitive positioning survey revealed that two key customer segments were at risk. Both segments valued high-quality customer service, and both had experienced problems with order fulfillment and billing accuracy.

Results of an internal survey conducted at the same time as the market study revealed that employees believed that service levels had declined. The survey also revealed high stress levels, a substantial decline in job security, and sharp differences between top- and second-tier managers' perceptions of the organization's ability to deliver high-quality service.

The findings of both surveys were linked to staff reductions and to heavy recruitment of outsiders for jobs at the top of the organization. The new senior managers knew that productivity had to be increased, but their lack of familiarity with work processes led them to make staffing decisions that compromised the ability to deliver. The longer-service, second-tier managers saw the problem, but they knew that a premium was being placed on cost reduction. They also felt that their jobs were at risk. As a result, they were reluctant to take strong positions on the staffing issues. Instead, they delegated the problem downward, communicating increased performance targets to a reduced customer service work force and avoiding direct dialogue with employees about emerging service problems. In effect, their coping mechanism compounded stress levels while avoiding the delivery problem.

Using the combined market and employee data as a foundation, the company has taken the following steps to address the problem:

- Communicating about business realities and the need for an accelerated pace of delivery. The communications are designed to get commitment from all levels throughout the organization.
- Closing the communications gap between top and second-tier management to encourage dialogue regarding important delivery issues.
- Reopening channels for upward communication from employees to second-tier managers to ensure that delivery problems surface quickly.
- Reexamining recent downsizing and outsourcing decisions to arrive at a staffing mix that is both lean and able to deliver.
- Developing communications and service enhancement programs aimed at the buyer values of the two key at-risk customer segments.

The solution represents an integrated effort across departments, based on a combination of market intelligence and internal organizational information, with actions designed to have an impact on both the market and the company.

SUMMARY: EFFECTIVE POSITIONING AND THE BENEFITS OF ALIGNMENT

Effective market positioning requires that management actively take the following initiatives:

- Secure effective baseline market measures of the business environment, buyer values, and competitive positioning and use them to determine whether changes are being triggered.
- Monitor the market on an ongoing basis, as the environment, buyer values, and competitive positions are continually evolving.
- Use this information strategically to accomplish the following objectives:

- Provide input for determination of the company's competitive set.
- Develop effective market communication strategies.
- Develop a unique high ground that represents a differentiated market positioning.
- Align the organization to deliver on buyer values.

The relationship between the company and the market is interactive and continually evolving. The process described here requires a systemic, integrated approach to the use of strategic market information. Those organizations that manage the alignment process effectively can expect a number of benefits:

- Intelligence that can serve as an early warning system to preserve the existing customer base.
- Information that can be used to attract new customers.
- Ability to maximize the value of strategic market information by translating it directly into action both internally and externally.
- Combination of the best resources of those most in touch with the marketplace with those who manage internal and traditionally inward-looking functions.
- An open feedback and communication system linking internal groups with each other and with the voice of the customer.

Most importantly, the organization that manages alignment effectively will enjoy a sustainable competitive edge over those organizations in which market positioning and organizational delivery are treated separately.

NOTE

1. A. Ries and J. Trout, *Positioning: The Battle for Your Mind* (New York: McGraw-Hill, 1981).

Chapter Seven

Pile Drivers of Change

Martin J. Sikora

O n e look at the vast external landscape on which businesses operate leads to the inescapable conclusion that the change paradigm espoused by Lance Berger in Chapter 1 is not important. It's critical, in the most extreme sense of the word, to survival.

A degree in rocket science is not necessary for a person to understand that the forces impacting the world in the 1990s mean we are living in an era of constant change. Business is not exempt. Business does not live in some insular world that allows it just to continue moving forward year after year making and selling its wares, paying its dividends, and planning for the future free of concerns and changes in the world at large. Rather, business may be at the forefront of those who are affected by the movements of external forces.

As a result, it is incumbent on every business to keep a weather eye on the outside world to determine how the evolution of its most influential forces will create the problems and the opportunities of the future. And that on-the-ball approach requires nothing less than a pervasive attitude that change is inevitable, coupled with a Berger-style system for capturing change triggers and making them work for you.

Admittedly, this is easier said than done. Finding change may be relatively easy for the corporate Sherlock Holmes who really is looking for it. Responding to it properly and effectively is a lot harder. There are many reasons for this slip between cup and lip. But within the confines of this chapter, I will focus on the difficulties in handling the macro forces driving change across the globe.

Most of these pile drivers are well known and recognizable:

Globalization of industries and markets—many companies taking on a true multinational character.

Leapfrogging technology—spinning out of constant streams of new products and processes, forging of new scientific breakthroughs, and continual pushing of the envelope of knowledge.

Industry transformations—herculean changes within key industries that involve myriad different directions, such as consolidation of key players for some; maturation and decline for others; rapid growth for still another group; and emergence for a final turn on the leading edge.

Sociodemographic shifts—wide-ranging series of developments that can include anything from stagnant population growth in some developed countries to rising standards of living in underdeveloped areas.

Political revision—an amalgam of events and trends linked generally by their roots in government/political initiatives and including everything from the opening of Eastern Europe to free markets to regulation and deregulation in developed economies to cross-border confederations such as the European Common Market.

Although this list is not exhaustive, it does capture the primary elements in which change in the 1990s and the early 21st century has its origins.

So, the question recurs: If we know all of these things why is it so hard for so many to cope with them? I will frame my response in the context of the Berger change paradigm and change management in general.

First, there is the sheer number of forces at play. Never in economic history have so many massively influential forces been operating at the same time.

Second, and almost a corollary to point one, these forces do not operate independently or individually in some kind of hermetically sealed vacuum. They often are interlinked or reactive to each other—the effect of one having a major impact on another. For example, a new technology breakthrough may send one industry to its funeral pyre as another leaps from its ashes to carry on with new products, processes, and services.

Already we see an extremely complex picture for even the most well-intentioned and skilled change manager. The forces impacting change are powerful and pervasive. There are a lot of them, and they work together. That fact should drive home a number of different points. Under the scenario, change is continual and potent; a business cannot escape the ravages or the benefits of these changes, and business desperately needs a Berger-style change paradigm to detect and decode the sometimes mixed signals from the world at large. The agents of change need such a systematic process so they can look at all forces simultaneously, filter out the most consequential, fix the interrelationships of importance among the macro forces, and then develop an intelligent knowledge foundation for action.

But there is at least one other important factor to weigh. The macro forces themselves are rarely change triggers. It is their specific consequences that tend to be the change triggers that can complicate the life of the change manager who flies blind. Just spotting the macro force, or a few of the relatively widespread subsidiary trends spun off in its wake, is not enough. The change manager must plumb deeper to determine exactly what business implications—problems and opportunities—are being illuminated by the broader developments.

Gary Fernandes of Electronic Data Systems, which is in the midst of an industry characterized by constant technological innovation, notes that technology advances by themselves are virtually nothing. "What is important," he says, "is how these breakthroughs are channeled into usable products and services—i.e., how they are commercialized—that businesses can sell."

Getting to that all-important bottom line—where the theoretical becomes the actual—also requires an understanding of the myriad and often conflicting lead-lag relationships between the key influences.

For example, globalization, which everyone knows is happening, is not so simple as the fall from a log that some commentators presume. It is, in part, driven by business itself. As various markets—food, automobiles, household appliances, many types of consumer products, electrical equipment to name some—have matured in "home" countries, their companies have pushed outward to carve out new operating territories in foreign countries. But this action has a political driver as well. The 12 European nations that officially formed the Common Market on January 1, 1993, formed a unified market that increased the attractiveness of the region for both native and non-EC companies. Meanwhile, at the other end of the continent, the fall of Communism has opened large and potentially lucrative markets that until recently had been off-limits for companies from other areas.

But sociodemographics cannot be overlooked. Why did the developed markets become mature? In most cases the answer is that population growth slowed and such markets as consumer and industrial durable goods became replacement markets rather than territories of continued fertile growth. And to go a step further, maturation has been a force in industry consolidations not only so strong companies can be created to compete in flat markets and gain the market share needed for survival but also so the strongest and fittest can assemble the clout to go overseas.

However, don't just dismiss technology. Would any of this cross-border spread have accelerated to the rapid pace now being clocked had it not been possible first to send faxes around the world in seconds or to fly from New York to Tokyo in 14 hours (12 hours back)?

Technology is another intriguing force of multiple dimensions. As noted in the comment earlier by Gary Fernandes, technology really has its impact when it is turned into usable products and services. But that impact is felt on many levels. Technological advances in miniaturization have allowed the development of smaller computers that have endangered the existence of IBM, with its near-obsession with mainframes. Technological breakthroughs have continued to advance space exploration programs, which have in turn spun off usable ideas and processes to sciences ranging from medicine to transportation. And of course technology is at the root of the pharmaceutical and medical industries.

An entire family of ripple effects is noticeable from the healthcare developments alone. In the sociodemographic sense, they have prolonged lives and conquered or tamed diseases that once were incurable. An older, often better-heeled population with the spending power to have great impact on a wide range of industries affected by their demand has resulted. So there is an economic kicker as well. Yet the cost of drug and medical device development is so huge that, even as the field is considered in the growth mode, consolidations have been necessary to create global players with the means to continue pushing forward.

The number of concentric circles that can be traced back to any single trend—macro or micro—is impossible to register. But it is not important to calculate an exact number. It is important for the change manager to realize that the circles can go into infinity and to dig as deeply as possible beyond the basics to develop the plan for his or her company to succeed.

The change manager with an established, flexible change system is the one who will have a leg up, as will his or her company. Finally, the change manager must always keep alignment in mind. This is tough when change may require moving into different countries with their different cultures or into new technologies with different operating schemes and skills. Indeed, it may not be possible to rework all of the basic elements in combination under that scenario. But at the very least, the change manager must ensure that the big four—strategy, operations, culture, and reward—are not in conflict with each other.

And if changes cannot be effected immediately to ensure alignment, the idea should not be pigeonholed or forgotten. It should be pursued at a slower pace—retained as a goal rather than projected as an immediate target—and fully effected at the right time.

In summary, the forces driving change are there and they are moving. They promise great and widespread volatility. That fact is more than a prescription for change. It is a formula for developing a system to keep on top of change, to manage it, and to make it work for you.

Chapter Eight

Measuring Change & Changing Measures

Frederick F. Reichheld

Our theories determine what we measure.

Albert Einstein

I n business, "You are what you measure." What a business measures shapes employee thinking, communicates company values, and channels organizational learning. As a senior manager, the most strategic decision you can make is determining what to measure and how those measures are linked to incentives. This decision focuses organizational learning on the dimensions that are truly important—the foundation of effective change.

However, most companies are using inherited, outdated measurement systems that warp and distort their business strategies, preventing them from responding to change effectively. Too many companies allow learning and change to be driven by vestigial measures established by accountants and regulators rather than by CEOs in pursuit of their business missions.

Is it any wonder then that we read stories such as the following day after day?

Procter & Gamble's food and beverage division apparently hasn't met performance targets and still severely lagged behind the rest of the company in fiscal 1992 (*Wall Street Journal*, August 31, 1992).

Toshiba Corp. and NEC Corp. lowered their previously optimistic earnings forecasts for the current fiscal year (*Wall Street Journal*, August 31, 1992).

On a single day in one newspaper, we read about three different companies reporting disappointing results. It happens so often that it is not even news. But it should be!

CEOs around the world are being embarrassed by bad results or are missing great opportunities because they are forced to manage their companies with the wrong information. They are like pilots who fly an airplane with nothing but the air speed indicator to tell them how they're doing. Without the use of an altimeter or compass, most planes would crash, and without the right measurements, most organizations face a similar fate. And because of the all-absorbing challenge of a successful flight, CEOs have little time and energy to address their real jobs, the redesign of the plane and its instrumentation.

CREATING VALUE

To succeed, businesses must systemically create value. This value must be provided to at least three distinct groups—stockholders (in the form of a return on investment), customers (in the form of a quality product or service at an attractive price), and employees (in the form of superior compensation and personal satisfaction throughout their careers).

However, 90 percent of the measurements used to manage a company are designed to report on short-term returns to stockholders. Most management decisions are biased toward delivering short-term value to shareholders because that is what is measured. An income statement or balance sheet tells us almost nothing about the firm's ability to create value for customers and employees and, therefore, long-term stockholder value.

This obsession with shareholder information is a holdover from the 19th century, when the survival of process industries such as steel and textiles depended on attracting the huge amounts of capital needed to power those firms. Those days are long gone, but the measurement systems they spawned are with us still. It is these partial measurements, not the stupidity or venality of the managers and workers, that lead to poor decisions, big surprises, and lost opportunities day after day. Nothing then can be more important to an executive than knowing what his or her employees should measure. Perhaps the most strategic decision a CEO ever will make is to determine which numbers are really important to the company's future.

Something that can be measured can be managed. The corollary is that whatever escapes measurement becomes an unknown variable and eventually wreaks havoc in an organizational system.

However, it's impossible to know which numbers matter if you don't understand the business system and the key relationships that propel it. If Einstein had studied what large corporations measure, he probably would have concluded management's theory of business success is that only short-term profits matter.

But business requires far more than merely short-term profits. It requires the *continuous creation of value*. Only information that tells managers whether the company indeed is providing value is critical. All other information is secondary!

MEASUREMENT MODELS AND CHANGE MANAGEMENT

Using measurement to anticipate and drive change implies that the manager has a perspective that includes the following elements:

- A clear understanding of the dynamic cause-and-effect relationships at work in the business.
- Key measures of performance for providing customer, employee, and long-term shareholder value that can be compared to target levels.
- Incentives for employees to react appropriately to new information.
- Continuous monitoring of responses and their effects to facilitate learning and adapt to change.

Above all, the manager must see change as the natural condition, not as an exception. Businesses are always in a state of change as they grow and as they evolve to adapt to their environment. They must change in order to survive. The manager indeed should be concerned when the organization is resisting change because it indicates that the right measures and incentives are not in place.

Measurements keyed only to shareholders' short-term needs are especially dangerous. They entice managers to make decisions that will improve the numbers for the short-term stockholders rather than provide value to the other stakeholders in the system.

Managers become manipulators who act on symptoms rather than deal with root causes. All too often, a negative symptom is merely suppressed by palliatives, only to come roaring back with greater destructive strength later on. Short-term cost reductions and price increases often boost this year's earnings but destroy long-term value.

Some companies have recognized that they need to extend the range of gauges used to keep their business flying on course. However, without a clear understanding of the kind of data that are useful, they generate information overload, which only exacerbates the problem. All measures must be linked together through their relationship to current and future cash flows or else the trade-offs cannot be evaluated.

For instance, customer satisfaction surveys have become standard practice in many industries. But their linkage to profits and value is unclear. For example, in the U.S. automobile industry, from 85 to 90 percent of customers say they are satisfied, but the average repurchase rate is less than 50 percent. Most consumer defectors say they are satisfied! Should the auto company invest $10 million to increase satisfaction or $100 million? What is the right amount? The discrepancy between satisfaction statistics and repurchase patterns has led Dave Illingsworth, general manager of Lexus USA, to state, "The only meaningful measure of satisfaction is repurchase loyalty."

The irony of this situation is that managers in the automobile industry clearly understand the economic value of customer repurchase loyalty patterns. However, most of them measure customer satisfaction—perhaps because it is easier—rather than repurchase decisions. Their historic measurement systems track cars by their government-required vehicle identification numbers—not by customers. Have regulators had more impact on measures or have managers?

The simple truth is that satisfaction surveys alone don't yield the information companies must have about value to customer. Would anyone trying to measure shareholder value question stockholders about "satisfaction" and consider the job to be complete? I don't think so.

MISSING THE POINT

The advertising jingle "You can count on me, Sears, Roebuck and Company" had the right message for customers, but the impact was lost when the company's behavior contradicted the image it was trying to create.

Recent problems with Sears, Roebuck's auto services centers clearly illustrate the fundamental failure to measure and motivate properly. Sears has been under excruciating pressure from stockholders to improve profits, and the company's initial response was to alter its incentives for repair workers.

Until 1990, workers had been paid on an hourly basis, but the plan was changed to base compensation on the number of jobs completed. The shift in compensation practices reflected a misunderstanding of what made the Sears business system work so well for so many years—value, value, value. The emphasis on artificially delivering a return to stockholders pressured employees to learn how to make unnecessary repairs at the expense of the customer.

In the words of one reporter, "Motorists wailed as repair profits soared." Customers went to the authorities, and investigations into overcharging were launched in New Jersey, California, and Florida. In response, Sears Chairman Edward A. Brennan announced that the incentive program would be restructured yet again, and he apologized to customers for betraying their trust.

Sears executives who measured the initial impact of their policy change on profits must have been delighted and certainly would not have understood that they were rushing headlong into a danger zone. Until the controversy broke, the auto repair division was among the company's fastest growing units, accounting for nine percent of the Sears merchandise group's revenue in 1991, exactly what the stockholders wanted to see. However, if the company had been measuring the number of customers returning for auto service, they certainly would have noticed the drop-off, as people stopped going to Sears and started going to state regulators with their complaints

The Sears debacle provides an excellent example of a company failing to understand the relationships that contribute to long-term business success. The problem of falling profits was perceived as "not selling hard enough" rather than "not delivering value to the customer." The cure turned out to be far worse than the disease.

Contrast this behavior with that of Staples Inc., an office supplies retailer that has recorded phenomenal growth in recent years. Staples carefully tracks purchasing patterns among key customers, and if the data change, the company is able to call customers directly to find out why they are defecting. This allows Staples to address root causes rather than symptoms and to take action quickly in its hotly competitive market.

WHO MEASURES UP?

The right approach to measurement as a tool for change management is finally emerging, as several companies have discovered many of the practices essential to making effective measurement. Central to this emerging new management science is the concept of customer and employee retention, or loyalty.

These companies have discovered that retention is a driver of costs, market share, and profits and wields greater impact than any other variable. Measuring loyalty has become the core of their change management efforts, because changes in retention rates (i.e., customer defection to competitors) are the surest early warning sign of where their financial results soon will be heading.

The insurance carrier USAA, for example, has nurtured a customer retention rate of 98 percent, and these results have not been achieved by accident. USAA has a family of measures for every department, which includes three dimensions:

- Quality to the customer.
- Employee capability.
- Costs and productivity.

It is no surprise that with these tightly focused measures in place, the organization is learning how to improve along each dimension and to make appropriate trade-offs among the three.

Additional learning and sharing of experience are provided by a "swat team" that goes through all of the departments every three years, taking a fresh look at how to make changes that improve each of the key measures. USAA has experienced dramatic increases in productivity, and employee turnover has dropped from 25 percent to a single-digit rate.

Meanwhile, as the insurance industry's costs have surged out of control, USAA's cost per policy continues to decline in real dollars. Simplistic cost and productivity measures used by others in the industry don't incorporate customer quality and loyalty, so their learning is stalled. Managers in each of those companies also are trying to reduce cost per policy but usually in ways that reduce quality to the customer. This increases customer churn, which more than wipes out the desired cost reductions. USAA has helped its employees learn by providing them with an integrated set of measures closely linked to customer retention.

MBNA Inc., a leader in the credit card industry, uses a scorecard composed of 20 different measurements that the company has determined are keys to customer retention. On days when they reach 95 percent of their targets, money goes into the bonus pool, and the news is posted on the bulletin board outside the headquarters' cafeteria, further motivating employees to make the measurements work. It should be no surprise that MBNA has learned how to maintain one of the highest levels of loyalty and profitability in the industry.

Consistent with Dave Illingsworth's philosophy, Lexus has developed seven measurements that it considers to be critical factors leading to repurchase loyalty. One of the most important of these is customer satisfaction with service. To facilitate learning across dealerships, Lexus established a central tracking system to provide any dealer with the previous history of a specific vehicle so it is fixed right. This also allows Lexus to measure which dealers are doing the best job at fixing it right—which also facilitates learning how best to satisfy customers. Not surprisingly (you are what you measure) Lexus is on a course to establish the highest repurchase loyalty rates in the auto industry.

Companies like USAA, MBNA, and Lexus that are using new measurements to achieve their business mission in very different industries share one thing in common: They are systems oriented. They see their own businesses as whole systems composed of mutually interacting parts. They never tinker with the parts alone, but make decisions based on an understanding of the entire enterprise.

Systems thinking based on an understanding of the importance of customer, employee, and shareholder loyalty lays the foundation for replacing outmoded measurement methods in use today. From a systems point of view, change management is not esoteric; it is the very essence of survival. Change management is the highest priority of all systems, in nature or in business, and it is a matter of perpetual concern.

Any system must measure conditions about the internal and external environments so that adaptations can be made. These shifts and changes are a form of learning, and all systems have a learning function.

For a business system, the major problem with having the wrong measurement systems is that the necessary feedback doesn't get to the right people and changes aren't made or, without closed feedback loops, actions are taken and their results are unclear. In short, the organization does not learn, especially at intermediate levels, where prompt actions could allow the organization to benefit from new opportunities or solve old problems.

When surprises come knocking at the CEO's door, it is usually because the organization does not have the tools or incentives to learn. Whenever a senior executive is brought in at the last minute to make a crisis decision, the system probably is not learning properly.

Systems thinking, although essential to success, will be insufficient if it is not oriented toward developing a loyalty-based business system. Loyalty is tightly connected to both organizational learning and longevity. Loyalty leaders such as USAA, MBNA, and Lexus have found that the most important learning revolves around customer retention. These measures of loyalty are the cornerstones of their systems.

DEFINING AND MEASURING CUSTOMER RETENTION

The most important player in a business system is the customer—the source of all positive cash flow. Therefore, a business focused on loyalty must, above all, attract and secure good customers. In broad terms, good customers are defined as those for whom the company can profitably offer the highest value product or service available. Once these customers are on board, the most important variable to measure is retention rates.

For most companies interested in building a loyalty-based business system, the right customers will be those who respond to product quality and long-term incentives such as extended warranties, rather than short-term price promotions. They also will be the types of customers who value and appreciate a stable and continuing relationship with sales and service personnel.

Once a high-quality customer base is established, the company should imitate the manufacturers who strive for zero defects by zealously pursuing "zero defections." Each company also must define how to measure retention and set targets for success that are appropriate to their industry. It is important to determine not only what should be measured but also how often and how it is reported to employees, shareholders, and other interested parties.

When you have good customers and retention rates begin to fall, you will know it's not because they are fickle, but because they are not receiving value. The solution is clearly to reestablish the quality connection between customers and employees, not to initiate layoffs or to sell harder.

DEFINING AND MEASURING EMPLOYEE RETENTION

If employees are well trained and given adequate incentives to secure and serve good customers, retention for them is also likely to be high. Working in such an environment, they will be rewarded by the value generated through their positive relationship with customers. A company with high customer retention rates also will have strong cash flows and profits, which can be invested in compensation and training for workers, further securing employee loyalty.

Aligning employee incentives with the true goals of the business system is critical for success. Inconsistent incentives, based on old ways of thinking, will thwart the best-intended efforts. In the insurance industry, for example, loyalty is recognized as being important to financial success. However, in most companies agents are paid a huge front-end commission for bringing in new customers but are not highly rewarded for retaining existing customers.

State Farm, by contrast, is a loyalty leader that avoids the mistake of high front-end commissions for agents. Instead, their agents are rewarded for the long-term profitability of the "book of business." This practice encourages agents to learn how they can most effectively customize the State Farm offerings to the needs of their local communities. They get the best customers—and they keep them. Intervention or crisis resolution by headquarters rarely is required, and unpleasant surprises are unusual.

Once a company has defined its own measurements of retention and begun to set targets for achieving success, it is important that senior managers keep the company focused on using the new measurements effectively. Most importantly, employees must understand how loyalty is linked to this year's and future years' cash flows. The microeconomics of loyalty can and should be clearly linked to costs, revenues, and profits.

What is the role of the CEO in managing change within a loyalty-based business system? Rather than reacting to crisis and coping with sudden shifts in the business environment, the CEO should be the "Chief Education Officer," helping employees understand how to deliver high levels of value to customers and what to measure to determine if they are delivering and giving them the right incentives for learning these essential lessons.

Today's CEO simply cannot and should not make all the key decisions. The systems are too complex. Time delays are too dangerous to wait for the CEO to tell people what they should do in more than a few situations. The CEO's job is to design a system that creates value and allocates it in a manner that sustains the system's ability to learn and respond to its constantly changing environment.

Although the CEO cannot escape the central responsibility of satisfying shareholder needs for return on investment, he or she also must be instrumental in educating investors regarding the requirement that long-term value be delivered for other contributors to the business system as well. Stability can be brought to the business by attracting long-term investors rather than speculators.

In most companies that have been successful in changing their measurement systems to manage change, a visionary CEO has been the catalyst for the transformation. Until the fundamental concepts that underlie the loyalty-based business system are commonplace, the need for a far-seeing CEO is likely to persist. Eventually, however, retention measures will become the norm, making it far easier for organizations to utilize them, just as they routinely use accounting information today.

SUMMARY

We have heard resounding calls in recent years for an expanded suite of measurements that go beyond traditional accounting figures. However, simply increasing the number of variables in a measurement system will not help managers run their companies unless the right dimensions are being measured and their interrelationships are understood.

CONCLUSION

Because of the strategic impact, organizational issues, and time frame required, the CEO's job is to redesign company measurement frameworks. By changing measures the organization will be able to manage change.

The role of measurement in managing change is critical but often overlooked or inappropriately delegated. It goes to the heart of organizational success. It is only through measures that organizations can learn, only through learning that they can create value in an ever-changing world, and only through creating value that they survive and prosper.

SECTION

III

THE GEARS OF CHANGE

Structure of *The Change Management Handbook*

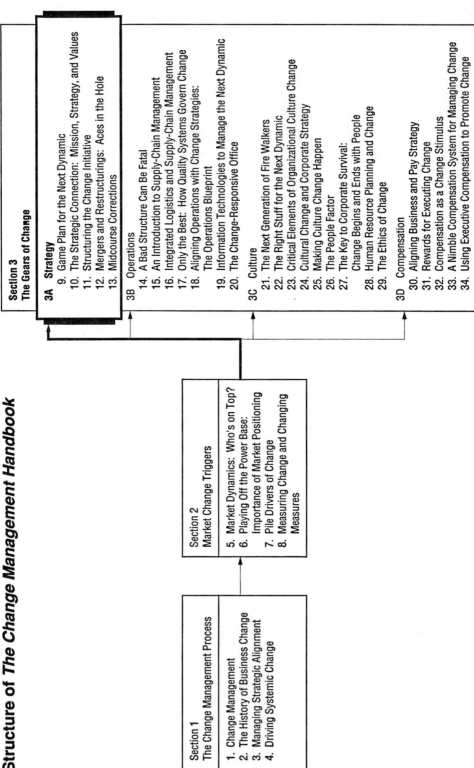

STRATEGY

Continual alignment of the firm to its market is at one end of the change management bridge. At the other is continual alignment of the internal gears so the firm is always ready to change (and to have each of the internal gears moving with the market in mind).

Sequentially, the first of the internal gears is strategy, which is the game plan of the firm for developing as a value-creating enterprise, the embodiment of its goals, its techniques, its timetable for progress. In the change-dominated 1990s and into the next century, strategy must accommodate change and be adaptable to change. It must be the polar star for encouraging and promoting change, rather than serving as a set-in-stone monument of the past (Rich and Mifflin, Chapter 9). The strategic plan must combat the musclebound and the philosophic rigidity.

One way of achieving such nimbleness is to make sure the strategic plan itself is well-balanced—that it displays its own type of alignment (Buchanan and Campbell, Chapter 10). How? By ensuring that the strategy is tightly wedded to the mission of the firm (and/or its business units) and its values, including ethics and ways of doing things. With those interconnections clear, the firm not only knows exactly how to manage itself amid great dynamism but also can communicate these specifics to people in the organization from top to bottom.

Keeping the firm's eye on the ball through a balanced, aligned strategy can pay great dividends in being the first either to adapt to change or to be ahead of it. In this respect market intelligence can be a great asset, providing a firm linkage between strategy and the marketplace. However, initiatives must be carefully executed within the company (Davidow, Chapter 11). Although the initiative is refreshing evidence that a firm is alive, it must take pains to ensure that the operations, culture, and rewards are properly adjusted when the strategy shifts in advance of the definitely provable need for great change. In fact, the pressure for alignment is even greater than if the change was so visible that everybody could buy into it from scratch.

These types of factors must be closely considered when the company must change suddenly and execute a midcourse correction, whether it is a pure initiative or a reaction to a change trigger (Rich and Mifflin, Chapter 13). But there are systems and procedures—Total Delivery Systems, Best Programs, etc.—that can make these corrections much easier to accomplish. They work best when they are in place at all times as part of an environment that expects and is geared to change at all times.

If the change requires rather extreme or decisive measures, the tools are there for the using (Sikora, Chapter 12). Disciplines exist for providing rewards in the case of mergers, acquisitions, and restructurings when they are necessary to reposition the firm. The message is that the more extreme these actions are, the more the firm needs to be riveted to continual alignment.

Chapter Nine

Game Plan for the Next Dynamic

Anthony C. Rich
Kenneth E. Mifflin

W hat was Jack Welch doing when he collapsed GE's portfolio from 350 strategic business units into 13 core businesses, issued corporate commandments demanding market leadership in each business, and installed management techniques that blew the old cultural model away?

Why did Procter & Gamble suddenly begin taking the lead in negotiating "partnerships" with retailers—after treating retailers with indifference for over 100 years? P&G's "partner" had always been the consumer, and "consumer pull" was the key to moving product through the channels. Historically, P&G's basic formula for success had always been "Superior Product + Effective Marketing = Category Dominance." A leading role for the retailer? This was totally new.

Both companies saw the handwriting on the wall—and did something about it. They accepted the need to take a broader view of the world, rejecting old business models and strategies as too narrow and inflexible. The solution, they knew, would require dramatic and comprehensive change. They needed to put new programs in place that would keep *every* part of the organization current, focused and on the move.

A key message emanating from these new business models is that the concept of strategy itself is now evolving to reflect the complexities of competing in the 1990s. Companies today are struggling to face this growing array of challenges:

- Continued abbreviation of life cycles for both products and skills.

- Fragmentation of customer expectations, forcing costly customization.

- Unexpected threats from substitute products and foreign competitors.

- Increasingly difficult choices to make regarding information technology.

- An uncertain public policy environment, reflecting the potential for major changes in areas such as environmental and trade legislation.

EFFECTIVE STRATEGIES

In the past, strategies were typically one-dimensional set pieces, focused on choosing a market and a business system that strategists hoped would result in long-term competitive advantage. Today, this approach to business strategy just is not enough. Today, effective strategies must be holistic, in that they have these properties:

- Multifaceted and multidimensional.
- Dynamically aligned, internally and externally.
- Designed for implementation.
- Adaptive over time.

Multifaceted and Multidimensional

Strategy defines the business today and tomorrow. What is our customer, market and product focus? What are our operational and go-to-market strategies? How should we organize? How should we allocate our resources? And what role should information systems play in enabling us to achieve competitive advantages? Our first tenet suggests that the many dimensions of strategy are inextricably entwined: *Multidimensional* strategies seek to establish harmony across the full range of these issues.

Importantly, the multidimensional concept does not imply creation of a laundry list, exhausting and unfocused. Successful companies have always recognized that good strategies focus primarily on one or a few critical strategic dimensions. In today's increasingly complex environment, corporate and business unit strategies need to be specific in defining an overall context that completes the picture with respect to all of the key strategic dimensions. Failure to do this often results in strategies that are unreliable or that do not address potentially fatal blind spots.

Our experience suggests that there are seven of these broad and interrelated strategic elements, which we call the Primary Strategic Dimensions (see Figure 9–1). What is new about this list is that, whereas "achieving competitive advantages" and "delivering superior value to customers" are *still* relevant objectives, the multidimensional approach helps to ensure success by putting these objectives into a workable framework. For instance, if customer relationship management has become an important new strategic focus at P&G, what are the implications for P&G's traditional focus on meeting consumer needs through superior product benefits? What new skills and capabilities are required, and how must our approach to supply chain management be changed to support the strategy? What must be redesigned or reengineered? If P&G succeeds in creating partnerships with retailers but loses sight of what the consumer wants, the new strategy fails.

Whatever dimensions a company chooses to focus upon, aligning all of the primary strategic dimensions and the individual components of these dimensions across the Total Value Delivery System will help ensure that all parts of the business and all external relationships remain in sync—which brings us to the *second tenet:* alignment.

Dynamically Aligned, Internally and Externally

The second tenet is that effective strategies should create *alignment* between all of the internal and external components of a company's total delivery system. Internally, the Total Delivery system encompasses the operations and the products and services that are produced by the business enterprise. Externally, it involves relationships with customers, suppliers, distributors, shareholders, and those who influence the market environment, such as government regulators—relative to competitors. Tying it all together is the company's shared vision, defining its unique role in the marketplace. As shown in Figure 9–2, the seven primary strategic dimensions already described are comprehensive in addressing alignment interfaces between these components.

To illustrate: In P&G's strategic focus on customer relationship management, what is the impact of selected retailer partnerships on the alignment of its operational elements with both suppliers and with customer requirements? What is the effect on other retailers, and can the partnership formula be transferred from one retailer to another?

P&G is a good example of how complicated and important the issue of alignment is becoming. For a variety of reasons—technological capability, customer demands, need for cost reduction, and competitive intensity—companies are seeking integration through closer, electronically linked relationships with suppliers, distributors, customers, and end consumers. One of the results of P&G's foray into partnership programs is that its processes are being electronically integrated with those of retailers. So the alignment of vendors, customers, and operations becomes more critical than it has ever been. P&G has even changed its approach to pricing, the better to fit the new pipeline management-oriented model.

Designed for Implementation

We all know that implementation is the key. The books are filled with strategies that failed because the organization could not execute them properly. But we assert that implementation must be built into strategy up-front—and that is the third tenet. For instance, continuously rising customer expectations may dictate a degree of process reengineering across the business system from inbound logistics to product development to delivery and postsales service, and that effort may have to be followed by ongoing programs of continuous improvement.

Adaptive over Time

Implicit in all of this is the capacity for ongoing change—and that is the fourth tenet. Given that most industries are in a constant state of change, adaptability is crucial to survival. To measure the impact of change continuously, we need to install strategy monitors at key points in our relationships, both inside and outside the company. Then, for us to respond to these changes early enough, the right organization, capabilities, and processes must be in place. The key is to view strategy as an evolving process, in need of continuous improvement.

FIGURE 9–1
The Primary Strategic Dimensions

Primary Strategic Dimensions	Potential Components of Competitive Advantage*	Total Delivery System Alignment Emphasis†
Customer relationship management	Customer service Channel management Distributor/retailer partnerships	Us ◄─► Distributors and/or retailers and/or consumers
Market/consumer focus	Portfolio Strategy Segmentation Proprietary customer/consumer insights	Us ◄─► Distributors, retailers and consumers
Superior product/service benefits	Product/service attributes and performance Innovation Specification management Brand image Benefit communication (advertising/promotion) Pricing strategy	Us ◄─► Consumers
Scale/cost/market power	Scale/cost learning curve Market power/control (bottleneck management) Horizontal integration	Us ◄─► Suppliers and/or retailers and/or consumers

Superior skills and capabilities	Total quality management (TQM)/continuous improvement	Us ◄─► Process/organization/technology/infrastructure
	Technology/R&D strategy and skills	
	Conversion process/cycle strategy and skills	
	Go-to-market/selling strategy	
	Organizational capabilities	
	"Hustle" as strategy	
Supply chain management	Integrated logistics (supplier partnerships)	Us ◄─► Suppliers, distributors, and retailers
	Sourcing control	
	Time-based competition	
	Vertical integration	
Industry forces management	Industry rivalry management	Us ◄─► Shareholders, regulators, other stakeholders, and competition
	Government/regulatory/trade management	
	Investor relationship management	

---

* Information Technology is an enabler for all strategic components

† Alignment with "Shared vision" and relative to "Competition" applies in each case

110

FIGURE 9–2
"Holistic" Strategies—Ensuring Alignment across the Total Delivery System

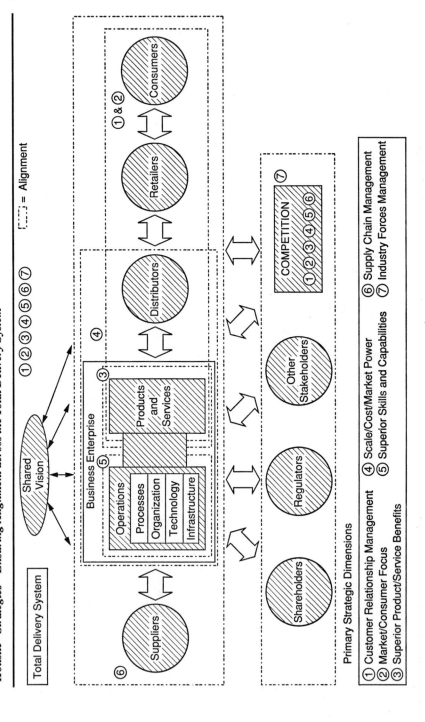

WHAT'S WRONG WITH THE OLD MODEL?

Based on past experience, some executives have little use for strategic planning at all, having concluded that most companies are hamstrung by the whole process. That response typically occurs because their strategies are the opposite of what we are talking about. They are one-dimensional, poorly aligned, static, and mired in archaic corporate views of the way the world works. And even if these firms do have sound strategies, studies have shown that, more often than not, implementability is an afterthought.

General Motors Corp. is a classic example of a company that thought it was seeing the world when it was in fact looking at its own old reflection. In the 1980s, unwilling to accept the realities of changes in the auto industry, GM spent 10 years automating its existing business system rather than disaggregating and redesigning it. GM did not run into trouble for lack of commitment or aggressiveness: The auto giant invested massive sums on new facilities, new processes, and new information technology capabilities. Nonetheless, management ultimately refused to rethink GM's traditional do-it-yourself system. To be sure, Saturn, as a greenfield operation, was given that luxury, but the separate venture underscored GM's inability and reluctance throughout the decade to make bold, long-lasting changes to its existing infrastructure. As a result, whereas some of the original equipment manufacturing operations were improved, by 1992 GM had not been able to match the low cost or high quality levels Ford and Chrysler had realized by using outside parts manufacturers. Further, with all that investment, GM still lagged in the movement toward flexible manufacturing, a serious weakness as the auto market splintered into smaller and smaller niches. To force GM to align itself with the realities, the board of directors finally overhauled top management in late 1992.

Sears, Roebuck & Co., despite all of its efforts to get in tune with the 1990s, is similarly bedeviled by its old model. Generally, Sears has lacked focus in recent years as it entered a variety of businesses and tried to beat off the new mass merchants, warehouse clubs and other discounters with strategies that have sometimes seemed in conflict with each other. Although Sears' recent reorganization into core businesses could significantly improve its market/consumer focus, it seems unlikely to help address the company's key problem: An inability to marry its new-found "low-price" strategy to a relatively high-cost business system and administrative structure. Historically, Sears made *purchasing* its core functional skill, with aggressive buyers and purchasing agents geared up to bash thousands of suppliers for the highest volume discounts and promotional deals. The Sears strategy, successful for decades, translated into a cost structure in which operations and administrative costs consumed 24 percent to 26 percent of sales.

In the 1980s, while management resisted the parting that was needed, new competition swept in, sporting a 12 percent to 14 percent overhead structure as well as a finely honed talent for buying at very low prices. Sears, under fire, decided to shift from a "high-low" pricing strategy to one that provides consumers with an everyday low price (EDLP). But by 1992, despite layoffs and other cost-cutting measures, the old institution's cost structure remained significantly higher than that of its major mass merchant competitors. Without that vital internal-external alignment, the EDLP strategy was doomed to failure.

Finally, there is United States Steel, or USX, a company that historically dominated its industry through sheer scale and power. In the late 1960s, it still controlled the market for steel. But in the tough market of the 1970s, its advantages were eroding, more because of failure to match new production methods pioneered by domestic competition than because of dumping by foreign manufacturers. U.S. Steel was ultimately the victim of its large scale, refusing and unable to move quickly into the new technologies and failing to recognize the growth of specialized steel producers and mini-mills. Oddly enough, while apparently fixated on labor cost and foreign competition issues, U.S. Steel virtually gave up on its area of historic strength and spent its funds on diversification into the oil and coal industries.

In 1986, the company became USX, relegating U.S. Steel to subsidiary status. Steel now accounts for just 30 percent of its profits. In the meantime, other American companies are competing very effectively with the so-called foreign dumpers on both a cost and a quality basis. One third of the market is now held by such stars as Nucor Corp. and Chaparral Steel, which have excelled in mini-mills. A ray of hope for USX is that, some 20 years after the new trends began, the U.S. Steel Group has finally cut costs and modernized to the point that some analysts believe it could again become a world leader in terms of costs and quality soon.

The common thread? These companies failed to recognize the importance of emerging new strategic dimensions—and paid the price.

THE ENDURING FUNDAMENTALS

In hindsight, these giants of industry obviously lacked the right strategic principles. This leads us to another question: Have the leading thinkers on strategic planning fundamentally failed American business?

As we said at the outset, the concept of strategy is evolving—but it is based on some sound and enduring fundamentals that have been enriched over the last 20 years. "How to Compete" and "Where to Compete" are still the fundamental dimensions of competitive strategy (i.e., "What am I trying to do?" and "How am I trying to do it?"). Competitive advantage continues to be the measure by which all business activities are gauged. We still need to articulate, in the simplest possible terms, a formula for delivering value to customers that is superior to what competitors offer.

But as we examine many of the current concepts and models for strategy, we again find the fatal flaw—which is that they are rarely holistic. They do not cover all the bases, and that raises the odds for failure, especially where change is pervasive. For instance, Michael Porter's[1] seminal work on competitive strategy is valuable for its analytic frameworks; however, his primary focus is on assessing the existing industry structure.

In recent years, major principles concerning implementation have been added to the concept of strategy. One is the "skill-based strategy" concept. For instance, Amar Bhide in his *Harvard Business Review* article "Hustle as Strategy" argued that in essence there is rarely such a thing as strategic superiority—there is little one can do that competitors cannot copy—so the advantage is gained by developing superior people and skills and energizing the organization to stay half a step ahead of the competition. You always come up with better ideas, you execute better, you recruit and train better, and you continue to evolve rapidly.

Skill-based strategies, with their emphasis on superior ongoing execution, are clearly an important dimension of modern strategy. But it is just one dimension. Bhide suggests that strategic planning can be dismissed in favor of "hustle." It is certainly true that strategic planning can be counterproductive if it is based on static assumptions and designed with the illusion of "permanent" advantages in mind. "Barriers to entry" rarely stopped competition in the past and still do not. We are finding that more and more companies are coming to terms with the impact of constant change on the concept of competitive advantage and through *holistic strategies* are developing new, dynamic ways to create that competitive edge.

Total Quality Management (TQM) and process reengineering incorporate some of today's most acclaimed and sophisticated implementation principles. These represent tools, techniques, and methodologies that can play a powerful role in enhancing capabilities, lowering costs, and realigning the components of a business. What is their problem? All too often, they are cast in the guise of a primary strategy. They become the focus rather than the means, and we have already seen companies that have relied on them as a panacea become disenchanted with the results.

Very simply, TQM is an incrementalist approach, oriented toward enabling the company to do better continually. But unless it is carefully positioned within a company's primary strategies, it is little more than a time-consuming set of activities that can drive employees to distraction.

Such careful positioning also applies to reengineering. In totally redesigning either individual or multiple business processes, reengineering aims at achieving relatively sudden and dramatic improvements, such as moving from average to world class, reducing costs by 40 percent, or achieving "six sigma" quality improvements, which is Motorola's goal. Reengineering can play a profound role in strategy, primarily by changing *how* a company competes. But its results will be unsatisfactory in any company that does not determine (1) what primary strategic purpose reengineering fulfills, and (2) how it will impact the alignment of relationships and strategies.

The point is that, piece by piece, we have been adding to and altering the many strategic principles organizations need to apply in this era that demands so much of them simultaneously and continuously: nimbleness, speed, quality; the ability to think global, act local, to be entrepreneurial and coordinated, to be innovative while efficient at execution.

All too often, the traditional one-dimensional strategic attack falls short. It is not enough for a company to decide to be the King of TQM (or Reengineering or

Customer Focus or Hustle). Such companies lack the framework for change. U.S. Steel and GM deteriorated when competition and technological changes eroded the advantages of their superior scale. Management failed to think about how their strategies needed to change—in terms of market focus, reengineering of the business, and redevelopment of the skill base. Sears somehow failed to appreciate that, in a highly competitive marketplace, a low price strategy also requires companywide low operational costs. Contrast Sears to the approach of Wal-Mart founder Sam Walton, whose corporate and personal principles were built around low price/low cost in every aspect.

THE PROCESS

If the problem is that we cannot continue to go at strategy piecemeal, then what is the process for developing a holistic strategy that contains the instruments for its own implementation and adaptability? As one might expect, it is a process that is continuous and its steps often overlap:

1. *Assess alignment.* Define the Total Delivery System and all the elements and relationships within it, both as they are currently and as they are evolving, and assess this profile relative to competitors. The idea is to create a dynamic picture of the Total Delivery System, factoring in all the elements within—and beyond—our control.

2. *Envision change.* Define an overall shared vision for the business that balances boldness with practicality. What constitutes a winning value proposition for our business, and what will it take to get there? Which of the Primary Strategic Dimensions (Figure 9–1) should we focus on, and what role should the other dimensions play? What financial targets should we strive for, and how can we get the whole organization behind the vision?

3. *Plan change.* Develop an operational strategy and a master plan for migrating to the new vision. Ensure that each aspect of alignment is addressed.

4. *Design, enable, and implement change.* Execute all programs and initiatives with discipline, registering interim "wins" along the way and maintaining momentum. As with earlier steps, unwavering top management commitment is required.

5. *Measure results and continuously improve.* Ensure that trends and events are continuously monitored. As change occurs, reexamine and refine strategies, alignments, and relationships within our own Total Delivery System and that of competitors.

The two key frameworks in the process are the Total Delivery System, which provides an overview of how the business and its key relationships are structured and aligned, and the seven Primary Strategic Dimensions, which define the focus and direction of the business. Let us take each dimension and the primary alignments it involves and show how some prevailing trends affect the development of a strategy.

Customer Relationship Management

This primary dimension offers opportunities to achieve competitive advantage via channel management, customer partnerships, and customer service. The main alignment is between our company and our customers and/or the channels.

What is happening today? Eroding customer loyalty in many categories is placing a premium on retaining and nurturing existing customers. Hence, the idea that "Customer Satisfaction = Increased Customer Retention and Revenue" is driving many companies into closer relationships with their customers and end consumers. This approach typically requires changes in operational alignments between suppliers and customers and affects other strategic dimensions or components, such as pricing, customer service, skills, and process redesign.

Market/Consumer Focus

A key component of this dimension is customer value segmentation. It has a primary effect, of course, on our alignment with the unique aspects of the needs of the various segments.

Because of increased competition in slow-growing markets, pressures to reduce costs, and growing customer demands, we are being forced to understand clearly what different customers value and to decide which customers should be targeted as key buyers. Hence, we are redefining how to segment customers and are developing tailored strategies—unique combinations of price and service—for delivering superior value against these segments. Value segmentation can lead to major changes in almost every other dimension, from customer relationships to configuration of product/service benefits to supply chain management.

Superior Product/Service Benefits

This dimension may include such components as technological and service innovation, customization, pricing, and brand image. Beyond alignment with the customer, the critical alignments are within operations and between operations and product development.

Both the increased pace of technological change and the fact that today most industries are buyer's markets mean that customer values tend to change constantly. Companies are having to respond with more than a superior product. They must offer a superior package of product, service, and pricing features and increasingly must customize these offerings for individual segments and/or customers.

These developments explain why it is more important than ever to keep R&D, manufacturing, sales, marketing, and distribution in perfect alignment with one another, working simultaneously rather than sequentially on creating the superior package. No operational entity can go off and "do its own thing" in this environment.

Scale/Cost/Market Power

This dimension has to do with achieving advantages based on size and/or image. Specific strategies here vary widely and typically have a critical impact on every relationship in the Total Delivery System. The strategies may involve market control, continuous cost reduction, horizontal or vertical integration, and/or global standardization.

The way Andersen views the advantages of scale has changed markedly in the last several years. Bigness still affords power, but the competitive and financial cost to many giants has been fierce in terms of bureaucracy and inability to respond to change. This has led them to intense, sometimes chaotic, efforts to achieve the best of all worlds: the economies and power of size and the nimbleness of the small entrepreneur. For instance, some have devised strategies to disintegrate their manufacturing and other operations, such as Ford has done in becoming an assembler rather than a manufacturer. Others, like Wal-Mart, are backward integrating, acquiring distributors to eliminate the costs and delays of intermediaries in the supply chain.

Superior Skills and Capabilities

We call this the implementation dimension because it includes many aspects of strategy that frame how we are going to achieve applicable goals in such areas as organizational redesign, communications, skills development, process reengineering, and total quality management. The main alignment is among the components of the business—processes, organization, technology and infrastructure—although, in partnerships, the strategies and tools of implementation cross corporate boundaries.

A fundamental shift in corporate thinking is occurring which often elevates this dimension to lead status. Earlier emphasis on portfolio strategy (i.e., "Which businesses should we be in?") is being transformed into a focus on core competencies and business process reengineering. That is, "What fundamental capabilities and skills do we have and should we have to keep up with our goals and the changes we foresee? How should my business system work to support those competencies?" The skills and capabilities dimension helps to close the loop in the alignment between where to compete and how to compete.

Supply Chain Management

Specific strategies in this area may involve integrated logistics/supplier partnerships, distributor/dealer partnerships, vertical integration, and sourcing control. The alignment is between logistics-related functions within the company and all external parties involved in inbound and/or outbound logistics.

Because of all of the recent market pressures, companies are rethinking the supply chain and pressuring their suppliers and distributors to become part of the solution in delivering high-value goods to their customers at low cost. This is taking many forms, including the compression and electronic integration of processes throughout the supply chain. In some industries cooperative efforts to cut total system costs (such as

"Efficient Consumer Response") are being encouraged. As we noted earlier, this has increased the criticality of the alignment of operations for all parties involved.

Industry Forces Management

This dimension has to do with managing the external influences that significantly impact our marketplace. Some of these key external influences include shareholders and the investment community in general, government regulators, and legislators who dictate national/international trade relationships and standards.

The pace of technological change, the global economic upheaval, and the growing body of environmental laws and regulations worldwide have vastly increased the importance of this dimension. To set and control technological direction demands involvement in setting standards, regulations, and laws. For example, cable TV versus phone company regulatory decisions and Federal Communications Commission standards for High Definition Television will likely determine the next winners in the TV manufacturing market.

THE PRACTITIONERS

It should be evident that no matter what our focus, all of the seven dimensions and all of the key alignment relationships need to be incorporated into effective strategic planning. It is also clear that we need to take a holistic view of our vision versus that of our competitors. How well or how poorly have *they* aligned their Total Delivery Systems and all the strategic dimensions?

Within our description of the model (Figure 9–2), implementation and adaptability are implicit, if not fully evident. When we align the corporate vision and strategies with employees and the organizational infrastructure, we are talking about lining up, on the one hand, the culture (values, commitment, and attitudes) and, on the other hand, skills and capabilities. Much of this is part of the Primary Strategic Dimension of *superior skills and capabilities,* which we labeled the implementation dimension. Potential components of competitive advantage in this area involve organizational redesign and communications, management leadership and style, business process improvement, critical skills development, information and information systems architecture, and performance measures and incentives systems, to name a few.

All implementation approaches have to be adopted with the idea that circumstances *will* change. When we define the Total Delivery System today and how it may look tomorrow, we are developing scenarios of what may happen to our markets and how that may affect us in order to prepare contingency plans.

When we identify all the critical relationships in our Total Delivery System, we are pinpointing where we must place *strategic monitors* to track any event or trend that will affect each alignment. The organizational structure is set up so that there is constant communication throughout the system—top down, bottom up and laterally—among individuals and teams. Business processes and information systems are designed to expect change that is continuous and often dramatic. When speed is critical, the management system empowers people to act to change tactics and at times to modify strategy.

And when we change strategy, we know every dimension that may be affected and how we have considered it in our contingency plans. And on the process goes.

Our model comes to life when we look at successful companies, those that have changed with the times by implementing a holistic strategy.

In 1985, Procter & Gamble began to experience a dip in earnings. Historically, P&G's approach toward building leading positions in new categories had been to identify a market where consumer needs are not particularly well met, introduce a product that is superior in performance, use channel and marketing leverage to make sure that customers understand the new product's benefits—and then watch the profits roll in. In this methodical way, over a period of over 100 years P&G *doubled* unit volume and profitability every 10 years. In all that time, starting with the first advertisement for Ivory Soap in 1882 and incorporation 1890, the company had only six chief executives. In 1985, the company had the number one brand in virtually every product category in which it competed. Could there be a problem?

Traditionally, P&G had considered only three issues in introducing a new product: What does the customer need? How will superior benefits be provided? and How much money will be made? Basically, the firm ignored the competition, typically running roughshod over it, and it did not pay much attention to the retailer. The feeling was that the brand image and the consumer would pull the products through.

By 1985, though, it became apparent that P&G was running into costly problems. They were indiscriminately taking on entrenched, hard-nosed competitors like Nabisco in cookies, Tropicana in orange juice, and Coca-Cola/Pepsi Cola in soft drinks. These giants were not rolling over when P&G thrust its "superior product" into their domains. And when it came to the retailer, P&G was faced with increasingly larger, more savvy merchants intent on low costs, discount prices, and ample profits.

P&G dramatically changed its successful formula by correcting its omissions. The company came out with what still appears to be the most effective program in the packaged goods industry for working with retailers. The most publicized of these partnerships, the one with Wal-Mart, has yielded a totally new relationship concept for P&G with its major retailers and for Wal-Mart with its suppliers. This once aloof manufacturer works very closely with retailers, sending in teams to trade ideas, work on reducing total system costs, and implement new processes and systems for managing orders and payments.

P&G has also developed a new respect for the competition. Rather than simply flinging itself into new markets by making small initial acquisitions and setting out to squash the competition with superior technology, P&G is refocusing on maximizing its potential in existing markets and utilizing larger acquisitions to enter new markets from a more stable base.

The point is that P&G, while not abandoning its emphasis on the consumer and on benefit performance, took a hard look at the relative focus and emphasis of every other dimension of its strategy. The result was realignment of relationships throughout virtually all of the Total Delivery System.

General Electric is another company that looked hard at its hodgepodge of businesses—neatly separated into 350 Strategic Business Units—and decided that a new model was in order. Despite GE's overall financial strength, the portfolio contained too many losing operations. That said, there were just too many SBUs to manage effectively. Certainly, there was little cross-business coordination and communication, but there was a great deal of internecine warfare over funding.

The transformation began in 1980, when Jack Welch was named Chairman and CEO. The primary strategy was to improve GE's market and customer focus dramatically, concentrating in those arenas that it could dominate globally and creating a new companywide emphasis on scale and market power. Welch thus spearheaded the divestiture of all businesses that were not first or second in their markets, representing 25 percent of total sales, and boiled down the remainder into 13 core businesses. By 1990, he had bolstered these core businesses with $17 billion worth of acquisitions and about $20 billion in capital spending.

But beyond this support, Welch paid careful attention to the alignment of strategies and relationships, particularly within the firm's highly entrepreneurial structure. An overlay of companywide principles, tools, and techniques was created to ensure that everyone was pulling in the same direction. Welch and his team said, in effect, "In addition to our strong financial foundation, the distinctive competence we as a corporation can provide to all of our businesses is management skills and techniques. That is how we are going to hold this corporation together. The strategic, where-to-compete issues will be the province of the different businesses."

The entire process was not painless, as GE reduced its payroll by over 130,000 employees through divestitures, plant closings, early retirements, and layoffs. But Welch motivated and energized those who remained by replacing the "be silent" culture with one that says "speak out." Throughout the company, employees attend two- and three-day action-oriented Work Out sessions to interact about better ways to run the business. One of the values being instilled through these sessions is to "stimulate and relish change." Such communication and cooperation runs *across* businesses as well, another 180-degree shift from the old model. As with P&G, GE's recent track record has been extraordinary

ConAgra, Inc. provides another case of successful transition. In 1976, this was a small ($500 million), sickly commodity firm known best for beef, pork, lamb, and flour milling. Today the Omaha-based company is a highly profitable diversified food organization; indeed, with about $20 billion in revenues in 1991, it was second only to Kraft General Foods in the U.S. consumer packaged foods industry. Although the corporate name is not yet a household word, its brand names are: Banquet frozen foods Hunt's tomato sauce, Armour luncheon meats, Peter Pan peanut butter, and most recently, the successful Healthy Choice line of inexpensive frozen foods, cheese, and other reduced fat/cholesterol/sodium products.

The architect for this dramatic change was chairman and CEO Charles M. Harper, a man known for his skill in acquiring good companies at excellent prices. When he took the reins in 1976, Harper set in motion a three-phase change:

1. Quickly revamp or eliminate all inefficient business, policies, and practices.
2. Redesign the business strategy to create a balance of commodity and branded packaged food products.
3. Focus on growth in selected target markets.

ConAgra poured its money into buying, innovating and expanding powerful brand names. By 1992, ConAgra had acquired more than 100 companies, including Banquet and much of Beatrice, and introduced enough innovations to grab the lead in many nutritional food markets. With 60 operating companies, each of them relatively autonomous, ConAgra has maintained control through strong financial standards and a focus on skill, execution, and quality. In essence, Harper had the vision to reinvent the entire company across virtually all strategic dimensions.

Johnson & Johnson, like GE, succeeded over the decades as a highly decentralized company. It consists of over 160 separately chartered companies that, until recently, were expected to act independently. The prevailing wisdom always had been that smaller, self-governing units are more manageable and nimble. A few years ago, however, J&J recognized a problem that the marketplace had been turning into a glaring weakness. There was no leverage for either the retailer or J&J when every account was called on by dozens of different J&J companies. Further, J&J was not able to react quickly to events that impacted several of its units. For instance, when distributor American Hospital Supply leaped into the lead in the hospital products market by implementing on-line order entry for customer (the ASAP system), it took J&J several years to respond.

These factors led corporate management to take a companywide look. The result has been to consolidate some functions by sector (pharmaceutical, professional, and consumer) so as to support new, increased focus on Customer Relationship and Supply Chain Management. For instance, within the consumer sector, integrated customer-support centers have been established to provide common order management and customer service support across all companies, with consolidation of distribution functions planned for the near future. Certain services to hospitals, such as contract administration and distribution, have been centralized under J&J Hospital Services. The company is devoting a great many resources to ensure that the balance between decentralization and cross-company coordination does not go out of whack. In summary, J&J saw how the world had changed and underwent the massive changes necessary to reestablish market leadership.

A final example: An important factor in Unilever's historic success in consumer and industrial products has been the strength of its country organizations. Half-British, half-Dutch, the organization has a mercantile tradition that has made it second to none in entering new lands, setting up shop, and leaving it to local management to devise appropriate strategies for each business (within the framework of a common corporate culture). The same laissez-faire approach typically was also adopted when deciding to enter new product categories. As happened with other companies in the 1960s and 1970s, this approach ultimately resulted in an odd grab bag of businesses, some performing quite well, others not. By the late 1970s profit growth was sluggish.

Unilever then sat down and asked how it could preserve the benefits stemming from its strong country organizations while improving its performance and prospects. One part of the answer was to shift its corporate strategic focus from portfolio management to a greater emphasis on transnational core competencies (skills and capabilities). This led to the designation of core businesses ("coordinations") in which Unilever could maintain superiority over the long term. Other businesses were divested. Subsequently, Unilever's food businesses, which had been organized into three coordinations based on product characteristics, were divided into five strategic groups, each carefully aligned with different types of consumer needs. Although the country organizations retained much of their independence, Unilever strengthened its matrix of regional/industry executives, each of whom was responsible for overall strategies and performance and for worldwide or regional coordination. Unilever's subsequent progress has been dramatic.

What is the lesson? P&G, GE, J&J, ConAgra, Unilever—in the 1980s these companies were ahead of the curve. In the 1990s, companies that fail to respond may not get another chance.

CONCLUSION

What is clear from these cases is that thinking holistically about strategy leads to continuous and sometimes radical transformation. Performance across the Total Delivery System is continuously being reviewed, refined, and altered to maintain alignment with each facet and each dimension of strategy. Every change in strategy automatically throws the wheels into motion to change other primary strategies and any components that are affected. Monitors are in place at every critical junction of the alignment equation. The methodologies, the structures, and the responsibilities for implementation are primed for change. It is a never-ending process that successful leaders for business and industry are adopting totally. One executive stated the mandate succinctly: "If we ever stop reinventing ourselves, we will not be around in the year 2000."

NOTES

1. Porter, M. E. *Competitive Strategy: Techniques for Analyzing Industries and Competitors,* (New York: The Free Press, 1980).

Chapter Ten

The Strategic Connection: Mission, Strategy and Values

Robin W. T. Buchanan

Andrew Campbell

W hat makes a company successful? There is no single answer although gurus have proffered a plethora of popular hypotheses, ranging from the need for chaos to drive the organization to success (Tom Peters) to the strict reliance on statistical process controls (Deming). The problem with these approaches is that they tend to be rather narrow, and, although appropriate for the companies sampled in developing the hypotheses, they cannot be accepted as universal or easily transferred to other organizations.

In working with companies to improve their businesses or develop plans for meeting future challenges, we have concluded that there is no one system that is all things to all organizations. However, we also have determined that it is useful to have a generalized analytical framework that provides a starting point for each company to develop an individual operating style that suits it best.

The framework contains the ingredients for a continuous linkage of the firm's mission—its purpose for being in business—and its strategy—the way in which it pursues the mission. It is designed to ensure that the two overriding themes of the business are in constant alignment. And most importantly, it allows the company to monitor whether that harmony is being maintained during periods such as the 1990s when there is an ever-pressing need to execute change.

This framework itself represents the linkage of two of our earlier research projects—on the importance of corporate mission[1] and the development of a strategic management construct called the Quality Pentagon.[2,3] The underlying thesis is that a sense of mission is central to a company's success and that the Quality Pentagon is a powerful tool for translating mission into reality and thus for achievement of success.

Our work was helped by an investigation by Ashbridge Strategic Management Centre. In November 1987, Ashbridge began a two-year research project into corporate mission statements in the belief that there was no clear understanding of what they are, what issues they should address, and what benefits they provide. The Ashbridge team reviewed the existing literature on the subject, collected nearly 200 mission statements from companies all over the world, and interviewed managers from 40 organizations in Europe and the United States.

The results were confusing. There was wide variation with respect to the format, contents, use, and effectiveness of mission statements. The variation in the *statements* seemed to be attributable to fundamental differences in each company's view of *mission* itself. The statements thus reflected the different views.

Some organizations took the view that mission was primarily a strategic tool, an intellectual discipline that defined their commercial rationale and target market, that is, mission is about defining the business the company is in and the strategy the management wants to follow. Others, more philosophically, saw mission as the "cultural glue" that enabled the firm to function as a collective unity, that is, mission is about values and behavior. According to the latter group, the mission defined the business itself, not where it was going or hoped to go.

These two views of mission placed the Ashbridge team in a quandary. Upon analysis, neither approach by itself seemed sufficient. "Mission" needed to encompass both strategy and culture.

As part of a different exercise, Bain & Co. also was coming to the view that successful companies were aligning culture *and* strategy. In the end, both Ashbridge and Bain concluded that mission *only* exists when strategy and culture are mutually supportive. The more closely integrated the two elements are, the more successful the company will be. When a sense of mission unifies strategy and culture, it becomes THE driving force of a successful company.

This insight brought us to the question of whether there was a way to ensure that a company's chosen mission imbues its strategy and culture. In other words, how could mission be translated into effective actions? In the course of answering this question, Bain developed the PDoubleSBV framework or Quality Pentagon. Based on a construct originally developed at Ashbridge,[1] the Pentagon has been further extended by Bain[2] in helping companies make sense of the enormous amount of advice they get on Total Quality Management. It has evolved into a tool to help companies transform their performance.

For the purpose of analysis and clarity, we shall describe the Quality Pentagon in terms of its five key headings of Purpose, Strategy, Standards, Behavior, and Values. In real life, of course, one must remember these concepts do not stand alone or work consecutively; behavior is conditioned by values and vice versa. What we are talking about, therefore, is not an abstract checklist but a dynamic, interactive system that describes human behavior in companies and that has a life all of its own.

PURPOSE

Purpose is important because it is the linchpin of a company's philosophy. Ultimately all activity must have a purpose and all component purposes must be linked to the overall company purpose if there is to be any sense of unity in the organization. Choosing a purpose has profound implications for choices in strategy, standards, behavior, and values.

Understanding a company's purpose involves questions like: What is this company for? For whose benefit is all the effort being put in? Why should a manager or an employee do more than the minimum required? For a company, these questions are the equivalent of a person asking, Why do I exist? The questions are deeply philosophical and are answered differently by different companies.

In the first type of company the company exists for one purpose, for example, maximizing the wealth of the shareholders. All decisions are assessed against the yardstick of shareholder value. Hanson PLC, a British conglomerate with widespread interests in the United States, falls into this category. Lord Hanson, the CEO, repeatedly states: "The shareholder is king."

Many managers are not so single-minded as Lord Hanson. In a second type of company, managers acknowledge the claims of other stakeholders such as customers, employees, suppliers, and the community. Faced with the question, "Is your company in business to make money for shareholders, make products for customers, or provide rewarding jobs for employees?" they will answer "yes" to all three.

Managers in a third type of company are not satisfied to aim solely at satisfying stakeholders' needs. They aim at what they see as a higher ideal. At the British retailer Marks & Spencer PLC, one manager described the company's purpose as "raising standards for the working man." This rings true for many others in the company who said that they felt, particularly after World War II, that they were improving the standard of clothing available to the average person because they were able to retail high-quality goods at affordable prices. The Japanese clothing and cosmetic company Wacoal aspired "To promote the creation of feminine beauty and to improve the culture of living." Such companies have reached beyond the stakeholder definition of purpose and shoot for a higher-level goal that potentially can be supported by all stakeholders.

Defining a clear purpose then is a starting point from which strategy, standards, behavior and values must flow. If 90 percent of the management cannot say what the company's purpose is, the company cannot progress to the next stages. Our research suggests that different kinds of purpose do not generate different results in terms of a company's success. Hanson and Marks & Spencer are both very successful companies. However, we have seen repeatedly that companies with an unclear or insufficient sense of purpose fail to meet the needs of stakeholders or to achieve any other goal.

A company's choice of purpose will be driven by its corporate history and by the values embodied in that history. The people currently managing the company will bring their own sense of purpose and values. The purpose of any company grows from that organization's history and from the determination of the current management team.

With purpose defined, management can move on to consider the first "S" on our framework: Strategy.

STRATEGY

To achieve a purpose, there needs to be a strategy. If the purpose is to be the best competitor, there must be a strategy that outlines how the best can be achieved; if the purpose is to create wealth, there must be a strategy aimed at creating wealth.

The principle applies all the way down the line. Strategy determines how the resources of the company are to be allocated so that customers can be served, quality improved, and costs managed. In short, strategy provides the commercial logic for the company.Without it, a sense of purpose, no matter how strong, will go for nothing. It is strategy that defines the business in which the company is going to compete, the position the company plans to hold, and its distinctive competence and/or competitive advantage.

In its apparel retailing business, Marks & Spencer seeks to offer the best value for the money by providing a broad range of classic quality clothing. Marks & Spencer's competitive advantage is based on large sales per square foot driven by better quality products at affordable prices. The strategy of Hewlett-Packard Inc. has been to succeed in high-value niches in the electronics industry and to be better than its competitors at innovation and product development. Its competitive advantage is based on strong innovation, high-quality staff, and a participatory management style.

Although the strategy for a particular company often depends largely on the particular circumstances in its industry, one decision is crucial to the strategies of all companies: the choice of its management team or its "People."

Field Marshall Bernard Montgomery said 25 years after the World War II battle of El-Alamein: "If it was considered that I was successful...I attribute it to three reasons: I chose good subordinate generals and trusted them. The second is that I built up a very high class staff. My staff was so good that I could confidently hand over the whole matter to them to implement, and get on with thinking about future operations. The third reason was that I had a very clear understanding of the importance of the human factor in war and of the need to preserve the lives of those under my command." John Keegan, a leading military historian at the Royal Military Academy at Sandhurst, identifies Montgomery's approach as: "The number one imperative of leadership."A tiresome debate that we are occasionally invited to join is "People versus strategy—which is most important?" They are of course totally intertwined. Often the most important strategic decision managers make is which people to hire and how to allocate their time.

But it is not just a question of choosing *good* people. It is a question of choosing the *right* people in terms of the requirements of all the levels of the Quality Pentagon—Purpose, Strategy, Standards, Behavior, and Values. Bain rejects many extremely bright applicants not because they would not be good consultants but because they don't have the entrepreneurial spirit so critical to helping the firm achieve its purpose of "Outstanding results for clients."

STANDARDS

Management must reinforce its strategy by setting and maintaining standards, that is, both targets for achievement and the policies that will ensure achievement. Purpose and strategy are empty concepts unless they can be converted into action, into the policy guidelines that help people to decide what to do on a day-to-day basis. Once standards are set, there must be some means of measuring the degree to which they have been attained, and mechanisms must be put into place to ensure that they continue to be met.

There are four fundamental sources of standards:

1. *Benchmark against the best.* To study how to improve its operations, Xerox Corp. sent its managers of quality programs to Milliken & Co., a textile company with a Baldrige award, and its marketing managers to Procter & Gamble Co. Managers in the billing department went to American Express Co. The managers were expected to learn about the standards observed in their host companies and the means by which the standards were to be met.

2. *Customer research.* For most companies it is the customer who will provide the most input to these standards—whether it be current, potential, or former customers. For example, Bain's banking, building (savings) society, and insurance clients regularly interview customers who have closed their accounts, or whose balances or activity have dropped significantly. Insights gained from this research have enabled these clients to improve customer service. At one client the number of customers defecting to competitors each year was reduced by half.

3. *A company's own imagination.* Former CEO Robert Galvin of Motorola Inc. set what seemed to be an almost unattainable standard for his organization—six sigma quality. That translates into only 3.4 defects per million or 99.99966% quality. It worked, and his successor, George Fisher, is thinking of raising the standard to 99.999994% or only 60 defects per billion, which is 56 times better than the original.

4. *Regulation.* Environmental, health and safety, and other regulations exist to lay down minimum standards that a company must meet. Some Bain clients use these standards as competitive weapons in their strategy. They plan to exceed the minimum significantly and then put pressure on regulators to raise the standards and damage competitors who haven't been so obedient.

Understanding what standards the strategy requires is only the first step. The challenge is to translate them into policies so that the standards are actually met in practice.

Some policies may lay out customer service practices in great detail, whereas others may provide only basic guidelines. British Airways is a practitioner of great detail.

The airline was striving for in-flight service and comfort as good as or better than competitors, a better on-time record, and more friendly and helpful ground services. These strategic objectives were then translated into specific policies. For example, in-flight services would be at least as good as those of competing airlines on the same route; managers and employees should be helpful and friendly at all times. Customer research identified attentiveness as a critical element in service quality. The airlines' *Passenger Care Standards Manual* translates this finding into a response program for cabin staff that includes being visible in the cabin, responding promptly to bells, offering assistance to the elderly, infirm, young children or their parents, and making contact with non-English-speaking passengers. British Airways provides a good example of how to convert purpose and strategy into tangible standards and actions that have dramatically improved its performance.

In the past, many service companies—McDonalds Inc. being an obvious example—have coupled detailed policies with sophisticated technologies to ensure that even uneducated and unmotivated workers could consistently deliver high-quality service. Modeled after assembly line production systems, the McDonalds' approach has effected a service revolution.

Walt Disney Co. has developed perhaps the most complete code of conduct for employees with policies ranging from "you are responsible for maintaining appropriate weight and size" to "hats should be worn with the brim two fingers above the eyebrows." The problem with such precise human engineering is that it lacks the flexibility to allow people to cope with unusual customer circumstances or to respond when something goes wrong. Measurement has replaced judgment, instead of supplementing judgment.

By contrast, some companies feel that they can rely almost totally on their employees. Nordstrom Inc., the fashion retailer, has a slim employee handbook. It has only two rules. The first states, "Use your good judgment in all situations." The second states, "There will be no additional rules." Despite the contrast, both Disney and Nordstrom are successful concerns.

The setting of targets and the promulgation of policies that contain and express standards are not sufficient to ensure that the standards are actually met. There must be a link between standards and performance. It has often been said, quite rightly, that "what gets measured gets managed." A recent Bain survey found a high correlation between unsuccessful service quality programs and a failure to measure and monitor service quality standards.

In the early 1980s one service company was focusing on quality circles. Its manager, an author of this chapter, complained: "I sat all my employees around in circles and we all had lots of interesting ideas which we wrote down. In reality it became a frustrating and negative exercise because none of us, neither they nor I, knew what service levels were necessary and how high our standards should be."

By contrast, Federal Express Co. has a clear hierarchy of performance. A package delivered even five minutes late gets one negative point. If the package is delivered on the wrong day, that's five negative points. A lost package or a missed pickup gets ten negative points. These negative points are closely monitored for trends in service quality.

Choosing the right aspect of performance to measure is critical to the effective use of standards. For instance, customer retention is a key measure of service performance, and for some companies is often as important as the level of profits. Managers should not underestimate the future profits lost and the wasted effort and investment when a customer departs unhappy.

Fred Reichheld (see Chapter 8), founder and director of Bain's customer retention practice, estimates that retaining an additional 5 percent of the customer base each year produces improvement in profitability ranging from 20 percent for mail-order companies to a startling 125 percent for credit card companies. Other Bain research shows that it may cost up to five times as much to win a new customer as to retain an existing one. Furthermore, evidence shows that long-term customers buy additional products or services, refer new customers, and contribute to greater employee morale and stability.

In addition to being an important measure of success in meeting service standards, customer retention is a relatively easy concept to analyze and to calculate. "Customers who defect to the competition," says Reichheld, "can tell you exactly what parts of the business you need to improve."

The retention level is derived in the bluntest possible fashion: divide the number of customers at the end of the year who also were customers when the year started by the total number of customers at the beginning. The benefits of choosing straightforward measurements that are easy to understand and use are obvious. Managers will apply them willingly, consistently, quickly, and correctly.

After the firm sets a standard, expresses it in a policy, and identifies effective means of measuring the level of attainment, rewards must then be devised that encourage the meeting of these standards. Mastercare, the auto service subsidiary of Bridgestone/Firestone, found that many former customers who took their business elsewhere said they did not like being pressured into repairs they had not planned on. Inadvertently, Mastercare's sales commission scheme had been working against customer retention by providing rewards for overly aggressive employees. By contrast, Great-West, a U.S. life insurance company, pays a 50 percent bonus to brokers who meet their customer retention targets.

BEHAVIOR

So far, we have described how the first three elements of the Pentagon—purpose, strategy, and standards—should be vital components of a company's efforts to achieve success and strengthen its sense of mission. Nonetheless, as we said at the beginning, mission is as much about culture as it is about strategy and direction. However strong a company's sense of purpose, however clear its strategy, however rigorous its standards, unless it succeeds in influencing or often altering the behavior of its employees, the mission is doomed to failure.

This question is complicated because human behavior in the work place is conditioned by a number of factors. It not only is governed by corporate imperatives but also is conditioned by the employees' own values. Thus, the success of the enterprise depends in large measure on the extent to which these two value systems—the corporate and the personal—are in harmony. Behavior and values, the final corners of the Pentagon, must be viewed in this context.

Although senior management sets the tone, it is not just a question of leading from the front. The decision to alter a company's culture or direction and therefore the behavior of its employees may at first glance seem to arise only from commercial considerations. We have found, however, that in most instances in which changes are successfully accomplished, an additional dimension arises from the company's sense of mission.

For instance, British Airways sent 20,000 of its staff on "Putting People First" training programs. There was a good commercial reason for "Putting People First," for it would help to retain customers, but there was also a moral reason. The company, in effect, was saying, "We are all people and life would be better for all of us if we took a little more care with each other." The new patterns of behavior described by the British Airways' trainers were presented as a philosophy of life as much as a way of improving the airline. Participants were asked to consider how they greeted their families when arriving home, as well as how they handled customers. In other words, employees of British Airways were being asked to compare corporate values with their own private values in order to realize a corporate mission that included caring and solicitude.

Different companies approach their employees in different ways, depending on who they are and what business they are in. What might be appropriate for a service-oriented company like British Airways might not work for a high-tech business like Hewlett-Packard. Hewlett-Packard's "The HP Way" describes the company's famous behavior standard of Management by Wandering Around (MBWA). To implement its strategy of innovation in high-value areas, HP needs to attract and retain the best engineers and product managers. These high-quality individuals do not like to be closely or hierarchically managed. HP therefore developed the MBWA policy as a management approach suited for these kinds of high achievers.

The MBWA behavior standard is based on good commercial logic, but it too has become a crusade of its own. Managers believe it is the right way to manage not only high achievers but also all personnel, because it acknowledges the innate creativity of individuals and underlines the manager's respect for people. It has its roots in the company's sense of mission and has become part of the value system. Whereas the objective observer can readily identify situations such as piloting a plane, where MBWA would be the totally wrong style of management, it is for managers committed to the HP Way in the HP context almost sacrosanct. Like putting people first at

British Airways, MBWA in Hewlett-Packard is not only good strategy but also the "right way to behave." Recall that our definition of mission includes two types of rationale for behavior:

1. The commercial rationale—do it this way because it will make us commercially successful.
2. The ethical rationale—do it this way because it is the right way.

This combined motivation for behavior is essential because human beings are fundamentally emotional. To capture the emotional energy of an organization, the mission needs to provide an ethical underpinning for commercially desirable behavior. The Body Shop, a chain of beauty stores, has a purpose of developing cosmetics that do not harm animals or the environment. Its strategy is to be more environmentally conscious than its competitors, hence attracting the "green" consumer and the "green"employee. Within the company, environmental consciousness has been translated into policies and behavior standards, one of which was almost unique when first introduced. All employees have two wastepaper baskets—one for recyclable and one for nonrecyclable products. Employees receive training in what can be recycled and what cannot. By ensuring that every aspect of company life is permeated by the company's ethic, management ensures consistent and motivated behavior. This would have been impossible to create with bonus systems or management exhortations.

VALUES

Values are the beliefs and moral principles that lie behind the company's culture and give meaning to its norms and behaviors. Management cannot change values through mission statements or company songs. But the change CAN be accomplished through management behavior. As management acts in line with the company's purpose, executes its strategy, enforces its standards, and hires people with the appropriate values, a new set of values emerges. When the emerging corporate values match the employees' values, a virtuous circle develops that embodies all five elements in the Quality Pentagon. One sure sign of success is when employees' values put them continuously ahead of management in finding ways to improve quality and service. At that point, the employees are helping drive changes in purpose, strategy, standards, and behavior.

In real life, of course, the loop embracing purpose, strategy, standards, behavior, and values does not operate consecutively. In particular, a company's choice of purpose is driven by the values of the people selecting that purpose. This interaction is evident in several of the case examples we have discussed. Much of the change involved is interactive. As new standards are achieved, the strategy may change, and as new values emerge, policies may need to be rewritten. However, it is still important to approach the *planning* of change in a phased way and to allow the interaction between these critical elements to happen.

LEADERSHIP

If a sense of mission is the driving force behind success and the Quality Pentagon provides the organizational framework for the development of a program to implement the mission, then one more key ingredient is needed. There must be some central catalyst that ensures that program and mission march hand in hand even when the firm faces the challenges inherent in an ever-changing business environment. An administrative alignment of the five elements of the pentagon will not alone create the success and the cohesiveness companies seek. The catalyst must be provided by the leadership of the company.

To be effective leaders, managers at all levels must demonstrate their own levels of commitment to the company's mission and program. Symbolic actions, particularly on the part of senior managers, are among the best ways of communicating a new mission or a continued belief in a mission.

For example, when senior executives of Anglian Water, a U.K. water utility, refuse to drink bottled water, they send the strongest of signals to employees and customers that the leadership personally believes in the quality of its product and service. Another example involves a Bain client, a successful British company whose profits rose 20 percent after we handled a quality and efficiency assignment. Two years after the changes, employees still talk about one gesture: the decision by the executives to give up their chauffeur-driven Mercedes. The gesture effectively communicated management's determination to cut all costs that were not essential to the company's success.

By the same token, inconsistent behavior at the top sends an equally strong message of noncommitment to stated goals. That was the message when a former British Transport Minister, whose domain includes U.K. railroads, went everywhere by chauffeur-driven car and nowhere by train. The more extensively and thoroughly that management embraces the company mission and its requisite behaviors, the more effective leadership by example is likely to be. At Rank Xerox PLC, quality training started at board level and cascaded down through middle management before it reached the front-line employees, who were thus fully aware of their superiors' commitment. If symbolic acts are not accompanied by real efforts to guide the company, they will be received as mere PR hype.

In addition to specific acts or gestures, managers, as leaders, have to recognize that they may have to adapt their overall style and methods to their employees. If both the employees' motivations and abilities are low, a military-style directional à la Walt Disney is required. If an organization is already excited by its vision, its strategy and the goals it is trying to achieve, managers must still lead from the front. But they should emphasize explaining why and how things are to be done and giving employees appropriate discretion. Managers dealing with subordinates who are capable but lacking in confidence must be not only teachers but also sports coaches, participating and encouraging, leading their teams from within, and being prepared to be lavish with congratulations and awards. As employees grow in confidence managers must gently let go of the reins, that is, "empower the employees," to use a fashionable buzzword. Striking the balance between overcontrol and underguidance may seem difficult and dangerous, but enormous rewards, both moral and financial, await managers who successfully walk the tightrope.

CONCLUSION

In this chapter the authors have outlined and explained the construct that we call the Quality Pentagon and its five corners—Purpose, Strategy, Standards, Behavior, and Values. We have also discussed ways in which leadership actions and style reinforce the company program to be implemented within the framework of the Pentagon. However, one must never forget that the Pentagon cannot be applied mechanically. Mere administrative alignment of its five elements will not guarantee success. The Pentagon is effective only if it embodies and furthers the sense of management and employee commitment that lies at the core of the company.

Commitment is, in the final analysis, an emotional issue. It is about the feelings an individual has toward the company. It is the sense of mission and the commitment that draw the elements of the Pentagon into a coherent whole. Conversely, a sense of mission without a comprehensive framework must remain a mere concept that lacks a means of consistent application or expression.

A sense of mission improves company decision making and communication, makes the right personnel decisions easier, and, most importantly, makes possible greater cooperation and trust. Employees with a sense of mission find it easier to work together, respect each other, and search for the solution that is in the best interests of the organization.

REFERENCES

1. A. Campbell, M. Devine, and D. Young, *A Sense of Mission*, London: (Economist/ Heinemann, 1990).
2. R. Buchanan, "The Bain Quality Pentagon," *Management Consultancy,* April 1992.
3. R. Buchanan, "The Bain Quality Pentagon," *Mortgage Finance*, April 1992.

Chapter Eleven

Structuring the Change Initiative

Robert Davidow

J ust as an effective change management program must encompass the four components of Strategy, People, Process, and Technology, the defining and monitoring of change strategies require the same components. Specifically, a broad array of tools, techniques, and systems can be employed effectively to implement a change program. And they all fall into the categories of Strategy, People, Process and Technology (Figure 11–1).

In this chapter, we cover the requirements for defining and monitoring change strategies, and discuss the following topics:

- Developing the change *strategy.*
- Structuring the change *organization.*
- Building the change *process.*
- Creating the *technology* to control the process.

DEVELOPING THE CHANGE STRATEGY

After carefully studying the need for change and identifying what has to be changed, an organization should develop a change strategy. The three basic components of this strategy are these:

- Change readiness assessment.
- Implementation plan.
- Communications strategy.

FIGURE 11–1
The Change Process Nerve Center

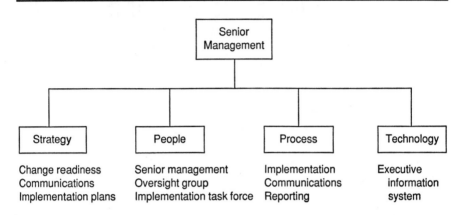

Change Readiness Assessment

One of the most significant obstacles to change is the organization's employees and their attitudes. By the same token, one of the greatest benefits from change is the ability to harness the creative and intellectual capabilities of the company's human resources and focus them on the common goal.

Companies have found that a change readiness assessment is invaluable in helping them overcome the obstacles and seize the opportunities of change. A change readiness assessment is a survey of employees at various levels to determine whether they understand the need to change, the direction of change and the benefits of change, and how willing they are to change. The assessment can point up the employee attitudes toward change and help determine what kinds of educational efforts must be executed during implementation of the change strategy. Once an organization understands the hurdles and potential pitfalls of implementing the change that lurk within its work force, it is in a position to address its employees' attitudes on change through vehicles such as education, training, communications, job design, incentive programs, and an entire panoply of human resources management techniques.

Implementation Plan

The implementation plan is the definition of who (the change managers) will do what (take change actions) by when (the change timetable) to carry out the change program. The implementation plan typically covers these points:

- Action steps.
- Major milestones.
- Responsibility assignments.
- Completion dates.
- Cost/benefit targets.

For the change program to have any chance of success, explicit tasks must be assigned to responsible individuals who are fully empowered to carry them out. The change program must have leaders or champions. In addition, the targets and metrics that the change program is supposed to achieve must become some person's responsibility. And attainment of the assigned goals must be key ingredients in determining how the individual is evaluated, advanced, and compensated for the period he or she is responsible for achieving the targets. The implementation plan then is management's main scorecard for ensuring that the change program is on track and yielding the intended benefits. Finally, any issues that surfaced in the change readiness assessment but were not immediately addressed can be dealt with in the implementation plan.

Communication Strategy

The communication strategy is a mechanism to let various stakeholders know what is going to change, why, and what benefits they can expect to derive from the change. The stakeholders can be a diverse group that include: shareholders, the investment community, regulators, directors, employees, suppliers, customers, and so on. Depending on the nature of the company's change and which of these stakeholders will be most impacted by it, the communications strategy should determine the following:

Who is to receive information—which constituencies are to be targeted and which ones are most essential to enlist in the change management effort.

What they are to be told—specifically, what information do the targeted stakeholders need to help with the efforts.

When the messages should go to the various constituencies—timing the release of the information to get the most effect (for example, conditioning a market or employees in advance for a change about to take place).

Who should communicate with *whom*—the specific individuals at both ends who will deliver and receive the messages, so the message has the biggest and most effective impact, so real people are talking to real people about real change.

Why the communication effort is important to the stakeholders—what is in it for them or how they will be affected by it.

What the stakeholders can expect to derive from the change program—what benefits will be distributed among the so-called "publics." Who will gain what?

Note the composition of the stakeholder bloc. It offers unique opportunities. The work force, for example, can be educated to participate actively in the change program and get their own benefits from its success. Customers provide the continuing opportunity to keep atop the market and keep in step with it. All can rally behind the designated change leader or champion.

STRUCTURING THE CHANGE ORGANIZATION

Three main organizational units are responsible for executing the change program: senior management, the change oversight group, and the implementation task forces. I will review the role of each and how they interrelate.

Senior Management

Ultimately, senior management—the CEO, president, division heads, functional heads, and so on—is responsible for effecting change in its area of responsibility. Without their enthusiastic support, change cannot happen. Unless they put the change responsibility firmly on their shoulders, the motivation and drive required to implement large-scale change will be absent. There should be no doubt in the organization about who wants the change to happen, who is responsible for the change, and who will have to be answered to if the change program falters. Clearly that is senior management.

Change Oversight Group

Although senior management is fully responsible for achieving the change, it may delegate day-to-day oversight and monitoring functions to an individual or a task force. I refer to these people as the change oversight group. This group uses the implementation plan as its guidebook to ensure that requisite steps are accomplished on time and on budget and that they yield the desired results. If there is slippage or if implementation plans fail to yield the desired results, the change oversight group can bring these situations to senior management's attention and obtain guidance in how to pursue a midcourse shift to put the effort back on track. This oversight group, therefore, keeps senior management informed, involved, and committed to the change process, while simultaneously allowing management to carry out its day-to-day responsibilities. Monitoring alignment of the key functions also falls to this group.

Implementation Task Force

The implementation task force, which in some cases may consist of only one individual, is responsible for actually making change happen. These groups may design the product, develop the new organization structure, change the compensation system, and so forth.

The degree of authority and responsibility will vary from situation to situation, but several common elements tend to characterize implementation task forces:

- They include the people directly involved with carrying out the steps in the change-response plan.
- They report to the oversight group.
- The task force memberships are of limited (often temporary) duration.
- If they perform well, they usually are rewarded with increased responsibility.

- The task forces generally include the mix of skills and disciplines necessary to complete the assignment. For example, a new product development task force usually will include sales, marketing, financial and production executives. This task force provides insight into whether the new product can be sold to a receptive market, manufactured and delivered in timely fashion, and earn enough money (beyond the cost of capital) to make the whole deal worth the time and effort.

BUILDING THE CHANGE PROCESS

A successful change program will require three key processes to be effectively implemented: ongoing communications, as outlined in the communications strategy; implementation, as described in the implementation plans; and continuous reporting to the oversight groups and senior management. The actual nature of these processes will be a function of the plans and strategies that mandate them. Effective execution of these processes is the essence of change.

Some organizations also will institute a fourth process called contingency planning, essentially a fallback position. Contingency planning comes into play when an event that clearly signals the change management effort is not producing the intended results triggers it. When that shortfall becomes evident, a group will be impaneled to recommend an alternative course of action that will direct the program toward intended results. If the contingency plans fail to generate desired results, the organization may have to reconsider whether the original goals were appropriate to begin with.

CREATING THE TECHNOLOGY TO CONTROL THE PROCESS

The final, but no means least important, task of a successful change program is to create the technology to control the process. Although technology can play various roles, the most common and most useful tool is an executive information system (E.I.S.).

The E.I.S. not only can provide management with the status of implementation but also report on the key metrics and goals an organization is trying to achieve. The system also can link results with responsibility assignments and report on actual versus planned outcomes.

Although the nature and development of an E.I.S. probably could be the subject matter of a complete book, suffice it to say that an effective, timely, accurate E.I.S. is an invaluable tool in monitoring a large-scale change effort.

Thus we see that to design an effective change program properly, the elements of strategy, people, process, and technology must be taken into account. Moreover, the same four elements must be employed in defining and monitoring change strategies. Absent any one, the probability of success declines. With all four operating in conjunction, achievement of the intended results is far more likely.

Chapter Twelve

Mergers and Restructurings: Aces in the Hole

Martin J. Sikora

M ergers, acquisitions, and divestitures are perhaps the most striking and dramatic symbols of corporate change. Certainly this is true for the people involved in them, and mergers and acquisitions have great weight in the observations of analysts, investors, customers, suppliers, and other external stakeholders. Although they are change events and tools of change, mergers and acquisitions are not usually change triggers. Rather, they represent dramatic responses to the threat of change—at least in the well-managed, change-oriented company.

However, change is so powerful that, in many cases, the surviving company may have to treat the merger as a change trigger. In the 1990s, and even in the high-powered M&A era of the 1980s, the typical merger, acquisition, and divestiture is a reaction to a change trigger. External outreach often makes sense because the buying company gets some desired or necessary attribute quickly, despite some stiff up-front cash outlays.

In other words, the merger is a vehicle for a swift and decisive response to a change trigger. Not surprisingly, many of these triggers emerge within the markets served by the acquirer or by both companies.

When Dennison Manufacturing and Avery merged in the office supplies field, their change trigger was the massive shift in the retail market to mass-merchandise distribution. AT&T was prompted to acquire computer manufacturer NCR Corporation by the increasing need to combine telecommunications with data processing and management information systems. Poor prospects for maturation in the cigarette market (because of growing emphasis on health problems) pushed Philip Morris and the former R. J. Reynolds into major food acquisitions. The merger of BankAmerica and Security Pacific was triggered by the consolidation of the banking industry, to meet demands for larger, more efficient financial institutions. Allied Corporation, an old-line maker of commodity chemicals, used acquisitions and divestitures to remold itself into the high-tech Allied-Signal because it saw a bleak future in its cyclical, hotly competitive, low-margin, and highly volatile traditional business.

Although most other strategic mergers are driven by the same overtly sensible initiatives, they often don't work as well as the strategic blueprints predict. The rate of failed or disappointing acquisitions is probably overstated, but an uncomfortably large number haven't panned out. Postmortems seldom blame strategic misjudgment (buying the wrong products or acquiring when a promising-looking market is about to peak out) or even overpricing, which may produce a hurdle rate on investment that is impossible to scale. Indeed, these should not occur when most strategically driven companies acquire through a finely honed process that generates a plethora of information on the rationale for the deal and the candidate companies best suited to achieve these benefits. The key problem is that, in general, the process stops with the closing of the deal. Many acquirers thus lack a clear vision of the capabilities and scope of the combined company and the actions needed to turn potential into real payoffs.

The principal manifestation of postacquisition problems is personnel attrition in the first few years after the deal. Surveys have found that acquired management is usually gone within three to five years—sometimes driven out, sometimes on their own volition. This is a good example of misalignment and unbalancing: The target was acquired for the people who made it worthwhile to get, and these people are no longer on the job. A target that was acquired to stabilize a potentially destabilizing situation can become, through mishandling, another source of destabilization. Thus, the major impediment to realizing the objectives of an acquisition is the failure to adhere to the principles of alignment in the wake of the deal.

Alignment is especially critical in the M&A context because, as other commentators note in this book, change (whether good or bad) tends to be resisted by a large part of an organization. Nothing conveys the idea of change with more force than a merger, acquisition, or divestiture. It changes the scene for the workers and executives in both camps.

Some bizarre reactions have been logged. In *Mergers & Acquisitions* magazine, psychologist Mitchell Lee Marks and organizational behavior specialist Philip H. Mirvis revealed their discovery of the merger syndrome. It was based on their work developing postmerger integration programs that emphasized the role of people in making deals successful. The syndrome, they reported, was manifested in stress and resistance, fear and uncertainty, and worries by target-company executives that they would have to prove their skills and abilities again to new bosses.

On the acquiring side, the syndrome often took on a "conquering army" tone—"if you were so great, how did we acquire you?" In the merger of two large eastern banks, for example, an integration consultant was called in to develop a fair plan for assigning personnel and integrating the organizations. One bank was among the largest in the country; the other was a large institution that generally had not performed as well as the acquirer but was far superior in some highly profitable segments. Although the acquirer talked about an equitable integration, a conquering army mentality lurked beneath the surface. When the consultant finally submitted his integration plan, the acquiring bank's CEO, with just a glance at it, threw it aside, saying "I don't give a shit about this." As it turned out, he should have. Firings resembled a reign of terror that defied logic—some terminated workers had to be brought back while others left embittered. Key managers in the high-performance segments at the bank left quickly. Computer operations were fouled by sloppy integration of management information systems. It took years before things were straightened out and the acquirer could finally realize the payoffs.

The deal was strategically well-grounded. It was part of the consolidation of the U.S. banking industry to create larger and more competitive institutions. It was nearly scuttled by personnel issues and the failure to adhere to principles of alignment.

Time after time, the strategically envisioned benefits of M&A are either negated or delayed by people problems. In the change management context, we would say that the acquisition was executed in response to a change trigger as a means of stabilizing the company.

Under our concept of change and alignment, an appropriate management of a merger—on a continuous basis well after the deal is completed—has to start with the exact strategic reason for the deal. Those first pitches in the M&A ball game are the identification of the change trigger that suggested a strategic initiative was needed and the exact reasons why a merger or acquisition (or divestiture) was chosen as the appropriate response.

A sampling of the strategic benefits available to intelligent acquirers includes the following:

- New or complementary products without the cost or time involved in developing them in-house.
- New technologies that can provide an advantage over the competition without a learning curve.
- Geographic expansion, including foreign countries.
- New markets, again by shortcutting de novo development.
- Going into complementary markets with somewhat different skills and knowledge bases.
- Expanding production capacity without waiting for the delayed payoffs in internal investment.
- Getting people with critical skills in every area, from the laboratory to the sales force.
- Playing competitively in consolidating industries; being the whale that gobbles the fish and gaining the share and mass needed to survive.
- Accelerating growth in expanding industries.
- Staking out growth niches in mature industries.
- Entirely remaking a company by getting out of a traditional business and going into entirely new fields with better prospects.

It takes people to produce the payoffs. The combined company has tricky personnel decisions to make from day one that ultimately affect its ongoing alignment. Without question, there will be personnel redundancy that may require some terminations. Doing this in a consistent way that will keep the survivors committed to the combined firm is a hard act. The task may be easier if the principles of alignment are kept in mind; alignment is an ongoing process needed long after the acquisition until the target company loses its identity as a newcomer and becomes an integrated part of the entire outfit.

Again, it is critical to keep sight of the change triggers that prompted the acquisition and the reasons the acquisition was chosen as the appropriate response to change. With these in mind, it can be acknowledged that real alignment may require the target to adapt to some characteristics of the acquirer, whereas other characteristics can be maintained. A checklist of the four points will show how this happens in the real world.

STRATEGY

Strategy can actually be like walking a tightrope before a decision can be reached. Certainly, the acquirer's strategy is paramount and the target, as well as the acquisition itself, must conform to the overall corporate strategy. However, the acquiring company must understand that differences in the way the acquirer and the target conduct their business may have to be retained—especially to meet the demands of the market. In other words, the target may need to keep its own strategy alive if its market is different from the acquirer's and thus demands a different style.

The two strategies may have to coexist in the same organization even if both constituents are in the same basic industry. The issue is segmentation in the industry. For example, Kmart's basic business is discount retailing, but a fast-growing and more profitable element (although smaller than the core), is specialty retailing—a number of retailers in pharmaceuticals, sporting goods, office supplies, books, and other markets. Kmart recognizes that the customer bases and the merchandising approaches must differ from those of the basic discounting business, so it allows these units to operate with considerable autonomy. However, the diverse retailing operations are still aligned with the market.

Aligning strategy does not require that everybody do exactly the same thing or that the target's strategy be perfectly tuned to that of the acquirer. Alignment does require that the strategies be examined to determine where harmony is appropriate and to recognize where the divergence is best. In short, strategies must be aligned to markets rather than to some arbitrary norm within the organization.

OPERATIONS

Alignment of operations must reflect the principle that divergence may be necessitated by the market. If the target has been acquired because it infuses something new into the acquirer—again, in response to a change trigger—it might be more appropriate for the target's operations to remain unchanged if this suits the market and has been a key to its success. Conversely, if the target is in the exact same industry and has been acquired to provide mass or scale, it may be necessary to change the target's operations to fit those of the acquirer to achieve economies of scale and reduce costs.

It is always a judgment call. For example, Philip Morris made three large acquisitions in the food industry (General Foods, Kraft, and Jacobs Suchard) in response to a change trigger: the flattening of the cigarette market. In many respects, food is a complementary industry because it is a consumer market and its products are distributed through the same channels as cigarettes. However, food processing and cigarette manufacturing are clearly two different businesses requiring two separate modes of operation.

There can be different modes of operation within the same industry. In food, distribution systems are different for baked goods and frozen foods, for fresh produce and canned items. Operating differences may have to be maintained when a commodities-oriented producer moves upscale to a higher-margined niche product, or a firm oriented toward premium-pricing buys a maker of off-the-shelf products that offers volume, cash generation, and economies of scale.

Again, the market may be the arbiter. If keeping the target in its original operation mode best serves the market, that may be the best way to go unless the need for in-house conformity is more important.

CULTURE

Culture is typically cited by M&A mavens as the single biggest problem in a merger, the corporate factor that most often trips up the deal makers and undermines the best strategies. In many cases a merger falls apart because the target's personnel are mistreated and not allowed to do what they do best. In plainer terms, the acquirer tries to dictate its culture to the target with a take-it-or-leave-it ultimatum.

A classic case of a deal that went astray because the acquirer insisted on doing things its way is the Schlumberger acquisition of Fairchild Semiconductor in the early 1980s. The acquisition was based on Schlumberger's desire to move up the technological scale from its core business of oil field and other industrial equipment. The business mix had some plausibility, but the human mix was a disaster. Paris-based Schlumberger, the epitome of old-line, hierarchical management, and Silicon Valley–based Fairchild, with laid-back scientific personnel, were from different worlds. But Schlumberger was adamant. The acquisition was a Pyrrhic victory. Fairchild's top people cut out rather than buy in. Scores of successful Silicon Valley enterprises were launched by former Fairchilders. Schlumberger lost the best and the brightest employees and Fairchild has been struggling to regain its former eminence.

At the other extreme on the success/failure meter is the approach of the Kmarts of the world. Kmart's decision not to tamper with its retailing subsidiaries' ways of doing business is a means of preserving their unique cultures as much as their modes of operations. In many cases, of course, operating style and culture are interwoven.

Other cases of culture clash are not as clear-cut. In the vast majority of cases, there is no easy answer. Some integration experts say it is not necessary to harmonize cultures perfectly unless there is an overpowering business reason. They suggest that it is feasible to let the target retain its culture, or at least most of the artifacts of its culture. In such cases, it is important to recognize that the culture differences exist and to manage them accordingly.

Is this another area where the market can be the corporate Supreme Court? Of course. This is the area where it is perhaps most important for the customer to prevail over internal egomania.

COMPENSATION

The fourth area, compensation or reward, may be the hardest issue to deal with. Managing compensation discrepancies cuts across many lines: incentives, employee and worker satisfaction, fairness, and, of course, financial reality. Moreover, anecdotal evidence reveals some bizarre results that often are in conflict with each other, even when the same compensation techniques were used.

For example, there is often a rush to equalize pay and compensation scales across the entire company. But what happens if the target's pay is higher than the acquirer's? Should the target employees be asked to take a cut just to get in step? Or should the acquirer's scale be raised—perhaps at a whopping cost? Leaving the differentials untouched can be a source of jealousy and low morale. Experience is not a particularly good teacher.

In a *Mergers & Acquisitions* article, Robin Ferracone of Management Compensation Group related the case of a manufacturer that acquired a retailer when a change trigger suggested that forward integration was important. The pay scales were markedly different; the acquirer's ranked much higher. To demonstrate fairness and a welcome-aboard environment, the acquirer lifted the pay scales at its new retailing subsidiary and brought them in line with its own.

The result was a disaster. The retail unit started slipping badly. What happened? The increased pay scales had so loaded up its cost structure that the retailer could not make its hurdle rate for profitability. A quick reversal had to be made.

In another case, costs were not that critical, but a pay harmonization plan still backfired. The merger partners were two insurance companies—the acquirer was an Eastern-based firm that paid its employees and managers well, and the target, a firm centered in the Midwest, had incredibly low base salaries and bonuses but extraordinarily liberal perquisites. First-class air travel, company-paid club dues, and top-of-the-line leased cars were all standard.

Instead of being pleased by the ability to earn much more, the target's personnel went into a funk. Performance dropped alarmingly. A backlash was evident. As it turned out, the target's workers preferred their perks to more cash in their pockets. They got their wish, as the acquirer went back to square one.

There is no easy answer to the compensation issue. Sometimes, alignment to market can help set the guideposts, but sometimes it can't. Compensation must be looked at in terms of its alignment with the other three planks of good corporate performance and determined on a case-by-case basis. However, there is no excuse for ignoring compensation issues or excluding them from the alignment process.

The market can light the beacon on another issue, one that cannot be fit neatly into one of the four main compartments but uniquely cuts across all four. That is the matter of maintaining the target after the deal is completed. Many target managements are lured by promises of increased investment to accelerate growth, but when it comes time for the piper to be paid, top management must choose between the investment requests of its subsidiaries, and the newly acquired unit doesn't get what it was promised.

The results—feelings of being shortchanged, lower morale, turf warfare with people at other subsidiaries, and the perceived inability to work all opportunities to the fullest—are the exact opposite of what was desired from the acquisition.

How can this be resolved? By going back to the market and examining the change trigger that led to the acquisition. Allocate funding on the basis of what units have the best prospects and can contribute the most to stabilizing the company. Even then, the decisions are tough, but nobody says that acquisitions or change management are easy.

Divestitures may be even trickier to handle from an alignment perspective. In some respects, they represent more dramatic change than straightforward mergers or acquisitions that combine two free-standing companies. In any event, divestitures can become complicated because they represent a two-edged sword in their effects on alignment.

From the selling company's perspective, the disposal may represent a clean break. That does not free the divestor from taking a new look at its alignment. Conversely, the buyer treats the deal just as it would any other kind of acquisition, and this touches off the need for reexamination of alignment.

Although various reasons are given for why companies sell businesses, most sell-offs are driven by the markets. The markets also may dictate the form of the divestiture. The most common type of disposal is the straightforward deal, in which the seller deals off a division or subsidiary for cash, and occasionally stock in the acquiring company. Other principal mechanisms include spin-offs, in which ownership of a business unit is transferred from the parent to a free-standing company controlled by its own shareholders via a stock dividend, and equity-carve-outs, in which partial interest in a subsidiary is sold in a public offering.

In a straightforward sell-off of a business unit from one company to another, the market invariably calls the shots. The rationale for a divestiture of this type is generally that the business is more valuable to the purchasing company than to the current owner. For example, a low market share that troubles one company can be a prime asset to a competing company that wants to add that slice of share to its competitive arsenal.

At the other extreme, the business may be an absolute jewel with great prospects in a growing market. The investment required to reap those rewards may be too great a burden to the parent, however. From a pure alignment standpoint, a good sale candidate is a business that is out of joint with the parent's core competencies and core strategies. The added value, of course, is an influx of cash from the sell-off that can be redeployed into the markets that are the primary centers of focus.

The selling company, to put the finishing touch on the deal, should check out the alignment of the surviving parts of its business. Are the four key management levers still functioning in harmony? Is the company realigned with the markets it has chosen to serve? For the buyer, as in any acquisition, there is the need to determine how absorption of another business will affect its alignment and whether any fine tuning is needed.

A spin-off actually demands similar disciplines. Although the spin-off is often used to get rid of unsalable operations, it has also been used to cut loose a subsidiary that will never fetch an optimum price because it is too good. The alternative is to give it to the shareholders, which is a way of saying that the newly independent company is capable of standing on its own feet and serving its market well. Spin-offs tend to be either stars or dogs.

In the late 1980s, Household International restructured back to its traditional financial services business by shedding its industrial operations. Six were sold, the other three spun off. The demarcation line was whether an independent company could compete in its market. In three cases, the answer was yes.

After spinning off its subsidiary, the parent company must look inward and determine whether its remaining parts are maintaining alignment. The new leaders of the spun-off company should check their primary elements of alignment as they leave the starting gate.

If the deal is an equity carve-out, in which the parent keeps control of the publicly traded subsidiary, the twin checks on alignment still are necessary. Indeed, they may be most critical for the subsidiary that is straddling the line between being a stand-alone company yet still a part of the old corporate family.

Even if a company doesn't change its configuration, good management demands a periodic alignment audit. When the company merges, acquires, divests, spins off, or executes an equity carve-out, an alignment check should be automatic.

Chapter Thirteen

Midcourse Corrections

Anthony C. Rich
Kenneth E. Mifflin

I n times of great and constant change, how can we tell who the corporate survivors will be? Why can some companies expertly navigate the churning water, execute successful midcourse corrections no matter what happens, and land at their chosen destinations unscathed? On the other hand, why do others founder, getting lost at sea or washing up on shores far from home?

And why is it that organizations can lay a solid strategic foundation—even the multifaceted, holistic strategy described in Chapter 9, "Game Plan for the Next Dynamic"—and still be less than successful in responding to change? Think about the annual list of "most admired companies." Why are so many revered names of yesterday missing from the rolls today?

Not long ago Andersen went in search of definitive answers by talking to 300 key executives across many industries in the United States, Europe, and Asia. We asked them how they adjust the company's business strategy to changes in the competitive environment—in essence, how they sense external change and then how they respond with internal changes.

Only a few of the sampled companies indicated that they could rapidly convert external change in the marketplace—caused by change triggers—to internal alignment of their strategies and operations. Each of these few companies had several elements in place to facilitate necessary changes, but the three major factors they shared were the following:

- The fundamental underpinnings—the culture, the strategy, and the systems that foster change.
- Feedback, constant and unfiltered, from the marketplace.
- The mechanisms that enable execution of midcourse adjustments.

For the majority that had difficulties, the problems were simply that they lacked these elements. Their answers were remarkably consistent. They talked about the general inabilities of their organizations to sense change in their competitive environments on a holistic and factual basis. Specifically they meant that they generally lacked the capability to weave bits and pieces of competitive and market information into a comprehensive view of changing competition within their industries.

In addition, even when the competitive picture was clear, they felt unable to make midcourse corrections to their strategies and operations quickly because of a variety of barriers to change. Most significantly they lacked the executive leadership for change. Although they had historically been successful, their values and beliefs had become frozen in time. The underlying philosophy of "If it ain't broke, don't fix it" had created inertia, and what change processes existed were inadequate. Not surprisingly their reward systems did not support change. They were mired in the zone of self-denial.

In short they had few instruments in place for converting external change into internal action. The vision, organization, operational processes, rewards, and leadership style all reinforced the status quo.

We have seen some very great names struggling with these barriers. With entrenched beliefs and unwieldy bureaucracies, General Motors, U.S. Steel, and Sears Roebuck have taken abysmally long periods and required some severe blows to respond to changes in their industries. At this writing they are still struggling.

In 1991, traumatized by its slipping performance, IBM dramatically reorganized itself into numerous smaller business units in an effort to pull out of its "mainframe mentality." Yet the reasons for its crisis—mainly the emergence of the personal computer and the definitive shift it caused in economics, technology, and application—were apparent a decade ago.

Although less intransigent, Xerox Corporation was a moment away from disaster in the 1980s. Early in the decade Xerox was so inward looking that it didn't even know Eastman Kodak was going to announce its entry into the copier market. It literally had no receptors in the marketplace. Japanese companies, of course, lulled Xerox by entering the low-end copier market that Xerox steadfastly ignored. The Japanese worked their way up with technological innovations and low pricing until a significant percentage of Xerox's large copier market had been stolen away.

After more than five years of setbacks in the market, Xerox broke out of the zone of self-denial and began an intense self-examination that resulted in major cultural and process changes. For instance, by simultaneously addressing the major issues of market leadership and customer satisfaction and retention, Xerox significantly compressed product development time and mounted several major programs for capturing customer feedback and responding to it.

The daunting task for corporations today is to have in place all the pieces that foster change and adaptability: the culture, strategy, structure, management practices and systems, and techniques. In Chapter 9, "Game Plan for the Next Dynamic," we established that our strategies must be holistic and multifaceted, and we now assert that the ability to change must be approached in the same all-encompassing fashion. Companies need a closed-loop system—one that features planning, executing, and reporting back. Further, a company cannot have a change-oriented culture unless everything it says and does supports change and adaptation.

Within this context we are going to deal with four fundamental parts of this process of setting up an adaptable business organization:

- Establishing the right culture.
- Ensuring a change-oriented strategy through scenario analysis and contingency planning.
- Placing strategic monitors, the mechanisms for feedback from critical points outside and inside the company.

CULTURAL IMPERATIVES

To reiterate, establishing and maintaining a corporate culture oriented to change requires a holistic approach, but it begins with creating and communicating the vision and the goals. The late Sam Walton, founder of Wal-Mart, was so good at it that talking about him has become a cliché. His guiding principle was simply "The secret of successful retailing is to give your customers what they want." He defined what that meant very succinctly: a wide assortment of quality merchandise, guaranteed satisfaction, the lowest prices, excellent service, convenient hours, and a pleasant shopping experience.

He communicated and supported his belief that the only way to keep abreast of what customers expect in each of those areas is to listen to them carefully and constantly. That is why Wal-Mart has 13 airplanes carrying executives and managers to stores around the country. That is why it pushes responsibility and authority down to the level of department managers in the store and brings them to Saturday morning meetings in its home base of Bentonville, Arkansas. That's why there are few management layers to impede decision making.

Walton also recognized that the culture must fit the vision. In his book *Mr. Sam,* Walton talked about the 10 basic rules he followed, most of which explicitly or implicitly established a culture that fostered change, not merely to keep aligned with customer demands and market movement but often to get ahead of them. They are, in brief, the following:

- Rule 1: Commit to your business. Believe in it more than anyone else . . . .
- Rule 2: Share your profits with all your associates, and treat them as partners. Together you will all perform beyond your wildest expectations.
- Rule 3: Motivate your partners. Think of new and more interesting ways to motivate and challenge your partners. Set high goals, encourage competition, and then keep score. Make bets with outrageous payoffs. If things get stale, cross-pollinate, have managers switch jobs with one another to stay challenged . . . . Don't become predictable.

- Rule 4: Communicate everything you can to your partners. The more they know and understand, the more they will care.

- Rule 5: Appreciate everything your associates do for the business. Nothing can quite substitute for a few well-chosen, well-timed, sincere words of praise. They're absolutely free—but worth a fortune.

- Rule 6: Celebrate your successes. Find some humor in your failures . . . .

- Rule 7: Listen to everyone in your company and figure out ways to get them talking. The folks on the front lines—the people who actually talk to the customer—are the only ones who really know what's going on out there. This is really what total quality is all about. To push responsibility down in your organization, and to force good ideas to bubble up, top management must listen to what associates are trying to tell them.

- Rule 8: Exceed your customer expectations. If you do, they will come back over and over . . . . Stand behind everything you do. The most important words I ever wrote were on that first Wal-Mart sign: SATISFACTION GUARANTEED.

- Rule 9: Control your expenses better than your competition . . . . For 25 years running . . . . we ranked No. 1 in our industry for the lowest ratio of expenses to sales. You can make a lot of different mistakes and still recover if you run an efficient operation. Or you can be brilliant and still go out of business if you're too inefficient.

- Rule 10: Swim upstream . . Ignore conventional wisdom. If everyone else is doing it one way, there's a good chance you can find your niche by going in the opposite direction.

Sharing partnership, motivation, empowerment, involvement, communication, humor, appreciation, innovation, customer focus—notice Walton was talking about his people in most of these rules. He gave them a piece of the company, involved them financially, mentally, and emotionally. He tried to treat them as well as he expected them to treat the customer, feeling that employees are THE key to doing whatever needed to be done—including major change and continuous improvement— to achieve the vision.

PLANNING FOR CHANGE

Walton was a stickler for keeping everything in alignment with the primary strategy of low prices, quality products, and great service. He ensured operational efficiency in hundreds of ways—keeping a lean organization, compressing and integrating processes with suppliers, encouraging new ideas everywhere. He worked with suppliers to improve products while maintaining low prices.

The Total Delivery System is the complete business model that extends from the suppliers at one end of the system, through internal operations and new product/service development, to people in the channel (distributors, dealers, retailers, and so on), and finally to the end customers. The seven primary strategic dimensions concern the decisions a company must make about where and how it goes to market—that is, where it will be superior (see Figure 9-1, pages 108–109). Those decisions in their entirety determine how every component of the Total Delivery System must function.

Again, ensuring alignment means that the firm sets itself up to know what to do when events challenge existing strategies. Every time the company senses a change and responds to it, the company has to deal with the domino effect that any adjustment may have on strategies and the company's business. The firm can't prepare for every eventuality, but it can set itself up to minimize surprise, respond quickly, and at times lead the charge.

Alignment is a continuing process that starts during strategy creation and planning for implementation. A company creates strategies based on critical assumptions about the marketplace and critical decisions about the role it wants to play and how it wants to play it. The firm hopes that it is making those assumptions and decisions based on good information, analysis, intuition, and projection.

The problem in a chaotic world is that there are invariably many different market outlooks. Therefore the firm may have to develop several different views of the world and alternative courses of action and then answer the critical question: Do we want to take the risk of selecting and optimizing one course of action, or do we want to minimize risk by suboptimizing in order to position ourselves to be able to move quickly from one course to another?

This problem has intensified the need for scenario analysis, a tool for identifying a range of events and their impacts. Among others, planning expert Michael Porter of Harvard University has detailed the following process for creating industry scenarios:[1]

- Identify the uncertainties that may affect industry structure.
- Determine the causal factors.
- Make a range of assumptions about each critical factor.
- Analyze the industry structure, the potential sources of advantage, and the competitive behavior that might prevail under each scenario.

The process can be very difficult considering that we have to make assumptions and project impacts based on both whether something will occur and when. The nature of the markets that open up early can shape the way products and technology evolve. The nature and resources of competitors can influence an industry's development; for instance, in its heyday, IBM's entry into a computing market would automatically accelerate that market's growth. The time period for standardization and those who influence the choice of standards can have great impact. For instance, the evolution of HDTV, which promises to revolutionize television, is highly dependent on the actions of two parties: the Federal Communications Commission in choosing a standard, and the company or consortium whose standard is chosen.

Another aspect of scenario analysis is to project the impact of each scenario on the Total Delivery System and our fundamental vision concerning core competencies and goals. How would each scenario affect our products and services, our supply chain, and our channels? What changes in the seven Primary Dimensions of Strategy would be dictated by different scenarios? What contingency plans must be in place to minimize surprise?

For instance, Eastman Kodak is trying to position itself for the developing battle in photography between silver halide and electronic imaging. Presently, the chemical products hold an edge because of resolution and low cost, but electronic imaging is gaining ground and already has penetrated many applications in which high-quality resolution is not needed and price is not a big issue. For example, in photojournalism the ability to transmit a digital image 10,000 miles across the telephone wires quite often surpasses the need for high resolution. If the use of the image is for television, high resolution also is not an issue.

That electronic imaging is already becoming a sizable business and that it will supplant silver halide in many applications are not in question. The key question is how the price performance of electronic imaging cameras and other devices will evolve. Will silver halide be obsolete? If so, when? A wide range of issues hinges on the outcome. If silver halide isn't obsolete, where will it find its markets and how big will they be? What are the hybrid (chemical/electronic) opportunities and how long will they last? What are the transitional markets in image capture, development, and output? What electronic imaging capabilities must Kodak develop, and what can Kodak develop? Is Kodak's core competence in photographic images or is it chemicals and coated papers?

So the alternative scenarios for this decade, highly complex and uncertain as they are, boil down to these:

- Rapid wholesale takeover of photoimaging by electronic imaging.
- Slow penetration with silver halide maintaining predominance in the amateur market and some professional markets.
- A long transition in which silver halide and electronic imaging exist side by side with sizable markets for hybrid products eventually developing.

Kodak currently has a hybrid product, the PhotoCD, for use by photofinishing laboratories. With it the firm can process the customer's film and provide the customer a compact disk with the images on it—a permanent record that can be played on television or turned into prints. Kodak also has developed electronic capabilities in color printers and other output technology. It has established a center for research and training on electronic imaging in Camden, Maine, and is engaged in a variety of alliances and joint projects concerning this technology.

If the worst-case scenario, a rapid decline in the use of film, occurs, will Kodak be able to take the route of transforming itself into an imaging company rather than a film company? And even if the best-case scenario occurs, a slow transformation of the imaging markets, that will not negate the fact that Kodak has been fighting off intense competition in film and processing supplies, which have rapidly fallen to commodity status. The issue for Kodak as of 1993 is to set itself up across the Total Delivery System for large-scale change. R&D investments and skills, manufacturing plants and capacity, sales and marketing programs, customer segmentation, the logistics system, the channel, and many more elements will be impacted.

STRATEGIC MONITORS

Wal-Mart historically has been successful in responding to change in part because it has, as Walton put it, "kept its ear to the ground." The dramatic industry changes facing Kodak suggest that its survival depends on the very careful placement of strategic monitors in all corners of its marketplace around the globe—customers, competitors, laboratories, academia, employees.

As was stated at the outset, a key deficiency at companies that cannot turn external change into internal responses is the lack of constant unfiltered feedback from the marketplace and the inability to piece it together into a meaningful picture of what is happening. Let's look at some of the places where we have to place strategic monitors.

Customers

The first priority obviously is to establish clear and constant communications with customers—communications that support the goals of each dimension of strategy. A major retail chain, eager to differentiate itself through innovative customer service and specialty offerings, maintains a panel of more than 10,000 customers to keep it informed about the market. Xerox surveys thousands of customers monthly.

Executive management must get out to where the action is—the customer's factory, the store, the office. Each year, the retailer Nordstrom's assigns its executives to stints on the front lines in its department stores. Japanese auto executives spend time simply watching customers use cars. They have been known to spend hours in supermarket parking lots, observing what station wagon owners go through to put packages into the car. Companies that make packaged goods for consumers are spending more and more time with the trade, analyzing not the needs and habits of each store's consumer population, but ways to add value and reduce costs for the retailer. For instance, Frito-Lay has a "Top to Top" program in which heads of key supermarket accounts are invited to regular meetings with the food maker's executive group. Chemicals and textile producers, such as DuPont and Milliken, are setting up forums for exchanging ideas with direct customers as well as with their customers and end users.

Competitors

Most companies lack a comprehensive strategic and structural view of the competitor that focuses on the newest products and their pricing and sales tactics. There are a variety of ways to gather competitive intelligence, ranging from published reports and funded studies to consumer roundtables on vendor performance. Some companies have literally assigned people to put themselves into "the shoes" of specific competitors; they have to become so attuned to the culture and strategy of the competitor that they can predict actions and reactions of competing firms.

Technology

Keeping abreast of technological developments that affect both the company's operations and its products and services is critical. This requires monitoring research institutions worldwide—universities, industrial research arms and consortia, government-funded laboratories, and joint projects. It also includes monitoring leading-edge competitors, new entries, and relevant companies in adjacent industries. And, we emphasize, it includes monitoring internal R&D.

As a technology goes into use, it is important to monitor the evolution of applications and technological refinement. This means monitoring leading-edge users—including internal users, competitors, and customers—and setting up internal laboratories to simulate applications.

Best Practices Companies

The modern firm must find benchmarks for excellence outside of its industry as well as in its own. These may be excellence in a particular strategic dimension, for example, in customer partnership or channel management or in the operation of the Total Delivery System.

Industry

Companies need top-down monitors that survey core and allied industries. They should seek out the influences that impact customer demand and requirements, technological development, materials and parts supply, barriers to entry, and other crucial elements. Monitors that capture a panoramic vision of the industry landscape will be the first to spot such critical change triggers as incursions from companies outside the industry or a shift in foreign government trade policies.

Employees

Employees are extremely sensitive gatherers of information on the marketplace. They are, after all, constantly sifting the sands to determine how market developments will impact their jobs and their livelihoods. Thus, companies have to set up formal mechanisms to extract potentially valuable information. The question is how to do that, particularly with people on the front line—the troops in sales, customer service, telemarketing, repair, and support. In some cases, the mechanism is there and all that must be done is turn it on. The telemarketers and service people who man the phones typically are armed with terminals and customer databases to record every transaction. It is relatively easy to incorporate that system and the plethora of detail it generates into a "satisfaction" monitor Indeed, employees may be a first line of intelligence to pick up change triggers.

Gathering the softer information on customers and competitors from the sales force and other personnel is much tougher, provided that information either is not a normal part of their jobs or, in the case of sales, often is perceived as a threat. This accumulation of data requires a dedicated top-down effort to promote the need for intelligence and to provide evidence that it is being used. Personnel must be given easy ways to submit the information. Finally, and perhaps most importantly, those who participate should receive something valuable in return, such as information feedback, involvement in the actions resulting from intelligence, and attractive rewards for the results.

Some of the best examples of management techniques for monitoring employees are at General Electric under the rubrics of Work-Out, Best Practices, and Process Mapping.

• The Work-Out has been likened to a town meeting. The manager assembles his or her personnel and sets an agenda of problems or new ideas to be addressed—initially, simple problems involving process, environment, and administration—and then leaves the employees to work out proposals to resolve them. The first Work-Outs within a business unit are held off-site over three days, with 40 to 100 people from different parts of the unit attending. At times suppliers and customers take part. At the end of the session, the manager returns and is given a few minutes to consider each proposal—to approve, disapprove, or ask for more information. Approved proposals are set into motion at the Work-Out. Subsequent Work-Outs may be on-site and address more complicated issues. The cumulative impact has been enormous, in terms of employee involvement and cost-saving improvements.

• Best Practices began with a study of several noncompeting companies that had faster productivity growth than GE and had sustained the improvement for 10 years or more. The focus was on the attitudes and management practices that had made them successful. They turned out to be the following: an emphasis on managing processes, not functions—in other words, how departments work together (that is, alignment); product leadership; partnerships with suppliers; and superior inventory management. As a result, GE shifted its focus to how things get done and to the concept of continuous improvement—which, of course, is a goal of the Work-Out sessions. Best Practices studies of other companies and information exchanges with these noncompetitors have become integral elements in the management of every business unit. GE's Management Development Institute also teaches a Best Practices course.

• Process Mapping is an old technique in which even the most minuscule step of a process is put down on a flow chart. The value comes not from the technique but from the people who are doing the mapping. Value is greatest when the mapping involves everyone both inside the firm and outside. The most inclusive participation would include managers and the workers they supervise in-house and key external blocs like customers, suppliers, and distributors. If used correctly, mapping allows everyone involved to develop a complete understanding of the process beyond his or her own job. It also fosters integration of all components and functions across the Total Delivery System. Process mapping then is a clearly proalignment technique.

IMPLEMENTING ACTION-ORIENTED SYSTEMS AND PRACTICES

How do we turn external signals for change from change triggers into internal action? What surfaced repeatedly in our survey of 300 executives around the world was their lack of confidence in their ability to make change happen. Whether the change meant major redesigns of their operations or the implementation of continuous improvement programs, the issue they raised was strikingly universal: "How do we execute major changes when the vast number of our employees do not see the need for change?"

Most agreed that the customers, and their changing needs and demands, are the pivotal points for redirecting the business. However, they were collectively confused about the specific processes and techniques that could be used most effectively and efficiently to execute the change.

Let's first make a distinction here. There is a fundamental difference between a company that is trying to effect a major change because the old ways are no longer working and a company that recognizes that change is a constant in its marketplace and is trying to develop a change-oriented organization.

Often the company forced into change is hoping to change just once. It fails to create a culture that encourages willingness to move, and shift, and pivot 180 degrees whenever it is necessary to achieve targets. Once management pushes the whole organization through the meat grinder of change, everyone breathes a sigh of relief and settles in for a long haul. When the next "major change" hits everyone goes into shell shock again.

Although the following techniques and practices may be used to swing a one-time change, they really are aimed at developing permanent change-oriented environments. The analysis will begin with the broad requirements an organization must meet to provide proper commitment and capability from top to bottom. This will lead to the specific solutions being achieved by companies that are widely using the three most powerful levers for change in the Total Delivery System, namely:

- New product and service development.
- Supply chain management, including all activities from the supply of raw materials, parts, and other in-bound components, through manufacturing, to sales and delivery to the end customer, distributor or retailer.
- Channel management, including distributors, agents, brokers, and retailers.

COMMITMENT AND CAPABILITY

The starting point for establishing and maintaining a change-oriented culture is creating and communicating a vision and a mission that key on the need for change. But understanding where the company is trying to go isn't enough. The cultural imperatives that include shared commitment and shared values must be actively promoted. Commitment and value can be shared at several levels, both internally and externally. This sharing can extend from the executive suite to the production worker, from the salesperson to the service agent, and from the suppliers to the channel.

Buy-in by the individual employee is essential. "We hear you. We want to go that way. We'll work cooperatively to implement our strategy. We'll do whatever it takes every day to make sure we keep up with, no, stay ahead of the market." Without buy-in, there can only be dictated or legislated change—which usually ends with disastrous results. The best people send their resumés out, major projects falter and die, and a desperate management begins wholesale layoffs and cost reductions that create an organization that's more mean than lean. Sound familiar?

Many successful companies have avoided such catastrophes by achieving shared commitment to doing whatever is necessary to stay on course. At Wal-Mart, the cheer is "Give me a W...A...L...M...A...R...T. What does that spell? Wal-Mart! Who's number one? The customer!" That's buy-in, but in more than words. Walton's actions, as seen through the 10 rules, supported and reinforced the vision and the idea of "change as needed" and motivated employees to match the words with deeds.

Walton showed commitment when he made the employees partners and gave them a voice and a piece of the action. He demonstrated that he was willing to change constantly to improve the supply chain and the cost structure. He worked in partnership with suppliers like P&G to integrate and automate the replenishment and payment processes, and he eliminated or bought up intermediaries in the distribution channel to bring down costs.

Wal-Mart's actions center around the second component of buy-in, which is capability. Three critical elements—people, process, and technology—must be clearly defined and aligned to gain requisite capability. The prescription for achieving and ensuring buy-in is to get everybody and everything moving in the same direction. Here is a partial checklist of how to develop optimum alignment:

1. *People.* Getting people at all levels in organizationwide change management requires the following:

   - Incentive systems that are aligned with the changing needs of the customer and that provide rewards for quick responses.
   - Strong leadership commitment to the vision, mission and shared values; to supporting it with the right structure, systems, and skills; and to sharing the vision, responsibilities, and benefits with employees.

- Training, precise job definitions, and core competencies that are in line with customer demands and a change-oriented culture.
- An efficient organization structure that reduces the time and complexity of decision making and focuses on results.
- Greater empowerment for personnel, pushing authority downward to facilitate decisions by people close to "where the action is"—near the customer, out in the regions, in the plants, and at the distribution centers.
- Forums and channels for expressing ideas and problems, and for expediting implementation, such as those incorporated in General Electric's Work-Out.

2. *Processes.* The change-oriented company features such operating techniques as these:

- Performance measurements dynamically aligned with changing customer needs and market conditions.
- Decision-making processes that are simpler and quicker than ones used by competitors.
- Effective work flows that eliminate non-value-added activities, compress cycle time, and reduce errors.
- Results-oriented integration of process, driven by outcomes and designed to take advantage of technology.
- Simplified procedures.
- Practice and structure to promote continuous process improvement.
- Quality at the source of each process.

3. *Information technology.* Information systems driving change management should be based on the following:

- An infrastructure that can be changed in a cost-effective manner.
- Integration with the business processes.
- Dynamic alignment with the decision-making processes to identify changes in required information continuously, provide exception reporting, and ensure that information is shared across functions, business units, and geographic territories.
- A continuous focus on eliminating paper and unnecessary information.

Wal-Mart historically has enjoyed the advantage of a stable vision and a leader who believed constant change was needed to achieve it. Many companies whose strategies and cultures were once successful need an overhaul, and it helps to see how they are changing their capabilities in terms of people, processes, and technology.

For instance, Apple Computer is renowned for offering innovative, user-friendly, high-priced products in the personal computer market—but not for its operational efficiency or its expertise in customer service. With the launch of the Performa PC line in 1991, Chairman John Scully signaled Apple's thrust into consumer electronics and everything that means in terms of product diversification, customer service, mass marketing, and wheeling and dealing with retailers and discounters. And he is doing it while maintaining Apple's position as an innovative product leader.

How does one take a free-wheeling club of high-tech geniuses and move it toward becoming a giant in 21st-century consumer electronics? Scully began by changing behavior in the Apple organization. He has worked hard to instill a more businesslike environment, change the reward systems, hire people with different attitudes and skills, de-layer the organization to speed decision making, and improve communication. At the same time, he is maintaining the spirit of innovation.

Producing for the consumer electronics markets demands operational efficiency, not a strong suit of innovators. Scully addressed that by guiding the reengineering and simplification of all processes in the entire value chain and setting in place a process for continuous improvement. Wherever Apple doesn't have well-developed competencies, it is being outsourced. Take service. Apple historically has delegated most of its service functions to its well-chosen independent dealer network. But when Apple moved into consumer electronics, that network obviously could not service the people who bought their box of equipment at Circuit City or Staples. Moving quickly—within weeks—Scully launched a new teleservice center operated by an outside firm, and in the process initiated another valuable capability—a centralized database of the consumers, including who they are, what they bought, and what problems they are having.

THE THREE LEVERS FOR CHANGE

As a firm zeroes in on the broad range of actions needed to make change and create a change-oriented culture, it begins to suggest still more specific actions throughout the Total Delivery System, namely through the three change levers: product and service development, supply chain management, and channel management. Here are some of the specific approaches successful companies are taking.

Product and Service Development

For companies whose survival depends on leadership through innovative products, quick reengineering of competitors' products, or their use of customization of products for particular groups of customers, the quick responsiveness of the product development cycle is critical. Some of the successful techniques include the following:

• Product simplification. A leading tractor manufacturer, fending off a low-price foreign competitor, reduced the number of parts in its equipment by over 20 percent.

The reengineering cut prices and significantly slashed the time required to get the tractors to market.

• Shortening the new-product development cycle through such techniques as concurrent engineering and cross-functional teams. The teams ensure that all needed inputs—design, manufacturing, marketing, and so on—are incorporated simultaneously rather than sequentially into the process of developing and getting a product or service to market.

• Speeding up commercialization by simplifying consumer testing. Rather than conduct elaborate research, the company does quick pilot tests and runs prototypes in representative locations in the field. J C Penney has electronically connected consumer panels with merchandisers to cut down the feedback time in testing new styles.

• Shortening the "organizational distance" between development and approval of any response to the market—be they ideas, strategies, technologies, or the products and services themselves. For instance, in 1990 Hewlett-Packard, in an effort to enter new markets and bring products out faster, began a reorganization that cut away three layers of management. Engineering experts in such technologies as printers, workstations, and mass storage now go directly to top management for approval of their product strategies. The company also has instituted the practice of dispatching research groups to work uninterrupted at sites away from the office. In 1991, H-P stationed 10 engineers and marketers in a trailer in Boise, Idaho, and directed them to come up with a minuscule hard disk drive installable in such instruments as telephones and game machines. Within a year, the group demonstrated a one-ounce "matchbox" that did the job.

The Supply Chain

How does the company facilitate midcourse corrections within the supply chain? There are innumerable approaches and techniques being used successfully, such as these:

• Elimination of isolated functional towers and viewing the entire chain as an integrated process. The goals and the performance measures are based on what the marketplace demands, and everyone shares responsibility for meeting those goals. For instance, Colgate-Palmolive developed a series of common measures for the supply chain including time to market, quality of the end product, and total costs. They became the common measures of all functions in the chain as well.

• Cost-cutting manufacturing techniques like focused factories, just-in-time manufacturing and Sony Corporation's new approach, which stresses common components across product lines and partially manufactured subassemblies.

• Quality programs. Quality programs have allowed such companies as Motorola to reduce their product failure rate to an extremely minuscule percentage.

• Information networks to compress processes and eliminate low-value activities across the supply chain. In industry after industry, companies have implemented electronic data interchange (EDI) systems to connect them with customers and suppliers for order management. Hospital supply and pharmaceutical distributors have sought competitive advantage by using these systems to become in effect the inventory control, ordering, and restocking arms of their customers. Many consumer goods companies, such as Coca-Cola, have gone to computer-supported telemarketing to eliminate the need for field sales personnel to handle small accounts.

• Joint improvement programs between suppliers and manufacturers. Often netting enormous benefits that couldn't be realized unilaterally, some makers of cans and plastic bottles are actually manufacturing them at the plants of soft drink manufacturers. Companies in many industries have used joint design teams with members from customers and suppliers to cut costs, speed development, and simplify components in the end product so rejects could be reduced.

• Rationalization of the physical design of the supply chain. This step results in fewer warehouses, focused factories, better-located plants that deliver better service, and lower manufacturing and distribution costs.

The Channel

Streamlining the channel may include these features:

• Integration of the selling channel through information technology. Haggar, the apparel firm, is using EDI to manage its inventories at individual stores, working with such retailers as Wal-Mart. This is yet another variation on the techniques used by wholesalers in some fields.

• Partnerships between manufacturers and retailers that aim at increasing value, lowering costs, and improving service. In their simplest form, they may involve the use of electronic ordering. However, many more comprehensive partnerships are being formed around such activities as customized packaging, direct delivery to individual stores, manufacturer management of inventory, reduced lead times, and customized promotional programs.

CONCLUSION

Keeping the company name on the "most admired" list in today's markets demands keeping the company in a constant state of readiness for change. Most critically, that requires getting buy-in from each employee. Sustaining shared commitment and shared values through the peaks and valleys is a full-time, never-ending job.

If a company is to minimize surprise and lead the market, it must base its strategies on well-considered assumptions. Fast-changing markets, such as those Kodak and IBM are facing, demand multiple views of the world, multiple courses of action, and complete understanding of the potential effects of these forces on business as well as every element of the Total Delivery System. In the end we are taking a gamble that the course we choose is the right one. But astute scenario analyses and contingency planning can cut the odds against failure.

At all times, the pulse of the markets must be measured through strategic monitors placed at every corner of the marketplace (external) and in the farthest reaches of the organization. The process of turning unfiltered feedback from the monitors into action has to be a closed loop. Information has to be funneled to wherever people are empowered to take action—through the Work-Outs, the cross-functional teams, the partnerships (internal). All the levers for change—product and service development, supply chain management, and channel management—have to be buttressed with techniques and systems that facilitate midcourse corrections.

Without such a comprehensive approach that embodies corporate alignment, the business cannot compete in the bitter, but still intensifying competitive environment of the 1990s.

NOTE

1. Porter, M.E., *Competive Strategy: Techniques for Analyzing Industries and Competitors,* (New York: The Free press, 1980).

Structure of *The Change Management Handbook*

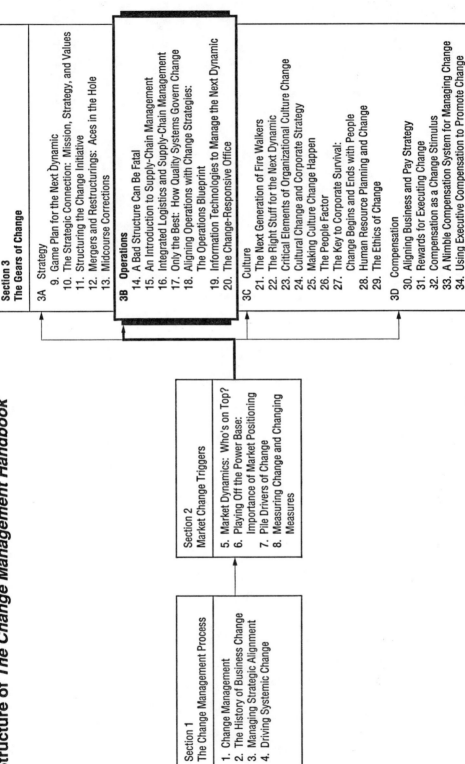

Section 1
The Change Management Process

1. Change Management
2. The History of Business Change
3. Managing Strategic Alignment
4. Driving Systemic Change

Section 2
Market Change Triggers

5. Market Dynamics: Who's on Top?
6. Playing Off the Power Base:
   Importance of Market Positioning
7. Pile Drivers of Change
8. Measuring Change and Changing
   Measures

Section 3
The Gears of Change

3A   Strategy

9. Game Plan for the Next Dynamic
10. The Strategic Connection: Mission, Strategy, and Values
11. Structuring the Change Initiative
12. Mergers and Restructurings: Aces in the Hole
13. Midcourse Corrections

3B   Operations

14. A Bad Structure Can Be Fatal
15. An Introduction to Supply-Chain Management
16. Integrated Logistics and Supply-Chain Management
17. Only the Best: How Quality Systems Govern Change
18. Aligning Operations with Change Strategies:
    The Operations Blueprint
19. Information Technologies to Manage the Next Dynamic
20. The Change-Responsive Office

3C   Culture

21. The Next Generation of Fire Walkers
22. The Right Stuff for the Next Dynamic
23. Critical Elements of Organizational Culture Change
24. Cultural Change and Corporate Strategy
25. Making Culture Change Happen
26. The People Factor
27. The Key to Corporate Survival:
    Change Begins and Ends with People
28. Human Resource Planning and Change
29. The Ethics of Change

3D   Compensation

30. Aligning Business and Pay Strategy
31. Rewards for Executing Change
32. Compensation as a Change Stimulus
33. A Nimble Compensation System for Managing Change
34. Using Executive Compensation to Promote Change

PART

B

OPERATIONS

K eeping a strategy limbered up and in alignment is one challenge. Getting the firm's operations in step with the shifts in the game plan may be even more complicated. For one thing, there are more subissues to be handled to ensure operations are changed properly and alignments are sustained. But even more basic is that whereas strategy is in the realm of ideas, operations represent actions—often easier said than done. A key element that can smooth the movement from talk to action is the structure of the organization (Duncan, Chapter 14). A stratified, rigidly constructed organization is the enemy of nimbleness and flexibility, an ally of the status quo. Whether horizontally structured around operating units or vertically built around functions, the traditional organization tends to create segmented parts that often don't work or communicate with each other. The mosaic of "turfdoms" blocks change. The organization of today and tomorrow has as few blocs and specific units as possible, as much interaction and team effort as can be achieved. Once the organization that elevates change to priority status is set up (and in all probability continually finetuned), how it makes use of its best assets is a critical step in executing successful change.

One of the greatest of these assets is technology (Kabat, Chapter 19). Technology is versatile and pervasive. It can cause change triggers, help a firm respond to change triggers, and provide mechanisms for thinking through appropriate responses to change. The change-oriented organization continually works with technology to cause its own change triggers or respond to change triggers set off elsewhere. It not only accepts technology and technological change as inevitable but also works hard to align the entire organization toward continual technological change and its great ripple effects on people.

Technology is one of many factors, therefore, that must be employed in aligning operations with strategy (Gunn, Chapter 18). Another significant link is supply-chain management, which covers the entire process from conceiving a product to getting it to the customer and embraces such interim steps as development, manufacturing, order fulfillment, delivery, and so on. Supply-chain management is one of those ever-present components that link an internal element with the market to help keep all parts of the firm market-centered. And the strategy/operations interlink can be continually monitored and measured through quality systems to ensure that it is on track (Weintraub, Chapter 17). Again, quality should be one of the hallmarks of customer service.

The change-oriented firm that means business can even go as far as to design its facilities—notably its offices—to work with change (Breading and Hall, Chapter 20). Indeed, the office may be an artifact of alignment. At the very least, the office should contain the physical attributes and strengths that allow the firm to install state-of-the-art technology—computers, faxes, copiers, and so on—that promotes free flow of information, quick analysis, and use of critical data for rapid decision making. The ultramodern office will go several dimensions further, incorporating in its layout the placement of offices, conference rooms, and such to encourage team approaches, quick actions, constant communications, and continuous contact with the field—all primary elements in managing change and balancing alignment.

Chapter Fourteen

A Bad Structure Can Be Fatal

Daniel M. Duncan

In the era of constant change the best structure that a business organization can choose must be keyed to survival and is likely to be dissimilar to anything it has used in the past. Instead of creating an elaborate series of interlocking units held together by a formalized chain of command—the essence of the traditional organization structure—businesses of the 1990s would be far better off letting their shapes and configurations be dictated by the work they do and the complex world they face. The epitome of the flexibility and agility needed for operating the streamlined organization demanded of premier competitors would be an organization structure that facilitates the firm's work process, a decision-making and communications process to connect the parts—and not much more.

Thus structure, and related cultural elements, would be driven by the work and the needs of the marketplace, not the other way around. In times of great change the structure must be vastly altered to properly respond to change triggers; simply rearranging the bricks won't do. The structural changes should be quick, pervasive, and meaningful, and relatively easy because they are a part of a continuous management of structure. This would not only keep the change managers focused on the alignment of structure with other primary organizational elements—they would not be awed and diverted by the job of shuffling structure alone—but they could constantly be plugged into their markets and their customers. By using the work process as the touchstone, the company is actually asserting its primary link to the market as a major driving force. Hence it can sustain an outward focus rather than get bogged down in internal technicalities that have no real relevance over the long run.

Traditional structures actually impede change. Regardless of their philosophical underpinnings, traditional structures tend to string together a series of boxes (i.e., divisions, departments, functions, and so on). On top are stacked layers of supervision and management, resulting in a vast hierarchy. Managers wind up with a series of narrow vertical units, and like the old series Christmas tree lights, when one unit fails they all fail. The firm is carved into a series of turfs with little reason to interconnect, communicate, and work in conjunction for real change and, more importantly, real required change.

Thus thinking in terms of structural units within a company limits creativity in how those units can be configured. How many options are there for stacking or patterning five wooden blocks? In the traditional approach the change managers' degrees of freedom are severely limited.

The trick in the 1990s and beyond is to forget about departments, divisions, and other structural units and take the key organizational cues from work processes. Again—and this can't be stressed enough—the work is the reason the firm exists, whether the firm manufactures, provides services or information, or generates energy. If the firm's customers value the output, the firm survives. If the firm can execute its work process better than a competitor, it profits handsomely. Keeping plugged into the customer is critical. If we accept that concept, we can readily accept the idea that it is our work process that counts and gets the job done. Thus the first job in defining the organizational structure is to clarify, refine, and then organize the work process. Otherwise some very strange anomalies result.

Take the example of a chemical plant—essentially one long pipeline punctuated by pumps, vessels, heaters, and coolers along its length. Does it make sense to break the pipeline and transfer products in buckets or wheelbarrows? If the structure design places jurisdictional boundaries across the continuous flow it will create conflicts that mar efficiency, get in the way of customer service, and block change.

As an even worse consequence of too tight a structure, consider our military services. They are organized around the medium through which they travel (the Army on land, the Navy at sea, and so on). During Operation Desert Storm problems at the boundaries between the services emerged with regard to the delivery of medical service. Can we afford to lose one soldier because the needed medical equipment is "owned" by the other service branch? Organization can kill you.

So the key to thinking about modern structure is to ignore structure from the very beginning by starting with work process and letting structure arise out of process. Let structure come second and be configured to facilitate process, not impede it. Structure should not become a plow harness on a race horse.

THE NEW MODEL: DECISION PROCESSES

Once the organization structure has been patterned to facilitate the work process, the decision-making dimension needs to be considered. Although every organization has a work throughput (a metabolism), it also needs a guidance system or management apparatus (rather like a nervous system or intelligence). As we design a system of decision-making mechanisms and communication processes, major points must be kept in mind.

- A primary set of decision processes and communication linkages is necessary for any management system to be effective.

- There are a variety of ways for accomplishing these primary processes and linkages, but they must be performed effectively to prevent the organization from being crippled by problems.

The traditional management system was built around parceling out the power and responsibility of the top person (owner, king, commander, CEO) to lower-ranked people. Ultimate power was retained at the top, and portions of that authority were successively delegated to the next lower tiers in the echelon until the bottom of the pyramid was reached.

Consider the typical chain of command. It consists of simple pyramids stacked on top of each other until the horizons of the firm are reached at the bottom. The logic is simple mathematics; seven (more or less) employees and you have a branch manager; seven branch managers and you have a region manager; seven region managers and you have a zone manager; then a sector; and so on. The hierarchy grows by addition of simple pyramid forms.

Some observations about this structure are important:

- As you go up the chain of command there is little *real* difference in function. The number of branches overseen in each successively higher level increases, but the task at each level essentially is the same (i.e., oversight of branch operations).

- The chain of command is prone to becoming bureaucratic. The firm's overall objective is managed only at the top. Goals and authority are parceled out in smaller and smaller bits and tend to become fragmentary down the line. Accompanying this will be rigidification of job role with a parallel reduction of job scope and responsibility.

- This type of layered structure generates pressure to standardize market approaches, materials, technology, and products. Routine overpowers adaptability. Tallahassee gets the same as Tacoma, whether it needs it, deserves it, or does as much.

- Management will likely feel it has to drive the system, or "ride it." People downstream become so accustomed to initiative from the top that when a high-level executive's hand slips from the throttle, the entire works may grind to a halt.

- Some traditionalists argue that the hierarchical structure is required because the branches need assistance, provided by close supervision or staff experts. This sounds good in theory, but people are hesitant to pass problems upstream, particularly if the troubles are of one's own making or inadequacy. Thus, branch personnel may ask for help on "safe," easy-to-fix problems, but nasty, hard-to-handle problems get buried. If the staff experts and others don't get enough real problems to solve, they will busy themselves on problems that *they perceive* to exist.

- Such systems soon become overburdened with "middle managers" and the vexing problems they contribute. Middle management has become a saddle-worn critter struggling under the pressure for change from a number of vantage points. The change itself isn't beyond handling; the problem is that each vantage point—each stakeholder—has a different agenda for change and middle managers are ensnared in a web of polemic perspectives.

Here are some of the conflicting and multidirectional pressures:

- *Top management:* It wants fewer middle managers because of the cost, yet it is reluctant to relinquish the control inherent in tight hierarchies.
- *Lower-level management:* It also wants fewer middle managers, arguing that the new work force is better educated and doesn't need all that "supervision" and overcontrol.
- *Product management (strategic business unit) personnel:* They find middle management insensitive to market shifts and a bureaucratic impediment to the quick responses that SBUs like to display. (Note the tug between quick changers and slow changers.)
- *Functional management types:* These people are notorious for trying to end-run other people's hierarchy and make direct demands to first-level supervisors, customer reps, et al.

Of late, organizations have somewhat arbitrarily whacked out a management layer here or there, ostensibly to cut costs and smooth communication flow. But some major problems have been caused. Of course, it's traumatic to the people involved, but the cutback is also traumatic to the organization itself and can even lead to major dysfunction.

When layers are haphazardly removed the organization can become like a person with a damaged spinal cord: Arms and legs may flail aimlessly, and the brain cannot control them. When this occurs in organizations, the employees (who often serve as the glue or "shock absorber" for poor structure) begin to build informal linkages to accomplish the functions necessary to ensure the survival of the firm. These informal sub-rosa links are of a patchwork nature and frequently inhibit the organization from getting its work done. Consequently, talent and energy that top management thinks is focused on the marketplace is instead absorbed in maintaining vital internal systems that were thoughtlessly removed with the erased layer.

The evils cited above result from what organizational experts call *additive simplicity* in the hierarchical structure. The numbness we experience with large size results from stacking simple pyramids one on top of the other. It is additive simplicity that results in repetitive decision making and the lethargy we all dread and condemn. The alternative is to replace simplistic redundancy with greater complexity and variety.

Step number one is to design functional differentiation into the vertical plane. We are all familiar with functional differentiation in the horizontal structure (i.e., one group engineers the product, another manufactures it, a third sells it, and so on). We need complexity and variety in the vertical organization just as much as in the horizontal, or "work," organization. Cookie-cutter sameness won't work. Complexity and variety should manifest itself in differentiated roles. Rather than everyone "overseeing the branches," different decision roles need to be carried out. In the book *My Years with General Motors*,[1] Alfred P. Sloan shed light on role differentiation by talking about the difference between the operating units and the corporate center. They are two separate entities with vastly separate work roles.

As communication and decision tasks are parceled out vertically, one inevitably comes to the topic of "staff." Of late there has been a fad to cut staff. Critics of staff organizations often provide more smoke than illumination. For example, Peters and Waterman in *In Search of Excellence*[2] hailed the virtues of "lean staff." But the typical company they praised for using these staffs was divided along product lines, and each division was different enough and large enough to support its own staff operations. Many companies in the United States are not diversified enough for product divisions, and the Peters and Waterman counsel is of little practical use and dangerous if ill applied.

As the duties in the vertical organization are shredded out, there should be units near the top that gather data both from the external environment (critical in change management) and from inside the firm and then package the information for top-level consumption. These are staff roles.

Staff units are a necessity, and they shouldn't be cut out as willy-nilly as the company picnic. A company with an undeveloped staff is like a dinosaur—all brawn, no brain.

Second, there are decisions that necessitate a corporate or overall view that isn't available to those down in the trenches. When a stock option plan or an internal audit system is developed, it will hopefully apply to more than just the shipping department, the engineering department, or any other single function.

CHANGE TRIGGERS

Inevitably, organization managers will be asked or challenged to link structural design to a wide range of variables. *Variables* means change, and a continuous stream of variables—newly emerging variables especially—means constant change. However, the new variables are often framed in narrow terms, as are their responses. For example, a marketing executive might advise, "The customer is asking for a faster response," and propose, "Let's keep the warehouse open longer and move our trucks out more frequently." Or a technical executive might note, "Our technology enables us to do design engineering and product prototyping at the same time," and suggest, "If we do that on a regular basis, we can get to market faster than our competitors."

These represent changes in the ways the firm does business. And any time some key element of the business changes, it is a potential trigger for structural change. For example, the faster customer response might require structural changes that link manufacturing and shipping as self-contained units in various product lines rather than as omnibus enterprises that deal with all products of the firm. Telescoping product development might require sales and marketing people to be brought into the process earlier so they can be more familiar with the new products and provide input gleaned from customers.

Often the question is asked, "When should structure be changed?" The answer is to continuously monitor the business and manage the structure as required. The easier question to deal with is "When should structure be fixed or locked in?" The answer is simple: Never.

In linking your organization structure to aspects of the business, most of your associations will likely be intuitive. Although some may be wrong, the fact that you are attempting a linkage is of countervailing merit. Fortunately, the use of intuition can be replaced by a more scientific approach.

Over the past 40 years, a great number of studies have been carried out by scholars and other researchers that link business variables to structural forms. They are absolute gold mines of design criteria. They give the designer a large set of "if-then" statements that can guide design decisions.

Some rules of thumb are as follows:

- If the firm's technology is stable, centralize.
- If the firm's market is dispersed, decentralize.
- If problem solving is continuous at the firm, divide departments along sector lines.
- If the task is ambiguous, use an organic structure with low control.

PAYOFF

Management is already more than a full-time job. If we add the burden of continuously managing structure, what payoff might we derive? In the main, every aspect of the business will benefit. No process can work well when encumbered by an inappropriate structure. Inappropriate structure always fails. And structure is always likely to be inappropriate unless it is managed.

To describe all of the positive fallouts from good organization would require a massive tome. Probably the greatest single benefit is that elusive creature called motivation—that invisible spark that all organizations need to survive.

The structure of the organization prescribes the larger playing field within which individual and group behavior occurs. If the organization is haphazardly wired together, then individual and team performance will be negatively impacted. As noted before, an inappropriate organizational structure is like a plow harness on a racehorse. A harness, or an organization structure, tends to facilitate some behavior and to constrain other acts. Neither the horse nor the jockey will be happy about trying to compete against the rest of the field and fight the harness at the same time.

How often have people gone off to training seminars only to return and behave exactly as they had before? This has to suggest that the variables in the person's job context, rather than the lack of certain knowledge, are the primary determinants of the behavior. How often have we seen new programs (MBO, performance evaluation, quality efforts, and so on) fail because they ran across the grain of the established structure?

We all know that employees can be "motivated" for short periods of time to overcome practically any type of impediment. But these moments of bravado and inspiration fade quickly, and behavior relaxes into its old mode. Our objective should be to provide an organizational framework that will enable a business unit to achieve its employee performance goals in the typical or normal range over an extended period. We can't sustain extraordinary performance from our personnel indefinitely. Further, we don't want to put our people in the position of having to use their energies to put up with inappropriate structural patterns or "de-motivating" authority systems.

Motivation falls into two general types:

- Extrinsic motivation, which is driven by external rewards.
- Intrinsic motivation, in which the drive for performance comes from within the person.

We tend to seek out employees who are self-starters and have considerable internal, or intrinsic, motivation.

It's often observed that new employees have a good deal of intrinsic motivation. They are eager, get to work early, show a lot of hustle, and tend to initiate activity on their own. Unfortunately, over time, this verve and vinegar often erode. In the worst case the energetic, intrinsically motivated person turns into a lethargic example of the bureaucratic personality.

What causes this transformation? The structure of the organization can have considerable impact on employee motivation and may be the biggest culprit. When the structure in place is too mechanistic, a negative cycle can begin. First, the rigidities of the mechanistic structure permit less self-determination. This causes a reduction of intrinsic motivation and less enthusiasm for the job. Unfortunately the management, observing that performance is beginning to sag, will often impose greater control, rules, formalization, and centralization rather than loosen the offending structure. This only increases the mechanistic nature of the structure and further depresses the intrinsic motivation. At this point we have bureaucracy breeding bureaucracy and extinguishing the new employee's motivation even faster.

For management to win in the marketplace all employees must feel they can "win" as well. When the organization structure fails to fit the goals, employees do not experience a feeling of job mastery and competence—there is no "winning." If the organization design is aligned to the objectives, employees can more easily get on top of their job and "win." As this occurs the atmosphere of success becomes contagious and spreads throughout the company.

When management puts the wrong structure in place the employees will build an "informal system" that operates in spite of the formal system and helps to get the job done. But this "unofficial" apparatus forces management to wrestle with two troubling concerns.

First, top management finds itself with a gnawing uncertainty about who is running the place. Somehow, some way, the company seems to have taken on a life of its own and stumbles along. As noted above, when a structure fails to fit, the feeling of mastery doesn't occur. A bad structure can eventually take the "winning" out of all jobs, including management's.

Second, management observes the lackluster performance in almost all functions and ranks and wonders if a bad case of laziness has set in. The contention that employees are lazy seldom has any merit. Most workers actually feel they could do more work than they are now doing.

In situations such as we've described, productivity—or the absence of it—has more to do with systemic demotivation than it has to do with personal motivation. Frustrated employees, employees who can't "win" regardless of how hard they try, still retain an innate common sense that tells them not to continue to battle uphill when there is no prospect of coming out on top.

Winning at the personal or corporate level requires that structure be right; and only continuous, judicious, and timely change management will get it there. Inappropriate structure will kill motivation, and that can be fatal to a company.

REFERENCES

1. A. P. Sloan, Jr., *My Years with General Motors* (Garden City, New York: Doubleday, 1972).

2. T. J. Peters and R. H. Waterman, Jr., *In Search of Excellence: Lessons from America's Best-Run Companies* (New York: Warner, 1984).

Chapter Fifteen

Introduction to Supply-Chain Management

Martin J. Sikora

How does the value chain react to market change triggers? Ideally, that question should not even be asked. The value chain—or the company's supply chain, embracing all functions from the production line to delivery at the customer's doorstep—should be sensitive to change triggers, which are the cues to top management that the company must be aligned with its customer base.

Unfortunately that ideal seldom exists. As a result, the answer to the question of how the value chain reacts depends on how well the company executes change management, how well it maintains the value chain itself, and how much of a workhorse the value chain is in driving both ongoing operations and change management efforts of all degrees. In the right hands, change management places a premium on a superior value chain, regarding it as one of the most valuable assets a company can command. An inferior change management program destroys the value of the chain while jamming the critical signals management should be fielding.

Why is the value, or supply, chain so pivotal? Because it serves a multiplicity of valuable functions in an era when change is constant but quality customer service will always be the target. First, the value chain is the most direct link between the firm and its customers—it is the pathway by which the customers are served. Thus, the chain should be highly sensitive to change triggers within the marketplace and/or the customer base and should be flexible enough to relay the signals back to the managers. Second, the value chain is a working mini-model of the total corporate alignment that is at the heart of sensible change management. The chain is a network of several functions and many people. If the chain is to work properly, all of these functions must be completely integrated and working in total harmony. Thus, it can be a prototype for companywide unification on a grander scale.

As a result, the smoothly humming value chain plays a dual role in the context of change management by maintaining alignment between the company and its customer base and by sustaining alignment in an especially vital multifunctional component of the company.

The key to building an efficient and nimble supply chain is to set up the logistics for moving goods, services, and people from function to function in a fully integrated manner. To put that type of potent system in place, management must do the following:

- Understand the service needs of their customers (and stay alert for making changes when the needs change).

- Design a logistics network and operating policies that get the most value and peak performance out of the chain.

- Design an organization that creates harmony and synergy among the key interdependent functions, such as strong linkage of sales and marketing (i.e., promotions, pricing policies, sales campaigns, etc.) with operations of the company (such as manufacturing, design, etc.).

- Install top notch information systems that tie the functions and the people together, help catch the change triggers and feed them back, promote team projects, and provide impetus for seizing a competitive edge.

- Forge integration across the entire supply chain channel by building bridges and linkages that stretch from suppliers through the company's functions and out the other side into the marketplace.

Of all of the five elements, the most important may be the information systems. A company cannot have an integrated, leading-edge logistics capability without a state-of-the-art information system to support the value chain. In particular, the information systems are critical in keeping the supply channel integration intact—not just from time to time but on a ceaseless, day-in, day-out basis.

Strong and aggressive management of the supply chain is a win-win situation. The fallout includes lower costs and premier customer service, which keep the company in a position to retain satisfied customers, gain new buyers, expand market share, and improve profitability.

Before one can understand the implications of the five critical elements of the supply chain, one must be familiar with the concepts of integrated logistics and integrated management of the chain. Logistics cement the integrated management of a company's supply, manufacturing, and distribution activities. Key components of the chain are interdependent and must be managed in a coordinated fashion. The mélange of activities to be coordinated includes purchasing, production, shipments, outbound deliveries, warehousing, order-taking and fulfillment, and customer service. A change in any one of these functions has ripple effects across many if not all of the others.

Cost management exemplifies interdependence. No single area may be attacked without weighing the implications for others. Putting a lid on one area may cause upward pressure somewhere else and actually raise total costs across the chain.

For example, the target at a company that experiences a seasonal demand pattern may be to reduce inventory levels. That would presumably reduce storage, interest, and materials purchasing costs. But if a reduction in inventory levels results in erratic production schedules and constantly changing levels of output, production costs may go up. A smooth and level production strategy may turn out to be the most economical in terms of total chain costs—even though the inventory costs may be higher than if the lean approach had been pressed.

In another area, the company may divide its inventories across regional warehouses to reduce transportation costs and gain such add-on bonuses as improved sales and delivery performance. Although this policy may raise inventory and warehousing costs, those increases may be more than offset by the other benefits.

Despite such clear arguments in favor of full-scale integration, many companies still assign the responsibility for logistics to one of the functions, such as marketing, sales, finance, or manufacturing. That decision not only works against the desired integration but also tends to create an unhealthy series of hermetically sealed, uncommunicative turfdoms. Each function may emphasize its own excellence without determining the trade-offs. Such insularity is self-defeating and diminishes the chances of getting maximum value out of the value chain. One of the most troubling threats is that the change trigger signals will get stuck somewhere or be shuffled on to some seldom-visited section of the company.

Customer service is the capstone for the entire value chain and the jumping-off point for the design of logistics capability. The best logistics enhance the nimbleness of the chain by allowing the firm to align with the service requirements not only of the entire market but also discrete customer niches—where, indeed, some valuable, albeit low-grade and sometimes hard to detect, change triggers may be in development. Supply chain management is a first among equals because it connects directly to the customer (see Gunn, Chapter 18, and Copacino, Chapter 16).

Chapter Sixteen

Integrated Logistics and Supply-Chain Management

William C. Copacino

The 1990s have been hailed as the decade of customer service. Many companies today (and many more in the future will) no longer describe themselves as being market driven but instead think of themselves as customer driven, focusing on serving their customers in the way their customers want to be served. To prepare for this intensified interest in customer service, companies need to build leading-edge supply-chain management capabilities.

To build an effective and efficient supply chain capability, companies must address five areas. First, they must focus on understanding the service needs of their customers. Second, they must design a logistics network structure and operating policies that maximize logistics performance. This generally also involves reengineering activities around core processes rather than functions. Third, they need to design an organization that creates harmony and synergy among all operating functions. This involves effective integration of sales and marketing programs (e.g., promotional programs, pricing policies) with operations. Fourth, and perhaps most important, information systems are becoming the enabler of leading-edge supply-chain concepts; information systems tie the logistics system together and allow a company to reach new operating levels of performance. A company cannot have an integrated, leading-edge supply-chain capability without effective supporting information systems. Finally, companies must focus on integration across the supply channel, thereby building bridges, operating linkages, and forging partnerships with suppliers, customers, and carriers.

By focusing on effective, integrated supply-chain management many companies have both lowered costs and improved the service they provide for their customers, and have thus positioned their companies to win new customers, expand market share, and increase their profitability. This chapter describes the opportunities, benefits, and paths to an integrated supply-chain capability that provides lasting competitive advantage. Before describing each of these areas, let me first define the integrated logistics management concept and the concept of supply-chain management.

FIGURE 16–1
Integrated Logistics and Supply-Chain Management

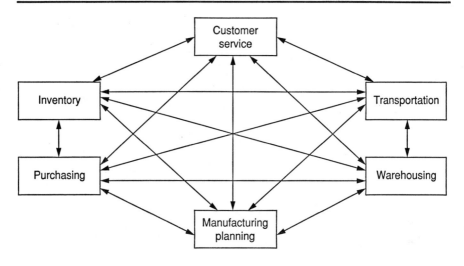

INTEGRATED LOGISTICS MANAGEMENT

Logistics focuses on the integrated management of supply, manufacturing and distribution activities. Put another way, purchasing, inventory control, inbound transportation, production setup, outbound transportation, warehousing, ordering, and customer service costs are interdependent (as outlined in Figure 16–1) and must be managed in a coordinated fashion. A change in any one of these activities influences the others, and an attempt to minimize any additional cost element may result in higher total logistics costs.

For example, setting a limit on inventory levels in a company with a seasonal demand pattern may result in lower inventory levels, but the additional costs incurred by manufacturing in adjusting production levels to match demand may more than offset these inventory savings. A level production strategy may well result in lower costs.

Similarly regional stocking may permit dramatic reductions in transportation costs through increased shipment consolidation, as well as expanded sales through better delivery performance. These improvements may be accomplished with only moderate increases in inventory and warehousing costs.

In many companies the responsibility for logistics is assigned to different functional units—marketing, sales, finance, manufacturing. Each function tries to optimize the performance of the logistics activities they have responsibility for, with no one assessing the overall tradeoffs. This focus on functional excellence works to the detriment of the company and results in inferior performance of logistics overall.

It is important to note that customer service does not appear at the top of Figure 16–1 merely by chance. Customer service is the jumping-off point for the design of

FIGURE 16–2
Supply-Chain Management

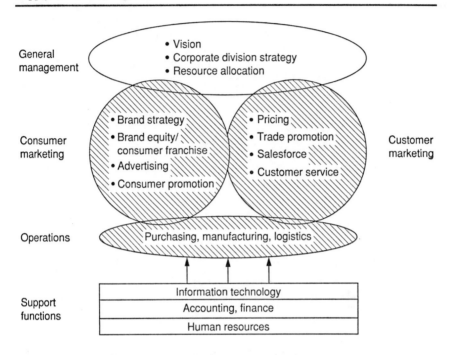

General management
- Vision
- Corporate division strategy
- Resource allocation

Consumer marketing
- Brand strategy
- Brand equity/consumer franchise
- Advertising
- Consumer promotion

Customer marketing
- Pricing
- Trade promotion
- Salesforce
- Customer service

Operations
Purchasing, manufacturing, logistics

Support functions
Information technology
Accounting, finance
Human resources

the logistics capability. Integrated logistics begins with the customer, not with distribution, manufacturing, or inventory management. The operations and logistics capabilities must be designed to meet the service requirements of distinct customer segments at the lowest possible cost.

INTEGRATED SUPPLY-CHAIN MANAGEMENT

Supply-chain management can be thought of as a broader concept than logistics management. It involves the coordinated management of the consumer marketing, customer marketing, and operations activities outlined in Figure 16–2, as well as the effective linkage with the general management vision and strategy and the integration with the full set of support functions.

Operations involves the core supply-chain activities of purchasing, manufacturing, and logistics. *Customer marketing* involves key interfaces with the trade, including pricing strategy, trade promotions, sales force management, and customer services. *Consumer marketing* involves the full set of traditional marketing activities. Most important to supply-chain management are advertising and consumer promotion.

These activities must be carefully linked as part of the supply-chain management approach. For example, forecasting, inventory planning, manufacturing scheduling,

FIGURE 16–3
Macro Processes Key to Effective Supply-Chain Management

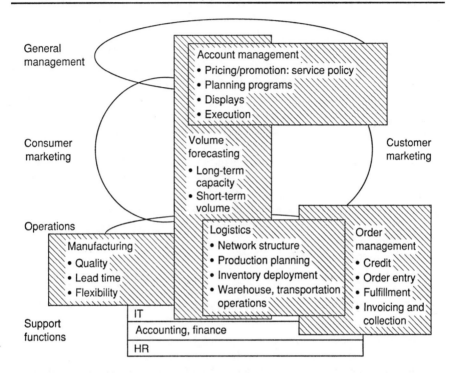

shipment planning, and channel inventory planning (at the retail levels) must be carefully coordinated with advertising trade promotion and consumer promotion schedules. Although most companies intellectually recognize the benefits and value of tight alignment of these activities, in practice most companies are very poor in executing aligned supply-chain approaches.

There are several reasons for these failures. Typically many companies have put a great emphasis on functional excellence—isolating each function and driving it to perform in a superior way. Although the search for excellence is admirable, the narrow functional focus preempts the vision and cooperation needed to achieve a higher level of total system performance. This critical flaw in organizational design is often reinforced by measurement systems that focus only on functional performance and by career path models that do not provide exposure to all aspects and functions of the business.

Key to providing a broader perspective to supply-chain management is a focus on core processes. Importantly there are five macro processes that must be well managed for effective supply-chain management. As noted in Figure 16–3 these processes are interrelated and span many functional areas, implying the need for thoughtful process and organizational design to achieve the proper level of integration.

THE OPPORTUNITY

The integrated logistics management and supply-chain management concepts have been discussed for many years but have been fully implemented in few companies. Three factors are motivating a new look at logistics, and leading-edge companies are now aggressively working to implement the integrated logistics concept.

The first factor is the increased importance of logistics as part of the overall marketing mix. Customer service, and specifically delivery service, has increased in importance. Leading companies are making quality, and particularly quality customer service, a cornerstone of their business. Many companies have learned that their customers will not tolerate poor customer service and that their customers will often pay a premium for superior customer service.

Thus effective delivery performance and the capability to provide value-adding services are becoming key to winning new customers and retaining existing ones. In studies across a variety of industries Arthur Andersen has documented that customer service performance correlates closely with market share positions. In my experience superior customer service has been the most consistently underexploited element of the marketing mix in company after company.

Second, logistics and customer service are becoming an increasingly important cost element. With manufacturing costs declining, logistics costs become more visible and more important. The full channel costs can account for 25 to 30 percent of the cost of goods sold. Therefore, integrated logistics management is important from both a cost and service perspective.

The third factor driving increased attention to the integrated logistics and supply chain management concept is the evolution of information technology. Advanced information systems make integration of the supply-chain functions possible. Companies can use advanced information to operate in new and fundamentally different ways, as outlined in the next section.

THE BENEFITS

Integrated logistics and supply-chain management allow companies to achieve more for less—to improve customer service while lowering costs at the same time. This powerful potential provides the keystone for competitive advantage. Consider these examples of the benefits companies have achieved through integrated logistics:

• *Consumer packaged goods:* A major food producer developed a fundamentally different way of delivering to its major retail accounts. The food producer previously sent full truckloads of individual products to the retailer's warehouse. The retailer would receive, put away, and store the goods in inventory and subsequently pick, pack, stage, and ship the goods to its stores.

Using advanced logistics and information technology concepts the food producer now sends mixed pallets of different products directly to the retailer's stores. This

FIGURE 16–4
Achieved Improvements in Both Cost and Service

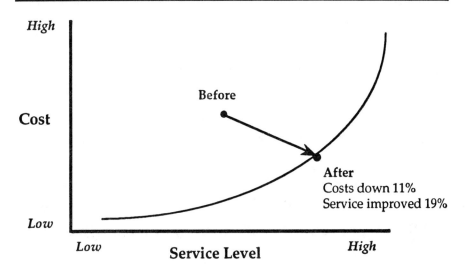

new delivery system dramatically reduces the handling, inventory, and transportation costs of moving the product through the channel and has been the stimulus to an entirely new relationship between the food producer and the retailer. Both parties have improved their profitability under this new arrangement.

• *Specialty chemicals:* A large specialty chemicals company was experiencing increasing logistics costs. Equally important, its poor delivery performance was souring customer relations. The specialized, highly trained sales force was spending almost half its time tracking the status of customer orders and reacting to customer complaints.

In response the chemical company reorganized the logistics activities into a single group that included inbound transportation, production planning, inventory management, forecasting, warehousing, and outbound transportation. They also upgraded their information systems so that they had accurate, real-time information on the status of inventory levels, production, and customer orders, as well as visibility of all logistics costs.

As noted in Figure 16–4 these actions reduced logistics costs by 11 percent, improved on-time shipments from 73 to 92 percent, and dramatically improved customer relationships. One customer commented that the company "is now our most reliable supplier. They deliver when promised and in the few cases where deliveries will not meet the planned schedule, they are able to let us know in advance. They are a real, value-added supplier and the kind of company we want to do more business with."

THE PATHWAY TO INTEGRATED LOGISTICS

From our experience in working to improve the competitiveness of scores of companies, we believe that companies must address five key areas to develop an integrated logistics management capability that creates lasting competitive advantage.

Customer Service Needs and Opportunities

As a starting point for building a differentiating logistics capability, a company must understand its customers' needs, specifically:

- Which of the 20 to 25 elements of customer service are important to the company's customers? Are different elements important to different customer segments?

- How is the company performing on each element of customer service, from the customers' perspective? What levels of performance are acceptable? How is the company doing in comparison to key competitors on each element of service?

- What value-added capabilities can provide the company with a distinctive edge? Modified packaging? Use of bar codes? Use of inner packs? Drop shipments? Pallets configured with mixed products?

Carefully designed, focused research involving key decision makers and a thoughtfully selected group of customers can provide invaluable insights about the service needs of your customers and how your company can position itself to be a more effective supplier.

Andersen's work has clearly indicated that companies can often gain competitive advantages through value-adding services, which in essence differentiate their product offering. Thoughtful research focused on understanding buyers' values is essential to identifying basic service requirements, as well as services that can add value.

When customer service needs are well understood, a company must then simultaneously address three areas in parallel, as outlined in Figure 16–5.

Structure and Processes

Typically, significant benefits are available from a reconfiguration of existing facilities. Geographic markets and sales volumes change over time; therefore the economics and tradeoffs among transportation, inventory, and facility costs also change, so that a logistics network that was right yesterday may not be appropriate for the future. Many companies can gain significant cost savings and customer service improvements from a redesign of their logistics network. A logistics network planning computer model may be used to address such basic questions as:

- How many warehouses should a company have? Where should they be located and how big should they be designed?

FIGURE 16–5
Framework for Logistics Operational Improvement

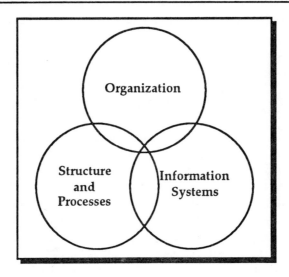

- What are the cost and customer service implications of alternative logistics network designs?
- What logistics network configuration makes best strategic sense for the company and for its customers?

In addition, a comprehensive assessment of the policies, procedures, and operating methods in the areas of logistics—such as forecasting, inventory control, transportation planning and traffic management, warehouse operations, customer service and order entry, manufacturing planning and scheduling, and purchasing—can uncover opportunities to improve efficiency and to build harmony among the operating functions.

Most companies can gain considerable leverage over their operating methods along process lines rather than functional lines. Key to this approach is the identification and redesign of core processes, such as those outlined in Figure 16–3. These process redesigns are perhaps best illustrated by example.

- A major consumer packaged goods company required 47 steps, the involvement of six functional areas, and over three days on average to process an order. The order flowed from the *Customer Service Department* for entry to *Sales Administration* for a pricing check to *Credit and Collections* for a credit sign-off to *Inventory Planning* for a check on availability to *Sales* for the allocation of low inventory and finally to *Distribution* for picking and shipping and then back to *Finance* for processing of the

FIGURE 16–6
Building an Effective Logistics Organization

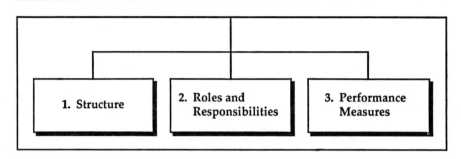

payment and the administration of deductions. The company reengineered the order management process by organizing into three order management teams—each cell staffed by individuals to handle all the order management activities. The three cells were designed by type of order: continuous replenishment, electronic data interchange (EDI), and traditional paper or fax orders. This arrangement lowered costs by 50 percent and reduced order cycle time to less than two hours for 95 percent of the orders.

• Similarly an industrial company reengineered the replenishment process (forecasting, inventory planning, capacity planning, manufacturing scheduling) along product lines with teams from sales, marketing, distribution, and manufacturing working together to manage the replenishment process for each product line. Inventory was reduced by 32 percent, and customer service increased 10 percentage points.

Organization

In parallel, the organizational issues should be thoroughly examined. Integrated logistics management does not necessarily mean centralization of the logistics activities into a single organizational unit. However, integrated logistics management requires careful design of three key elements, as indicated in Figure 16–6.

Organization structure. There is no single organizational structure that is best for all companies. The assignment of the responsibility for purchasing, inbound transportation, forecasting, inventory planning, inventory control, order entry, customer service, outbound transportation, warehousing, and manufacturing planning to the marketing, manufacturing, finance functions or to a logistics or distribution function must be determined with the key competitive factors, customer needs, culture, and philosophy of each individual company taken into account.

Roles and responsibilities. The structuring of logistics activities is often less important than how they work together. In designing organizational relationships Andersen generally follows an important rule. In a stable environment, design for functional efficiency; let each function manage more independently with the goal of achieving functional excellence and the greatest functional efficiency.

In an uncertain or dynamic environment design for functional integration; develop an organization that has close working relationships among functions and operates in an integrated way. Tactics to achieve this goal include teaming by product (for example, Procter & Gamble has created a Supply Manager position to manage fully the supply-chain activities for each product family) and conducting the sales and operations planning meeting (SOPM), where all key functions meet weekly to monitor and manage carefully the production and distribution plans in light of the changing market conditions.

Over the past decade most companies have faced a more uncertain and complex operating environment. Therefore the need for and benefits of effective, functional integration has increased and will continue to increase for most companies.

Performance measures. To have an effective, integrated logistics system a company must align performance measures with desired results. It is foolish to ask a purchasing manager to work to lower the total costs of a purchased item (purchase price, transportation, inventory, quality, returns, administrative costs) if he or she is evaluated solely on purchase price. Similarly, a transportation manager will not set up the most effective and efficient logistics system if bonuses are paid based on transportation cost reduction targets alone. Performance measures are the most overlooked area of logistics and offer considerable opportunity in most companies.

A few companies are effectively using process measures of performance. A new, simple, and comprehensive measure of customer service and logistics effectiveness has been employed by a handful of companies. It is called the Perfect Order.

The Perfect Order is designed to measure process effectiveness, not functional effectiveness. In simple terms it is the percentage of orders that proceed through all steps of the order management process without fault, exception handling, or intervention.

Every step in the order management process must go right for the order to be considered perfect. These steps include order entry, credit clearance, inventory availability, accurate picking, on-time delivery, correct invoicing, and payment without deductions. If anything goes wrong (or requires manual intervention, exception processing, or expediting) the order is not considered perfect. Figure 16–7 lists some examples of problems that can prevent achievement of the Perfect Order.

Companies are beginning to measure the percentage of their orders that meet the criteria of the Perfect Order. Surprisingly they are finding that less than 10 percent of their orders are perfect. These companies are reengineering their order management and logistics processes with a focus on eliminating unnecessary steps, aligning functional objectives, speeding order cycle times, and using the Perfect Order as the measure of success.

One major consumer packaged goods company has achieved remarkable success. They have increased their Perfect Order percentage to the 55 to 60 percent range,

FIGURE 16–7
Sample "Busters" of the Perfect Order

Nine (or more) of ten orders in a typical company get "busted" for such reasons as:

• Order entry error	• Late shipment
• Missing information (e.g., product code)	• Late arrival
• Inventory unavailability (of a single item)	• Incomplete paperwork
• Credit hold	• Early arrival
• Inability to meet ship date	• Damaged shipment
• Picking error	• Invoice error
• Inaccurate picking paperwork	• Overcharge error
• Error in payment processing	• Customer deduction

---

with a goal of reaching 90 percent within two years. With competitors operating at one-sixth of this effectiveness, they have a growing competitive advantage.

Measures of process effectiveness will become commonplace in companies in the 1990s. The Perfect Order is an effective measure of order management and logistics effectiveness, and it provides a lever for companies to increase customer service and reduce costs at the same time.

Information Systems

Information systems are the enabler of the integrated logistics concept. Companies cannot effectively manage costs, provide superior customer service, and be leaders in logistics performance without leading-edge information systems. These capabilities will be a requirement for the 1990s.

Advanced logistics information systems involve three aspects, as outlined in Figure 16–8. First, timely and accurate information is essential. This requires source data capture (input of each transaction at the time and place of occurrence) and real-time information-processing capabilities. For example, a warehouse worker should not have to send pick documents to an office for keypunching and batch processing but rather should scan or keypunch each transaction as it occurs.

Second, integrated applications software with full functionality is a key part of an effective logistics information system. Full functionality will differ for each company but may include capabilities such as the ability to allocate inventory to a specific customer or lot traceability.

Third, advanced decision support is an important part of a logistics information system. Capabilities in this area include logistics network planning models that allow a what-if simulation of the cost and customer service impacts of alternative logistics network structures and policies, routing and scheduling analytic programs that can be

FIGURE 16–8
Pyramid of Hierarchical Logistics Information Systems Needs

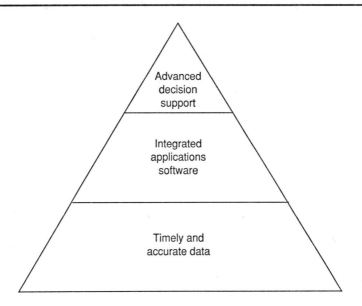

used to reduce transportation costs, order consolidation programs that can design the best shipping strategies, and analytic software to evaluate alternative inventory deployment and management strategies.

Channel Integration

Leading-edge companies have gone beyond the integrated logistics concept. For many companies the quantum improvements in logistics performance are available no longer from fine tuning their own logistics systems but instead from the integration of their logistics system with those of their suppliers and customers, as outlined in Figure 16–9. This approach has been referred to as Quick Response, Efficient Consumer Response, Intercorporate Logistics, or Channel Supply-Chain Management.

One company's distribution system is another company's supply system. It makes no sense for a manufacturer and a distributor to hold inventory in warehouses next door to each other. If they can manage the inventory in a joint way they have to be able to improve the performance of the entire logistics channel. The same lesson applies to coordinated management of the transportation activities of companies across the channel. Similarly, if a manufacturer knows the real usage or takeaway rate at the retail level and the channel inventories, he or she has to be able to do a better job of forecasting and production planning.

FIGURE 16–9
Channel Integration Approach

Suppliers	Manufacturers	Wholesalers	Retailers	Consumers
• Forecasting • Production planning • Inventory • Transportation • Information systems • Order processing • Billing	• Forecasting • Production planning • Inventory • Transportation • Information systems • Purchasing • Order processing • Billing	• Forecasting • Inventory • Transportation • Information systems • Purchasing • Order processing • Billing	• Forecasting • Inventory • Transportation • Information systems • Buying • Shelf replenishment	• Demand • Usage rate

The challenge in developing integrated channel management lies in cooperation and trust among the channel partners. This is often a substantial challenge, but companies who can find ways to build these channel partnerships will enjoy both operational and strategic advantages.

SUMMARY

Superior customer service performance will be a competitive requirement for all companies in the 1990s, necessitating an intensified focus on integrated logistics management. Companies will use integrated logistics and supply-chain management to improve customer service performance dramatically while reducing costs at the same time.

Achieving an integrated supply-chain capability requires that companies understand customers' service needs; build a network structure, operating policies, organization, and information systems that are oriented to integration and excellence; reengineer around core processes; and focus on building channel partnerships. These actions will create a leading-edge supply-chain capability that provides an enduring, difficult-to-duplicate competitive advantage.

Chapter Seventeen

Only the Best: How Quality Systems Govern Change

Donald L. Weintraub

W hy has the Roman Catholic Church survived for nearly 2,000 years when many competing theologies either disappeared or failed to achieve as much breadth or power?

And how is it possible for a business to endure after scoring an overnight success with a new product or service that became a fixture of modern life? How were Apple Computer, MTV, Federal Express, Xerox, Nike, and others able to follow up on their initial breakthroughs with enough additional successes to keep operating and thriving?

Why do other companies, both fast starters and outfits that logged considerable mileage, ultimately stumble, fall, and drop out of the competitive race for good? What caused such companies as Eastern Airlines, Drexel Burnham Lambert, Wang Laboratories, and Bell & Howell to fade out even after enjoying impressive spurts of prosperity?

The one major trait that distinguishes the aforementioned survivors from the extinct is *alignment*. The winners hanging in for the long pull have it. The dropouts were in disarray at the very end.

Alignment most simply means that all key elements of the organization are operating in harmony with each other. But the companies that perform impressively year in and year out practice a version of alignment that transcends mere functions and units. Their concept of alignment is a multidimensional approach that includes the following:

- Clear vision, mission, values, and goals.
- A well-set deployment process to help achieve the goals.
- Key methods of measuring progress (and alignment), including process, results, and customer satisfaction.

- Commitment within and throughout the organization—top down, bottom up, side to side—on what the critical goals are, how the goals will be reached, and how employees will be involved, appraised, and rewarded.
- Recognition of the outside world, including customers, suppliers, competitors, and benchmark performers.

In short, alignment is signified by a corporate culture that is clear on where the company is going and by consistent communication and reinforcement of the culture message within and outside the organization.

CONTINUAL CHANGE

Alignment that is so complete and so comprehensive is critical at the modern corporation where leaders are continually faced with change on every front. There is change within the organization that may or may not be wanted and change in the external environment that may not be fully knowable or controllable. It is one thing to have an aligned organization but quite another to maintain alignment in the face of rapid and substantive change. Thus the company that carries the concept of alignment to its broadest dimensions is the company that can keep itself in sync while managing great change.

So how can an organization's focus be kept on the viewpoint that constant change is the "half-full glass?" One method is to keep tabs on alignment by using the Contingency Diagram in planning for successful change. The Contingency Diagram is unique in that it puts the typical planning process—from data gathering to implementation—into a reverse scenario. It makes the worst case the standard and shows what it takes to make change management fail. By highlighting what to do wrong the Contingency Diagram aims to point out what should be avoided as the change process goes forward, and, more importantly, dramatizes by reverse English what really has to be done.

Contingency diagramming works because it draws upon our vast experience in screwing things up. It makes us think about the steps we would take if we wanted to guarantee failure and about how we would ensure the absence of alignment. Figure 17–1 shows a Contingency Diagram completed in answer to the question, "What would we do to *guarantee the failure* of a major change in our organization?"

If we reverse each of the contingency arrows so that the focus is on *achieving* a successful change effort, we see the need for the following:

- Current, accurate, and "customer-driven" (external and/or internal) data.
- A well-conceived plan that is communicated throughout the organization.
- A strategy to follow up, measure, and reinforce performance.
- Adequate resources and training.
- Leadership and accountability.
- Recognition for those who perform well.

FIGURE 17–1

Contingency Diagram Example

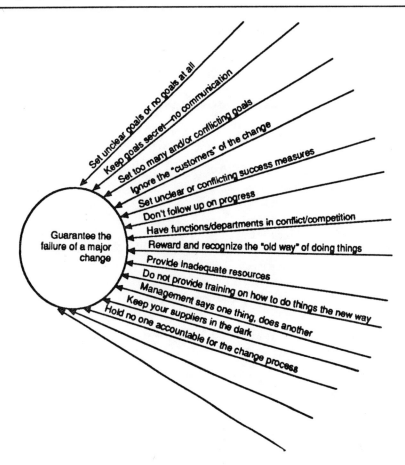

In other words we need to have all arrows moving in the same direction, focused on success, unconflicted, and *aligned*. The absence of alignment—which takes place when various arrows are moving in different directions—guarantees suboptimal results or, in the worst case, total failure.

To increase the chances for a fully aligned and therefore successful change effort, change managers must key on 11 strategies for implementing change. Eight of these strategies are internally focused. Three are externally focused. Figure 17–2 outlines them.

For each strategy there is a series of questions. As the managers of the change process begin to plan implementation of their program, the answers to these questions

FIGURE 17–2
Outline of the 11 Strategies for Implementing Change

Eleven Strategies for Implementing Change

Internal

    Leadership and Commitment

    Infrastructure

    Focus and Rollout

    Measurement

    Education

    Resources

    Information and Communication

    Systems Alignment

External

    Public Responsibility

    Customer Alignment

    Supplier Alignment

provide guidance for what needs to be done. A plan that addresses all 11 strategies is likely to be aligned and successful.

Figures 17–3 and 17–4 point out some questions that would provide useful information under each strategy in addition to serving as a monitor of whether the strategies are moving together (i.e., are in alignment).

Planning for change is critical to the success of the endeavor. There must be committed leadership, data-driven decision making, involved customers and suppliers, adequate resources, an educated work force, a carefully targeted implementation plan

FIGURE 17–3A
Useful Questions—Internally Focused Strategies

Leadership and Commitment

When implementing a major change, how effectively does senior management

	Very Well			Very Poorly	
	1	2	3	4	5
a. Become visible spokespersons in support of the change?	1	2	3	4	5
b. Remove obstacles and conflicting priorities?	1	2	3	4	5
c. Visit locations throughout the organization to see firsthand how the change is working?	1	2	3	4	5
d. Reinforce changes through rewards, recognition, and promotions?	1	2	3	4	5

and accountability for success, effective measurements, and rewards and recognition for a job well done. In many cases changes also need to be carefully positioned and communicated to all those who will be impacted and involved.

MARKETING CHANGE

Managing the change process becomes much easier if the pending change is "attractive" to those involved in and affected by its implementation. Certainly there are attractive and unattractive "candidates" for change, in politics as well as in organizational life. The organizational changes implied by a need for downsizing, cost cutting, and mergers and acquisitions inspire anxiety if not outright fear. Fearful people

FIGURE 17–3B

Infrastructure

Infrastructure

When implementing a major change, how effectively does your organization

	Very Well 1	2	3	Very Poorly 4	5
a. Create a process to manage change?	1	2	3	4	5
b. Assign accountability for carrying out change?	1	2	3	4	5
c. Identify, train, and empower internal change champions?	1	2	3	4	5
d. Develop a process for reporting and monitoring change?	1	2	3	4	5

FIGURE 17–3C

Focus and Rollout

Focus and Rollout

When implementing a major change, how effectively does your organization

	Very Well 1	2	3	Very Poorly 4	5
a. Identify and focus on customer priorities?	1	2	3	4	5
b. Target the key processes you want to improve?	1	2	3	4	5
c. Target the departments, functions, and individuals who will implement this change?	1	2	3	4	5
d. Target the key locations in which this change will be implemented?	1	2	3	4	5

FIGURE 17–3D
Measurement

Measurement

When implementing a major change, how effectively does your organization

	Very Well			Very Poorly	
	1	2	3	4	5
a. Review existing measures in the light of new priorities?	1	2	3	4	5
b. Develop process and results measures and customer and internally driven measures? (See example — Figure 3)	1	2	3	4	5
c. Develop a change measurement tracking and reporting system?	1	2	3	4	5
d. Benchmark changes against world-class performers?	1	2	3	4	5

FIGURE 17–3E
Measures Matrix

Measures Matrix

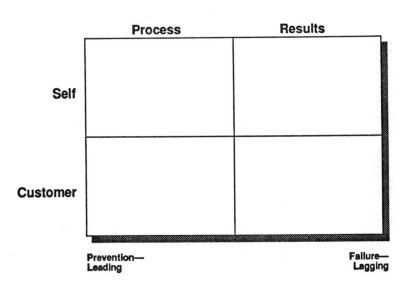

FIGURE 17–3F
Education

Education

When implementing a major change, how effectively does your organization

	Very Well 1	2	3	Very Poorly 4	5
a. Audit employees' current skills and knowledge levels?	1	2	3	4	5
b. Provide training to compensate for skill and knowledge deficiencies?	1	2	3	4	5
c. Educate customers and suppliers?	1	2	3	4	5
d. Develop measures of training effectiveness?	1	2	3	4	5

FIGURE 17–3G
Resources

Resources

When implementing a major change, how effectively does your organization

	Very Well 1	2	3	Very Poorly 4	5
a. Identify and provide required financial support?	1	2	3	4	5
b. Identify and provide required staff resources?	1	2	3	4	5
c. Identify and provide adequate time to plan and implement change?	1	2	3	4	5
d. Reduce or eliminate competing priorities?	1	2	3	4	5

FIGURE 17–3H
Information and Communication

Information and Communication

When implementing a major change, how effectively does your organization

	Very Well			Very Poorly	
	1	2	3	4	5
a. Gather and integrate critical information?	1	2	3	4	5
b. Develop a change communication plan focused on employees?	1	2	3	4	5
c. Develop a change communication plan focused on customers?	1	2	3	4	5
d. Develop a change communication plan focused on stakeholders?	1	2	3	4	5

FIGURE 17–3I
Systems Alignment

Systems Alignment

When implementing a major change, how effectively does your organization

	Very Well			Very Poorly	
	1	2	3	4	5
a. Align this change with the current strategies and goals?	1	2	3	4	5
b. Align this change with the budget?	1	2	3	4	5
c. Align this change with organizational rewards and recognition?	1	2	3	4	5
d. Align this change with performance appraisal and promotion?	1	2	3	4	5

FIGURE 17–4A

Useful Questions—Externally Focused Strategies

Public Responsibility

When implementing a major change, how effectively does your organization link this change with

	Very Well			Very Poorly	
	1	2	3	4	5
a. Health, safety, and environmental issues?	1	2	3	4	5
b. Corporate image, marketing and communication strategies?	1	2	3	4	5
c. Corporate ethics policies?	1	2	3	4	5
d. Community service efforts?	1	2	3	4	5

FIGURE 17–4B

Customer Alignment

Customer Alignment

When implementing a major change, how effectively does your organization

	Very Well			Very Poorly	
	1	2	3	4	5
a. Identify current and future customer requirements and expectations?	1	2	3	4	5
b. Develop and use customer satisfaction measures?	1	2	3	4	5
c. Create partner relationships with key customers?	1	2	3	4	5
d. Gather continuous feedback from customers?	1	2	3	4	5

FIGURE 17–4C
Supplier Alignment

Supplier Alignment

When implementing a major change, how effectively does your organization

	Very Well 1	2	3	Very Poorly 4	5
a. Identify key suppliers?	1	2	3	4	5
b. Develop a supplier alignment strategy and plan?	1	2	3	4	5
c. Identify current and future supplier requirements and expectations?	1	2	3	4	5
d. Create partner relationships with key suppliers?	1	2	3	4	5

usually make fearful decisions, and fearful decisions usually lead to unsuccessful changes.

Attractive candidates for change are improved customer satisfaction, improved employee satisfaction, and improved shareholder value. These are the "constituencies" that John P. Kotter and James L. Heskett continually refer to in their book *Corporate Culture and Performance* in describing performance-enhancing cultures (i.e., cultures that give the voices of the customer, employee, and shareholder fair volume).

Kotter and Heskett differentiate between *performers*—companies that have done reasonably well over time—and *better performers*—companies that have consistently outperformed their competition. "What seems to differentiate the two groups is this: in the cases of the better performers, the leaders got their managers to buy into a timeless philosophy or set of values that stressed both meeting constituency needs and leadership or some other engine for change—values that cynics would liken to motherhood, but that when followed can be very powerful. Those people and their successors then perpetuated the adaptive part of their cultures—the values/philosophy part relating to constituencies and leadership—because they worked at it." A values-driven change process focused on customers, employees, and shareholders is synonymous in many ways with a Total Quality Management (TQM) process.

FIGURE 17–5
The Five Pillars of Quality

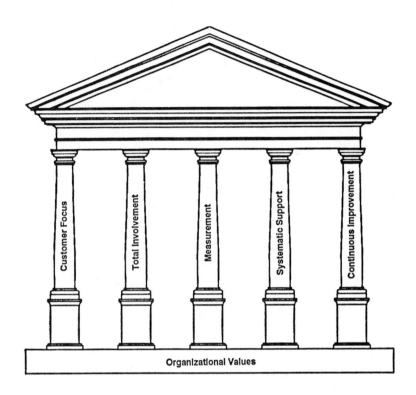

TQM: AN ATTRACTIVE CANDIDATE FOR CHANGE

So, enter TQM. It is the ideal vehicle for aligned change. Its goals are consistent with those of any organization that wants to run at maximum efficiency, improve its work processes, be more profitable, increase customer and employee satisfaction, and promote a concept of continuous improvement that is woven into the daily work of all managers.

TQM works because its stated goals (see Figure 17–5) are unassailable and because it provides leaders of change, and those they purport to lead, with a common language free of the emotionally loaded baggage of the past. The old conflicts of worker versus boss, field versus headquarters, individual versus team, function versus function, and customer versus supplier die hard. But they have to go sooner or later because they are anathema to an aligned, customer-driven, fully competitive organization. The cancerous nature of internal conflict was summed up by a senior vice president of a major international food company who once told me that "if the senior management in my company spent less time competing with one another and more time competing against the competition, they would be far more successful."

These conflicts die more quickly and less painfully if the voices of the customer, employee, and shareholder are aligned to direct successful business activity and resultant rewards. TQM, which includes customer, employee, and shareholder components, is well described by the Five Pillars of Quality and the concepts that anchor them:

1. Customer Focus: Inside an organization employees supply products, services, and information to each other. These exchanges link co-workers as internal customers and suppliers. An organization can best meet the needs of its final, external customers when it also meets the requirements of its internal customers.

2. Total Involvement: TQM is not just the responsibility of management or Quality Control. Everyone in the organization must be involved in achieving quality—top down, bottom up, and side to side.

3. Measurement: An axiom of Quality is "You cannot improve what you do not measure." An organization cannot meet quality goals unless it establishes baselines and charts progress against them. Decisions about what to measure and who will do the measuring should be heavily influenced by customer requirements.

4. Systematic Support: All systems in the organization, including planning, budgeting, scheduling, and performance management, must support the quality effort. The right alignment of systems can reduce internal conflict and the time required to get work done.

5. Continuous Improvement: To progress, organizations need to do things better tomorrow than they did yesterday. They must constantly be on the lookout for ways to prevent problems, correct flaws, and make even the smallest improvements. Through continuous improvement, organizations foster creativity and breakthroughs that increase credibility with their customers.

SUCCESS STORIES

Companies of all sizes and shapes have proven that alignment, often practiced through TQM, works. Kotter and Heskett list firms such as General Electric, ICI, Nissan, Xerox, Bankers Trust, First Chicago, American Express Travel Related Services, British Airways, SAS, and ConAgra. These companies have outpaced their competition over many years. What they all have in common is strong leadership and a business strategy that aligns and balances the needs of customers, employees, and shareholders.

Aligned Change at Federal Express

Another excellent example of success through aligned change is Federal Express. The delivery service company's longstanding "People—Service—Profit" philosophy provides a balanced focus for all employees because workers at all levels and in all functions understand the value of delighted customers. They know that in the highly competitive overnight shipping business, costs must be contained and steps that don't add value must be eliminated. Federal Express has long focused on its people, with the idea that empowered employees take good care of the customers. Federal Express employees are expected to provide an accurate bill and to deliver packages intact, among other courtesies. Different kinds of service failures had different impacts, depending on the severity of the miscue. A package delivered a few minutes late hurts but doesn't cause the same level of dissatisfaction generated by a lost package. A customer complaint hurts, but a "reopened complaint"—a second complaint made by the customer after the initial inquiry, despite promises, did not gain satisfaction—hurts much more.

In response to the findings of wider customer expectations, Federal Express developed the Service Quality Index (SQI), which tracks 12 types of events that trigger customer dissatisfaction. Each event is weighted to reflect the degree to which it negatively affects the customer—that is, by the severity and intensity of the trouble it produces. For example, a missed package pickup or a lost package is assigned five points. An invoice adjustment generates one point. (See Figure 17–6.)

Significantly the SQI score reflects the real number—not an average—of service failures that occur each day, thereby putting an intense spotlight on the relatively few instances of service breakdowns. SQI results are broadcast weekly over FXTV, the company's private television network, so everyone can track progress toward the ultimate goal: an SQI score of zero.

But Federal Express does not emphasize customer satisfaction at the expense of employee satisfaction or profitability. To the contrary, all three are stressed simultaneously. For example, the company sets both annual profitability targets and leadership improvement goals at the same time. Leadership is regarded as critical to employee satisfaction and is monitored through a survey instrument that measures how well employees believe they are being led.

In the spirit of alignment Federal Express's Executive Quality Board moved another step further by recently adopting an aggressive new corporate Quality Deployment Plan. This plan, which has the buy-in commitment of senior management, plots the business goals and objectives for the coming years. It is a clear plan, balanced between people, service, and profit, that has been communicated to all employees. Taking the alignment concept one step further, the new Federal Express plan provides bonus compensation when people, service, and profit targets have been met. This puts teeth into alignment and deployment and gets everyone working in the same direction—much like the process sketched by the contingency diagram.

FIGURE 17-6
Federal Express Quality Index

___

Federal Express Service Quality Index

Service failure type	Weighting **X** factor	Estimated daily occurrences	Weighted **=** daily failure points
Right-day late-service failures	1		
Wrong-day late-service failures	5		
Traces not answered by COSMOS	1		
Complaints reopened by customers	5		
Missing PODs	1		
Invoice adjustments requested	1		
Missed pickups	10		
Lost packages	10		
Damaged packages	10		
Delay minutes/aircraft ("0-based")	5		
Overgoods	5		
Abandoned calls	1		

Total Daily Failure Points   _____

Moore Canada: Deployment at Its Best

A different example of balance and alignment is practiced at the Canadian division of Moore Business Forms, which began a major quality initiative in 1991. Pat Allin, president of the company, took the lead not only by touting the tools and concepts of quality, but more importantly by serving as a model for the desired behavior. On his business card and on the newsletter circulated monthly to Moore employees he is identified as "President and Chief Listener." His newsletter reflects his own customer focus—both internal and external—and stresses that he regards his role as being a sole source provider of an environment that encourages employees to do things right.

Allin has lived up to his title of Chief Listener. He held 50 meetings with Moore employees in just a few months, touching base with 1,600 workers and fielding their concerns about the company. He followed up by communicating the employees' concerns through his newsletter and then distributing a survey that solicited more information on their views.

Employees were asked to react to a "fix-it" list of problems considered by management to be most pressing. But Chief Listener Allin also asked his employees about their expectations of him, about their preferences on how to change and implement change at the company, and about their views of the organization's strengths and weaknesses.

Response was plentiful, strong, and substantial. Most interesting was Allin's willingness to act on what he heard. One of the employees' main concerns was compensation. Allin responded by developing a new incentive compensation pilot plan tied to quality objectives, such as reduction of late shipments, fewer errors, productivity increases on presses and collators, waste reduction, fewer accidents, and improved attendance at work.

The program was piloted at three of the company's sites, chosen because they represent a broad spectrum of products manufactured by Moore. Interestingly Allin commented, "We will not implement this plan in locations unwilling to change. We only want programs which will result in a payoff to employees, and this will only happen where employees use their quality training and focus on their customers."

Finally, as part of the marketing of the program, Allin developed the slogan "Dedicated to Customers/Driven To Excellence." More than just a slogan, it is backed up by a substantial investment in training and in Quality Action Team efforts to tackle Moore's toughest problems. But the goal is clearly alignment—alignment through TQM—with senior management taking an aggressive lead but leading by building consensus and reinforcing the desired goals of change.

CONCLUSION

Although change is difficult and directed change is often threatening, it can happen if company leadership develops meaningful consensus for change. Leadership must be sincere and must avoid potentially disastrous mixed messages—the incongruities of saying one thing and doing another. TQM provides the basis for aligned change over time. When done well, it works.

The key is the simplicity of the vision—the basic tenets of Roman Catholic theology, for example, can be stated in about four short sentences—and willingness to immerse the organization in the unending complexity of the work. Roman Catholic theologians promised an eternity in paradise. TQM goals are more prosaic, but they represent a future that more organizations might regard as heavenly. That mix would include an aligned, efficient operation; responsible, empowered employees; senior management leadership rooted in care and concern for key organizational constituencies; and prosperous, profitable adaptation to a competitive, changing global structure.

NOTE

1. J. P. Kotter and J. L. Heskett, *Corporate Culture and Performance* (New York: Free Press, 1992).

Chapter Eighteen

Aligning Operations with Change Strategies: The Operations Blueprint

Thomas G. Gunn

CREATING THE LINKAGE TO FUNCTIONAL STRATEGY

T he successful linkage of business goals and measures to operational strategies requires the continuing alignment of several key company functions. A typical and quite visible chain of interlinked events, for example, is needed to get an ordered product to the customer. Such functions as product and process design, materials and components purchasing, and manufacturing must be operating harmoniously with each other and with the two terminal functions, receiving the order and shipping it out. That sounds rather axiomatic, but keeping these elements working together is extraordinarily complex. Coordinating the relationships requires careful development of a detailed plan that explicitly translates the company's business strategy into clear operational goals and measurements.

Once in use the plan can also be a significant frame of reference if it is necessary to execute major change in the company. By acting as a coordinating agent the plan reminds managers of the need for changing several different components in concert so that these components will remain in alignment with each other. Moreover, the plan can identify any misalignments that need correction.

The purpose of this chapter is to create a detailed operations planning framework that will guide senior executives toward successfully developing the functional linkages necessary to implement their corporate strategy. This framework is graphically illustrated in Figure 18–1, and the eight steps that follow will serve as your road map through its sectors.

FIGURE 18-1

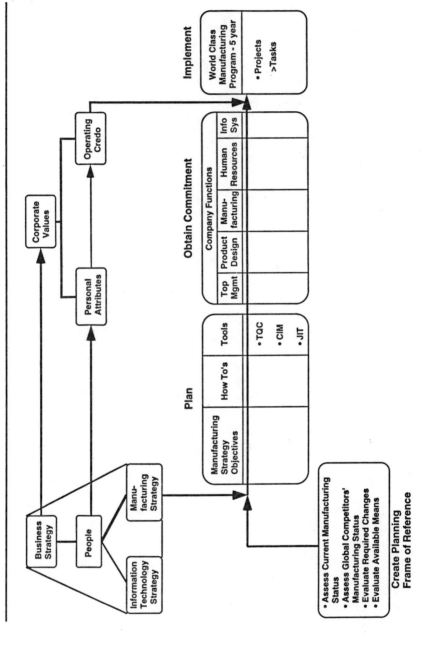

STEP 1: ESTABLISHING THE PLANNING FRAME OF REFERENCE

The first step in the planning process is to establish the basis for the company's performance improvement strategy. This will become a reference point for specific performance improvement measures.

A key step in creating this performance-planning frame of reference is to conduct an operations audit. To avoid provincial perspectives in both the audit and its resulting recommendations it is useful to have an external change agent as well as adequate representation by change managers within the company who are capable of anticipating and responding to changes implied by the audit. This objectivity will provide an important sense of perspective to the audit that is simply not available when the company's own executives—some of whom may have been with the company or industry for 20 to 30 years—perform the work; however, the internal change agents are more suitably oriented toward implementing recommendations.

The operations audit should include interviews with key customers and suppliers. It should also focus on the factors in time-based competition, not just cost-based competition. The lead time involved in each of the fundamental business processes must be identified as a basis for performance improvement. It is also essential that the audit examine the corporation's business performance in the context of the external world, comparing it against peers and competitors. An inward view compares the company's performance only on a historical basis against itself, that is, how well it did this year against the year before or earlier years.

The operations audit can generally be performed by interviewing 10 to 20 key managers in the organization and by observing operations for one to two days each in a few of the corporation's plants. Even gathering responses to a well-designed questionnaire can provide the basis for a valuable snapshot of the business unit's current operating status. At most the audit should require no more than four to six weeks to perform before the findings are presented to the corporation's senior management.

STEP 2: PLANNING

In regard to Figure 18–1, once the implications of a Strategic Business Unit's (SBU) business strategy and the parent company's current competitive position are well understood by the complete management team, it is time to formulate the operations strategies. Emphasis should be on performance factors rather than on structural factors (i.e., how many plants and where they are located, what kind of organization structure, etc.). Performance factors are related to creating business process excellence, maximizing customer satisfaction, improving quality, minimizing lead times, increasing return on assets, enhancing productivity, and increasing operations flexibility. These strategies must be stated in specific terms that spell out what actions to take, the amount of improvement required, and the deadlines for achieving objectives. Representative Manufacturing Strategy Objectives for operations might be as follows:

- Reduce new product/process design lead time by 50 percent in two years.
- Double total inventory turns in 18 months.
- Improve product quality by a factor of 10 by reducing the current defect rate of 50,000 defective parts per million to 5,000 defective parts per million in two years.
- Reduce the lead time in the customer order to delivery cycle from three weeks to three days in 12 months.

The next step shown in the Plan box is recognizing that there are many broad ways that the selected strategies can be carried out—the How To's. In general some can be accomplished with new manufacturing or information technology. Others can be carried out by reorganizing the work or the organization structure more effectively. Still others can be implemented through new education and training programs for specific employees. So the How To's are created as detailed steps in understanding how management will achieve the strategic objectives articulated on the left side of the Plan box.

Finally, in the Tools column, the specific tools—that is, competitive advantage enablers or operations concepts—are selected so that they will contribute to the accomplishment of the chosen strategic objectives.

To reach a particular design objective, for instance, the How To might require reorganizing the work or business process itself. The Tool to be used in this case could be concurrent (or simultaneous) product and process engineering. Another How To might be the use of modern information systems to accomplish the objective. In this case computer integrated manufacturing (CIM) tools such as computer-aided design (CAD), computer-aided engineering (CAE), group technology (GT), and computer-aided process planning (CAPP) will probably be some of the items employed to ensure the company's future competitive advantage in product and process design.

Note that contrary to the practice of many corporations we have moved "top down" in this planning process so that management understands what it wants to do or must do before it selects the tools to accomplish its objective. In many companies tools are being implemented in helter-skelter fashion. There is little understanding of how each will contribute to the attainment of the company's business strategy and how much each tool will deliver to the success.

STEP 3: OBTAINING UNDERSTANDING AND COMMITMENT

The most critical step of the planning process is one that most companies omit: obtaining genuine understanding of the performance improvement plan and a steadfast commitment to implementing it throughout the company. As a result most companies never get their operations aligned, or fully implement their operations improvement program, or achieve the financial and strategic benefits of the total performance improvement program.

When the Tools are developed in the Plan box, they are allocated to particular functions involved in operational strategies (including top management) on the basis of two criteria:

- Which function(s) will have the primary implementation responsibility?
- Which function(s) will be impacted by the Tools' implementation?

The purpose of this crucial allocation is to make sure that the head of each function understands exactly what his or her unit must do to successfully implement the How To's and Tools that will lead to attainment of the Manufacturing Strategy Objectives. Each functional manager also gets to see how functionally interdependent the business performance improvement solutions are and how important it is for all the functions' managers to place the SBU's welfare above their own narrow interests. Showing the Tools in this manner also shines light on the complete scope and magnitude of each task so that adequate thought is given to the resources required to implement each Tool and the total performance improvement program.

Most companies skip the crucial step of obtaining commitment, only to discover during implementation an incomplete understanding of the scope and magnitude of each task and of the resources required to successfully implement each part of the overall program. As Michael Beer maintains, "There will be no business success if there is compliance but no commitment." Thus the implementation bogs down because it lacks enough resources from the start. Corners get cut, major parts of the program are eliminated, or the entire implementation fails to reach objectives. Yes, the commitment step is a learning process that lengthens the planning process. But managers must remember that the total committed time to successful implementation is what counts, not how quickly the planning stage can be completed just so that people start doing something. Time invested in obtaining commitment will be rewarded downstream in the implementation process with a quicker, less expensive, and smoother execution. It's the old story of pay me now or pay me more later if the commitment step is avoided.

STEP 4: PULLING THE PERFORMANCE IMPROVEMENT PROGRAM TOGETHER

The Tools spread through the Obtain Commitment box can now be sorted and grouped into a number of projects—generally about 15 to 30, with 3 to 6 major tasks in each. The projects may be organized functionally or from a business process standpoint. Each project has to be laid out in further detail as to expected duration and timing, human resources requirements, costs, and benefits. Experience says that at the outset it is best to estimate costs of the entire program at the margin in order to be as conservative as possible. This can be relaxed later if senior management decides that company managers can be shifted from less essential tasks to implementation of highly valuable improvement programs.

STEP 5: UNDERSTANDING THE HIERARCHY OF BUSINESS NEEDS

Part of the challenge in developing an operational performance improvement strategy in which related functional strategies are aligned with the business strategy and the total work force is aligned with the goals of the business unit or the corporation, is to achieve an understanding of the way each Tool in the program contributes to the company's overall success. The improvement program is highly synergistic, and the benefits from implementing each Tool often accrue in ways that are complex and subtle.

Abraham Maslow's hierarchy of human needs can serve as a model for the development of a similar chain of corporate business needs, thus bringing a sense of order to how we think of and array business benefits. As shown in Figure 18–2, the business chain that should lead to a company's overall success starts out, just as Maslow's human need chain begins, with the need for survival. After survival the links in descending order of importance are the needs for growth, prosperity, and ultimately "market presence"—a recognition by industrial and personal consumers that a company is a world leader with its established brand names or products. Companies that enjoy such market presence are Coca-Cola, Honda, Sony, Apple, Levi Strauss, Caterpillar, Lexus, and Canon, among others.

At the second level, companies seek a group of high-level generic business benefits—call them "meta-benefits." There are, I believe, just six that really count:

- Greater customer satisfaction.
- Higher profitability.
- Increased sales.
- Greater return on assets.
- Higher productivity.
- Employee environment of continuous learning and improvement.

Just as meta-benefits can be mapped to their higher-level success factors (and many to more than one success factor), all of the more specific enterprise benefits can be mapped to the six meta-benefits.

The third level of the benefit chain comprises specific enterprise benefits, which include at a minimum the following:

- Increasing amounts of timely information to manage an increasingly complex business more effectively.

FIGURE 18–2
Sustainable Competitive Advantage through the Manufacturing Performance Benefit Chain

Enterprise Success	Enterprises "meta benefits"	Specific enterprise benefits	Specific concepts/enablers applied to leverage points in the enterprise regarding cost, quality, and time
• Survival • Growth • Prosperity • "Market presence"	• Greater customer satisfaction • Higher profitability • Increased sales • Greater return on assets • Higher productivity • Employee environment of continuous learning and improvement	• More *and* more timely information to manage increasingly complex business more effectively > Global scope > Faster pace > SKU* proliferation > Quality emphasis > Regulatory compliance • Higher product quality > Less risk of performance disappointment, degradation, or failure > More value-added in product[†] • Greater flexibility • Lower inventories • Lower costs • Better customer service > More reliable delivery performance to date/time needed > Reduced order to deliver lead times > Quicker time to market	• Better information and telecommunication systems • Better process automation • Quicker line changeovers • Smaller lot sizes • Statistical quality control • Education and training • Better manufacturing technology • Empowered employees • Taguchi methods[§] • Enterprise logistics planning

* SKUs—Stock Keeping Units—are more differentiated end items or products in stock.

† Product means product *plus* value-added services.

§ Taguchi methods are modern quality tools used to ensure robust product and process quality and to minimize loss to society caused by defective products.

- Higher product quality to reduce the risk of performance disappointment, degradation, or failure and to input more value added in the product.
- Greater flexibility.
- Lower inventories.
- Lower costs.
- Better customer service that emphasizes more reliable delivery performance in relation to the date and time set by the customer and reduces the lead times between the order and delivery.
- Quicker introduction of new products and services to market.

As noted earlier these specific benefits map to the company's meta-benefits. For instance, lower inventories will result in a greater return on assets. Higher product quality will result in greater customer satisfaction, higher productivity, more reliable production and delivery schedules, and perhaps increased sales and profitability.

Finally we can look to specific world class business concepts and enablers that will be implemented in the operations performance improvement plan and map them to the specific benefits each produces with regard to quality, cost, time, and information value. In most cases the implementation of these tools and concepts will produce specific benefits in several areas.

Thus the corporate benefit chain can map both ways: from corporate success factors to application tools or from the applications tools to the specific and ultimate benefits they produce. Benefit chain mapping represents a powerful way to understand and help justify the application of world class performance concepts and tools to a manufacturing company from a strategic and financial viewpoint.

STEP 6: RATIONALIZING THE OPERATIONS IMPROVEMENT PLAN

Many companies get bogged down in justifying costs of the program. They try to justify the cost of each tool or task or project in the program rather than justifying the overall program once and getting on with the implementation. In such cases each "cost-justified" project is generally ranked by return on investment (ROI). The projects are then arranged in order from highest return to lowest, and a few projects at the top of the list are "cherry-picked" for initial implementation. Unfortunately the projects toward the bottom of the list never seem to get implemented, and the company never realizes the benefits of the total performance improvement program. Most performance improvement programs can be justified in their totality just by looking at improvements in quality, asset utilization, better purchasing, and improved productivity. The only way to obtain all the benefits of the program is to implement the entire program.

In addition many companies get so caught up in financially justifying the performance improvement program that they forget about enumerating the strategic benefits of the program such as greater flexibility, shorter lead times, and greater ability to attract and retain high-performance employees. Then too, many managers forget to consider the grim alternative to not launching the performance improvement program: "What if we continue at our current (too slow) pace of improvement or do nothing?"

In my experience the companies that have problems justifying an operations improvement program either don't consider the program from a broad perspective or fail to understand the strategic benefits of the program.

STEP 7: MAKING PLANNING LINKAGES EXPLICIT

It is critical that all current and future managers and employees of the business unit understand why they are implementing some element of change—such as new manufacturing or information technologies, new processes, or new policies and practices. For this purpose it is beneficial to create an indexing scheme in the planning process so that every element of the plan is linked to its predecessor and to its successor. Thus when someone asks why a specific part of the improvement program is being implemented, the indexing scheme can lead them all the way back to the functional strategy objective that created the need for the tool to be implemented, and even back to the business strategy that created the need for the functional strategy.

STEP 8: GETTING PEOPLE BEHIND THE OPERATIONS IMPROVEMENT PROGRAM

As we have noted, the commitment step goes a long way toward promoting understanding of what has to be done to improve the performance of the business unit, and why. It is a learning process that promotes understanding and real commitment toward a shared vision and common goals. But it is only part of the people-oriented solution. The alignment of three other factors is essential to gaining effective support from both the white-collar and blue-collar components of the business unit's work force. People must be selected, guided, and motivated by overall corporate values, desired personal attributes, and performance-related operating principles.

Many firms have statements of corporate values that establish or reinforce an umbrella of "goodness" over the corporate culture. Typical statements of corporate values include the following:

- Customer satisfaction comes first.
- Teamwork is our style.
- Innovation is a way of life.

- The highest ethical standards are our guides.
- Quality is in everything we do.

Unfortunately, although they are valid and positive, these values often are difficult for people to grasp in the conduct of their everyday work because they are too emblematic of "motherhood and apple pie" unless they are built into the selection, appraisal, and succession points. Although they may represent valuable aspirations for the corporation's employees, maximizing the performance of people in the business unit requires selection and retention of only the best "raw material." This means retaining or hiring people with the best supporting attributes, such as:

- Drive.
- Leadership.
- Excellent character.
- Integrity.
- Vision.
- Efficiency.
- Responsiveness.
- Effectiveness.
- Perseverance.

In addition to those attributes many companies utilize an employee-screening process that identifies people with good problem-solving, team-building, and interpersonal skills, as well as good attitudes about work and life. With these characteristics for starters, the company claims it can impart all other skills the employees need through internal education and training programs.

Finally it's important that people be given some guidelines for the way they think about performance in their day-to-day jobs. This can be accomplished most effectively through an operating credo that usually includes such principles as:

- Anything that adds cost but not value to our products is waste. The nature of competition will not tolerate waste; neither must we.
- Low cost is a dependent variable; it results from doing other things well. Our goal is to always be the low-cost manufacturer in our marketplace.
- Excess complexity in our products, procedures, or organization exponentially adds cost—both in dollars and time. We will pursue simplicity as a key to our competitive effectiveness.
- Time is our most precious competitive asset. A sense of urgency must permeate all of our activities.

These kinds of principles help shape the thinking of people throughout the organization about performance—their own and the entire organization's. They constantly reinforce desirable job performance by focusing on continuous improvement. When incorporated into people's performance evaluations they can become more than just another set of slogans on the wall. The operating credo can be a powerful catalyst for change in the organization.

A third item that is effective in changing the behavior of people in the organization is education and training—that is, improving the intellectual capital of the business unit. Both words are important because most companies don't recognize the difference between the concepts or acknowledge the importance of both education and training in changing the performance of the business unit. Training is the "how." Education is the "why."

Company training programs often emphasize only the "how" and neglect to explain "why" to the work force. Explaining "why" may involve key questions. Why do we have to change? Why do we need new technology? Why do we (all) need new skills? Why do we need to enter joint ventures with companies in other parts of the world? Why is our current performance no longer satisfactory?

Most employees are reasonable people who, when confronted with the facts about their company's competitive position, will realize that their futures are at stake. They will respond by doing whatever is necessary to further their company's competitive position and preserve their jobs.

Besides failing to emphasize the education aspect of education and training, most companies woefully under-invest in this area. Leading U.S. companies—such as General Electric, IBM, Hewlett-Packard, ATT, Xerox, and Motorola—spend anywhere from $1150 to $3500 per employee annually on education and training. But the average U.S. manufacturer spends less than $150 per employee per year—or a fraction of the amount spent by those corporate leaders. Yet Motorola, in documented studies, has shown it receives $33 back for every dollar it spends on education and training. What better investment can a company make than in its people? In the end they are the ultimate competitive differentiators—given that the same technology is available to everyone today. Ray Stata, President and CEO of Analog Devices, Inc., sums it up well when he says, "The rate at which organizations learn may become the only sustainable source of competitive advantage, especially in knowledge-intensive businesses."

The companies in which operations are most aligned have three people-related processes in place to support their alignment: obtaining commitment as a step in their planning processes; using the right items to select, guide, and motivate people and their operating performances; and establishing continuing programs of employee education and training. It takes all of these to win in business today—to establish a culture of innovation and high performance that empowers people under a vision, strategy, and structure to drive peak business performance in the company.

Chapter Nineteen

Information Technologies to Manage the Next Dynamic

Donald J. Kabat

C orporate change managers cannot go very far without bumping into technology. Technology not only comes at the transitional company from a multitude of directions but strikes on a variety of levels. An advance in technology can be a change trigger that threatens to destabilize not only a single company but an entire industry and perhaps a cluster of industries. Technology can also be the means for countering that danger and driving the response that restabilizes the company. Or technology can provide the tools for thinking through the implications and for helping develop the intelligent response. And in still another of its seemingly infinite guises, a technology shift by a single player can be the change trigger that destabilizes not only competitors, customers and suppliers, the entire industry in which the company competes, and related industries but even the very firm that forged the breakthrough.

All of these roles demand that the modern company manage technology and manage it well. For example, in the case where the leading-edge company can actually sow the seeds of its own destruction, the firm will pay for rather than benefit from its achievement if it blazes the path and just stops there. To capture the real payoffs of a breakthrough a firm must crank up all parts of the organization to go along—the product development people who can commercialize it, the operations people who can produce it, and the sales and marketing people who can convince customers of the superiority of the products. This requires new skills, alteration of the organization to speed delivery and prepare for the next breakthrough, rewards for improved performance, and so on.

Even if the technology change is less than a breakthrough, perhaps something as simple as installing a computerized process to speed an assembly line or reduce its costs is no less critical.

Regardless of where the technology change originates or what form it takes, it will invariably send shock waves through the organization. In that kind of environment, the company accepts that it is in transformation and that a change management process must be launched to both align the new technology to the rest of the company and revamp the four key organizational elements—strategy, operations, culture, and reward—so that they are synchronized with each other and with the new technology. Management of technological change, in short, requires the company to stay focused on alignment.

This can be a tall order. It requires many organizations to think about technology management in a way that has been virtually ignored over the last four decades of the technology "revolution."

Despite all of the time and money expended on technological improvements, the results have not measured up to the investment. To a large degree this is because managers have failed to come to grips with what technology can do for companies or have short-changed technology investments. Many companies have expected too much from technology advancements and been sorely disappointed. Still another group of "failures" includes the companies that got bitten by the technology bug and bet the house on expensive equipment and processes—whether they needed it or not. These are the "overinvestors."

Recent studies of American manufacturing companies show that an overwhelming percentage of corporate technology initiatives fail and that a high percentage of these fizzles resulted not from deficiencies in the technology but in non-technology areas. The principal cause of failure has been problems with people and organizations charged with operating the new technology (in other words, misalignment after introduction of the technology).

Perhaps the best way to approach technology management is to start by casting it in purely business terms—that is, what type of return does the company want or expect from investing in technology? That will in turn represent a key step in getting the ball rolling toward alignment. From the very start concepts and pure business purposes that are framed in the language of the main line manager will be interlinked. This will enable technology and operating managers to choose the optimal equipment, processes, and techniques for achieving such aims as becoming the low-cost, premium-service, high-quality provider of products and services and for keeping focus on external markets. That would drive investment in technology systems to allow rapid sharing of information among a more educated, more highly skilled, and increasingly entrepreneurial work force.

In that position technology can streamline business processes by doing the following:

- Eliminating redundancies.
- Shortening the time to do work.
- Improving quality.
- Improving productivity and effectiveness.
- Upgrading communications.

- Cutting costs.
- Improving service.

The management approach that will get technology users to these goals is a "holistic" effort that knits together these corporate functions:

- Business strategy and planning.
- Technology strategy and research.
- Business process reengineering.
- Human resource planning.
- Education and training.

The contents of the complete approach thus tie together the four key elements of alignment—strategy, operations, culture, and reward. But this directs us to another major flaw in technology management of the past. These functions have not come together but have operated independently, an unwelcome insularity that has prevented the melding of disciplines, forces, and skills required for synchronization and alignment.

In an effort to weave these components together Andersen Consulting has isolated "The Four Pillars of Technology," which include the following:

- *New Age Architecture:* highly customized information and solutions through the use of *cooperative processing, client/server,* and *open systems* that depend on a network of hardware and software linked together.
- *Human Metaphor:* a concept that makes computer technology a natural, even invisible, everyday experience, based on human characteristics and need rather than the requirements of a given system.
- *Universal Network:* a transparent, seamless link that delivers myriad services anytime and anyplace and sustains large numbers of portable and mobile subscribers.
- *Smart Systems:* systems that make use of a company's most expensive, valuable, and underutilized asset—knowledge. Many programs in these systems will initiate aspects of human reasoning. Integrated Performance Support Systems are an example of the use of technology to support the knowledge worker of the future.

Putting these concepts into practice requires management to do the following:

- Know how and when to use technology as part of the change process.
- Align technology in support of its business strategy, processes, and organization structure.
- Understand its leadership role in the critical technology assimilation process.

- Be familiar with the various business integration change models and know how to align technology with the components of the models.
- Reengineer the information technology (IT) function to facilitate and contribute to overall business process change.

The CEO must not allow the pursuit of technical excellence to take precedence over providing a true business benefit to the organization. An excellent system that is not or cannot be used is a poor investment. Technology can be a disruptive power if not managed properly. The primary mission of all those associated with this computing revolution is as vital as it is complex: to turn existing and evolving technology into strategic competitive advantage.

WHAT TO THINK ABOUT IN ALIGNING TECHNOLOGY SYSTEMS

The potential for achieving superior organizational performance cannot be realized solely by the use of superior technology. Studies have shown that large investments in technology in the 1970s and 1980s produced little in the way of productivity gains. Research and personal technology implementation experience clearly indicate that most of the reason for this failure falls outside the realm of technology "issues." One study concluded that 55 to 90 percent of all technology failures are due to human and organizational problems.[*] Thus expected technology projects often fall short of producing benefits because they are misaligned with other elements of the company, chiefly in the non-technology areas.

The business integration model (Figure 19–1) shows how technology must relate to the other components of the business in order to achieve superior organizational performance. The model underscores the need to align an organization's people, processes, and technology with its business strategy in order to meet or exceed performance goals. The following "alignment" issues should be understood in trying to integrate or upgrade technology within an organization:

- *Strategy.* Historically business strategies drove information technology requirements. Now information technology capabilities are key influences shaping and carrying out business strategies. Simply stated, technology can drive what people should do and enable them to do their job better. The "enabler" strategy of the 1980s is now being replaced by a "driver" strategy that focuses on the next technology to fundamentally change the way a company conducts its business. The question for management is how to select the right information technology strategy to support the business strategy. The driver versus enabler distinction is critical because the costs and risks are quite different. It is also a major issue in change management because the form of technology chosen can determine how quickly executives pick up change triggers and how quickly and effectively they respond.

---

[*] APICS, Society of Manufacturing Engineers, Office of Technology Assessment.

FIGURE 19–1
Business Integration Model

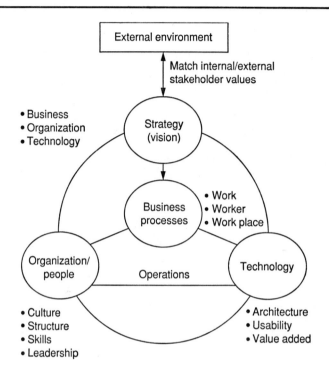

• *Business processes.* How does technology facilitate business processes in terms of the work performed, worker performance, and the environment in which the work is done? The popular term *business process reengineering* refers to a method for sorting out internal and external technology issues. The driver should always be the customer needs. It is these needs that ultimately dictate the scope and the level of technology investment. The issues that need to be reconciled include time, quality, customer perspective, people empowerment, efficiency (i.e., eliminating non–value-added activities), and flexibility. In change management the right use of "reengineering" can keep an all-important focus on customers and markets.

• *Organization/people.* How does technology facilitate how people are organized and how they work, communicate, and learn? Technology has the capacity to create new organization structures without physical or geographic boundaries. Therefore putting technology to work in creative ways can break old mind-sets of how to organize. The knowledge worker of the future will be supported by a combination or blending of all forms and functions of data, sound, text, and image (e.g., phones that process images and the marriage of television and computers). The human senses of sight and hearing are the ways we receive information today. The "information age" will continue to develop with further integration of computers, television, and telephones. As we add other senses to the equation (e.g., touch, taste, and smell) we can see how technology and people are inexorably intertwined in "aligning" appropriate technology solutions.

The alignment of technology with all the components of the model is no small feat. In fact, it is a continuous process of modifying and balancing longer-term strategies and goals with the communication and execution efforts required to realign the organization, business processes, and technology.

LESSONS FROM THE PAST!

Some tips for handling the technology changes of the future can be gleaned from the painful mistakes of the last four decades.

Don't Automate a Lousy Process!

Do not install a technology before doing a trial run on the business process affected by the change. In fact, it is wise to stack the technology-based plan against an alternative that minimizes or doesn't even need a technology component. Sometimes a better process or a new policy is more effective than a better technology solution to the current environment.

Experience has shown that the biggest paybacks occur when a process is simplified. The preferred sequence is to simplify first, automate second, and then integrate. The effort and cost of simplification are significantly less than the effort and cost for systems integration, and the benefits are greater (see Figure 19–2).

Once a New System Is "Converted," Expect the Hard Work to Begin

Many companies go through so much pain to get a new technology to work that insufficient time or money is devoted to the "inevitable" changes that need to take place after the technology is installed. The change curve is shown in Figure 19–3.

The simple picture says that change always introduces some element of concern, confusion, realignment, and even despair, so that assigning an organized program to deal with these issues is essential. It is an example of one of the many subsets that must be in alignment to achieve total corporate harmony.

Target Performance Improvement Goals as Part of Technology Investments

In general, companies do a poor job of redefining the new performance levels "expected" from technology investment. It is not enough to measure success by on-time or on-budget criteria. The real test is whether the technology contributes to the

FIGURE 19–2
Don't Automate a Lousy Process!

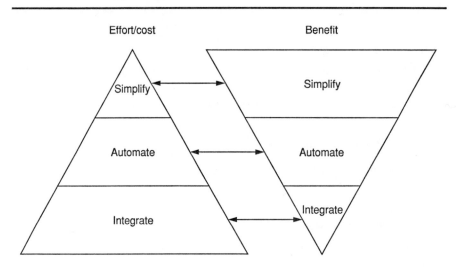

FIGURE 19–3
Change Curve

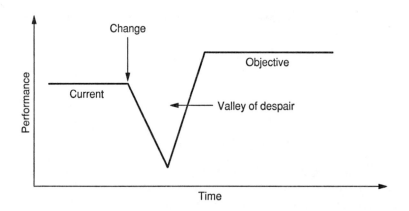

performance of the organization. These "numbers" tend to be lost in the shuffle when there is a rush to get the job done. The measurement of success should include both interim and longer-term results, particularly if a major transformation or change will be phased in over a period of time.

FIGURE 19–4

Aligning the Magnitude and Scope of Technology Change

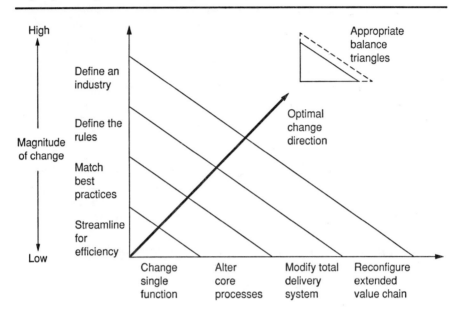

Align the Magnitude and Scope of Change

Understanding and balancing the magnitude and scope of change is essential to a successful technology introduction. There is a major difference in effort between introducing a driver technology, for which the transformation includes myriad organization, process, and strategy changes, and introducing an enabler technology that calls for considerably less change and risk.

Figure 19–4 depicts the balance issues. The magnitude of change, which varies from high to low, establishes an organization's goal for change. Do you want to introduce driver technology to redefine an entire industry (at the most ambitious level)? The scope of change—from narrow to broad—represents the second dimension. Is the objective as daring as reconfiguring the entire value chain from suppliers to customers, or is it as relatively routine as revamping a single low-level function?

Targeting levels of technology investment to get the biggest bang for the buck involves not only a trade-off (i.e., cost versus capability) but a true assessment of risk in terms of the organization's ability to handle the change issues.

Do Not Short-Cut Training and Education

Only people make change work. Therefore, in the end, improved performance from technology investments are highly dependent on how people buy into and utilize their new "tools" on the job. Unfortunately the human component of a successful technology introduction is frequently not addressed with the necessary skills and scope of attention it deserves. It is often essential to arm workers with skills in the areas of leadership development, organization development, communication, human-computer interaction, and instructional design if they are to take to and properly operate the new systems.

The key to training is to focus on simplicity and usability, from a worker's perspective. To achieve the desired performance improvement the company must support the worker with the best tools and techniques available. A growing trend is to integrate the training into the systems environment so that it becomes an integral part of the work environment. Indeed, integrated performance support systems are keys to long-term success in harnessing technology to work toward an improved organization.

Technology will create competitive advantage only if the company sports a "competitive" work force with required skills from top to bottom. When success depends on producing a high-quality, low-cost product, the education of the bottom 50 percent of the work force is critical because this group must operate the new processes. If they cannot learn effectively, new high-tech systems and processes won't work.

Don't Forget the Human Resources Function

When major technology programs are introduced there is a need for a better balance between technology and human resources (HR) systems. Technology change will shift work flow, job content, required skills, performance measures, compensation, and a whole list of human resources issues. The idea is to involve the human resources function early in the technology change cycle before irreparable damage is caused. In this regard the idea of technology-centered alignment is carried several strides further than just training.

One idea would be to concentrate on the critical jobs that will be introduced, changed, or eliminated as part of the introduction of new technology. This would center attention on the critical path and the priorities of the human resources initiatives needed to support the technology shift. The HR changes that need to be dealt with may very well affect the time frame and size of the effort required to adjust the remaining jobs impacted by the new technology and their related business processes and workflows. This represents a top-down, gradual implementation.

CHANGE READINESS (THE POTENTIAL FOR ANTICIPATING, RESPONDING TO, AND SUSTAINING CHANGE)

The culture of an organization can play a large role in deciding how far a company is able to go in implementing a new business or technology solution. The major characteristics of culture can be defined by the diagram in Figure 19–5—leadership, structure, process, and work force shape the culture of an organization. This change model depicts the need to align the organization culture with the strategy in order to achieve

FIGURE 19-5
Change Model

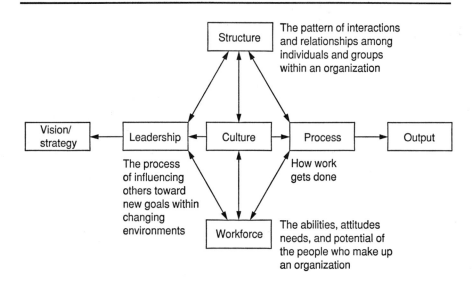

the desired outputs. The alignment issues demand an analysis of the underlying change drivers that require professional analysis.

Andersen Consulting has developed a change readiness questionnaire that is extremely useful in assessing the risks and barriers to change. An overall change readiness index based on the results has been developed. The index of the subject firm may then be compared with that of other companies in similar industries, including competitors. The goal was to identify the change issues and risks in implementing a new technology. In this systemized way of finding flaws that would cause resistance to change and programs that would build on strong points to promote, acceptance to change could become an integral part of the technology change process.

LEADERSHIP

Technology decision making starts at the top. No CEO should delegate major technology decisions without providing appropriate direction, policies, checks, and balances. Technology affects the entire business, from organizational structure to product marketing strategies, and the CEO as chief alignment officer cannot hand the ball off without information on the whole superstructure.

Technical experts do not generally have a comprehensive understanding of where the overall business is going. On the other hand, the CEO needs to know in what direction technology is going, how it can best be used, and what the associated risks

FIGURE 19–6
Integrated Technology Change Process

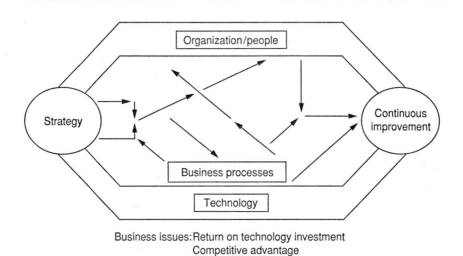

Business issues: Return on technology investment
Competitive advantage
Performance improvement

are with the evolving system. Modern companies need a new approach to decision making that blends the technical knowledge of the computer experts with the vision of senior management.

INTEGRATED TECHNOLOGY CHANGE PROCESS

If a company is to implement a technology change successfully, the change process (consisting of approach and methodology) must be understood and accepted. Just like a pilot preparing for takeoff, the firm should use checklists to make sure it covers all the key bases. Exceptions cannot be prescribed by methodologies, but must be managed by experience, judgment, and "tools" that can be used to ensure that alignment is complete.

Figure 19–6 depicts the need for getting from a strategy to a steady state of continuous improvement and the complexity in building this bridge. If the business goal is getting an appropriate return on technology investment, management must recognize the need to involve all parts of the organization *simultaneously* as it moves from strategy formulation to implementation. Sequential involvement will cost a lot more in the long run because the cost of backtracking in a complex process, a common occurrence when alignment is mishandled, is very expensive.

COMMUNICATION

Most companies underestimate the need for communication to "sell" the new technology. Everyone assumes that the need for change is clear throughout the business and that all the newsletters, speeches, and training got the message across. However, the need for direct, consistent, and constant communication is essential for people to feel they are part of the technology change. In fact, management knows it has full support when the people start to drive the change process rather than be driven by it.

Misalignment of technology with the organization processes occurs when only a handful of employees can identify with the goals or define their roles or contributions in accomplishing those goals. It means that most people are in the dark or out in the cold, a bad way to recruit the mandatory buy-in that is required. What needs to be communicated is how the changes will impact people's roles and responsibilities. People must know what is expected from them to accomplish the stated goals of the organization.

WHAT YOUR TECHNOLOGY CHANGE PROCESS ENTAILS

The potential for achieving organizational performance will be realized when people, business processes, and technology are addressed in conjunction. If we look at the technology assimilation process a little more closely, we see some of its key interfaces with organization, people, and processes (see Figure 19–7). This is a gross oversimplification of the number and types of issues that must be reconciled in the process of moving from technology strategy formulation to implementation and continuous improvement. The model does, however, provide insight into the complexity of the process.

In the final analysis successful technology implementation can and should be measured by the improvement in overall work force performance. The process of technology assimilation and ultimately organizational performance requires many plan, design, develop, implement, and support cycles throughout the life of a major technology change program.

Most technology groups have their own defined methodologies for designing and implementing new systems. But their methodologies are seldom integrated with the methodologies used by the other parts of the organization involved in the assimilation process. Some of the units that should be included in the change loop are strategic and business planning, human resource management, quality control, industrial engineering, finance and accounting, and product development. In effect a change process must be developed for each technology program to incorporate the appropriate level of involvement for each function that should participate. Again, keep a weather eye on alignment. However, the allocations of funding and responsibility are difficult to decide in advance because the firm often doesn't know what the issues are and whether it has the right "tools" to deal with them.

FIGURE 19–7
Technology Change Process (Assimilation)

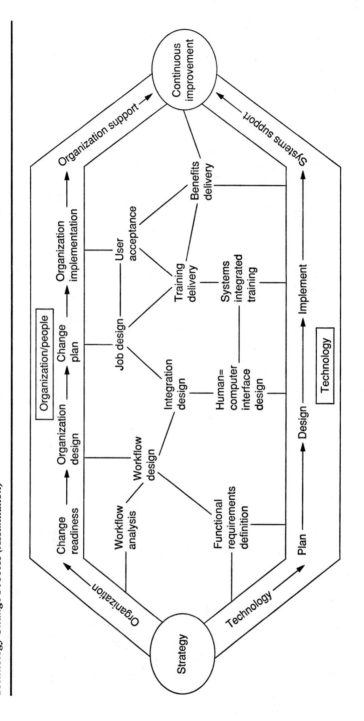

TECHNOLOGY ASSIMILATION

Over the past several years Andersen Consulting has been working diligently on defining the frameworks, approaches, methodologies, and deliverables for a coordinated and realistic approach to solving business system problems. Because the problems are usually not clearly identified at the beginning of a consulting assignment, a multidisciplinary diagnostic approach is highly desirable. Experts in technology, people, and processes work together to define the problems so that management can decide what to change, figure the costs and benefits in accomplishing the change, and determine the priorities, risks, and resources necessary to be successful. In today's complex world the answers are often surprising, and compromises are continually needed to keep major technology programs on track. Thus it is best at the outset to approach study and solution with a team that symbolizes the alignment of elements required to execute beneficial change.

Technology assimilation starts with an understanding of the impact required to achieve stated performance objectives. The process of transformation is different, depending on the type of change, or more specifically, the performance expected. The chart below illustrates the increasing level of complexity in moving from a relatively simple streamlining or efficiency transformation to defining a new approach to competing in an entire industry (see Figure 19–4).

Transformation type	Area impacted	Example
A	Technology	Conversion to a new technology platform
B	Work force	New customer information system that requires reps to exhibit new behaviors
C	Organization	New management and financial reporting system that supports a decentralized profit responsibility
D	Environment	A new approach to health care delivery by introducing a focused health-care facility

Each successive level of transformation encompasses the prior levels. As a result the complexity of the change effort increases geometrically as the project goes up the scale and/or widens in scope.

The process required for successful technology implementation (type A) involves effective *substitutions* of an "as is" (existing) technology architecture with a "to be" (future) one. However, the process required to succeed in the people areas (types B and C) requires *evolution* of the existing "as is" environment to the expected "to be" one. There are vastly important differences between the luxury of discarding the old (substitution) and the more painstaking approach of transforming the old into the new (evolution). In both cases innovation is of increasing importance, as shown in the following table:

Substitution process	Evolution process
Design the new.	Design the new—what will remain?
Build the new.	Define the gap—how much change is required?
Install the new.	Design the tools—support the evolution process.
Dispense with the old.	Build the tools—examples include training, participation in the change process, and communication.
	Empower the process—build a change process (systematic, controlled, and evolutionary).

A major trade-off is involved in moving from a type A to a type D "transformation;" the benefits get greater, but their realization increasingly depends on evolutionary processes that are more expensive, unpredictable, and difficult to manage. The evolution of the right work force, organization, and environment (culture) is an ongoing process that in some cases may never succeed.

In transformation the necessary resources and leadership are substantial, and in many cases they are not sustained for the length of time required to complete the transformation. This is understandable if the firm has a short-term, quick-fix management style. But at some point the underlying problems need to be fixed if the company is to survive. Leadership ability is then the key ingredient to successful management of a technology change that requires changes in the company's human systems (i.e., the work, the worker, and the work place). This is a key area where the CEO can assert his or her authority as chief alignment officer.

TECHNOLOGY ALIGNMENT: A CONTINUOUS PROCESS

Alignment of technology with the rest of the organization is a continuous process of assimilation. The key functions that should always be part of major technology initiatives include the following:

- Technology principles.
- User impact analysis.
- Business process review.
- Organization and critical job review.
- Technology organization review.

Technology Principles

Technology experts seldom have an in-depth understanding of the business issues that top management is dealing with. On the other hand, top management does not generally understand technology or know what technology can do to help it. Delegating these decisions to the chief technology officer or the management information systems director does not ensure that technology investments will advance the company's business strategy. They may be technically adept but out of touch with the business results of their decisions. One way of bridging the strategic and technical camps is to create a task force to develop principles for guiding technology investment decisions.

Those principles—10 to 12 would suffice—would reflect basic management beliefs on how the company should use technology over the long term. By translating the main aspects of a company's business strategy into the language of technology managers, these principles can span the communication gap between top management and the technical experts. The guidelines should be reviewed periodically, particularly when the company changes its basic business direction or undertakes widespread change or restructuring. The statements would also frame for operating management exactly what it wants from technology upgrading.

An example of a principle would be "All product data should be accessible through a common order-processing system." The mission handed the technology people is clear, and their time and money can be directed toward development of what appears to be an efficiency-enhancing tool. Often the mandate is fuzzy, and the work must be redone because the operations people didn't know what they wanted to begin with. But certainly a principle centering on a common and compatible order-entry system would be of benefit to a multidivision company whose various units serve the same basic markets.

User Impact Analysis

When a firm implements technology, users (i.e., the workers) must be well prepared with the right business processes, structure, and skills to achieve the full benefit of the technology. The goal is getting the users equipped with the skills and positioned in the organization so that they can use the technology to its fullest potential. Required comprehension and abilities are broad-based. Successful system implementation and system operations over the long term require users that:

- *Know more*—they understand the company's business direction, strategies, concepts, etc.
- *Can do more*—they have the skills, processes, and environment to perform their required jobs and tasks.
- *Want to do more*—they have the motivation and desire to continually improve and are rewarded for doing more and doing better.

Assimilating technology in the work place requires an analysis of the unique changes that the new business applications will produce among different user groups. The results will drive change programs that are tailored to the specific needs of each user group. For each user group/business application combination four critical components must be integrated, planned, and managed:

1. *Organization*
   - Reporting structure.
   - Communication program.
   - Performance evaluation criteria/reward programs.
   - Quality assurance issues.
   - Staffing requirements.
2. *Job*
   - Work force skill mix.
   - Task assignments.
   - Level of business and technical knowledge.
   - Decision-making and problem-solving abilities.
3. *Process*
   - Work flows.
   - Automated versus manual processes.
   - Number of departments or work groups involved.
4. *Technology/tools*
   - New applications.
   - New technologies.
   - Complexity and criticality.

The degree of change across each component/user group combination must be incorporated into the overall technology assimilation program. An additional tool to assist in the scope, priority, and content of these change programs would be the use of a tool such as the change readiness questionnaire that was referred to earlier.

Collectively these four categories further spotlight the pieces that must be synchronized for alignment.

Business Process Review

The business process should not be changed to fit the technology unless the users feel it is simpler and easier for them to use. Simplifying the process in many cases eliminates the need for complex technology solutions. In fact, the question that should be asked is whether the process adds value to the ultimate user and whether the cost/benefit relationship can be justified.

Work simplification, business process reengineering, and industrial engineering techniques are all applicable tools and methods for evaluating business processes. The business process alignment to a company's strategic objectives has to be understood before the technology alignment process can be completed.

Organization and Critical Job Review

An understanding of the critical jobs for each of the company's major functions is an excellent way to frame the elements of technology alignment. Given an efficient business process, the configuration of the organization and critical jobs that are necessary to execute the process provide a good framework to align a new technology with the people who operate the process. The connection will pinpoint how the technology supports the critical job performance and whether it adds value to the business processes it is designed to help.

Technology Organization Review

Examination of the technology organization itself is useful in assessing how well it is equipped to deal with the technology assimilation program. New technology, business communications, and process skills will be required if the designated technology managers are to do the right job. How much is available within the company? If there are deficiencies, who will be given training or what skills will be "purchased" from outside the organization? The answers are ingredients for success.

The role of the technology group is changing rapidly. As system development tools move closer and closer to users the role of the technology department will either expand through addition of new skills or narrow its sphere of expertise to the advanced technology tools and techniques. Top management should have a lot to say in making this decision.

ROLE OF TECHNOLOGY IN FACILITATING WORK FORCE PERFORMANCE

In today's business world the performance of the organization is what counts. Individual competence so as to meet changing customer needs and the reduction of work force shortages and turnover so as to sustain high levels of quality customer service are the keys to improved work force performance.

Traditionally organizations focus on training to improve performance. Training costs went from $40 billion in 1980 to more than $200 billion in 1990. This has led to a common problem that many organizations face, that is, *too much* education and training *too soon* before it is needed on the job and *too little* support provided *too late* while on the job.

However, integrated performance support systems (IPSSs) will change the way systems are built. Instead of fixing the worker to "fit" the technology, we are now moving to flexible systems that can be adjusted to meet the needs of the knowledge workers of the future. IPSSs align the supply of *knowledge* (gained through education) and *skills* (developed through training) with demand on the job when needed and where needed. IPSSs teach and inform as well as anticipate and coach the workers in order to meet or exceed performance requirements in a given job, recognizing that job requirements in today's environment are constantly changing.

The six key elements of an integrated performance support system are as follows:

Worker who will perform the work.

Advice the worker needs.

Work to be performed.

Skills the worker must have to do the work.

Knowledge the worker requires to do the work.

Tools the worker will use.

Although each component is invaluable in itself, integrating the performance support services with the business system applications offers maximum benefits to the work force and the organization.

The hardware/software platform for the IPSS utilizes some of the latest advances in multimedia presentation and process technologies, including image processing, artificial intelligence (AI), interactive video, wireless mobile networks, portable computers' windows-based delivery environments, "intelligent" user interfaces, interactive instruction, on-line reference tools, and access to technical documentation, to name a few.

In the future the most significant advances will come not from the evolution of new, more sophisticated technology but from the manner in which technology is applied to solve business problems. The IPSS concept is just the beginning, but a new, exciting one.

WHEN TO REENGINEER THE TECHNOLOGY FUNCTION

As information technology (IT) has matured, the IT function has become more like an independent business unit and less like a pure prop of the entire organization, especially with the advent of external technology competitors and a rapid move to client-server environments. Therefore, IT must review itself in the same context as a business, using all four elements of the business integration model described in Figure 19–1. In effect, the technology function is like a business within a business and must maximize its performance by aligning its people, process, and technology with the overall business strategy and stakeholder values.

Chapter Twenty

The Change-Responsive Office

Robert P. Breading
Germaine Hall

T he office of the future has a strong role to play in successful change management. As the nerve center of the modern business organization, the office not only houses but also interconnects a multiplicity of functions heavily used in arriving at change decisions. They range from sustaining the vital information systems that supply executives with up-to-date facts and figures on markets, operations, finances, and such to providing the right environment for managers to interact.

Thus, the change-responsive office must be developed from a combination of the right physical and the right atmospheric elements. Physically, the office of the 1990s must have all of the facilities that are needed to link the computers, fax machines, copiers, and other equipment needed to form the information system and keep the information flowing in timely fashion. These can include appropriate strength in the building structure, the right wiring, and the proper alignment of the equipment, as well as maintaining the equipment's quality. Atmospherically, the office must be configured to promote managerial and employee interaction with its individual offices, meeting rooms, and other components.

These elements can allow the people within the office to respond quickly and flexibly to the seemingly unending series of changes that impact business. The modern office must promote teamwork and communication, not stifle it; must facilitate interaction, not present barriers to it. If properly constructed, the office can be a significant instrument of alignment.

As a creature of the information age, the modern office must, first and foremost, be construed as a component of the smoothly functioning communications and information network. Beyond the physical properties needed to ensure that the network is created and sustained, the office must be influenced by additional concepts and elements, such as the interchangeable building, effective lighting, and proper noise control.

However, the office also can reflect the culture of the firm and how it is organized —decentralized, hierarchical, and so on. The office even may mirror the operational mode of the firm—fast growth, moderate growth or slow growth. These elements may be too subtle for the company itself to handle, but they are well within the expertise of architects and designers.

The growing trend of employee empowerment, through charging individual employees with increased responsibilities and setting up project teams to develop needed solutions, requires an office that promotes interaction to the fullest. The architect or designer in those settings will try to provide flexible work spaces that allow for a variety of tasks.

If the firm is enjoying rapid growth—it is in the *grow* mode—it likely will have an entrepreneurial orientation. Image and office amenities will not serve as incentives to energize workers. Thus, the architectural/design team would think in terms of providing flexible facilities that could be changed to accommodate sporadic, unpredictable, and large increases in staff and equipment needed to support continued growth.

A firm experiencing a moderate growth (earn mode), by contrast, needs a design that permits changes in work situations on a fairly regular basis. New people and new equipment will be brought in with some regularity and work groups and facilities are often relocated.

In the slow-growth situation, the firm must emphasize efficiency and tight cost controls, and these typically include a reduction in human resources. The architect assigned to redesign facilities in the slow-growth firm would think of revising existing areas, consolidating functions, and providing systems for the flow of information between equipment and people.

FACILITATING CHANGE IN THE INFORMATION AGE

Today, the pressures of the Information Age drive and inspire the designs of work spaces. Personal computers, once the domain of support staff and programmers, are becoming a fixture in executive suites across the country. Electronic tools such as the copier, the fax machine, and the terminal are consuming increasing quantities of space. Entirely new kinds of ancillary spaces—more conference rooms to support smaller offices, copy areas and computer tools, teleconferencing spaces and social niches—are serving new kinds of workplace needs. And as the demand for electronic devices and networks grows, buildings are being asked to absorb literally miles of cabling, provide unprecedented numbers of outlets and dedicated lines, and utilize vertical and horizontal ductwork to mitigate the growing emissions of equipment-generated heat.

Other factors being brought to bear on the shape and feel of office buildings and interior spaces include the following:

- The leaner and increasingly team-oriented structure of corporate America.
- The changing face of the American work force, which is growing older, more culturally diverse, better educated, and more task focused.
- The unceasing pressure to streamline workflow, enhance internal communication lines, and encourage new ways of thinking and doing.

For building owners, facility managers, and corporate executives, the lesson is clear: the most effective buildings of our times will incorporate designs, space plans, and support systems to accommodate, encourage, and nurture change at every possible level. A building's skin and structure, primary mechanical and electrical systems, and interior partitions and fittings are all affected by the new mandate. Innovative, far-seeing design is the modern imperative.

BUILDING SYSTEMS IN THE INFORMATION AGE

The ability to respond to change is one aspect of a building suitable for the Information Age office. The design parameters of the 1960s were primarily influenced by organizational efficiencies. In the 1970s the energy crisis led to resource efficiencies. During the 1980s, more attention was paid to the human factors in office design, relating to the more highly educated and skilled Information Age personnel. And in the 1990s and on toward the next century, the office environment will be strongly influenced by the needs of technology, the efforts to organize office workers into ever-changing project teams, and the encouragement and support of organizational changes.

The office building must be able to support many requirements and rapid technological evolutions. Not all buildings will be able to meet these challenges. Office buildings should be reviewed on three major levels, each of which has a life cycle and should be somewhat independent of the others:

1. Shell, skin and structure should be designed to last approximately 50 years.
2. Building services—primarily mechanical, electrical, heating, and ventilating systems—should have life spans of approximately 20 years.
3. Partitions and interior fittings generally should have life spans of 7 to 10 years.

Many existing buildings will not be able to adapt to and support the needs of the advanced electronic office. The extensive renovations necessary to retrofit the edifice will be very costly and would possibly be best expended on new construction. Consider these examples:

- Floor heights must be tall enough to accommodate necessary ducting and cabling. The installed ceiling height should be 10 feet or higher to support the indirect lighting system and diffuse the light evenly to the work surfaces.

- Heating, ventilating, and air-conditioning systems will be zoned in small areas of the floor (200 square feet) to control hot spots generated by concentrated equipment.
- Raised floor areas will be required for computer and support facilities, allowing for easy access to cabling and for power to accommodate future changes and repairs to equipment.
- Ample space for vertical ducting must be provided, with shafts transporting plumbing, ducting, and cabling.
- Enough power to support a high density of electrical outlets will be a necessity.
- Location of furnishings and location and types of window treatments are important details. Window coverings may cover or interfere with supply air diffusers or other heating units near a window.

The challenge for architects, designers, developers, building owners, facilities managers, and corporate executives is to design buildings, spatial layouts, and support systems that allow the organization to function, reorganize, and evolve without costly revisions every time small organizational change is effected. Some suggested approaches follow.

Consider the raw building shell—the unpartitioned, unfinished volume that tenants must subdivide, finish, and furnish before it can be usefully occupied. Not long ago, such shells were designed to house only one or two specific functions; office buildings housed office activities, for example, whereas retail merchants occupied retail strips. Adapting traditional shells to sustain new kinds of activity usually required comprehensive and expensive renovation.

The current requirement for far more flexible shells needs to be met by what can be termed the *interchangeable building,* an adaptable structure that can be modified to hold such diverse functions as the standard office, research facilities, light manufacturing and parts assembly—or to house all of them simultaneously. The key to flexibility in the interchangeable building lies in several architectural and structural features:

- A structure that supports heavy equipment loads.
- Large areas of open spaces that are free of excessive or erratic column spacings.
- A basic building plan that reflects a practical modular concept of four or five feet. Window elements generally establish the modular dimensions and all primary building features—ceiling modules, office dimensions, the placement of partitions—reflect the overall dimensional concept.
- Mechanical and electrical systems that support future power and data requirements and readily facilitate change.

The interchangeable building can contribute to an organization's productivity and profitability. Smart companies are rethinking the way they work and utilize their sophisticated information technology. The U.S. service industry, employing approximately four fifths of the work force, is losing its edge in productivity to rival nations. The Bank of Boston, cited as an example by *Fortune* magazine, consolidated 6 separate operations in 11 different locations into one facility. Computer cables that run across the ceiling in a large open space providing flexibility for changing the layout overnight enabled this consolidation to occur. The idea was to mimic a just-in-time flexible factory. Productivity soared: after two and a half years, with 17 percent fewer employees, the division does 80 percent more business.[1]

Mechanical systems are assuming greater roles in the building that supports information technology equipment. The key is to integrate all systems at the very beginning of the project so plans can be set for maximum needs and future flexibility.

REQUIREMENTS FOR THE CHANGE-ORIENTED OFFICE

Beyond structural systems and facade treatments, interior partitions and furniture systems, architects/designers, and facility managers must expend great effort on developing effective design solutions for what are, in fact, a building's lifelines—information technology, lighting systems, and acoustic treatments.

Information Technology

In tomorrow's office, a computer will be on almost every desk. A corporation's competitive advantage will depend on the speed with which information is generated and analyzed, on international/global communications in seconds, instead of hours or days, and on increasingly sophisticated technological breakthroughs. As management structures adapt and market strategies shift, data will be manipulated by increasingly skilled knowledge workers.

Communications will be the major logistical challenge. Each office will need to accommodate a growing and complex network of voice and data cabling, fiber-optic cables, satellites, local area network (LAN) interconnections between equipment, modems, and fax machines, as well as technologies as yet unheard of.

What Do We Do with the Cables and Wires?

Office spaces of the future will be larger than company managers may think—or wish! There must be more shaft and piping spaces and more conduit spaces for miles and miles of cables and wires. Provisions must be made for both vertical and horizontal ducts and interstitial spaces. Floors will have to be strong enough to support the concentrated loads of computer rooms and equipment, high-density filing, workstations, and personnel.

Recent advances in technology have quickened the rate of change in the office in an unprecedented fashion. A proper response is to design the technological support system to accommodate equipment and its cabling for what may occur in the future, for example, to provide spaces for installing new conduit and provide power/data outlets for flexible arrangements in the spaces. The additional expense at installation will be more than offset as equipment is added and relocated overnight. Many relocations of personnel and their equipment are done on a weekend so that all systems can "go" on Monday morning. Today's corporation cannot afford downtime!

An example of a new technology that might alleviate the space/access problem and help in realignments is fiber-optic data transmission. Fiber-optic cables transmit voice/data information by means of light impulses instead of the electrical impulses of standard cabling. According to Herman Miller's research, a pair of copper wires can transmit twenty-four transmissions at a time; a single pair of fiber-optic cables can transmit 8,000 simultaneous transmissions. Many of the newer buildings—certainly the construction of the future—will be providing empty conduit for fiber-optic utilization. A major disadvantage, however, is that fiber-optic cables are very fragile, and it is very difficult to bend, stretch, or splice the cabling. Future office layouts and workstations must be designed to accommodate long, uninterrupted runs of the cabling, which may result in yet another evolution in office layout and management organization.

As Herman Miller's research paper "Information Age Challenges the Office," states:

> The best .... solutions will incorporate as much flexibility as possible into their design in order to accommodate both today's and tomorrow's technology. They will allow for easy installation and rewiring. They will provide efficient, unobtrusive options for entry and termination. They will supply enough capacity both in terms of space and in terms of amps and circuit types. And they will do all this while still enabling users to adjust and reconfigure their environment readily so that it can continue to support a constantly revolving kaleidoscope of work styles and activities.[2]

Video teleconferencing is becoming a reality in office planning as the costs of equipment and skillful enhancement of the facility are far outweighed by the savings in travel by corporate management and the speed with which information can be disseminated and resolved. The teleconferencing space must be supportive through its lighting, acoustics, building systems, and even its colors, materials, and furnishings.

Enlightened Lighting for the Flexible Office

Providing effective lighting solutions for the flexible electronic office is both an art and a science, with emphasis on visual comfort, aesthetic concerns, and energy conservation. Successful lighting design applications begin with a determination of the user's needs, goals, and objectives and then provide the design solutions that will satisfy the requirements.

Lighting design for the office environment of today and the future must consider the magnitude of technological equipment on hand, the functional tasks performed, and the parameters of the workplace. Lighting design that promotes employee health and comfort supports enhanced performance and productivity.

The proliferation of computer equipment and resulting problems with glare on the VDT screens have made office workers and management increasingly aware of the inadequacies of their lighting. Lighting design must support the relocation of workstations and technological equipment and allow the workstations to be broken down and reconfigured as frequently as necessary for the right worker/team interactions. Lighting must provide a consistent, balanced level of brightness so that the terminal screens do not bounce reflections back into the eyes of the user.

As the open office concept came into use, the preferred lighting systems saw the office softly lighted with light from ambient fixtures on the tops of workstation storage modules bouncing off the ceiling. Although uniform lighting levels were maintained in the initial configuration, dark areas and "hot" spots resulted when the stations were reconfigured. The next generation of fixtures was recessed fluorescent models with acrylic lenses, later updated with parabolic baffles to direct the light down. Although reducing glare on the VDT screens, the overall lighting level often seems too dim for many workers. Variable level task lights thus are utilized at each workstation for the individual worker's use and control.

The trend now is toward the use of indirect lighting to provide the balanced glare-free brightness required for the Information Age office. Indirect pendent fixtures require a higher ceiling—10 feet at minimum—so that light will be more evenly distributed on the ceiling plane before it is bounced into the work area. Maximum office flexibility results. No matter how work teams are broken down and workstations are reconfigured, evenly balanced lighting for the work environment remains. Individually controlled task lights remain. The combination results in a saving of energy costs.

A building's design can incorporate the use of daylight in the interior spaces by such means as skylights, atria, and reflectors to direct natural light deep into the work space. Successful use of daylight requires knowledge and an understanding of climate, site, building orientation, building configuration, and a concern for the persons and their activities in the work space. Daylight is not a stable source of illumination because sunlight's orientation, intensity, and color are constantly in a state of change. Psychologically, however, the effects of natural light on the persons working in the office space are significant.

Lighting systems can also be designed with flexibility and energy conservation in mind for types of activities and use patterns. By installing sensors that are activated by the presence of body heat, motion, or sound, lamps can be dimmed or turned off when the space is not in use. One example of automatic switching can activate the system when workers are present during working hours, turn light levels down while maintenance workers are in the space, and turn fixtures off during the night hours.

Another lighting factor to consider is the demographics of the aging office population. As the worker ages, his or her eye lenses become more opaque and sensitive to glare. The physiological condition affecting the eyes of aging workers is the loss of elasticity of the lens (called presbyopia), which restricts the ability of the eye to focus on close objects. Workers older than forty can use glasses to improve their focusing abilities but require increased lighting levels for reading and detailed tasks.

Acoustics in the Flexible Office Environment

However invisible sound may be, its presence can be a defining force in a place of work. Too much of it can be disruptive, stressful, an impediment to productivity. Too little can stifle—even deaden—the atmosphere.

It was the introduction of workstation cubicles with highly sound-reflective surfaces that focused the architect/designer and the facility manager on the issue of sound. As objectionable variations overtook the work place, two related priorities emerged:

1. To reduce the transmission of unwanted sound, and

2. To maximize the use of sound-absorptive materials throughout the worksite.

The CEO and the planning team should analyze the company's objectives and functions, products and services, and communications patterns before considering acoustical solutions. Despite the documented adverse effects from the wrong noise, when sound is used in a positive way, workers function in a more productive manner.

Two types of acoustics must be dealt with in planning the office. (1) Sound transmission is a problem—it occurs when unwanted sounds are heard in an office or work space. There are methods for determining how much sound will get through various materials and there also are relatively simple steps, such as filling cracks under doors and installing slab-to-slab partitions, that will help to stop sound from escaping a work space. (2) Sound absorption by contrast is not a problem but a key factor in selecting materials for the office, for different materials have different sound absorption capacities. Generally, thick, porous, and soft materials are best for absorbing sound.

Guidelines for Sound Systems

The office environment cannot be so quiet as to seem deathly, nor so noisy that workers are distracted by nearby conversations and operating equipment. A few sample guidelines are useful in developing the flexible and productive Information Age office:

- As much sound as possible should be absorbed by a ceiling system made of materials with high absorption ratings, or noise reduction coefficients (NRC).

- Elements of the HVAC (heating, ventilating, and air-conditioning) system and the lighting system must be considered as to how well they deflect sound.

- Insulation batting in dry-wall partitions and extra layers of gypsum board are good for privacy or sound control.
- Similar areas should be next to one another. Provision should be made of zones for heavy and noisy equipment, with buffer zones such as corridors and closets to separate the zones or areas.
- Sound-absorptive materials or vertical surfaces on the quiet side of the wall should be provided.
- A soft floor covering—such as a carpet—will be a major factor in absorbing sounds as will acoustical panels, screens, and barriers.
- Room shapes that reflect or focus sounds, such as vaulted corridors and circular rooms, should be avoided.
- Hollow-core doors transmit more sound than solid-core doors. The tightness of the closure and use of sealers at the sill also moderate sound.
- Single pane windows can be replaced with double panes if too much noise is generated on the exterior of the space. Window closures can be tightened by caulking compounds.
- Space above the ceiling is often a transmitter of sounds from one space to another. Sound-absorbing or sound-blocking blankets or baffles can be used in some cases.
- A background sound-making system can be installed to cover residual sounds not absorbed by ceilings, floors, and partitioning.

Providing the optimum acoustical system—which encompasses all of the elements discussed—can be very costly and perhaps not totally necessary. In the modern office, levels of privacy and confidentiality are required, so planning the executive offices and conference facilities for maximum acoustical privacy should be a prime objective. Remaining offices need not have such high levels of acoustical privacy for typical tasks; conference rooms can be used when meetings are confidential. Open plan spaces will be covered by thoughtful planning of layout, acoustical panels, and masking sound to cover the noise of voices and equipment.

FUTURE DIRECTION

Futurist Marvin Cetron provides several insights into the office of the year 2000 in Herman Miller's research summary "An Introduction to Project Team Management." Cetron predicts that by the beginning of the next millennium information-based knowledge will be the "valued commodity." Each organizational worker will become more and more specialized in a narrower field of expertise. Project teams will be groups of "experts" in various areas, all working together to more quickly produce the solutions that will become their business's comptetive advantage. An important factor for those specialists involved in office planning will be the challenge of designing and providing flexible and responsive office environments to support the project team as the members work together on specific tasks, break apart, and reconfigure for the next project or task.[3]

There may be less of a need for the individual office or workstation as we now know it. Instead, a variety of team settings and options will be planned and designed to accommodate a multitude of functions: conferences, informal meeting spaces, bullpen settings for individual work areas, and facilitating communication between team members. A loose framework of team work spaces will be provided so that work surfaces, chairs, and equipment can be easily rearranged by project teams as they break up and reassemble for new assignments. And offices will be designed for unprecedented flexibility.

The results of basic research studies support the philosophy that office workers' productive output can increase as much as 15% when the staff works in an *ideal environment*—one that supports their functional tasks and communications interrelationships. The best of office designs will provide a variety of activity settings, each of which will provide a setting for limited activities rather than meeting all needs.

Identical workstations will be designed for the staff. For personnel relocations—and some people may be reassigned every few months—the staff member need only have his or her telephone number and data connections reassigned. Settlement into the new workstation will be facilitated by the fact that all file pedestals and storage units will be located in the same positions as the former stations. The future workstation may become a smaller unit—large enough to house only the technological equipment supporting the tasks and to provide an area for writing reports, making phone calls, and filing information.

Small rooms or areas will be provided for private conversations or when a project requires intense concentration. Larger open areas will be for team activities, shared tasks, and staff intercommunications.

Private offices will not disappear, but they will be components of the flexi-office. They also will be identical modules that will be used by management to serve as conference, team meeting, or support spaces when not assigned to executives. Identically sized modules with standard furnishings also will allow executive level personnel to relocate easily to another office or department and quickly adjust to the new space.

Furnishings will support the technological equipment and be adaptable to future additions and changes. As with the individual staff workstations, identical furniture components will be used and each executive can rearrange components to suit his or her particular needs or work style. Additional private offices will be provided for future expansion or as shared stations for staff members in the office less than 40 hours a week.

Flextime/Job Sharing: The At-Home Office

Increasing diversity in the workplace also will affect the changing office and will require greater emphasis on the human factors in the work environments. Furnishings are being designed for smaller-scale office spaces and people. Designers are beginning to incorporate more people-oriented features such as flexible heights of work surfaces and keyboards that support wrists and arms to prevent injuries. High technology is advancing to voice-activated computers that will type words and perform functions in response to verbal commands as another way of preventing injuries.

Because of the information technology in the home office, staff members might come in only a few hours each week, performing their functions and communicating with co-workers on their PCs at home. Or they may commute to a satellite office minutes away from home, saving time and commuting expense and, as a result, increasing their productivity.

As the work force expands and diversifies, the physical appearance of the office space probably will not change radically from what we know today. Behind the furnishings and layout, however, will be a multitude of sophisticated technological systems—power/data transmission systems, improved lighting and acoustics solutions, and energy conservation solutions. These systems innovations will more effectively supplement existing planning concepts and equipment.

Consideration must be given to factors of health, safety and well-being. Not only must the work place be accessible to all visitors and staff but also the interior materials must be selected with regard to nontoxicity and flammability standards and codes. The "sick building syndrome" is very much a concern of the work staff. Inadequate air flow and building odors not only cause illness but also consume great amounts of complaint and discussion time, taking efforts away from productive output.

MANAGEMENT CULTURE AND THE CHANGING OFFICE

As we have been developing the concept that the physical office environment evolves and adapts to changes in philosophies and technology, the cultural environment also has evolved and adapted. The traditional approach operated with the master-apprentice relationship and task assignments that conformed with prevailing customs. As Western culture has developed into an ever-more industrialized society, business organizations have become concerned with more impersonal tasks and with objectives to which all members are to be equally committed if success is to be achieved.

The organization head—whether as in the past a king or chieftain or today as a president or chairperson—plays a major role in determining the firm's cultural values. His or her definition of the hierarchy of the business and the status levels of management and workers determines how the office planning concept will be developed. As an example, the firm with heavy emphasis on hierarchy will require a floor or area for executive offices and conference facilities. Additional amenities reflecting the executives' enhanced status also may be desired.

An organization with a value system emphasizing a less formal and a more functional work environment might prefer locating executive and management offices in the same places where lower-level workers labor. Not only are spatial considerations affected in those two examples but also the working relationships of management and their workers.

Corporate culture must adjust to change, and change managers must realize that their organizations must respond to developing technologies and management philosophies. For any change to be significant in the development of the firm, the decisions have to derive from and be supported by top management. One way that management communicates its values to employees is through architecture and design. Decisions on office planning and responsiveness to staff needs will reflect how management ultimately regards the person working with them. These values and attitudes are quickly picked up by the staff, and their satisfaction or dissatisfaction with the environment and working conditions most certainly will be reflected in their level of productivity.

There are two main attitudes pertaining to the culture of an organization: dictatorial/authoritarian and democratic/participative. Today's values and managerial philosophies lean toward participation group-centered management. The evolution of office furnishings, for example, provides for project work teams, the sharing of information, and participation in decision making. Research data indicate, however, that managerial personnel in the United States have a greater tendency to share information with their underlings than to elicit participative decisions.

According to the research data of Haire, Ghiselle, and Porter, critical perceptions are what the manager feels is appropriate and inappropriate behavior in his or her role as a manager and the values of those persons considering management as a career. The research study reviewed data on cultural patterns that affected the role of managers in 11 countries. It found that there was an overall similarity in what managerial personnel considered important needs to be satisfied in their careers and that these objectives were relatively unaffected by their international cultural environments. This data could also be applied to workers in different firms with their differing cultural climates. The five types of psychological needs to be satisfied by both managers and staff as determined by Maslow's Hierarchy are these:

- *Basic Needs*: Relating to security or the manager's/worker's feeling of safety in a particular position or situation.
- *Social Needs*: Relating to the need for developing friendships and for giving and receiving help from others.
- *Esteem Needs*: Relating to the need for self-esteem and the opportunity for esteem to be received from co-workers.
- *Autonomy Needs*: Relating to the degree of authority connected with a position in a firm and the opportunities available for independent thought and action.
- *Self-Actualization Needs*: Relating to feelings of self-fulfillment and accomplishment and opportunities afforded for personal growth.

As is generally well known, once basic levels of needs are satisfied, the manager/worker seeks the next higher level. The needs of both managers and staff members arise from human nature and do not vary from culture to culture or from one organization to another. The staff's needs do not vary, but their satisfactions do, according to the situations encountered in the work environment. Wages or salary, benefits, and working conditions do not motivate staff members to contribute their best efforts; they only upset workers and destabilize organizations if they are considered inadequate. Maslow's list of needs are the true motivators. Recognition and opportunities for achievement and increasing levels of responsibility are requirements of the work involved and of the corporate culture and philosophy.

We are probably at a critical turning point as we approach the 21st century. As the international scene becomes more interrelated and interdependent, nations and corporations will need to shift from competition to increasing global cooperation. Within the office environment as well, managerial staff and their co-workers will need to shift their values from internal competition to teamwork and cooperative interrelationships.

Productivity will become the rallying cry of the future. The team of architect/planner and corporate management will need to determine designs for the organization that will support the work force in its quest to perform tasks efficiently. Planning solutions must also be able to satisfy the workers' psychological needs within the scope of their job responsibilities.

To maintain a competitive position in the marketplace, business cultures must provide both the environment and the opportunities that will encourage their personnel to remain. The environment is—and will continue to be—a key element in attracting and retaining high-caliber staff. Understanding one's role and responsibility in the organization takes time, as does performing assigned tasks with confidence and ability. Constant turnover in personnel interferes with the progress in achieving objectives and causes heavy costs in interviewing and hiring replacements, training new hires, and bringing them up to peak productive levels.

WHAT CAN THE EXECUTIVE DO TO ACHIEVE THE OPTIMAL OFFICE?

We have discussed several important elements in planning an office environment that will both satisfy the needs for today's tasks and provide flexibility to meet the needs of future change. What are the factors to be considered in establishing the planning procedures and arriving at workable decisions?

Initial Decision to Plan for Change

The decision generally arises from a change in the business situation of an organization and its need simultaneously to align its facilities, equipment and technologies, and people with a new strategy for market competitiveness. A continual audit of the existing workplace against current and future needs is a mandatory change management process.

Selecting the Architect/Planner

There are three key factors that the executive should weigh in selecting a design team:

1. *Compatibility*. Find someone that you can work with and that you like. The architect/planner will be empowered to make important and costly recommendations—the CEO must feel that the person is trustworthy as well as competent. If your organization is hiring a large design firm, make sure that you are comfortable with the individual who is working with you. If a small firm is to be hired, verify that the managing partner will be involved in design as well as direct supervision of staff.

2. *Technical Expertise*. The architect/planner must have recognized technical expertise in the areas necessary to perform the work that your organization needs. The architect does not need 10 years or more experience in the specialty nor is it necessary that he or she have millions of square feet of completed projects in a résumé. The architect/planner simply must have the expertise to provide the spaces, facilities, and systems that will solve your special problems.

3. *Proficient Contract Documentation*. The CEO should select a professional design team with demonstrated technical expertise in producing documents that the contractor can work with in an efficient fashion. These are contract documents that are highly buildable and provide the type of construction, materials, and systems that fit your requirements and your budget. The architect must be knowledgeable about the construction industry and understand how the project will be managed and constructed.

Establishing Project Guidelines

• Final budgets should be developed from the needs of the project, and include in the initial planning stages the quality of the interior environment and the flexible furnishings to support the worker while performing the tasks.

• Empowered employee representatives should be a part of the project team. Being involved and assisting in decisions on their work spaces and furnishings will result in their support of the completed project. Staff involvement will fulfill the opportunity to be meaningful contributors to the organization's objectives.

• Employee surveys are important techniques that can be used to collect data useful in designing facilities.

• Emphasis should be on an interior environment that promotes team work spaces and social interaction spaces and that provides private areas for concentration and confidentiality as well.

The office environment that does not allow for change invites its own obsolescence. The office environment that does not support and encourage the work force through its concern with the human factors of design and participative management philosophies diverts energies from productive endeavors. The firm's competitive advantage—as well as its survival—may be at stake!

NOTES

1. T. A. Stewart, "U. S. Productivity: First but Fading," Fortune, October 19, 1992, p. 52.
2. Herman Miller Inc., Research Summaries, Information Age Challenges the Office (Zeeland, MI: Herman Miller Inc., 1990), p. 16.
3. Herman Miller Inc., Research Summaries, An Introduction to Project Team Management (Zeeland, MI: Herman Miller Inc., 1989), p. 9.

FURTHER READING

Haberstroh, C. J. "Evolving Organizations." In *Culture & Management: Text and Readings in Comparative Management,* ed. R. A. Webber. Homewood, IL: Richard D. Irwin, 1969.

Haire, M., E. E. Ghiselle, and L.W. Porter. "Cultural Patterns in the Role of the Manager." In *Culture & Management: Text and Readings in Comparative Management.* ed. R. A. Webber. Homewood, IL: Richard D. Irwin, 1969.

Harris, D. A., A. E. Palmer, M. S. Lewis, R. Gerdes, D. C. Munson, and G. Meckler. *Planning and Designing the Office Environment.* New York: Van Nostrand Reinhold, 1981.

Herman Miller Inc., *Research Summaries.* Zeeland, MI: Herman Miller Inc.; 1990: *Aging Workers in the Office;* 1990: *Beyond Four Walls and a Door;* 1990: *Facilities for Project Teams;* 1990: *Information Age Challenges the Office;* 1989: *An Introduction to Project Team Management;* 1989: *Lean in the Middle: The Changing Role of Middle Managers;* 1989: *The Office Personalized: The Home of the Soul.*

Kleeman, W. B., Jr. *Interior Design of the Electronic Office: The Comfort and Productivity Payoff.* New York: Van Nostrand Reinhold, 1991.

Oxford Dictionary of Quotations, 2nd ed., London: Oxford University Press, 1953.

Palmer, A. E., and S. M. Lewis. *Planning the Office Landscape.* New York: McGraw-Hill, 1977.

Pulgram, W. L., and R. E. Stones. *Designing the Automated Office.* New York: Whitney Library of Design, 1984.

Roth, L. M. *A Concise History of American Architecture.* New York: Harper & Row, 1979.

Saphier, M. *Office Planning and Design.* New York: McGraw-Hill, 1968.

Schwartz, B. "Committing to Energy Efficiency," *Interiors.* July 1992. Vol. CLI, Pg. 21.

Steelcase Inc., *Office Environment Reports.* Grand Rapids, MI: Steelcase/Louis Harris & Associated, Inc.; 1987: The Office Environment Index (1987 Summary Report); 1988: The Office Environment Index (1988 Summary Report); 1989: The Office Environment Index (1989 Summary Report); 1991: Worldwide Office Environment Index (Summary Report).

Steelcase, Inc., *The Healthy Office: Neocon 23 Discussion Summaries*. Grand Rapids: MI: Steelcase, Inc.; 1990.

Steffy, G. B. *Architectural Lighting Design*. New York: Van Nostrand Reinhold, 1990.

Veneklasen, W. D., and P. T. Cornell. *The Human Component in the Healthy Office*. Grand Rapids, MI: Steelcase, Inc., 1991.

Weisbard, M. *Productive Workplaces/Organizing and Managing for Dignity: Meaning and Community*. San Francisco: Jossey-Bass Publishers, 1987.

Williams, C., D. Armstrong, and C. Malcolm. *The Negotiable Environment*. Ann Arbor, MI: Facility Management Institute, 1985.

Structure of *The Change Management Handbook*

Section 3
The Gears of Change

3A Strategy
9. Game Plan for the Next Dynamic
10. The Strategic Connection: Mission, Strategy, and Values
11. Structuring the Change Initiative
12. Mergers and Restructurings: Aces in the Hole
13. Midcourse Corrections

3B Operations
14. A Bad Structure Can Be Fatal
15. An Introduction to Supply-Chain Management
16. Integrated Logistics and Supply-Chain Management
17. Only the Best: How Quality Systems Govern Change
18. Aligning Operations with Change Strategies: The Operations Blueprint
19. Information Technologies to Manage the Next Dynamic
20. The Change-Responsive Office

3C Culture
21. The Next Generation of Fire Walkers
22. The Right Stuff for the Next Dynamic
23. Critical Elements of Organizational Culture Change
24. Cultural Change and Corporate Strategy
25. Making Culture Change Happen
26. The People Factor
27. The Key to Corporate Survival: Change Begins and Ends with People
28. Human Resource Planning and Change
29. The Ethics of Change

3D Compensation
30. Aligning Business and Pay Strategy
31. Rewards for Executing Change
32. Compensation as a Change Stimulus
33. A Nimble Compensation System for Managing Change
34. Using Executive Compensation to Promote Change

Section 2
Market Change Triggers

5. Market Dynamics: Who's on Top?
6. Playing Off the Power Base: Importance of Market Positioning
7. Pile Drivers of Change
8. Measuring Change and Changing Measures

Section 1
The Change Management Process

1. Change Management
2. The History of Business Change
3. Managing Strategic Alignment
4. Driving Systemic Change

P A R T

C

CULTURE

A change-oriented culture is the strongest glue in melding strategy to operations—the ideas and the actions—when a company must shift gears. This is true whether the company is undergoing a midcourse correction, creating the change on its own initiative, or, in the purest manifestation of change-oriented culture, phasing in the adjustments in fairly small and highly palatable increments. Shapers of change-oriented environments must start with the premise that most people—that is, change resistors—don't welcome adjustments in the status quo, whether they are good or bad.

The solution is coming up with the cultural environment that makes change a perennially acceptable and inevitable norm. That environment has to start at the top. It must begin with a CEO who not only delivers the message of change but also lives, breathes, and acts it (Conner, Chapter 21). The CEO must be the primary agent of change, the chief alignment officer—a position requiring such nimbleness, agility, and quick wittedness that he or she is a true fire walker.

A change-driven CEO must next assemble the team that will work with him or her to make the vision of change a reality. The team should mirror the CEO's penchant for proper change—that is, the right stuff to move successfully into the future (Spencer, Chapter 22). Of course having them arrayed across a loose and flexible organization is helpful. When the generals and the troops are moving in the same direction and at the same pace, cultural change to support strategic change can be clicked into place (Laud, Chapter 24).

A focus on the employees is critical, an internal version of keeping focused on the market in the external context. Moreover, this internal policing is necessary to ensure that lower and middle management and the population on the shop floor are as customer-oriented as the people at the top claim they are. The complete culture for change and customer alignment will ensure that the organization constitutes a committed supporting cast—or bench strength (Bowman, Chapter 26); that management has instilled the idea of change in all parts of the organization because it is really the people closest to the field who form the tightest bonds with customers (Smye and Cooke); and that not only are the people armed with the message of change but also they are in the right jobs to put their change skills to optimum use (Ulrich, Chapter 28).

And the primary connecting factor for the entire cultural mindset may very well be the ethics and values that accompany the message of change to managers and employees at all levels (Darcy, Chapter 29). In an increasingly competitive era, a firm's commitment to operating honestly and ethically may very well be a competitive edge, especially if it is fortified by quality products, attractive pricing, and premier service. At a time when customers are themselves beset by the forces of change, they have no time to get into disputes with their suppliers. Ethics and superior performance may be synonymous.

Chapter Twenty-One

The Next Generation of Fire Walkers

Daryl R. Conner

T he fire walker's eyes are focused on a specific point, straight ahead and slightly above his normal line of vision. His concentration is so intense that the noise of the spectators around him and the chilly night air have disappeared from his awareness. His bare feet are almost lost in the thick grass as he stands motionless, like a scarecrow in an open field.

Then, as he slowly and deliberately leans his body forward, he takes one small step and then another, until he gains the precise momentum he desires. Like an airplane just before leaving the runway, he reaches that certain point where aborting the effort is no longer an option. At this moment, his appointed task keeps him firmly on the ground instead of soaring into the air, and he walks, not runs, down a long bed of red-hot coals. He exits at the other end, not only unhurt but also exhilarated by the experience.

The first question that comes to a spectator's mind is, "How does he do that?" But long before the question is answered, a more compelling issue surfaces: "Why would he do it?" Why would an apparently sane person willingly attempt what appears to be a nearly impossible, painful, and thankless task?

People often have the same reaction when they view the chief executive's role in the modern, perennially challenged corporation. To many spectators, the task appears nearly impossible, painful, and thankless. Yet these same people would agree that, unless this leadership role is performed well, an organization has little hope of surviving the competitive demands of today's marketplace. Customers, shareholders, and employees are not sure how successful CEOs work their magic, or even why they desire the role with all of its headaches, but nearly everyone agrees that the job must be done, and done well.

Like the samurai of feudal Japan, CEO fire walkers are considered a special breed. They possess certain inherent traits that, in combination with the lessons they have learned at key points in their lives, have resulted in both conscious and unconscious skills on which they rely to succeed.

Not all who aspire to be fire walkers possess the characteristics and the discipline to do so. Some who think of themselves as capable never find a bed of coals on which to walk. Either they are never given the opportunity to head an existing organization or they are unable to build their own organization to lead. Other would-be fire walkers take their turns standing at the edge of the coals but freeze when it is time to lean forward into the task. Then there are those who have the motivation and courage to face the heat but halfway through the challenge find themselves lacking certain technical, managerial, or political skills to complete the task. In such situations, the intense heat of the coals is unforgiving. Finally, there are those who endure the experience, but fail at the mission. They complete their walks, but during the process mere survival becomes the goal, and they, along with their organizations, finish maimed and depleted.

Most of the people who seek the role of CEO fall into one of the preceding characterizations. In the face of these odds, however, there is evidence that certain men and women are true fire walkers. These are the people who willingly enter the bed of coals and not only complete their tenure, alive and exhilarated from the experience but also leave a legacy in the form of a healthy, prosperous organization.

Despite the evidence, for many people the question remains: "Do they really exist, or are fire walkers only mythical figures we contrive to satisfy our hunger for leadership?"

When the strengths we admire are manifested by only a few people, it is natural to wonder if the presence of such people is fact or fiction. After nearly 20 years of observing organizations throughout the world to determine what factors distinguish those who succeed from those who fail during major change, I can, with confidence, declare that fire walkers really do exist.

Although I can confirm their existence, I also must report that true fire walkers are a rare breed. As the world has become more complex, the ante has gone up for those who wish to lead. The breed is not extinct, but it is an endangered species.

Here lies the critical problem: Though the number of true fire walkers has never been large, the need for leaders of this caliber has accelerated proportionate to the escalating demands now being placed on organizations. Never in human history has so much changed so fast and with such dramatic implications. Nowhere are these implications of change more evident than in the workplace and with the executives, managers, supervisors, and workers striving to compete. Marketplace volatility of this magnitude can be confronted successfully only with strong leadership displayed at every level of management, but particularly at the CEO level. Yet as the demand for such leadership has increased, the number of people prepared to manifest the fire walker's profile does not meet the demand.

To address this leadership deficit, we must not only correctly position the men and women who already possess the necessary strengths to lead in uncertain times but also learn how to nurture and develop these traits in those who will lead in the future.

The next generation of fire walkers must be identified now and primed for the time when it is their turn to stand poised at the edge of their organization's bed of coals.

There are many talents that must be fostered in order for the next generation of CEOs to be prepared for their tasks, but none is more important than the ability to manage others successfully at the speed of change.

THE SPEED OF CHANGE

Each of us is designed by nature to move through life most effectively and efficiently at a unique pace that will allow us to absorb the major changes we face. I refer to this as our *speed of change*. When we assimilate less change than our optimum speed will allow, we fail to live up to our potential. When we attempt to assimilate more than our optimum speed will permit, complications arise.

Regardless of age, position, wealth, status, motive or desire, no individual or organization can adequately absorb life's inevitable transitions any faster than his or her own speed of change will allow. People can face an unlimited amount of change, but when their absorption thresholds are exceeded, they begin to display signs of dysfunction, such as fatigue, emotional burnout, inefficiency, sickness, and drug abuse, among other problems. People whose lives are challenging but productive and healthy typically remain within the bounds of their individual and collective speeds of change.

There is a basic change axiom by which humankind operates, regardless of whether we are conscious of it. The axiom is, our lives are most effective and efficient when functioning at a speed that allows us to assimilate the changes we face appropriately. This is not the velocity at which our individual and organizational environments are changing, or the speed at which we wish to change, but the pace at which we can recover from disrupted expectations with a minimum of dysfunctional behavior.

As the world grows more complex, the pressures mount for the CEO to manage more change at increasing speeds. To do this at the fire walker's proficiency level, the successful CEO must have a working understanding of how to reach his or her organization's optimum speed of transition.

FUTURE SHOCK IS HERE

In the 1960s, social observer and author Alvin Toffler was the first to popularize the term *future shock*, referring to the potentially debilitating effects of major change. After years of observing organizations suffering from these problems, I define future shock as *the point at which humans can no longer assimilate change without displaying dysfunctional behavior.* Let's focus on the last part of this definition: *without displaying dysfunctional behavior.* People don't stop changing when they have entered future shock; they just become less and less effective, both on the job and in their personal lives.

Dysfunctional behavior in the workplace is any behavior or feeling that diverts resources away from meeting productivity and quality standards. Today, we are seeing more signs of future shock and the attendant dysfunctional behavior than ever before. These are a clear indication that people are confronted with more change than they can realistically absorb.

There are many symptoms that reflect varying degrees of dysfunctional behavior, ranging from the inconsequential to the extreme. The onset of future shock, and the accompanying low levels of dysfunction, may be signified by these signs:

- Brief irritation, which may divert attention from work.
- Poor communication and reduced trust.
- Reduced honesty and directness.
- Defensive and blameful behavior.
- Reduced propensity for risk taking.
- Poor decision making.
- Increased conflict with fellow workers.
- Decreased team effectiveness.
- Inappropriate outbursts at the workplace.
- Venting of job frustration at home.

As the seriousness of the dysfunctional behavior progresses, the following additional psychological and physical symptoms may manifest themselves within the individual:

- Feelings of victimization and disempowerment.
- Lower morale.
- Headaches.
- Stomach pains.
- Chronic absenteeism.
- Apathy or noncompliance behavior.
- Feelings of resignation.

An extremely high degree of future shock may result in any of a number of severe dysfunctional reactions:

- Destructive behavior.
- Overt blocking of company tasks or procedures.
- Covert undermining of organizational leadership.
- Active promotion of a negative attitude in others.
- Strike.
- Sabotage.
- Chronic depression.

- Substance abuse or other addictive behaviors.
- Physical or psychological breakdowns.
- Family abuse.
- Suicide.

SATURATED SPONGES

The individual experiencing future shock is like a saturated sponge. Although he or she is already soaked, someone walks in with another 2-gallon pitcher of major change and pours it on. In organizations around the world, change typically is poured onto the physically and emotionally saturated sponges of the work force, and management watches helplessly as the intended objectives run down the drain.

Many men and women spend their entire careers struggling to reach the CEO position, only to be disillusioned. Some comments mirror the disenchantment: "I've worked my way to the top; I am making the right decisions and pushing the right strategic buttons, but the lights are not coming on down in my company. There seems to be a short in the circuitry somewhere. Either the lights don't come on at all when I push the buttons, they blink off and on, or they light up only while I'm watching."

When you make the right decisions but the lights don't come on, you may be dealing with people who are overwhelmed with change. A saturated sponge can no more absorb spring water than it can sewage; hence, the correctness of ideas, or change objectives, do not alone ensure effective response. Across every industry we have studied, CEOs are frustrated because they cannot successfully implement their decisions on time and within budget.

Senior officers can no longer flip a switch and pour on the changes. The "spray-and-pray" approach—announcing a major change and *hoping* that it will take hold—is out of date and insufficient. Instead, leaders must carefully orchestrate the flow of change, guiding their actions by asking such questions as: Where will this change have its greatest impact and at what speed? Should we proceed? Who is going to absorb it first? How do I prepare that part of the organization for what will happen?

RESILIENCE IS THE KEY

By understanding how certain factors affect the assimilation of change, we can increase the likelihood of achieving the optimum speed of change for ourselves and others. The single most important factor necessary for individuals to increase their speed of change is *human resilience*. Resilience is the ability to absorb high levels of disruptive change while displaying minimal dysfunctional behavior.

Resilient individuals and organizations experience the same stresses and challenges as other people when confronting the crises associated with change. However, they typically regain their equilibrium faster, maintain a higher level of quality and productivity in their work, preserve physical and emotional health, and achieve more of their objectives than people who experience future shock. In fact, when resilient people confront the ambiguity, anxiety, and loss of control that accompany major change, they tend to grow stronger from their experiences rather than feel depleted by them.

The pliability that resilient people demonstrate and the nimbleness and heartiness that resilient people display in the face of adversity reveal an elasticity that allows them to remain relatively calm in unstable environments. For this reason, they often avoid the dysfunctions of future shock.

Every person, group, and organization has a unique capacity to absorb change. To demonstrate, this capacity can be represented by the concept of *assimilation points*. For illustration purposes, imagine that a person has 600 assimilation points to spend for absorbing all of the changes that will take place in his or her life over the next year. During the year, the number of assimilation points expended on a given change depends on the degree to which change and its implications are matched by what was expected. Major disruptions in expectations will cost many points, whereas minor adjustments cost fewer points.

There are two things resilient people do that appear to reduce their susceptibility to dysfunctional behavior during change:

They increase the number of assimilation points they have available, thus raising their future shock threshold.

They minimize the number of assimilation points needed for the successful implementation of any single change.

Increasing Available Assimilation Points

The resilient person will engage in activity that increases his or her ability to absorb change, thus moving the individual's threshold from 600 points to a higher level, perhaps 800, 1,000, 1,500, and even beyond. Just as continuous quality improvement never stops, resilient people never can be satisfied with a static assimilation capacity; they continually strive to increase their capacity for change. In addition, fire-walking CEOs look for ways to increase the resilience of their employees by teaching them the dynamics of change and the tactics by which they can manage the process. In this way, they actually increase the threshold at which the organization faces the symptoms of future shock.

Decreasing Assimilation Points Used

Resilient people also minimize the number of assimilation points required to execute change. Although a certain number of points are necessary to absorb the implications of any major change, an equal or greater number often are consumed because of such things as ignorance of how people change, inadequate planning, inept organizational communications, and mismanaged resistance. Awareness of these important factors and thorough preparation for the introduction of change allow resilient CEOs to minimize unnecessary consumption of assimilation points—both for themselves and for others in their organizations.

FIGURE 21–1

The Competitive Advantage of Resilience

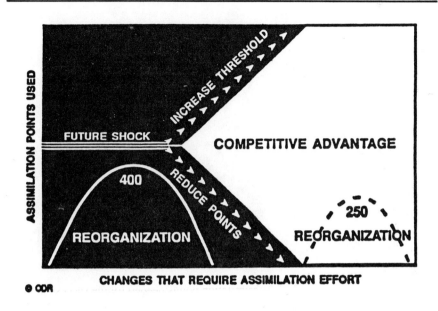

Increasing the number of available assimilation points while simultaneously reducing the number expended on any single change project thwarts the onset of future shock to yield a dramatic competitive advantage: the resilience to adapt continuously to shifting circumstances (see Figure 21–1).

TWO ORIENTATIONS TO CHANGE

Resilience is not a characteristic that either does or does not occur in individuals. Resilience is a combination of traits that are manifested to various degrees in different people. To understand the varying degrees of resilience that may be demonstrated, it is helpful to view people as having a preference toward one of two orientations to change.

Change produces a crisis when it significantly disrupts expectations about important issues or events. It is interesting to note that the Chinese express the concept of crisis with two separate symbols (shown in Figure 21–2). The top character represents potential danger, the lower one conveys hidden opportunity. By combining these two symbols, the Chinese seem to be characterizing change as a paradox.

In observing how people respond to the stress produced by the crisis of change, my research found two common orientations, each with a particular perspective on the

FIGURE 21–2

crises induced by change. Whereas one tends to see primarily dangerous implications, the other typically focuses on the promise of new opportunities. Let's use the Chinese symbols as reference points in describing the orientation of two very different groups of CEOs.

Danger-Oriented CEOs

Danger-oriented, or Type-D, CEOs view the crisis of change as threatening and generally feel victimized by it. I found that such people usually lack an overarching sense of purpose or vision for their lives and, therefore, often find it difficult to reorient themselves when unanticipated changes disrupt their expectations.

They tend to interpret life in binary and sequential terms and believe that change should progress in a logical and orderly fashion. Since the world rarely offers major change in such a simple package, a Type-D person's tolerance for ambiguity usually is not fully developed. For them, change is an unnatural, unnecessary, and unpleasant departure from the comforting stability of the status quo.

During turbulent periods, danger-oriented people typically feel insecure about themselves and their ability to manage uncertainty. They are unaware of the dynamics of human change, often feeling the need to defend themselves against what appear to be mysterious, random, emotional reactions that they and others sometimes have when facing disruption. They also are often reluctant to acknowledge the need for change. Some of the most common defense mechanisms used are these:

- Denial—"I don't see anything that would suggest the need for an alteration in our planned course."
- Distortion—"Well, the information does not look that bad to me."
- Delusion—"All this global competition is nothing but hot air. We don't have to worry; our markets are secure."

When faced with change, Type-D CEOs generally respond in reactive rather than proactive fashion. They tend to deny the forces of change in themselves and others as long as possible. When a major change no longer can be ignored, they have too little time to plan appropriate response strategies. Since the need to change invariably is acknowledged late, they are left with only knee-jerk reactions to defend themselves, their families, organizations, industries, or countries.

Such last-minute reactions to change are typically ineffective. Even worse, I believe that Type-D personalities would be only slightly more effective if they took the time to plan for change. They simply lack the knowledge and skill to anticipate the need for change accurately, diagnose the potential resistance problems, design a plan of action, and manage the implementation process.

To avoid their fears of change and lack of knowledge about what to do, Type-D persons often react to significant disruptions in their expectations by throwing up smoke screens. For example, they sometimes interpret unexpected change as resulting from personal vendettas or conspiracies with statements like "The government is out to get us." At other times they may try to shift the focus of attention to someone else, with something like "If only Jones had done his job, we wouldn't be in this mess."

Regardless of the mechanisms used, Type-D people often blame and attack someone else or something else for the problems caused by change. This behavior not only inhibits problem solving and demoralizes others but also is counterproductive. The energy that should be devoted to addressing the change instead is diverted to face-saving activities, usually resulting in increased anxiety and hostility.

In the past, the rate of change was of a magnitude that could better accommodate Type-D CEOs. Changes were more isolated and evolutionary in nature. Thus, the organizational impact was less disruptive and more manageable. In today's chaotic market environment, Type-Ds, with increasing frequency, experience gaping holes in their defenses against the stress, ambiguity, conflict, and disequilibrium brought on by change.

As the reality of change crashes in on them, they feel more and more overwhelmed and incapable in a world they perceive as unpredictable, confusing, and contradictory. They see that their responses to events and issues are no longer adequate. They futilely apply all the skills and knowledge that may have brought them success in the past but that now may tend to yield failure, humiliation, and defeat.

A Type-D response to organizational transition has less to do with a person's age than with issues such as his or her perspective on change or the resources available to assimilate change. Because the need to train people in change tactics and resilience strategies is not recognized as part of a required core curriculum by most public schools, colleges, graduate schools or management-training programs, many young people today demonstrate Type-D characteristics. Even more problematic is that most parents place a greater emphasis on competitive sports than on cultivating the resilience capabilities of their children. Educational agendas and parental priorities become increasingly important when evaluating the prospects of developing a new generation of fire walkers.

The Type-D orientation toward change is not limited to individuals. Entire organizations can display a danger orientation, which may be embedded in the corporate culture. This sort of organizational mind-set can dramatically inhibit strategic change initiatives and limit an organization's ability to manage transitions at its optimum speed of change.

Opportunity-Oriented CEOs

The opportunity-oriented, or Type-O, response to the crisis of change is dramatically different. Although recognizing the dangers, these people view change as a potential advantage to be exploited, rather than a problem to be avoided.

Type-O CEOs usually have a strong life vision that serves as a source of meaning and as a beacon guiding them through the turmoil and adversity of change. When the unanticipated throws them off course, they are able to regain their bearings by realigning their senses of purpose. Whatever its manifestations, this vision functions as a compass that allows the Type-O to navigate through any ambiguities that may arise as he or she strives to stay on a charted course.

Type-O CEOs view change, even major unanticipated change, as a natural part of human experience. Type-D CEOs develop expectations devoid of significant change and, therefore, they suffer a shock when realities suddenly shift. The Type-O group is spared some of the shock's intensity because change does not shatter their presumptions. They are far more likely to see the rationale that so often lies below the surface of what appears to be a situation filled with contradiction.

The Type-O ability to respond in a constructive and positive way to change does not occur because of any special immunity to the problems associated with change. When faced with disruptive change, they are as vulnerable to the discomforts of confusion, anxiety, and stress as Type-D people. But Type-O people feel less of a need to defend themselves against such feelings. The main difference between the two groups is not the feelings of discomfort generated by change, but their reactions to these feelings.

Type-O people are quicker to determine that a change is inevitable, necessary, or advantageous. Therefore, they engage their coping mechanisms faster when old frames of reference no longer appear relevant and move to a problem-solving mode. They incorporate what they have learned from the disruption into new frames of reference that lead them to a fresh understanding of the situation.

A salient characteristic of Type-O people is their tendency to "compartmentalize" the stress caused by disruptions and, in doing so, they are able to contain the strain of change they may be feeling in one area of their lives and prevent it from causing disruptions in another. Not only does this prevent the inappropriate release of these emotions to unsuspecting associates and loved ones but also it helps the individuals as well by allowing the Type-O person to avoid the drain on resources that would result from escalating problems in other areas of his or her life.

Type-O people also protect their assimilation capacity by not engaging in change efforts that require resources they do not possess. They know the limitations of their personal and organizational resources and refuse to waste their time, money, and such pursuing change initiatives that cannot be successfully supported. Though they are cautious about overextending themselves, they also tend to be creative about how to maximize the use of their resources. They are constantly challenging their own assumptions and frames of reference about how something can be accomplished.

A related aspect of how Type-O people operate is that they recognize when to ask for help. These people are often independent and self-sufficient, yet they know when to tap the special skills of those around them in order to achieve common change goals. In this way, they conserve their own assimilation capacities and liberate new team resources to absorb change.

Another mechanism that Type-O people tend to use to bounce back from the strain of change is a reliance upon nurturing relationships. Such relationships provide a "safe haven," where love and acceptance are available to rejuvenate energy and regain perspective. For some people, this nurturing is provided by their family or close friends. For others, it is secured through religious organizations or support groups.

Type-O people have an ability to achieve balance in their perspectives. They see such things as opportunities hidden within dangers, the humor of serious situations, the order embedded in chaos, and the patience necessary in urgent circumstances. They see the alterations necessary for things to remain the same, the constancy that exists within a transition and the fact that, even as people strive toward perfection, they must accept its impossibility.

As solutions are generated, stability and productivity are regained. Of course, it is only a matter of time until the disruption of change once again alters expectations and the process begins anew.

THE FIVE BASIC CHARACTERISTICS OF RESILIENCE

The general description of Type-O people can be organized into categories that reflect five basic characteristics of resilience, which are manifested by certain beliefs, attitudes, behaviors, skills, and areas of knowledge. Type-O resilient people have these traits:

- Display a sense of security and self-assurance that is based on their view of life as dynamic, but generally rewarding (Positive).
- Have a clear vision of what they want to achieve (Focused).

- Demonstrate a special pliability when responding to uncertainty (Flexible).
- Develop structured approaches to managing ambiguity (Organized).
- Engage change rather than defend against it (Proactive).

Resilient people, therefore, are positive, focused, flexible, organized, and proactive.

Implications

This list of attributes can be more overwhelming than helpful if it is not viewed in the proper light. When attempting to recognize your own potential for resilience, or someone else's, a word of caution is warranted. Resilience is a relative term. I have found no one person or group that was purely Type-D or Type-O. When faced with significant change, the majority of people most often will respond according to a preferred orientation. Think of Type-D and Type-O as representing two ends of a resilience continuum. People unconsciously move from side to side on the continuum at all times, although most individuals clearly show a preference for a particular end of the spectrum.

When facing major disruption, a fire-walking CEO should not have as his or her objective to display all of these attributes all the time, but rather to be capable of marshalling many of them most of the time. The key to enhancing resilience is learning, or teaching others, to display as many of these Type-O actions as frequently as possible. Any attempt to hold yourself, or others, up to the unrealistic standard of displaying all of these attributes all of the time would be futile and counterproductive.

Another important implication that can be drawn from the list of resilience attributes is that everyone has both D and O tendencies, but it is our life experiences that tend to mold what we believe to be true and what we expect to happen regarding change. These beliefs and expectations have powerful effects on our actions. Once individuals believe and relate to change in a manner consistent with Type-D thinking, they often maintain that orientation for the rest of their lives, unless they make a concerted effort to see things differently, or someone else makes them.

It is important to note that someone with a Type-D preference is not bad and that there is nothing wrong with resistance to change per se. Resistance is a natural, healthy response to disrupted expectations. An individual defines his or her personality, and a corporation defines its culture, as much by what is rejected as by what is accepted.

Given the strong human need for control, some Type-D responses are just as legitimate and appropriate as Type-O reactions in certain circumstances. In fact, there are many situations in which change should be resisted passionately. The primary problems arise when Type-D responses become predetermined, instinctive, and habitual, regardless of the situation.

Fostering Resilience

For organizations to survive and prosper in turbulent times, Type-O attributes must be essential parts of leadership at every level, but especially for the CEO. This calls for nimble, fire-walking leaders who know how to manage transitions effectively. They must successfully implement change for themselves and others, consistently apply the mechanisms they use, and be able to relate to these methods as a structured discipline so that the lessons they have learned can be transferred to others.

As the demands of change increase, so will the need for resilient people who are able to travel successfully through their personal, organizational and societal lives at an ever-increasing speed of change. To meet this need, we must foster a new generation of fire-walking CEOs that can enhance Type-O characteristics within the men and women of the organizations they direct. Only with proper education and practice will these individuals be prepared to meet the challenges that lie before them and successfully walk the organizational beds of coals they will inherit.

NOTE

This chapter is adapted from Mr. Conner's book *Managing at the Speed of Change* (New York: Villard Books, a division of Random House, 1993).

Chapter Twenty-Two

The Right Stuff for the New Dynamic

Lyle M. Spencer, Jr.

INTRODUCTION

B usinesses that carry out strategic, organizational, and other sweeping changes to meet challenges of the future often tie their programs to core competencies of their personnel. At times, change decisions are made solely to take advantage of existing core competencies that may provide the company with great competitive strengths. These firms know what they do best and try to base their value maximization efforts on these skills. Other firms, however, may require totally new core competencies to ensure the success of their revised game plans.

In this chapter, I will define and explain core competencies, especially those that are needed by the people in a changing organization. I also will demonstrate how to identify and assess these competencies and point out a *systems* approach to thinking about how each human resource function in the company must cause or reinforce people changing.

DEFINITION OF A COMPETENCY

The concept of competence offers a foundation and common language for the design of human resource systems that support change efforts.

A competency is defined as an *underlying characteristic* of a person which is *causally related* to *effective* or *superior* performance in a job. These characteristics can include *motive, trait, self-concept,* and generalizable *knowledge* and *skill* variables that can be reliably measured.

Competencies are enduring "master traits" of people, which predict their behavior in a wide variety of situations, in *future* jobs as well as in present capacities. More than a person's present knowledge or skills, competencies determine one's ability to adapt to change. For example, "ability to program in FORTRAN" (a third-generation computer language) is not a competency. "Analytic thinking" and "motivation and ability to learn *new* computer languages" are competencies that predict which mainframe programmers can learn the fourth-generation graphical user interface (GUI) applications on personal computers in a distributed, networked data processing environment.

ORGANIZATIONAL CHANGE = PEOPLE CHANGES

Virtually all **organization** changes require changes **by** or **of** the **people** within the organization. "By" or "of" implies the choice for individuals in a changing organization is to "change" or "leave" (and be replaced). This sounds harsh but is a reality of every organization change. Disciplined thinking about the people consequences of any organization change effort is essential to its success.

Figure 22–1 shows the "people subset" of any organization change effort. After the question "How must the organization change to take advantage of its opportunities or fix its problems?" is the question "How must its **people** change to make this change happen?" This question is followed by two others: What are the firm's human resource functions doing to make these people changes happen, and what remains to be done?

Recently I went through all the organizational changes I had observed and tried to list two associated factors: the people change issues and the responses required by the company's human resources personnel. The results of this analysis are in Figure 22–2. Note that the matrix is almost completely filled in. Thus, we can conclude that every organization change raises the same people change issues and nearly all changes require effort by all of the firm's human resource functions.

Each organizational change involves the basic question: **Do we have the people (or people with the competencies) needed to make the change happen?** This question usually leads to this conclusion: "We (the firm) need **better** and/or **different** people" to be successful in carrying out the desired change program. For example, a firm may remain in what is generally called the computer market but shift its strategic focus. It may be a company that traditionally has produced and sold hardware, but the changing characteristics of the market suggest that its future prospects are better in selling systems integration consulting services. If it makes the strategic shift, its core competency must be similarly adjusted from a technology-driven organization to a customer-service-driven firm. That may require new people or, at the least, retrained or refocused personnel.

A subset of the question "Do we have the people?" is "Do we have the **management** to lead and manage the change process and/or the new and different people in the future organization?" The different people in the hypothetical example cited previously will be marketing-driven, customer-service-oriented consultants. They may require a very different managerial style from what was appropriate for managing technical engineers.

FIGURE 22–1
Human Resource System Change Planning

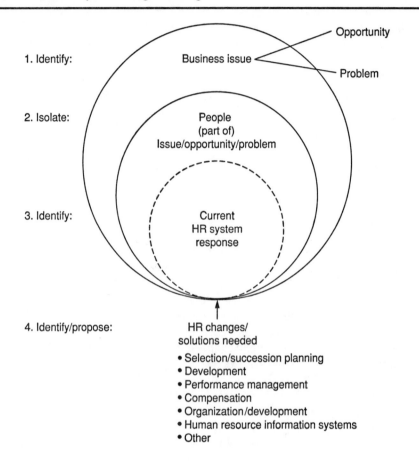

In downsizing (or "rightsizing") and in mergers and acquisitions, the question invariably is, Who do we **keep?** That means, Who has the competencies to do more with less, or to be effective in the new "lean and mean" environment? Responses to these questions involve the firm's recruitment, selection, and succession planning systems. Present employees must be assessed and assigned to one of three categories:

1. Competent now to perform in the future job.
2. Can be competent to perform in a future job with proper training.
3. Not likely to adapt to a changed business environment, and hence a candidate for termination or early retirement.

FIGURE 22–2

Human Resource Systems Involved in any Organization Change

Organization Change/Programs: Growth, downsizing, change, TQM, service quality, productivity/work, reengineering, innovation/entrepreneurship, globalization, new technology, privatization, merger/acquisition, self-managed work groups, networked teams, participative "empowered" vs. authoritarian culture, etc.	Competency-based Selection	Succession Planning	Development	Performance Management	Competency-based Pay	Organization development e.g., Venting/Problem-solving Session	IHRMIS Integrated Human Resource Management Information System
DO YOU HAVE THE PEOPLE for the FUTURE? e.g., the new, changed organization?	P*	P	s†		s		s
• Need BETTER people?	P	P	s	s	s		s
• Need DIFFERENT people?	P	P	s	s	s		s
• DO YOU HAVE MANAGEMENT in place? Capable of managing change? new/different people?	P	P	s	s	s		s
If DOWNSIZING or merging duplicated							
• Who to KEEP? needed for the future? able to do more with less?	P	P	s	s	s	s	s
DO PEOPLE KNOW WHAT TO DO? HOW TO DO IT?	s	s	P	s	s	P	s
ARE PEOPLE MOTIVATED to make needed changes?	s	s	P/s	P	P	s	s

* P = Primary human resource function

† s = secondary or supporting human resource function

273

If the firm's existing people are judged to have the competencies needed for success in the changed organization, the next question is: Do they know **what** to do and **how** to do it? Repeated, compelling communication of the firm's future mission and vision is needed to convey the "what" of change. The firm's training and development systems must communicate the organization's strategic intent and teach employees the knowledge and skills needed to do future jobs. Organization development sessions, goal progress reviews, and problem-solving meetings often are used to reinforce training interventions.

Finally, the question is: Are people **motivated** to change in the ways the firm needs so it can be successful in attaining its strategic objectives? Employee motivation directly involves the firm's performance management and compensation systems. These functions provide feedback on and incentives for changed behavior. Employee motivation also is affected by the selection of co-workers, a process that sends a message on what type of people are preferred in the changed organization. For example, are the workers motivated toward entrepreneurial initiative or toward being order takers? And are the managers participative team leaders of "command-and-control-oriented" bureaucrats? Various types of organization development interventions may be needed to increase motivation for change. An example is the venting/problem solving session, at which employees get the opportunity to express their feelings about change. The energy of those resisting the change can be rechanneled to more productive actions such as sorting out their positions, finding places in the new order, and participating in problem-solving efforts to determine how (not whether) to make the needed changes.

As will be noted in the final section of this chapter, all human resource functions are most effective when each reinforces the changes promoted by all the others. The emerging method of coordinating human resource functions is an integrated human resource management information system (IHRMIS).[1] This involves a "smart" (expert system) database of information about the competency requirements of jobs, the assessed competencies of people, and organizational outcomes.

COMPETENCIES IMPORTANT IN THE FUTURE

Most observers agree that the future business environment will include the following:

- An ever-increasing pace of technological and societal change.
- A further shift to an information economy requiring highly skilled knowledge workers.
- Intensifying global competition.
- Fragmentation of markets into specialized niches.
- Diversity, with employees and customers of every race, sex, country, and culture in the world.

Simultaneously, the United States labor force will be *less* educationally well-prepared for technical information economy jobs[2] and *less* committed to work, because of increased concern about a "balanced life style" that emphasizes family and leisure. These trends will create a tight labor market for critically needed knowledge workers.

Organizations will need to respond to these changes by innovating more rapidly; continually improving service, quality and productivity; and marketing to, managing, and motivating more diverse kinds of people. Successful organizations will be flatter and leaner, with fewer managerial levels and fewer middle managers than in the early 1990s. Responsibility and decision making will be pushed down to workers closest to customers and production. Much work will be done by empowered knowledge workers formed into ad hoc multidisciplinary teams.

Competencies that researchers,[3] including the author,[4] regard as increasingly important for executives, managers, and employees of the organizations of the future include the following:

For Executives

- *Strategic thinking.* The ability to understand rapidly changing environmental trends, market oppportunities, competitive threats, and strengths and weaknesses of their own organizations, and to identify the optimum strategic responses.
- *Change leadership.* The ability to communicate a compelling vision of the firm's strategy that makes adaptive responses appear both feasible and desirable to its many stakeholders and that arouses their genuine motivation and commitment; the skills to act as sponsors of innovation and entrepreneurship and to allocate the firm's resources optimally to implement frequent changes.
- *Relationship management.* The ability to establish relationships with and influence complex networks of people who can be regarded as coequals or are internal or external business associates. Their cooperation is needed for the organization to succeed. This diverse group includes product champions, customers, stockholders, labor representatives, federal, state and local government regulators, legislators, and interest groups in many countries.[5]

For Managers

- *Flexibility.* The willingness and ability to change managerial structures and processes when needed to implement the organization's change strategies.
- *Change implementation.* "Change leadership" ability to communicate the organization's needs for change to co-workers; "change management" skills, including communication, training, and group process facilitation to implement change in discrete work groups.
- *Entrepreneurial innovation.* The motivation to champion new products, services, and production processes.

- *Interpersonal understanding.* The ability to understand and value the inputs of a diverse group of people involved in or impacted by the change process.

- *Managerial behaviors that are empowering.* These include sharing information, participatively soliciting co-workers' ideas, fostering employee development, delegating meaningful responsibility, providing feedback, expressing positive expectations of subordinates, and rewarding performance improvement. These steps make employees feel more capable and motivate them to assume greater responsibility.

- *Team facilitation.* Group process skills needed to get diverse groups of people to work together effectively to achieve a common goal; e.g., establishing goal and role clarity, controlling "overtalkers," inviting silent members to participate, and resolving conflicts.

- *Adaptability.* The ability to adapt rapidly to and function effectively in any foreign environment so that a manager can quickly move into a position regardless of where it is located geographically—Nairobi, Jakarta, Moscow, or anywhere else in the world. Research indicates this competency is correlated with such competencies as liking travel and novelty, resistance to stress, and cross-cultural interpersonal understanding.[6]

For Employees

- *Flexibility.* The predisposition to see change as an exciting opportunity rather than a threat. An example would be treating the adoption of a new technology as "getting to play with new gadgets, the latest and best!"

- *Motivation to seek information and ability to learn.* Genuine enthusiasm for opportunities to learn new technical and interpersonal skills. An illustration is the secretary who, when asked to learn to use a spreadsheet program and take over department accounting, welcomes the request as job enrichment rather than an additional burden. This competency transcends computer literacy and other specific technical skills future workers will need. It is the impetus for lifelong learning of *any* new knowledge and skill required by the changing requirements of future jobs.

- *Achievement motivation.* The impetus for innovation and "kaizen," which is the continuous improvement in quality and productivity needed to meet and preferably move ahead of ever-increasing competition.

- *Work motivation under time pressure.* A combination of flexibility, achievement motivation, stress resistance, and organization commitment that enables individuals to work under increasing demands for new products and services in constantly shortening periods of time. This often is expressed as: "I work **best** under pressure—the challenge really gets my juices flowing!"

- *Collaborativeness.* The ability to work cooperatively in multidisciplinary groups with diverse co-workers. This involves positive expectations of others, interpersonal understanding, and organization commitment.

- *Customer service orientation.* A genuine desire to be of help to others, interpersonal understanding sufficient to hear customers' needs and emotional states, and the initiative to overcome obstacles in one's own organization to solve customer problems.

IDENTIFYING COMPETENCIES NEEDED TO SUPPORT SPECIFIC ORGANIZATIONAL CHANGES

There are three ways to identify the competency requirements for future jobs: criterion studies, task-competency databases, and expert panels.

Criterion Study

This study identifies people currently doing all or part of the future job and examines a sample of superior and average performers to determine competencies that predict if they will do the job *well*. For example, one firm identified managers known for exceptional competence in seven "strategic situations likely to be important in the future." Among the seven were these:

- *Managing diversity.* Getting high productivity and morale from minority and female employees, and developing an unusually high percentage of them for classification as "promotable."

- *Managing foreign turnaround situations.* Taking over failing overseas operations and restoring them to profitability and market leadership.

The competencies of exceptional managers who already enjoyed these skills were assessed and compared with those of average colleagues. Behavioral Event Interviews (discussed in more detail in the next section) were used in these assessments to identify the specific competencies successful managers used in each "strategic situation for the future." These competencies are then used to guide the firm's future hiring selections, succession planning, and development programs.

Task-Competency Database

Tasks that people in the future job will perform are identified and a competency model database is analyzed to identify competencies that in previous studies predicted if the jobs would be done well.

For example, an American telecommunications firm planning to sell digital switching systems in Europe wanted to know the competencies to use in selecting an international sales force. Because the firm had never marketed its products outside of the

United States, it had no superior performers to study in-house. Analysis of tasks required to do the job indicated that a sales post combined the tasks of a diplomat with those of a high-tech salesperson. Extensive competency data from previous studies existed for both diplomats (e.g., cross-cultural empathy, speed of learning foreign political networks) and high-tech sales people (e.g., achievement motivation, direct persuasion skills in citing the economic value added to a customer's business in proposals for hardware sales). The firm was able to produce a composite of these known job tasks that formed the heart of a competency model for its international salespeople.

Expert Panels

Managerial and technical experts identify the firm's strategy and critical success factors in accomplishing it. Invariably, the critical success factors have implications for the competencies the firm's employees will need to be successful. For example, the critical success factor "unparalleled customer service" implies that the firm's customer contact employees will need a reasonable level of two competencies:

1. *Interpersonal sensitivity.* Hearing accurately what people say and understanding their underlying concerns.

2. *Customer service orientation.* Feeling rewarded by helping others and being willing to go beyond expectations to see that customers' needs are met.

Competencies identified by an expert panel often can be validated by searching a database of competencies developed for one or more companies (the task-competency database method). Sometimes an expert panel can identify people inside or outside the firm who exemplify one or more of the competencies hypothesized to be important for the future. If these persons can be questioned in Behavioral Event Interviews, a sample study can also be used to verify the expert panel's hypotheses.

ASSESSING COMPETENCIES FOR CHANGE

Competencies can be assessed by a special type of interview called a Behavioral Event Interview (BEI). The results are based on "360-degree" ratings of an individual by co-workers all around him or her (e.g., by the subject's boss, the boss's boss, peers, subordinates, clients, and customers). Other sources of information include psychological tests, biographical data, and assessment center observations.[7] The BEI is the most flexible, cost-effective and acceptable method of assessing most competencies.

A Behavioral Event Interview consists of asking a person to describe the most critical events with which he or she has been involved in his or her job in the past two years. In most cases 20 percent of the work incidents account for 80 percent of performance. Interview subjects are usually asked to describe both significant successes and significant failures. The type of incident doesn't matter since critical competencies are equally present in success and failure events.

The subject describes the event in great narrative detail.

- What led up to the incident?
- Who was involved?
- What did the person think, feel, and want to have happen?
- What did the person actually do?
- What was the outcome of the incident?

These narratives, usually tape-recorded and transcribed, can be scored for most competencies by trained psychologists. Responses to the "think, feel or want" probe can be scored for cognitive style and self-confidence motivation. For example, Figure 22–3 shows a scale for one motive competency, achievement motivation, that is important to success in many technical, quality, productivity improvement, entrepreneurial, and innovation change efforts. This scale can be used to score the following passage from the BEI of a data-processing manager at an apparel manufacturer:

> When I took over the EDP [electronic data-processing] shop, it took us **six weeks** to get inventory reports out of an antiquated mainframe. We had to wait until the end-of-month financial reports got done to consolidate the data. That kind of inefficiency drives me nuts; I just knew I could do better. So, over the next 18 months, I spec'd [determined requirements for], designed, sold to senior management, developed, and installed a new distributed financial and inventory management system worldwide, setting up a WAN [wide area network] using Sybase on Sun SparcStation 2s. Now I can get an inventory report on any store in the world **overnight**—and the day I pulled the plug on the mainframe, I saved the firm $3 million.
>
> The high point of all this? I think it was getting the sign-off from the Investment Committee of the board. I'd lobbied for months. I pitched the new system to each function that had clout with the board. To the bean counters I emphasized the straight-to-the-bottom-line head count and dollar savings we'd get the day I shot the mainframe. To marketing I sold the competitive advantage we'd get with virtually daily market research. What was and wasn't selling any- and everywhere in the world. What trends in teenage consumers' tastes were emerging, so we could identify coming fads and shift production to take advantage of them *fast*… at least faster than our competitors….

This passage can be scored as follows:

- *Achievement motivation,* characterized by wanting to <u>do better</u> against an objective standard of excellence, citing time contraction ("six weeks" to "overnight") and $3 million cost savings, and, perhaps, sustained entrepreneurial initiative to make an innovative change happen.
- *Technical expertise,* characterized by knowledge of hardware and software that would permit downsizing of mainframe operations.
- *Change leadership,* or at least the use of influence strategies at levels of **direct persuasion,** characterized by convincing others by citing the benefits of the

proposal, and **assembling of political coalitions,** characterized by lining up support for the position from two or more decision influencers.

The assessment power of the BEI is based on this psychological principle: *The best predictor of what someone will do is what he or she has done in the most similar critical situations in the past.* For example, if the manager just cited is asked to manage a similar situation—another data processing operation with an inefficient mainframe—it is highly likely that she will find a way to improve systems productivity. Even in a somewhat different situation, such as an assignment in marketing or human resources, this manager's assessed achievement motivation and influence skills make it likely she will initiate changes to improve operations.

A COMPETENCY-BASED HUMAN RESOURCE SYSTEMS APPROACH TO CHANGE

As shown in Figure 22–2 and noted previously, human resources (HR) functions and programs are a system, that is, interconnected and interdependent. The following laws of systems apply:

- Single inputs don't work. Changes in one human resource function without supporting changes in others are unlikely to be effective.
- Change is most likely when *every* part of the human resource system changes to reinforce the changes in all other parts.

Figure 22–3 is an example of Human Resource System Change Planning for a computer firm that underwent a major change, from selling hardware, a business in which it was no longer competitive, to selling systems integration consulting services. Future consulting jobs were to be conducted by multidisciplinary, self-managing teams consisting of systems professionals from many parts of the firm as well as third-party vendors, clients, and even competitors, working together to create complex technical solutions. After losing several billion dollars, this firm closed all of its manufacturing facilities and cut its staff from 30,000 to 8,000, a downsizing of more than 70 percent. This drastic organization change, essential to the firm's survival, required a human resource systems response. Figure 22–3 shows the firm's **business issue,** the **people** parts of this issue, the firm's **current HR system**, and the **changes needed** by each HR function to support its change effort.

Recruitment/Selection and Succession Planning

The firm's most pressing human resources concern was to identify which of its hardware "box" salespeople and technical support staff had the competencies to sell and deliver consulting services. This evaluation was needed to determine who to keep, who to retrain, and how many to recruit to perform and manage the future consulting business.

FIGURE 22-3
Human Resource Change Planning Form [Organization: Major minicomputer (MMC)]

Business issue Problem/Opportunity

Change from selling hardware to selling reengineering and systems integration consulting. Future work to be done in multidisciplinary self-managing teams: people from many parts of MMC, third-party vendors, clients, even competitors. Major 70% downsizing: issue is who to keep and who needs to be recruited to do new jobs.

People (part of problem/issue opportunity)

Need people able to analyze complex BUSINESS (vs. just technical IS) problems; identify and sell "reengineering" solutions; sell "higher" in client organizations; "comfortable in the boardroom"; with collaborative team skills.

	Selection/Succession Planning	Development	Performance Mgmt	Compensation	Organization Development	Integrated Human Resource Management Information System
Firm's Current HR SYSTEM	Recruit for sales and technical skills—but not consulting competencies	Have sales and reengineering training but not team building or consulting competency training	Sales quotas met only—nothing regarding competencies needed in changed organization	Low base salaries, commissions based on hardware "boxes" sold	TQM effort includes some team building	Have data base of technical skills, but not competencies or job-person matching
Changes needed in firm's HR system to make strategy happen	Need competency models for new jobs: sales, business consultant and technical positions; competency assessment training for HR staff and managers	Need training in "collaborativeness," team building, group facilitation and leadership competencies; BEI training; consulting firm management training	Performance Management system should include measures of consulting effectiveness and new competencies especially collaborativeness and team leadership	Need professional service firm compensation system for "consultants:" competency-based and team performance incentives vs. sales quotas only	Need team building for multidisciplinary teams and reinforcement for team skills training	Need system that can inventory and match people to jobs on technical, industry and competency requirements

The firm traditionally recruited for technical and sales skills. Human resources' first task was to develop competency model criteria for five critical jobs in the future organization: reengineering business consultant, consultant manager, reengineering sales consultant, sales manager, and technical support consultant. Competencies identified as important for reengineering consultants included the following:

- The ability to analyze complex business problems as opposed to purely technical problems.
- The achievement orientation and creativity needed to develop radical reengineering solutions to client problems, which would improve productivity or cut costs 50–90 percent.
- The ability of consultants who are "comfortable in the boardroom" to sell these solutions to persons at higher levels in client organizations, that is, to senior executives.
- The collaborative team skills needed to work in and/or manage multidisciplinary groups of professionals from many organizations.

Once competency models were established for key jobs, human resource professionals and key managers were trained in competency assessment methods. They assessed present employees and potential recruits for the competencies needed to do the jobs in reorganized firms.

Development

Reengineering sales people, consultants, and technical support staff needed to know the following:

Hardware and software platforms, not only the firm's platforms but also those of 100 other manufacturers. They also had to know how to link all of these systems together in local and wide-area networks.

Vertical market reengineering applications, or how system integration could be used in the banking, insurance, local government, manufacturing, and other sectors to improve customer productivity.

Selling consulting services competencies.

Consulting competencies, especially team collaboration in multidisciplinary work teams with members of the firm, competing firms, third-party vendors, and client reengineering teams.

Members of the firm had technical, sales, and reengineering principles training but needed, in addition, training in consulting and elements of "collaborativeness" such as team building and facilitation and leadership of multidisciplinary teams. The focus of its management training programs had to change from sales management to management of professional service firm units and consultants.

Performance Management

The firm measured and rewarded customer contact personnel for meeting hardware sales quotas. To motivate and provide feedback to employees on their success in their new consulting roles, the firm changed performance management systems to include consultant utilization, or billing, rates (the percentage of a consultant's time he or she can charge a client), consulting projects sold, project profitability, and appraisal of demonstrated consulting competencies, especially the contributions made to project teams.

Compensation

The firm's compensation system reflected its sales emphasis. There were relatively low fixed salaries and large variable incentives based on meeting or exceeding sales quotas. To reward employee changes in role and behavior, the firm needed to change its compensation system to resemble a professional service firm more closely. That involved larger fixed salaries with "pay for competence" opportunities or salary increases when new consulting skills were acquired and variable incentives based on team project performance rather than individual sales accomplishments.

Organization Development

The firm's Total Quality Management (TQM) program included some team building and training in group facilitation skills. To reinforce new training in team building and leadership skills, the firm's OD (organization development) consultants offered team building and problem-solving process facilitation services to multidisciplinary teams working on reengineering projects with clients.

Integrated Human Resource Management Information Systems (IHRMIS)

The firm's existing Human Resource Information System included an inventory of employees' technical skills (e.g., who could program in COBOL computer language) but had no information on employee competencies to sell or do the consulting tasks essential in future jobs.

To support its move into reengineering consulting, the firm developed a data base with three sets of competencies: technical, industry, and interpersonal. An expert job-person matcher enabled sales and project managers to find consultants who had the combination of technical, industry, and interpersonal skills to work on complex projects.

For example, one project involved the merger of two major banks in the southeastern United States. The resulting megabank faced the complicated task of integrating two MIS departments that used different computers and software and had numerous line operations that were in conflict. Appropriate consultants needed the following:

To know how to interface two computer communications local area networks (LANs).

To determine how imaging systems can be used to speed transaction processing in banks.

To have the interpersonal skills to consult in a highly politicized environment.

The firm's IHRMIS can search its staff of more than 1,000 sales, business, and technical consultants and identify employees with competencies that match this complex job profile.

SUMMARY

Knowledge of the competency requirements of future jobs can, with assessment of employees' competencies, provide the basis for systemic human resources planning for change in evolving organizations. Each HR function can identify what it is doing and what it needs to do to support the recruitment, selection, assessment, reward, and organizational reinforcement of people with the competencies needed for the changing firm's success in the future.

NOTES

1. See R. Page and S. Spencer, "Integrated Human Resource Management Information Systems," in *Human Resources Management and Development Handbook,* ed. W. Tracey (New York: American Management Association, 1993).

2. W. B. Johnson and A. E. Packer, *Workforce 2000: Work and Workers for the 21st Century* (Indianapolis: The Hudson Institute, 1987).

3. L. M. Spencer, "Job Competency Assessment," in *Handbook of Business Strategy*, ed. H. Glass (Boston: Warren, Gorham & Lambert, 1991).

4. A. Howard, "New Directions for Human Resources Practice," in *Working with Organizations and Their People: A Guide to Human Resources Practice*, ed. D. W. Bray (New York: Guilford Press, 1991); and A. Howard "Personal Characteristics for a Post-Industrial Society," paper presented at the Personnel Testing Conference of Southern California Spring Conference (Ontario, CA: April 12, 1991).

5. As anticipated by J. Kotter, *Power and Influence* (New York: Free Press, 1985).

6. R. S. Mansfield and S. Mumford, "A Competency-Based Approach to Intercultural Relations" (Boston, MA: McBer and Company, undated).

7. See L. Spencer and S. Spencer, "Competency-Based Selection Methods," *Competence at Work* (New York: Wiley-Interscience, 1993).

Chapter Twenty-Three

Critical Elements of Organizational Culture Change

W. Warner Burke

R arely if ever does significant societal change or organization change occur randomly. Leaders step forward or are selected to do something about society's needs—for example, Lenin, Lincoln, Gandhi, DeGaulle, or Churchill—or to respond to an organization's needs—such as Lee Iacocca at Chrysler, Jack Welch at GE, Mike Harper at ConAgra. In other words, events occur and a need for change may arise in society or in an organization, but for the needs to be met, leadership must be exerted. The leader is *responding* to this need, not creating the need. Usually what leaders must create is motivation on the part of the people to respond in a direction that will address the need.

Such was the case at British Airways (BA) during the early 1980s. BA at the time was a government organization, the result of a merger between British European Airways (BEA) and British Overseas Airways Corporation (BOAC) in the early 1970s. These two organizations in turn had been spawned from Britain's Royal Air Force. The BA of 1983, when Colin Marshall arrived as president and CEO, operated largely as a function of its history—rather like the military—and was draining the British treasury with financial losses year after year. Moreover, passengers referred to BA as "bloody awful." Prime Minister Margaret Thatcher had decided earlier that BA was to be privatized and brought in Lord John King, a successful businessman, to be chairman. King recruited Marshall from Avis Rent-A-Car in 1983 and gave him the charge and the authority to change BA so that it could survive privatization.

In addition to the pressure on British Airways by Prime Minister Thatcher and her government administration, another key environmental change was the growing deregulation of international air traffic. Many airfares no longer were set by governments.

Internally, BA had to change its mission and strategy as well as its corporate culture. BA's mission was to serve with distinction as the UK's flagship airline and, strategically, to compete both domestically and internationally. The mission and strategy would need to change so it was directed more toward customer service, and BA would need to become much more competitive. With respect to the culture, BA would have to be transformed from a bureaucratic and militaristic organization to a service-oriented and market-driven one.

Before I describe the culture change effort at BA—with a particular focus on the leadership role—let us examine the model or organizational framework that guided the change activities.

THE BURKE-LITWIN MODEL OF ORGANIZATIONAL PERFORMANCE AND CHANGE

The model that we propose for orchestrating culture change and that will be described in this chapter resulted from five years of work at BA—from 1985 to 1990 when the heart of the airline's change process was underway. As G. H. Litwin and I, the model's codevelopers, noted in an article in the *Journal of Management*, we learned "what changes seemed to have worked and what activities clearly did not. It was from these experiences that our model took form."

The model is based on two distinct sets of organizational dynamics. One set primarily is associated with the transactional level of human behavior, or the everyday interactions and exchanges that create the *climate* of local work units. The other set of dynamics is concerned with processes of organization transformation—that is, sudden "leaps" in behavior. These transformational processes are required for genuine change in the *culture* of an organization. Efforts to distinguish transactional and transformational dynamics in organizations have been influenced by the writings of James McGregor Burns (1978), who described transforming and transacting leaders, and by our consulting efforts to change organizations.

The Burke-Litwin model owes its original development to the work of Litwin and his associates (Litwin and Stringer, 1968; Tagiuri and Litwin, 1968); it has been refined through a series of studies directed by Burke (Bernstein and Burke, 1989; Fox, 1990; Michela, Boni, Schechter, Manderlink, Bernstein, O'Malley and Burke, 1988). Recent collaboration has led to the current form of this model, which attempts the following:

- To specify the interrelationships of organizational variables.
- To distinguish transformational and transactional dynamics in organizational behavior and change.

Figure 23–1 summarizes the model.

In accordance with accepted thinking about organizations from general systems theory (Katz and Kahn, 1978), the external environment box represents the input and the individual and organizational performance box represents the output. Feedback loops go in both directions. The remaining boxes of the model represent the throughput aspect of general systems theory.

FIGURE 23–1

The Burke-Litwin Model of Individual and Oranizational Performance

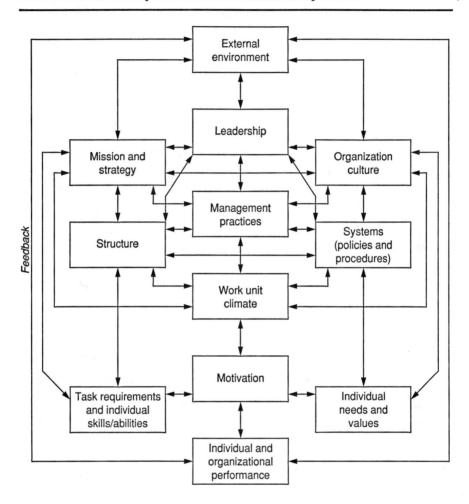

The model is complex, as is the rich intricacy of organizational phenomena. However, this model, exhibited two dimensionally, is still an oversimplification; a hologram would be a better representation.

Arrows in both directions convey the open-systems principle that change in one factor eventually will have an impact on the other factors. Moreover, if the model could be diagrammed so that the arrows were circular (as they would be in a hologram), reality could be represented more accurately. Yet this is a *causal* model. For example, although culture and systems affect each other, culture has a stronger influence on systems than systems have on culture.

The model could be displayed differently. External environment could be on the left and performance on the right, with all throughput boxes in between. Displaying it as shown, however, makes a statement about organizational change: Organizational change stems more from environmental impact than from any other factor. Moreover, with respect to organizational change, the variables of strategy, leadership, and culture have more weight than the variables of structure, management practices, and systems; that is, just having leaders communicate a new strategy is not sufficient for effective change. Changing culture must be planned as well as aligned with strategy and leader behavior. How the model is displayed does not dictate where change could start; however, it does indicate the weighting of change dynamics. The reader can think of the model in terms of gravity, with the push toward performance being in the weighted order displayed in Figure 23–1.

In summary, the model, as shown in Figure 23–1, portrays these features:

- The primary variables that need to be considered in any attempt to predict and explain the total behavioral output of an organization.
- The most important interactions among these variables.
- How the variables affect change.

Transformational and Transactional Dynamics

The concept of transformational change in organizations is suggested in the writings of such people as Bass (1985), Burns (1978), McClelland (1975), and Tichy and Devanna (1986). Figure 23–2 displays the transformational variables that are shown in the upper half of the Burke-Litwin model. *Transformational* refers to areas in which organizational alteration probably is caused by the interaction of customer and competitor forces with internal capabilities and that require entirely new behavior patterns on the part of organizational members.

Figure 23–3 shows the transactional variables of the model, those displayed in the lower half. These variables are very similar to those originally isolated by Litwin and Stringer (1968) and later by Michela et al. (1988). They are *transactional* because alteration occurs primarily through relatively short-term reciprocity among people and groups. In other words, "You do this for me and I'll do that for you."

A brief description of each category or box in the model follows:

External environment. Any outside condition or situation that influences the performance of the organization. These conditions include such things as marketplaces, world financial conditions, and political/governmental circumstances.

Mission and strategy. What employees believe is the central purpose of the organization and how the organization intends to achieve that purpose over an extended period of time.

FIGURE 23–2
The Transformational Factors

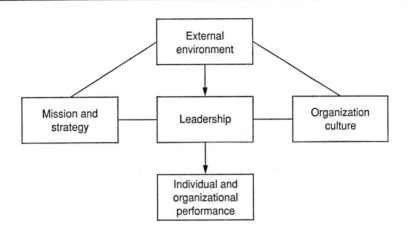

FIGURE 23–3
The Transactional Factors

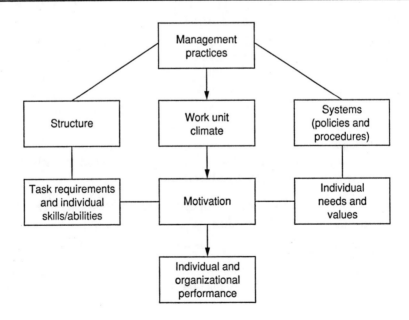

Leadership. Executive behavior that provides direction and encourages others to take needed action. For purposes of data gathering, this box includes perceptions of executive practices and values.

Organization culture. "The way we do things around here." Culture is the collection of overt and covert rules, values, and principles that guide organizational behavior and have been strongly influenced by history, custom, and practice.

Structure. The arrangement of functions and people into specific areas and levels of responsibility, decision-making authority, and relationships. Structure ensures effective implementation of the organization's mission and strategy.

Management practices. What managers do in the normal course of events to use the human and material resources at their disposal to carry out the organization's strategy.

Systems. Standardized policies and mechanisms that are designed to facilitate work. Systems primarily manifest themselves in the organization's reward systems and in control systems such as the organization's management information system, goal and budget development, and human resource allocation.

Work unit climate. The collective current impressions, expectations, and feelings of the members of local work units. These in turn affect members' relations with supervisors, with each other, and with other units.

Task requirements and individual skills/abilities. The behavior required for task effectiveness, including specific skills and knowledge required for people to accomplish the work assigned and for which they feel directly responsible. This box concerns what is often referred to as the job-person match.

Individual needs and values. The specific psychological factors that provide desire and worth for individual actions or thoughts.

Motivation. Aroused behavioral tendencies to move toward goals, take needed action, and persist until satisfaction is attained. This is the resultant net energy generated by the sum of achievement, power, affection, discovery, and other important human motives.

Individual and organizational performance. The outcomes or results, with indicators of effort and achievement. Such indicators might include productivity, customer or staff satisfaction, profit, and service quality.

Climate Results From Transactions: Culture Change Requires Transformation

In the causal model, day-to-day climate is a result of transactions related to such issues as these:

- *Sense of direction.* The effect of mission clarity, or lack thereof, on one's daily responsibilities.

- *Role and responsibility.* The effect of structure, reinforced by managerial practice.
- *Standards and commitment.* The effect of managerial practice, reinforced by culture.
- *Fairness of rewards.* The effect of systems, reinforced by managerial practice.
- *Focus on customer service rather than internal pressures or standards of excellence.* The effect of culture, reinforced by other variables.

In contrast, the concept of organizational culture has to do with those underlying values and meaning systems that are difficult to manage, to alter, and even to be realized completely (Schein, 1985). Moreover, instant change in culture seems to be a contradiction in terms. By definition, those things that can be changed quickly are not the underlying reward systems but the behaviors that are attached to the meaning systems. It is relatively easy to alter superficial human behavior; it is undoubtedly quite difficult to alter something unconscious that is hidden in symbols and mythology and that functions as the fabric helping an organization to remain together, intact, and viable. To change something so deeply embedded in organizational life does indeed require transformational experiences and events.

USING THE MODEL: DATA GATHERING AND ANALYSIS

Distinguishing transformational and transactional thinking about organizations has implications for planning organizational change. Unless one is conducting an overall organizational diagnosis, preliminary interviews will result in enough information to conduct a fairly targeted survey. Survey targets would be determined from the interviews and, most likely, would be focused on either transformational or transactional issues. Transformational issues call for a survey that probes mission and strategy, leadership, culture, and performance. Transactional issues need a focus on structure, systems, management practices, climate, and performance. Other transactional probes might involve motivation, including task requirements (job-person match) and individual needs and values. For example, parts or all of "The Job Diagnostic Survey" (Hackman and Oldham, 1980) might be appropriate.

A consultant helping to manage change would conduct preliminary interviews with, say, 15 to 30 representative individuals in the organization. If a summary of these interviews revealed that significant organizational change was needed, additional data would be collected related to the top or *transformational* part of Figure 23–1. Note that in major organizational change, transformational variables represent the primary levers, that is, the areas in which change must be focused. The following examples represent transformational change (concentrated at the top of the model, as illustrated in Figure 23–2).

- An acquisition in which the acquired organization's culture, leadership, and business strategy are dramatically different from those of the acquiring organization, even if both organizations are in the same industry; this will necessitate a new, merged organization. For an example of how the model has been used to facilitate a merger, see Burke and Jackson (1991).

- A Federal agency in which the mission has been modified and the structure and leadership changed significantly, yet the culture remains in the past.

- A high-tech firm whose leadership has changed and is perceived negatively, whose strategy is unclear, and whose internal politics have moved from minimal before the shift to predominant after the new leaders took over. The hue and cry is, "We have no direction from our leaders and no culture to guide our behavior in the meantime."

For an organization in which the problem can be addressed by problem fine-tuning or an improvement process, the second layer of the model (shown in Figure 23–3) serves as the point of concentration. Examples include changes in the organization's structure; modification of the reward system; management development (perhaps in the form of a program that concentrates on behavioral practices); or the administration of a climate survey to measure job stratification, job clarity, degree of teamwork, and so on.

British Airways is the best example of an organization in which almost all of the model was used to provide a framework for executives and managers to understand the massive change they were attempting to manage. BA became a private corporation in February 1987, and moving from operating as a government agency to a market-driven, customer-focused business enterprise is a significant change. All of the boxes in the model have been, and still are being, affected. Data have been gathered based on most of the boxes and summarized in a feedback report for many BA executives and managers. This feedback, organized according to the model, helped these executives and managers understand which of the boxes within his or her domain needed attention.

To summarize: Considering the model in horizontal terms emphasizes that organizational change is either *transformational*—significant if not fundamental change—or *transactional*—fine-tuning and improving the organization rather than executing a change that is significant in effect. Considering the model from a vertical perspective entails hypothesizing causal effects and assuming that the "weight" of change is top-down; that is, the heaviest or most influential organizational dimensions for change are external environment, first and foremost, followed by mission, strategy, leadership, and culture. It is interesting to note that executives and managers typically concern themselves with the left side of the model illustrated in Figure 23–1—mission and strategy, structure, task requirements, and individual skills/abilities. In contrast, behavioral scientists are more likely to be concerned with the right side and middle of Figure 23–1—leadership, culture, systems (especially rewards), management practices, climate, individual needs and values, and motivation. Any change leader should be concerned with the entire model and with a more effective integration of purpose and practice.

CHANGE AT BRITISH AIRWAYS

Back to our story. Having explained already the internal forces impacting BA at the time Colin Marshall took over as CEO in 1983, I will move forward to describe the changes that took place in the mission and strategy, leadership, and culture boxes of the Burke-Litwin model, in other words, the transformational changes.

- *Mission and strategy.* To make BA more competitive and to reduce costs, Marshall first reduced the size of the work force from about 59,000 to 37,000. The downsizing was done with a certain amount of compassion, primarily through early retirements with substantial financial settlements. Marshall's background was marketing in a service industry and he began to change BA's strategy accordingly. BA was to become "The World's Favourite Airline," with a strong emphasis on the customer by providing superior service.

- *Leadership.* The major change here was the hiring of Marshall. He in turn hired Nicholas Georgiades, a psychologist and former professor and consultant, as head of human resources. Georgiades developed the specific tactics and programs required to bring about the culture change.

- *Culture.* Through a series of programs and activities, the culture gradually shifted from too much bureaucracy to a genuine service orientation. The first program was called "Putting People First." "Aimed at helping line workers and managers understand the service nature of the airline industry, it was intended to challenge the prevailing wisdom about how things were to be done at BA" (Goodstein and Burke, 1991; p. 12).

The next steps were to focus even more intensely on the culture. Georgiades conceptualized the process metaphorically as a three-legged stool. The "seat" was the new, desired culture (customer-service-oriented) and the three legs were these:

- The "Managing People First" (MPF) program, a five-day residential experience to help managers learn about how to manage their people (more participatively, for example) so that they would be more service oriented.

- Performance appraisal techniques in which half of a manager's evaluation was based on results and half on how the results were achieved. The *how* incorporated the behaviors and practices emphasized in the MPF program.

- Pay-for-performance systems to reward managers according to how they were rated in their performance appraisals.

In summary, since the BA change was clearly fundamental and transformational in nature, concentrating on the top three boxes of the Burke-Litwin model (which were changed in response to external environment demands) was the appropriate approach for the airline. Subsequent efforts concentrated on these areas:

- The climate, enhanced through team-building processes.
- Support systems, such as those established by modifying rewards (pay for performance).
- Training human resources people in consulting skills to help managers apply what they had learned in the MPF program.

To state that BA has changed is now a matter of record (Goodstein and Burke, 1991). It is one of the most profitable airlines in the world, and its significantly improved service has caused a change in what passengers call it—from "bloody awful" to "bloody awesome" (see *Business Week*, October 9, 1989, p. 97).

CONCLUSION

The programs that helped to move BA toward the intended change goals were extremely important. To conceptualize the change effort and to help determine the phases of change, the Burke-Litwin model was indeed useful. Most important of all, however, was the leadership of the change effort. Marshall not only specified the change goals, but also reinforced them by personally speaking at each of the initial "Putting People First" programs. They were conducted numerous times with 100 people at a time attending these one-day sessions. Marshall was at each of the MPF programs to conduct a question-and-answer session. There were more than 200 of these programs over a three-year period. In other words, Marshall made an incredible commitment to "staying the course" for the change. Georgiades provided significant leadership through creative changes in the human resources function, and Gordon Dunlop, the chief financial officer, played a critical role in getting BA not only financially sound but also eventually highly profitable.

Effecting culture change requires the combination of a clear plan with phased programs, activities, and modifications in key aspects of the system, for example, rewards *and* leadership throughout the organization but critically at the top.

REFERENCES

Bass, B. *Leadership and Performance beyond Expectations*. New York: Free Press, 1985.

Bernstein, W. M.; and W. W. Burke. "Modeling Organizational Meaning Systems." In *Research in Organizational Change and Development*, Vol. 3. Ed. R. W. Woodman and W. A. Pasmore. Greenwich, CT: JAI Press, 1989.

Burke, W. W.; and P. Jackson. "Making the SmithKline Beecham Merger Work." *Human Resources Management* 30 (1991), pp. 69–87.

Burke, W. W. "Leadership as Empowering Others." In *Executive Power: How Executives Influence People and Organizations.* Ed. S. Srivastva and Associates. San Francisco: Jossey-Bass, 1986.

Burke, W. W.; and G. H. Litwin. "A Causal Model of Organizational Performance and Change." In *The 1989 Annual: Developing Human Resources.* San Diego, CA. University Associates, 1989, pp. 277–278.

Burke, W. W.; and G. H. Litwin. "A Causal Model of Organizational Performance and Change." *Journal of Management* 18, no. 3 (1992), pp. 523–45.

Burns, J. M. *Leadership.* New York: Harper & Row, 1978.

Fox, M. M. "The Role of Individual Perceptions of Organizational Culture in Predicting Perceptions of Work Unit Climate and Organizational Performance." Ph.D. dissertation, Columbia University, 1990.

Goodstein, L. D.; and W. W. Burke. "Creating Successful Organizational Change." *Organizational Dynamics* 19, no. 4 (1991), pp. 5–17.

Hackman J. R.; and G. R. Oldham. *Work Redesign.* Reading, MA: Addison-Wesley, 1980.

Katz, D.; and R. L. Kahn. *The Social Psychology of Organizations.* 2nd ed. New York: Wiley, 1978.

Leahey, J.; and J. P. Kotter. "Changing the Culture at British Airways." Harvard Business School Case No. 491-009, Boston, 1990.

Litwin, G. H.; and R. A. Stringer. *Motivation and Organizational Climate.* Boston: Harvard Business School Press, 1968.

McClelland, D. C. *Power: The Inner Experience.* New York: Irvington, 1975.

Michela, J. L.; S. M. Boni; C. B. Schechter; G. Manderlink; W. M. Bernstein; M. O'Malley; and W. W. Burke. "A Hierarchically Nested Model for Estimation of Influences on Organizational Climate: Rationale, Methods, and Demonstration." Working Paper, Teachers College, Columbia University, New York City, 1988.

Schein, E. H. *Organizational Culture and Leadership.* San Francisco: Jossey-Bass, 1985.

Tagiuri, R.; and G. H. Litwin (eds.). *Organizational Climate: Explorations of a Concept.* Cambridge, MA: Harvard University Press, 1968.

Tichy, N. M.; and M. A. Devanna. *The Transformational Leader* New York: Wiley, 1986.

Chapter Twenty-Four

The Tortoise and the Hare: Cultural Change and Corporate Strategy

Robert L. Laud

INTRODUCTION

The widespread interest in corporate culture as a key to organization success is driven by a simple idea: Human behavior has a direct and measurable impact on organization effectiveness. The application of this concept is growing in terms of both significant and costly corporate culture initiatives as well as hard data and empirical research.

It is becoming clear that the successful implementation of corporate strategies depends on the ability of the organization to change culturally. Both corporate strategy and organization culture are inextricably linked and symbiotically related to each other. As corporate leaders seek new means to improve competitiveness, they are more frequently turning to strategic cultural intervention to obtain tangible financial payoffs. New knowledge bases about organizations are helping to create business environments that are strategically responsive to human work behavior and in turn, are providing maximum advantage to the organization in its efforts to achieve its business objectives.

Business analysts long have focused the attention of corporate America on excellence, often noting the essential attributes that characterize the culture of successful businesses. Implicit in these discussions is a general belief that a strong culture is essential for market leadership and long-term success. A decade ago, Peters and Waterman highlighted these findings, stating that "without exception the dominance and coherence of culture proved to be an essential quality of the excellent companies."[1] Recent research has indicated that the implementation of corporate strategies and achievement of financial objectives are linked to the cultural and organizational characteristics of companies.

However, most American companies traditionally have addressed business problems by providing targeted resources either to the most pressing and apparent need or, more often, to secondary needs consistent with the historic power base of internal decision making. As a result, the type of excellence achieved often has been an isolated functional excellence that has not been integrated into the entire company. As economic history bears out, this isolated functional excellence, whether it is in product development, finance, information systems, marketing, distribution, or human resources, has created a corporate leap-frogging effect. The result has been a failure to develop clear long-term leaders in most industries where excellence in one area produces a short-term king of the hill that is displaced as soon as a competitor finds the secret of creating a narrowly based excellence of its own.

Although these change strategies and tactics have provided some companies with the means to play global catch-up, the ability to dominate markets over time has been elusive, if not impossible. Long-term industry dominance and the complex ways in which it must be approached are only beginning to be understood. One reason may lie in the difficulty of identifying and investigating the full complement of factors that impact bottom-line effectiveness, with present research suggesting that the cultural or "soft" factors may be at the core of organizational excellence. Milliken & Company, a Baldrige award winner, vehemently believes in the importance of the cultural base as noted in one of its many slogans: "The hard stuff is easy. The soft stuff is hard. The soft stuff is more important than the hard stuff."

CULTURE AND ADAPTATION STRATEGY

If organizations are to measure and diagnose their cultures to ensure control and support during times of strategic change, they first must understand exactly what "culture" is. Organizations also must understand the dual nature of corporate culture, that is, both its *formal* and *informal* elements. Over time, members of an organization collectively generate meaning as they help build their firm. In turn, the emerging pattern of values that uniquely characterizes a particular organization will impact and be impacted by management practices and behaviors that exemplify and reinforce the organization norm.[2]

Thus, we may define corporate culture in this manner:

- The *informal* and collective values of the people of an organization.
- The *formal* methods and systems by which management reinforces behavior that is derived from these values.

Corporate values, or elements of culture, are composed of both real and symbolic items. Strong cultures exist when there is a widely shared view of appropriate behaviors and specific beliefs, and when the norms and practices are clear and consistent. This type of environment can provide an internal screen for judging workers' reactions and responses to new situations. The strategic implications of widespread agreement about practices and procedures, when coupled with high ideals and lofty

FIGURE 24–1
Behavior-Values Matrix

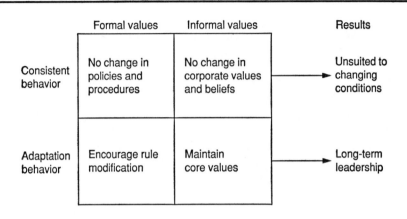

ambitions, are likely to result in a highly competitive and energetic organization that performs well.

A subtle yet important factor in cultural development is the trade-off between consistency of behavior and diversity, or *adaptation strategy*. Apparently organizations that can maintain the core values of their cultures while encouraging new behaviors in response to changing conditions are more likely to maintain leadership position over time. The following matrix (see Figure 24–1) demonstrates this relationship and its outcomes.

As many organizations have sadly learned, new strategies have little impact if they are road-blocked by older and stronger corporate cultures. Some experts empirically argue that well-entrenched cultures may take from 6 to 15 years to change, whereas others contend that some very strong cultures may never fundamentally change.[3] Executives from some oil and telecommunications companies argue that changing culture takes many difficult years and that it usually involves an exhausting and wrenching process. Strong cultures that were once sources of success in a static environment may become heavy anchors when new strategic directions are needed quickly.[4]

WINNING ORGANIZATIONS AND THE CULTURE-EFFECTIVENESS LINKAGE

Today's powerful new organizations are radically different from yesterday's slower-paced companies. The conceptual framework for organizations of today and tomorrow incorporates flat, lean structures with high-performance teams doing work that has been redesigned around processes. For example, spans of control, which were once thought to be limited to about 7 members, have now been eclipsed by spans from 20 to 50 members. Service organizations with well-integrated technologies, such as Shearson American Express, Merrill Lynch, and Federal Express, have already pushed the spans to several hundred, while at the same time decreasing organizational levels from CEO (or COO) to nonmanagement employees to a maximum of five.[5] Therefore, decision making is being pushed lower and lower in the organization, with empowered workers at the lower levels gaining new access to information through just-in-time and other training programs provided on a continuous basis. Performance and reward are being linked to customer satisfaction and team performance instead of traditional internal standards and individual contribution. New leadership is focusing on high-involvement work forces and complete process flows instead of functional boundary control. Yet two central questions remain: Are there organizational characteristics or human behaviors that predict financial health? And if these predictors exist, how do organizations undergo the difficult process of transforming their cultures to include these characteristics?

Historically, the organizational excellence of Japanese companies has been attributed to corporate cultures that support high levels of employee participation, open communications, job security, continuous training, and quality improvement. Additional evidence on U.S. companies was generated by a study of 34 large American companies.[6] The analysis linked financial performance with cultural attributes and tracked performance over a five-year period. The measures of financial performance included debt-to-equity ratio, working capital, current ratio, R&D spending as a percentage of sales, earnings per share, profit margins, return on equity, and investment as a percentage of income. The financial data were then compared with the following measures of organization, culture, or work behavior:

- Organization climate—work design, communication, and degree of emphasis on human resources decision making.
- Organizational context—bureaucracy, job challenge, rewards, and clarity.
- Leadership—team building, participation, and peer support.
- Outcomes—satisfaction and goal integration.

When the two sets of measurements were correlated, the results demonstrated that a "strong" culture, both real and symbolic, is an asset to the company that stresses values that are widely shared and consistent and that provide a framework by which people can address new situations. What these results translated into quantitatively was that the companies in the sample that encouraged employee participation in making decisions, in formulating flexible work methods and designs, and in setting clear and meaningful goals scored higher on the financial measurements than firms without participative cultures.

Some characteristics, such as participation in decision-making practices and emphasis on human resources, showed their differences in effectiveness only after two to three years. Since other elements of culture showed their effects after one year, this *lag factor* suggests the need to sustain cultural change programs over several years, perhaps three to five, to be effective. Thus, long-term investment is required for the benefits of strategic cultural change to be fully realized by the organization.

This cultural lag factor is strategically important. The strong and static culture that is an asset during times of stable growth can be the greatest impediment to organizational effectiveness during times of strategic change.

Consider, for example, that most mergers and acquisitions do not last beyond three years. Consider also that approximately 25 percent of the Fortune 100 companies in 1980 are no longer in existence. The major cause of failure in these cases has been the inability of management to integrate new and diverse cultures and ways of doing business.

Top management has lacked appropriate frameworks and skills to deal with the complex business requirements of the 1990s. Resistance to change, whether due to mergers, new technologies, or new processes, is attached to human and cultural characteristics that, studies indicate, account for 55–90 percent of failed strategic efforts. Put simply, *cultures change more slowly than strategies.*

Thus, culture and strategy are linked in what may appear to be a "tortoise-and-hare" relationship. Ironically, as we know from the traditional fable, the slowness of the tortoise didn't make it any less a threat to the hare. By not paying enough attention to the competition, by not taking the threat seriously, the hare lost the race, even though it was, in most respects, the stronger competitor. This outcome may sound sadly familiar to the large number of once enthusiastic and bold executives whose efforts to facilitate mergers resulted in dismal failure. In today's marketplace, companies will find their abilities to implement strategies increasingly dependent on their effectiveness in accelerating and controlling the pace of cultural change.

THE MISSING STRATEGIC ELEMENT IN THE PRODUCT LIFE CYCLE: CORPORATE CULTURE

The classic S-curve of the product life cycle has received considerable attention in describing the process of new product introduction from initial launch through the stages of growth, maturity, and decline. This curve has been an extremely effective tool for conducting industry and strategic analysis as companies also pass through natural evolutionary stages (see Figure 24–2).

According to this traditional understanding of how an industry evolves the stages are defined as inflection points in the rate of growth of industry sales. In the introductory phase, buyer appetite needs to be generated through the stimulation of initial sales and consumer trials. During the growth period, companies will seek to gain maximum market share and optimum pricing. As market share stabilizes, the product maturity stage is entered and strategies to maintain or rejuvenate sales are developed. Finally, products enter a decline phase as competing products enter or new technologies lead to new substitute products.[7]

FIGURE 24–2
Product Life Cycle

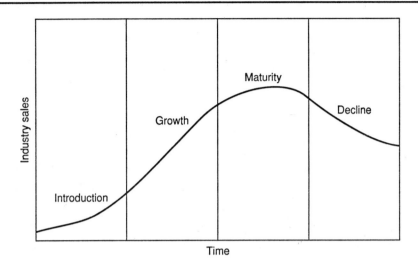

Michael Porter of Harvard University has effectively built upon the evolutionary framework in his summarization of common predictions on how industries will change over their life cycles and what strategies may be applied against the forecasts. A summary of Porter's chart is in Figure 24–3[8]. Porter notes that industries will migrate toward their evolutionary or potential structures based upon the underlying technology, product character, buyer nature, and R&D marketing innovations, among other factors. However, as evidenced previously, it also might be argued that among the most influential of the change drivers will be corporate culture and its impact on strategy. The inclusion of "cultural change drivers" will enhance management's ability to dictate on a more accurate basis effective strategies to move or control organizations as they move through their natural evolutionary curves. The key cultural or organization change drivers are noted in Figure 24–4.

CHANGE STRATEGIES AND THE CHANGE EFFORT CURVE

A company can modify the height and length of the product-life-cycle S-curve by employing a variety of change strategies as noted in the Charge Effort Curve (see Figure 24–5).

FIGURE 24-3

Prediction of Product-Life-Cycle Theories about Strategy, Competition, and Performance

	Introduction	Growth	Maturity	Decline
Overall strategy	• Increase market share (d) • Emphasize R&D, engineering (h)	• Emphasize marketing (h) • Good time to change price or quality image (h)	• Emphasizing marketing effectiveness (f) • Competitive costs are key (i) • Bad time to change price image or quality image (h)	• Emphasize cost control (f, h)
Competition	• Few companies (a, i, j, k)	• Entry (a) • Many competitors (a, c, i, k) • Many mergers and casualties (k)	• Price competition (a, h, i, j) • Shakeout (i, j)	• Exits (a) • Fewer competitors (i, k)
Risk	• High risk (a)	• Growth covers up risk (h)	• Cyclicality sets in (i)	
Margin/profits	• High prices and margins (b, i, k) • Low profiles (f, h)	• Highest priority (g) • Fairly high prices, but lower than introductory phase (b, i) • Good acquisition climate (i)	• Falling prices (b, h) • Lowest prices and margins (k) • Lower profits (k) • Poor acquisition climate (i)	• Falling prices, though might rise in late decline (b, i, k) • Low margins (a)
Buyers	• Buyer inertia (a) • High-income purchaser (i, j, k)	• Widening buyer group (i) • Consumer will accept uneven quality (h)	• Mass market (k) • Saturation (a) • Repeat buying (a, i)	• Customers are sophisticated buyers of product (h)

Products	• Poor quality (k) • Product design, development are keys (f) • Much product variation (j) • Basic product design, frequent design changes (i, j, k)	• Technical and performance differentiation (g) • Reliability is key (f) • Good quality (k) • Competitive product improvements (i)	• Superior quality (k) • Less product differentiation (b, e, h) • Standardization (e, j) • Less rapid product changes (h, i)	• Little product differentiation (g, h) • Spotty product quality (k)
Manufacturing/ distribution	• Overcapacity (k) • Short production runs (i, j) • High skilled-labor content (j) • High production costs (i)	• Undercapacity (k) • Shift toward mass production (i, j) • Scramble for distribution (i)	• Optimum capacity (k) • Increasing stability of manufacturing process (d) • Lower labor skills (j) • Long production runs (j) • High physical distribution costs (i)	• Substantial overcapacity (a, k) • Mass production (g) • Specialty channels (k)

(continues)

FIGURE 24–3 (continued)

Prediction of Product-Life-Cycle Theories about Strategy, Competition, and Performance

	Introduction	Growth	Maturity	Decline
Marketing	• Very high advertising/sales (b, g) • High marketing costs (i)	• High advertising, but lower percent of sales than in introductory (b, g) • Advertising and distribution key for nontechnical products (f)	• Market segmentation (a, i, k) • Efforts to extend life cycle (c, h) • Service and deals more prevalent (a, i) • Packaging important (a) • Advertising competition (a) • Lower advertising/sales (a, b)	• Low advertising/sales and other marketing (b, i)

(a) T. Levitt, "Exploit the Product Life Cycle," *Harvard Business Review,* November/December 1965, pp. 81–94.

(b) R. D. Buzzell, "Competitive Behavior and Product Life Cycles," in *New Ideas for Successful Marketing,* ed J. Wright and J. L. Goldstucker (Chicago: American Marketing Association, 1966), pp.46–68.

(c) R. D. Buzzell, R. M. Nourse, J. B. Matthews, Jr., and T. Levitt, *Marketing: A Contemporary Analysis* (New York: McGraw-Hill, 1972).

(d) B. Catry and M. Chevalier, "Market Share Strategy and the Product Life Cycle," *Journal of Marketing* 38, (October 1974) pp. 29–34.

(e) J. Dean, "Pricing Policies for New Products," *Harvard Business Review* 28, no. 6(November 1950).

(f) D. K. Clifford, Jr., "Leverage in the Product Life Cycle," *Dun's Review,* May 1965.

(g) J. W. Forrester, "Adertising: A Problem in Industrial Dynamics," *Harvard Business Review,* 37 no. 2 (March/April 1959) pp. 100–110.

(h) A. Patton, "Stretch Your Product's Earning Years," *Management Review* XLVII, no 6(June 1959)

(i) T. A. Staudt, D. Taylor and D. Bowersox, *A Managerial Introduction to Marketing* 3rd ed. (Englewood CLiffs, NJ: Prentice-Hall, 1976).

(j) L. T. Wells, Jr. "International Trade: The Product Life Cycle Approach," in *The Product Life Cycle in International Trade,* ed. L. T. Wells, Jr. (Cambridge, MA): Division of Research, Harvard Graduate School of Business Administration, 1972).

(k) J. E. Smallwood, "The Product Life Cycle: A Key to Strategic Market Planning," *MSU Business Topics* 21, no. 1 (Winter 1973) pp. 29–36.

Source: Adapted from Porter, pp. 159–161.

Change Effort Curve

As seen on the curve, change efforts range from rather small and incremental steps, such as in adaptation strategies, to major initiatives, such as programs necessitated by turnaround situations. At either extreme, the probability of significant change appears low. This occurs because slower-paced adaptation strategies are designed for only moderate change, whereas the major change initiatives required for turnaround situations often occur too late to have a significant impact. Thus, the risk for management to take action is low when changes are incremental, and high when changes become extensive.

The curve demonstrates that the extent of the change effort does not always yield proportional results. Instead, the results are more related to the type of change required than to the change effort expended. Therefore, companies can better protect their investments, or change efforts, by effecting the desired changes when their organizations are basically healthy, that is, in either an adaptation or revitalization stage. These changes will be further explored.

Adaptation

Adaptation may best be thought of as a continuous series of incremental changes in the context of a relatively stable environment. Adaptation may be a fine-tuning in which companies refine policies, methods, and procedures; increase attention on unit costs and marginal utilities; or clarify established rules, status, dependencies, and allocation mechanics.[9] Colleges often fall into the adaptation category. After all, how does one speed up the time it takes to read Shakespeare?

Revitalization

Revitalization strategies, although substantial, are nevertheless compatible with the organization's prevailing structure, systems, and processes. Revitalization efforts then may take the form of aggressive programs for expansion within existing sales territories, a shift in emphasis and investment within a product line, or improved processing technology in the production chain. As one analyst puts it, "The overall system adapts, but it is not transformed."[10]

Companies such as Marriott Corp. and Avis Inc. embraced expansive revitalization programs to gain and hold market share in highly competitive industries. Both organizations focused on customer responsiveness and designed internal processes to support their initiatives.

Transformation

Transformational change also may be thought of as large-scale change in response to major environmental shifts. These changes may be prompted by new governmental policies, technological advancement, process innovations, new product creation, or powerful global competition.[11] The concept of change under any of these conditions is that success will depend on quantum advances, not incremental steps. Companies like United Parcel Service and Wal-Mart Stores are excellent examples of organizations

FIGURE 24–4

Cultural and Organizational Change Drivers and the Product Life Cycle

	Introduction	Growth	Maturity	Decline
Skills training	• Hire external experts • Develop pilot training programs • Identify/hire key trainees	• Increase trainee hiring • Develop training program roll out • Measure training effectiveness • Provide training incentives	• Maintain measured and constant flow of trainees into program • Continuous improvement of training program	• Decrease training efforts • Decrease investment costs
Reward systems	• Equity-oriented • Low base • High incentives, bonus-oriented	• Base increases • Individual performance merit increases • Long-range incentives	• Profit sharing and stock options • Individual/Team bonuses • Tight incentives • Midpoint control • Cost control administration	• Reduced competitive compensation • Tight cost control • Short-term incentives
Appraisal systems	• Focus on increasing growth activities • Identify high-potential individuals	• Develop performance appraisal programs by individual level • Build linkages with human resource functions • Focus on discriminating between high and low performers	• Tightly linked to compensation • Tightly linked to human resource functions • Performance-based incentives/pay for knowledge	• Focus on cost control activities • Reduce/relocate staff

Structure	• Centralized and functional • Few staff functions	• Decentralization increases • Geographical focus • Numerous product groups • Duplicate staff functions by product line • Vertical hierarchy buildup	• Matrix structures emerge • Combined multiple product groups • Flat structure • Streamlining of staff functions	• Decentralized local control • Individual product phase out • Elimination of staff support funtions
Leadership	• Visionary and entrepreneurial	• Entrepreneurial and participatory	• Participatory and delegative	• Delegative and "watchdog"

FIGURE 24–5
Change Effort Curve

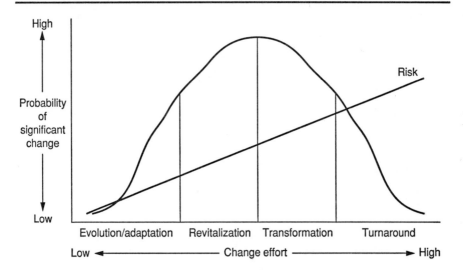

that have invested heavily in major transformations that enabled them to set industry standards in service to customers.

Turnaround

Turnaround change programs usually have the shortest time frame of all change strategies, usually under one year. This time constraint, coupled with financial exigency, often precludes cultural transformation, which then exacerbates the organization's ability to implement change successfully. For these and other reasons, turnarounds are difficult to effect, come at a high price, and have a low probability of success. Because significant change is not likely, organizations in this category are at high risk. Defunct companies such as Pan American, in airlines, and Drexel Burnham Lambert, in investment banking, were organizations whose longstanding cultures, values, and management practices could not adapt quickly enough to meet changing market forces.

ORGANIZATION DIAGNOSIS AND CULTURAL CHANGE

Successful organizations continually assess their condition to determine the potential impact of anticipated changes and their own readiness to address the changes. These assessments begin with a rigorous examination and diagnosis of the organization's major characteristics, underlying systems, and business strategies. It should be remembered that an organization diagnostic study is an essential prerequisite for

FIGURE 24-6
Andersen Consulting's Organization Change Model

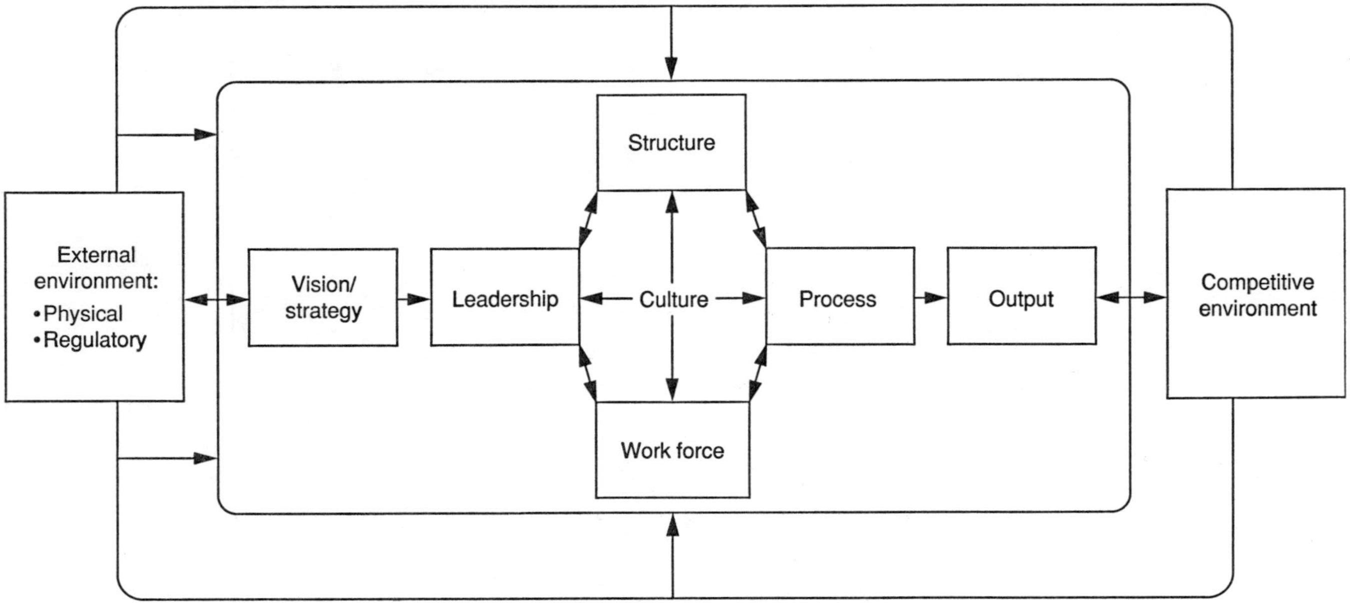

FIGURE 24–7

Leadership Influence Systems

Dimensions			
Leader	*Structure*	*Process*	*Work Force*
Influence systems			
Vision	Role	Planning Values	
Image	Relationship	Operations	Skills
Power	Form	Control	Knowledge
Innovation		Communication	Motivation
Style		Automation	Commitment
Risking		Education	
		Allocation	
		Rewards	

accommodating transformation. When the diagnostic review is completed, the organization should be better positioned to exploit its available resources and channel them to where they will be most needed to maximize results of change efforts.

Within a business world that appears chaotic, a diagnostic model that takes a quantum leap forward is needed. It should portray the organization quantitatively and in sufficient detail to set the stage for subsequent planned change. It also must provide a comprehensive framework that can be used to investigate the complex relationship between the formal and informal workings of the organization. The diagnostic model in Figure 24–6 draws on a rich legacy of research and experience from the fields of management and organization behavior.

This model is based upon four primary dimensions: leadership, structure, process, and work force. These primary dimensions may be defined as follows:

1. *Leadership.* Leadership is the process of skillfully and responsibly guiding and influencing others toward the accomplishment of a goal or goals. When the organization faces change, good leadership recognizes the necessary changes that will satisfy people's needs and supports and encourages these changes.

2. *Structure.* Structure refers to the formal pattern of interactions among individuals, groups, and functions within an organization. The structural aspects of an organization may include rules, policies, formal communication relationships, organization charts, job descriptions, and defined work flows. Structure also refers to the manner in which resources and authority are distributed throughout an organization and how its tasks and patterns of relationships are organized.

3. *Process.* Process is the collection of activities performed by an organization, including the planning, organizing and activating of operations whereby the material and human resources are coordinated to achieve specified results. Processes are what people and groups "do."

4. *Work Force.* Work force refers to the characteristics of the people in the organization. Work force is a collective term for the individuals that make up an organization, including top-level executives, middle management, operative or first-line management, and operating employees.

Beneath the primary dimension level is another level of detail termed *influence systems.* Research and experience have shown that influence systems affect whether and to what extent change can be implemented and sustained. During the present analysis, such influence systems as rewards and appraisal have been highlighted as key cultural levers of change strategies. A comprehensive diagnostic, however, now demands that all relevant characteristics and their interaction effects be analyzed. The chart (see Figure 24–7) shows how the influence systems relate to the four primary organizational dimensions.

Although each influence system relates primarily to one organizational dimension, the systems are highly interactive and interdependent. Their purpose is to help target specific changes and systematically coordinate their impacts. Therefore, changes to any single influence system often will cause changes in another—sometimes planned and sometimes unplanned.

The following are the definitions of each influence system:

Leadership Influence Systems

- *Vision.* What the organization imagines or what it wants to achieve in the future. It provides a reason for existence and helps ensure stability and continuity of direction. It embodies the goals, values, and characteristics the organization strives to attain. Visions are long-term and should transcend temporary changes.

- *Image.* The perceptions that individuals or groups have of the organization. It is considered a long-term phenomenon, stable and resistant to change. A goal of any organization's change effort is to determine and align existing images with the organization's vision of itself in the future—and then reinforce these images throughout the transformation process.

- *Power.* The ability or capacity to influence the behaviors of others. Power can be vested in individuals or in groups, and can be real or perceived. Power is evidenced by an individual's ability to influence the organization's direction.

- *Innovation.* The process of bringing new problem-solving or value-adding ideas into use. It can involve trying new business strategies or developing new products or processes. Innovation is not limited to new technology; organizational innovation is equally important. Many productivity improvements are due to innovations regarding job design or other social issues.

- *Style.* The pattern of behaviors throughout the organization, often reflective of its management or leadership.

- *Risking.* The tendency to take chances when conditions are uncertain. Since change involves a confrontation with the uncertain or the unknown, the propensity of organizations and individuals to risk is an indicator of their ability to change.

Structure Influence Systems

- *Role.* The "expected-perceived-enacted" behavior patterns attributed to a particular job or position. Each person's or group's role is to add, protect, enhance, or expand value to the organization.
- *Relationship.* The interactions among organizational units and their members. Relationships are the interpersonal component of a job. They can be based on expressed policies, procedures, and rules, and they also can be assumed through custom, personality, or indirect association. They may be formal, as with reporting relationships from subordinates to supervisors, or informal, as with networks of co-workers with common interests and shared goals or values.
- *Form.* The configuration or shape of an organization. Structural form is typically depicted on organization charts. Forms are the strategies of organizations to (1) increase their ability to preplan, (2) increase their flexibility to adapt to their inability to preplan, or (3) decrease the level of performance required for continued viability. Exactly which strategy is chosen depends on its relative costs to the organization.

Process Influence Systems

- *Planning.* Determination of what factors are required to achieve goals before an activity takes place. Planning involves the choice of achievements, as well as decisions among strategic, operational, and production alternatives and preparation for action. It takes place at many levels and for many purposes. Ideally, all plans are consistent and synchronized, and contribute to the attainment of collective goals.
- *Operations.* The primary prescribed processes conducted by any organization. Operations are those activities directly contributing to service, production, and creation of wealth. Although other processes may be crucial, their value lies only in their contribution to operations. A critical aspect of operations is the thorough understanding of the actual work flow. In addition to helping in the assessment of the impact of technology, this sets the stage for examining issues related to changes in roles, needed skills, and optional organization redesigns such as innovative work systems (e.g., self-directed work teams).
- *Control.* Adherence to plans and standards to achieve objectives. Controls exist at all levels (strategic, operational, or production) and apply to all organizational units (corporate, division, department, project, or work teams). By these mechanisms deviations from plans and standards are prevented, detected, and

corrected. Controls are enforcing and regulating. They may be positive, such as inspection to detect production irregularities, or negative, such as contractual terms requiring cost penalties for late delivery by vendors.

- *Communication.* The exchange of data, information, or meaning. Communication can occur between people, between people and information systems or automated processes, and among information systems or automated processes. It can be effected verbally through printed matter, by demonstration, or by nonverbal signaling, electronically or visually.

- *Automation.* The use of technology to enhance the work of people. Processes are automated when there is a conversion to the use of automatic machines or devices designed to control various processes. Automation attempts to improve the conduct and outcome of processes by changing the ways they work.

- *Education.* The development of abilities into specific, required, or desired skills, knowledge, or attitudes. The object of education is to increase an individual's performance and potential. When skills are taught, performance should increase, and when knowledge is advanced, potential advances as well. Training is often associated with skill development (e.g., how to use a computer system), whereas education is associated with knowledge advancement (e.g., learning the fundamentals of information system design). Motivation and commitment within a work force can be directly affected by education.

- *Allocation.* The distribution of resources within an organization. Resources include money, time, information, people, authority, material, equipment, and attention. Ideally, managers will attempt to predict changes in operating conditions, revise the exchange of inputs and outputs, and continually develop mutual agreements with resource contributors.

- *Rewards.* Incentives such as salary, bonus, stock, benefits, perquisites, promotions, transfers, training, security, opportunity, and autonomy. Rewards and the systems that generate them provide positive reinforcement in shaping the work behavior of individuals. When examining reward systems, we seek to identify those that promote or retard the planned organization change and those that affect the sustainability of change.

Work Force Influence Systems

- *Values.* The principles, enduring beliefs, and customs held dear by individuals and groups in an organization. They are what individuals consider to be good, important, and right. They may be moral, ethical, or social in nature and commonly reflect cultural norms, belief systems, or personal codes of behavior.

- *Skills.* Abilities that contribute to performance. Skills may be multiplied or leveraged through equipment, computers, or other people, but they reside in individuals. A primary objective of training and experience is to exercise and improve individual skills.

- *Knowledge.* Familiarity with facts, conditions, or principles. Knowledge pertaining to the conduct of certain processes or work tasks is termed skill for our purposes. The term *knowledge* is reserved for processes or work tasks not specifically related to the particular work at hand. Skill is what one must do or know at any given time; knowledge is what one does know, regardless of whether it is put to use.

- *Motivation.* A state of mind that causes one to behave in certain ways. Motivation is process oriented. Whatever process an individual goes through (choices, goals, directions), motivation is concerned with how the behavior begins, proceeds, or ends. It also refers to the type of subjective feelings one has during a certain behavior.

- *Commitment.* The desire to persist. It refers to the degree of connection one feels to a certain position. Commitment is a very strong perception. It affects resistance to change (commitment to the past or present), propensity to change (commitment to the vision or to the new organization), and leadership (commitment to others).

This organization change model highlights several variables that have not always been included in earlier prototypes. First, the concept of vision is introduced as a key factor for managing the formation of the future state of the organization. Clearly, this model develops a relationship between the organization's vision and the supporting strategy necessary to execute successful change. Second, the model draws a clear demarcation between internal variables and outputs and external variables and inputs. It draws attention to the fact that organizations are not entirely powerless over the entire spectrum of external forces. This is a key assumption and one that deserves further attention, especially in terms of today's global marketplace and the need to build better alliances between businesses and government.

The diagnostic requirement for change is extremely important. This factor, above all, has been cited by experienced transformational leaders as the key to what will set the course for either success or failure. By examining the organization's major characteristics and underlying systems, the potential impact of change can be more accurately anticipated. Resources can be allocated where they will generate the most return and help ensure the likelihood of transformation.

CONCLUSION

Clearly, the successful implementation of corporate strategy depends on the ability of the organization to change culturally. Both corporate strategy and organization culture are inextricably linked. Each is interdependent and symbiotically related to the other. Organizations must operate in a highly complex and competitive business environment in which the relationship between required stability and change is often ambiguous, confusing and, therefore, risky. Fortunately, the social sciences are maturing and lending new and useful insights to equip a new generation of leaders and managers with powerful and sophisticated change management tools. To meet the challenges ahead, corporate captains will need to balance traditional business acumen with new organizational knowledge bases. How well they combine their abilities not only will separate the "tortoises" from the "hares," but may also redefine how each plays the game.

NOTES

1. T. J. Peters and R. H. Waterman, *In Search of Excellence* (New York: Harper & Row, 1982), p. 75.

2. See C. J. Fombrun, "Of Tribes and Witch Doctors: The Anthropologist's View," in *Corporate Culture and Change: Highlights of a Conference,* ed. M. A. Berman (New York: The Conference Board, Inc., 1986), p. 7. See also C. J. Fombrun, "Corporate Culture and Competitive Stratagy," in *Strategic Human Resources Managment,* ed. C. J. Fombrun (New York: John Wiley & Sons, 1984), p. 203. On the relationship between management practices and cultural values, see D. R. Denison, *Corporate Culture and Organizational Effectiveness* (New York: John Wiley & Sons, 1990), p. 2.

3. B. Uttal, "The Corporate Culture Vultures," *Fortune,* 17 October 1983, p. 70. Cited in E. Huse and T. G. Cummings, *Organizational Development and Change* (St. Paul, MN: West, 1985), p. 352.

4. Huse and Cummings, p. 351.

5. J. B. Quinn and P. C. Paquette, "Technology and Services: Creating Organization Revolutions," *Sloan Management Review* 31, no. 2 (Winter 1990), pp. 67–78.

6. D. R. Denison, "The Climate Culture and Effectiveness of Work Organizations," Ph. D. Dissertation (University of Michigan: Ann Arbor, 1982).

7. M. E. Porter, *Competitive Strategy: Techniques for Analyzing Industries and Competitors* (New York: Free Press, 1980), p. 158.

8. Adapted from Porter, pp. 159–161.

9. M. Tushman, W. Newman, and E. Romanelli, "Convergence and Upheaval: Managing the Unsteady Pace of Organizations" in *The Management of Organizations,* ed. M. L. Tushman, C. O'Reilly, and D. A. Nadler (New York: Harper & Row, 1989).

10. Ibid., p. 482.

11. Ibid., pp. 483–84.

Chapter Twenty-Five

Making Culture Change Happen

Craig Eric Schneier
Richard W. Beatty

THE CHANGE IMPERATIVE

The drivers of change in companies of the 1990s are well documented. They include an aging, diverse work force; relentless foreign competition; frequent mergers, acquisitions, and divestitures; repeated downsizing and de-layering; continually rising customer expectations; accelerated technological obsolescence; and unstable political and economic environments, to name a few. As Figure 25–1 notes, at least half of the world's largest companies have made major changes in their structures, strategies, work processes, and/or sizes in the late 1980s and early 1990s. Hence, for most companies, the tough decision is not whether to change but what to change and how to change.

STRUCTURE CHANGE ALONE FAILS

The strategies and tactics companies use to make the tough decisions about change are often, by their own admissions, not terribly innovative. Despite the fact that most companies have marshaled considerable resources in the areas of quality, customer service, work process redesign, self-directed teams, and learning organizations, they still rely largely on replacing people and/or changing structure when performance must improve.

Research (cited in Schneier et al., 1992) has found that restructuring, including downsizing, when used as the primary change strategy, has not been particularly effective. At more than 50 percent of the companies sampled in one large study, restructuring, de-layering, and/or downsizing has resulted neither in lower costs nor higher productivity (see Bennett, 1991). Furthermore, after downsizing, loyalty and

FIGURE 25–1

Major Change Is Now Routine for Companies around the World

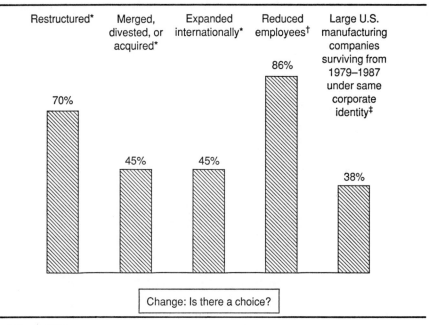

* Kanter (1991
† Fortune (1991)
‡ Forbis and Adams (1991)

morale of the work force and credibility of management suffer greatly (see, e.g., Filipowski, 1992). A "vicious cycle" (see Schneier et al., 1992) sets in as a demoralized work force does not innovate. Rather, it protects and even exalts the status quo. But for most companies, even heretofore successful ones like IBM, the status quo has shown that it cannot produce the order-of-magnitude improvements needed to compete. Without innovation, cost positions deteriorate further and lead to additional downsizings.

WORDS WITHOUT ACTIONS
WILL LEAD TO FAILURE

In addition to reorganizing or downsizing, companies often adopt a tactic for change that centers on values. In their attempts to stay competitive by reducing cycle times, enhancing customer service, and/or improving product quality, many organizations have changed, or at least reaffirmed, their visions or values. Some, for example, have moved from a production-focused to a market-focused company. Others have explicitly articulated teamwork, leadership, empowerment, and/or diversity as their core values.

Companies in trouble also redefine their strategies to become "niche players," "global" companies, or the "lowest-cost" manufacturers. But as numerous CEOs have found, a revised corporate values statement, even if emblazoned in a poster on the wall of every conference room or a card inside every employee's wallet, ensures neither change nor improvement. Values must be translated into behavior and visions must be implemented effectively for change to occur, and to endure.

These key questions remain:

What is different as a result of the new value?

What must each person do differently tomorrow to demonstrate the new value or execute the new strategy?

Exhortations about values do little, but actions consistent with them can do a great deal.

IMPLEMENTING SUCCESSFUL CHANGE: STRUCTURES, SYSTEMS, AND SKILLS

Corporations, like the people who constitute them, are dynamic and organic—they grow, they decline, they adapt. They constantly change, albeit with varying degrees of speed, intensity, and success. Corporate culture, defined as persistent shared values and behavior patterns, helps explain companies' reactions to change. Kotter and Heskett (1992), in their empirical study of the impact of culture on performance, identify "performance degrading" and "adaptive" cultures:

> We found that [high performance adaptive] firms with cultures that emphasized all the key managerial constituencies [customers, stockholders, and employees] and leadership from managers at all levels outperformed firms that did not have those cultural traits by a huge margin. Over an eleven-year period, the former . . . grew their stock prices by 901 percent versus 74 percent, and improved their net incomes by 756 percent versus 1 percent. Performance-degrading cultures have a negative financial impact for a number of reasons, the most significant being their tendency to inhibit firms from adopting needed strategic or tactical changes. (p. 11)

What distinguishes the adaptive cultures? For one thing, leaders have skills to initiate change, take risks, reduce bureaucracy, and communicate why new behavior is needed. Adaptive cultures are also evidenced by operational systems. A key set of systems is that related to decisions about people: Who is promoted, how, and why? Or, who is rewarded, how, and why?

Kotter and Heskett (1992) note that in adaptive cultures, criteria for rewards are changed to fit values, goals, and the competitive environment. Hence, promotion systems are mechanisms for change. Adaptive cultures typically are not overly hierarchical structures; boundaries between levels are permeable and facilitate flexibility.

FIGURE 25–2
A Model to Start, Maintain, and Sustain Culture Change

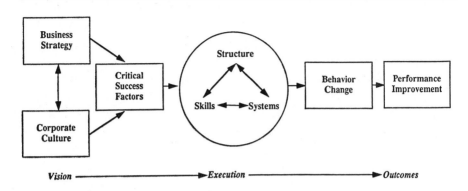

Separate studies of successful change (e.g., Ulrich and Lake, 1990; Waterman, 1989; Beer et al., 1991) are consistent. Change results from alteration of organization systems (e.g., measurement), structure (e.g., reporting relationships, span of control, hierarchical layers), and skills (e.g., coaching). All three are effective levers for change when they are utilized in conjunction with each other. Ignoring any two, for example, by putting one too far ahead in the change agenda, is a prescription for adherence to the status quo or for producing change that quickly evaporates.

How does lasting culture change happen? A change road map or model is proposed here (Figure 25–2) that describes the related use of the three levers. Examples of the model's use in different companies also are presented. The rest of this chapter deals with a summary of key results from an extensive analysis of numerous successful change efforts, as reported in the business press, academic journals, and company documents. The following two sections present vignettes describing actual culture change efforts in two companies and provide the context for the change road map.

WESTERN COMPANY: SYSTEMS, STRUCTURE, AND SKILLS LAG CHANGE EFFORTS

Western Company, a large manufacturing business, seemingly had the important ingredients for successful culture change, including these components:

- Significant declines in market share and profit provided a compelling need to change behavior, processes, and structure.

- There was a history of rallying around a problem, and through considerable effort, eventually solving it.
- Top management not only was committed to change but also was the architect of the change vision.
- The CEO participated in all key change activities, not merely to introduce them but actually to lead them.
- Skilled and experienced internal and external change consultants were identified and assigned.
- Ample time and resources were budgeted to make needed improvements.
- Key business problems were identified and analyzed; data from customers, employees, and suppliers were obtained.
- Cross-functional teams were formed; each developed specific goals, and each was charged with specific tasks.

After 18 months of activity—training sessions, team meetings, focus groups, task force reports, speeches, discussions, reorganizations, and even some managerial replacements—a dispassionate assessment concluded that a few problems (e.g., faster manufacturing changeovers for new models) had been solved, but that fundamentally little in the culture (or the firm's overall performance) had changed.

Western Company's culture still emphasized functional boundaries, crisis management, a concentration on cost over quality, and a shoot-the-messenger managerial style. Results of focus groups found that the culture change activities were successful at raising consciousness about the need for change and communicating the vision. But no broad-based ownership existed, no consistent, day-to-day behavior change was evident, and no sustained performance improvement was attained.

Western's change initiative for culture change succeeded as an *event*, but failed as a *process*. Why? There were several complex causes, including some external competitive issues. But mechanisms to put the vision into operation were not put in place; and systems and structure—key mechanisms that control behavior—were omitted from the change strategy. Hence, behavior changes required by the new vision did not develop. Activity, but not results, and treating problems, rather than preventing them, were still the behaviors that were rewarded at Western.

SOUTHERN COMPANY: SYSTEMS, STRUCTURE, AND SKILLS LEAD CULTURE CHANGE EFFORTS

Southern Company, another large manufacturer, used many more ingredients for successful change than Western:

- A once-advantaged market position slipped as foreign competitors offered higher quality, lower cost, faster order-to-ship cycles, and more innovative services. Southern thus had a compelling reason to change.

- Top management understood the ends and means to their culture change. Competitive advantage via customer service was the goal and employee empowerment was a means of getting there.

- Top management painted a clear picture of how cross-functional teams would operate on the shop floor and across the business.

- Top management sent managers and selected teams to visit companies where self-directed work teams were performing successfully.

- The production management team spent six months listening to customers, suppliers, and employees to identify problems and to build trust.

- Specific high performance targets and behavioral expectations were set and communicated.

- The work teams and the customers' names were placed on each subassembly produced by each team. Team members visited and called customers to provide them with status reports.

- Union members were sent to other company sites to meet with union and nonunion employees working in self-directed work teams.

- "All employee" meetings were held on company time to celebrate accomplishments and publicize how the production process had changed. Shop level employees participated in running these meetings.

- The first-level supervisory position was eliminated and the title of supervisor changed to Team Leader. That position was rotated among team members.

- Team Leaders received extensive training in problem solving, group interaction, and team building.

- Spans of control were broadened—made so broad in fact, that little "control" can actually be exercised. That was the intent, because self-control replaced supervisory control.

- Customer plant tours were initiated.

- Teams were given more influence in hiring, firing, paying, and promoting.

After 24 months, significant improvements were evident in work process simplification and managerial behavior at Southern, and they were created mostly by Southern's employees. Jobs were designed very differently; all employees work in teams. The material process flow through the plant has been streamlined, the production cycle time has been improved significantly, and customer satisfaction is up substantially.

Southern's change effort stressed *how* the change was to occur. It took place by simultaneous change in structure (e.g., job design), systems (e.g., performance measurement and assessment), leadership style and skills (e.g., interpersonal, decision making, teamwork), and work process flow. Even the symbols (e.g., job titles) used to communicate status were altered. Results, not activity and effort, first were defined, then were expected, and finally were rewarded at Southern.

A CULTURE CHANGE MODEL

The lessons learned from these two cases suggest that successful culture change efforts hinge on changes in the systems, structure, and skills that govern behavior. A model of culture change consistent with this view, therefore, would have at its core these three levers for change (see Figure 25–2).

CRITICAL SUCCESS FACTORS (CSFs)

As the culture change road map (Figure 25–2) shows, culture and strategy interact to suggest a set of critical success factors (CSFs). They are what a business must master to execute its strategy (Irvin and Michaels, 1989). For example, McDonalds Inc. succeeds because it is astute at selecting winning sites. The Limited Inc. succeeds because it excels at quickly distributing large quantities of the fastest-moving apparel to its stores. Frito-Lay, the snack food maker, succeeds because it gathers and uses real-time information on customer purchases to influence delivery, forecasts, and product development. Minnesota Mining & Manufacturing Co. (3M) succeeds because it encourages and rewards entrepreneurial behavior in a large and diversified corporation, resulting in numerous innovations and, hence, numerous new products. Caterpillar succeeds because it provides service worldwide within 24 hours. As these examples show, each CSF is operational, not merely conceptual. Each determines or identifies new behaviors, rewards, or structures.

Several recent analyses have described aspects of organizations critical to attain and sustain competitive advantage, that is, core competencies (Prahalad and Hamel 1990), core skills (Irvin and Michaels, 1989), capabilities (Stalk et al., 1992), and driving forces (Tregoe et al., 1989). Although there are differences in each notion, all propose that the keys to strategy execution—what it takes for a specific company to win in the marketplace—must be identified and become the focus of strategy (see Figure 25–3).

CSFs are, therefore, a starting place for change efforts. If corporate performance is inadequate, the wrong CSFs are very likely being emphasized or the execution of the CSFs is not measuring up to that of the competition. As Figure 25–2 depicts, the levers for change—structure, systems, and skills—are mechanisms to execute and improve performance on CSFs. As an example, assume that a CSF for Merck is research productivity and for Wal-Mart Stores it is warehouse distribution speed. The skills change lever at Merck would operate through a more effective recruiting and selection system to bring in the best research chemists. The structure change lever would lead to a more streamlined structure and eliminate work steps in Wal-Mart's warehouse distribution process.

Whereas CSFs identify how to execute strategy, actual execution, coupled with lasting culture change, requires a link from CSFs to individual-level and organization-level behaviors (see Figure 25–4). Western Company failed to address specific organization-level CSFs and did not put systems and structures in place to ensure behavior

FIGURE 25–3

Critical Success Factors (CSFs): How Culture Change Efforts Become Concrete

Company	Potential/Illustrative CSF
Merck	Research and development cycle time
Federal Express	Package tracking information system
Wal-Mart	Warehouse distribution system
3M	Entrepreneurial culture and rewards
Domino's Pizza	Order-taking process and delivery
Motorola	"Six-sigma" (% defects) level quality
Honda	Small engine capability
Cascio	Flat display screen technology
Fidelity Investments	Telephone-based customer service
PepsiCo	Penetration of overseas markets
Caterpillar	Twenty-four hour worldwide service

change. Culture change efforts were visible events, but events ultimately lose momentum. Southern Company, by contrast, was able to initiate and sustain culture change because structure, systems, and skills were addressed together and early. For example, supervisors were trained in coaching skills and the vertical structure was altered via new titles.

As the change model in Figure 25–3 demonstrates, not only was Southern Company's business strategy made clear, but consequences for individual employees and managers if the business was not successful were also made clear. Thus, required new behaviors on the part of both management and operating employees were clarified. Southern's CSFs were communicated continually by the CEO through public announcements, the weekly company newsletter, videotaped messages, and most of all via his numerous informal discussions. Local managers also provided a critical and credible communication link by continually listening and talking to their peers, suppliers, customers, subordinates, and superiors. They communicated success measures of the self-directed teams and individual performance expectations.

Figure 25–4 provides examples of how organization-level CSFs translate to individual-level behaviors and skills. Without putting CSFs into behavioral terms, their powers are seldom realized. CEOs can exhort their managers to innovate, but unless they arm subordinates with relevant marketplace information, provide rewards and recognition for taking prudent risks, and organize their teams effectively to take prudent risks, innovation is stifled. 3M, for example, addresses the translation issue successfully by these alterations:

- Structure (i.e., breaking business units into separate entities when they reach a certain size, reducing hierarchy, and liberally using ad hoc teams).

FIGURE 25–4
Execute Strategy via Organization-Level Success Factors...
Institutionalize Culture Change via Individual-Level Behaviors

Organization success factors	Individual success factors
McDonald's: Site selection ⟶	Real estate valuation
	Traffic pattern analysis
	Negotiations
	Long-range forecasting
3M: Innovation ⟶	Rewarding risk taking
	Empowering subordinates
	Building teams
Caterpillar: 24-hour service ⟶	Initiative
	Self-confidence
	"Do what it takes"

- Systems (i.e., rewarding, not punishing, risk takers by allocating funding for their projects).
- Skills (i.e., toward leading, encouraging and coaching, versus controlling).

Figure 25–5 notes those key aspects of structure, systems, and skills offering significant leverage as lead variables in culture change. A continuum is provided to illustrate the range of choices available in using structure and systems to facilitate behavior and, hence, culture change. For example, many companies' structures and systems are still quite bureaucratic, with numerous hierarchical layers and differentiated titles that hinder the push toward a lean, responsive organization. If responsiveness is desired as both an outcome and a characteristic of the culture, numerous layers are a structural deterrent. Changes in structure, systems, and skills that lead to culture change are discussed below.

CULTURE CHANGE AND STRUCTURE CHANGE

Job Design

At Southern Company significant changes occurred in the jobs on the shop floor; the notion of a job has been totally redefined. All employees now are members of teams. There are very few foremen, whose roles have been redefined so that they now serve as "suppliers" of resources, information, and authority to employees—who in effect have become their "customers."

The transformation process, however, evolved as the teams themselves, with management's assistance, began to redefine the roles of all employees in the production process. Considerable time was invested in determining the duties of each team member and each team (i.e., job design). A questionnaire was used to determine what

FIGURE 25–5

Organization Structure, (Human Resource) Systems, and Skills as Lead Variables in Culture Change*

Structure	Systems	Skills
Hierarchy Many levels→Few levels Vertical interactions→Horizontal interactions **Job design** Narrow responsiblity→Broad responsibility Rigid→Fluid **Organizing principle** Internal focus→External focus By function→By process By product→By customer	**Performance management** Annual rating→Ongoing assessment Measure costs→Measure value Boss evaluate→Customer evaluate **Compensation/rewards** Pay for tenure→Pay for performance Individual rewards→Team rewards Money→Recognition **Career development** Courses→Experiences Teach→Mentor Up is the only way→Horizontal and vertical paths lead to sucess	**Leadership** Individual accountability→Team accountability Motivate via threat of loss of security→Motivate via challenge, autonomy Manager→Coach **Communication** Written→Verbal Top down→Top-down, bottom-up, sideways **Change management** Followers, resister of change→Leader, champion of change **Technical expertise** Narrow, functional→Broad, cross-functional One per career→Multiple specialties, careers

*Illustrative list; other systems, for example, may include planning, budgeting, selection.

management, employees, and internal and external customers expected of the team and to identify the extent of decision making that was to be exercised at team levels. The broadening of the plant-level jobs in Southern Company is described in Figure 25–6 and the role of the Team Leader appears in Figure 25–7.

Organization Design

Functional "walls" or boundaries are still powerful forces in most businesses. Functional boundaries typically determine compensation, career paths, technical expertise requirements, information flow, and status. Cross-functional moves are made in many companies, but the process is rarely institutionalized and typically occurs at relatively high hierarchical levels and for high-potential employees. Yet, functional barriers and the parochial views they foster are deterrents to speed and customer service. General Electric, for example, has mounted an all-out frontal attack on internal boundaries, those that separate function levels, business units, domestic and overseas units, and customers and suppliers. General Electric's culture change initiative is aimed at becoming a "boundaryless" company (GE Annual Report, 1991). Several approaches are being used to disassemble change impediments.

Process-based organization designs. Organizing tasks around work flow, as opposed to functions, breaks down "walls" between functions. However, it requires a fundamental shift toward organizing around business processes, rather than functions. Value is added as raw materials (e.g., information, people, material) move through the organization, undergoing a transformation to become outputs (e.g., durable consumer goods, financial analyses, capable human resources).

In essence, the shift is from a vertical to a horizontal organization architecture (Nadler, 1992). Key processes—"flows of activity, information, decision, and material" (Ostroff and Smith, 1992)—are identified. Then such objectives as reducing order cycle time or increasing the number of new products generated are set and driven by strategy and CSFs. Specific work processes, such as order entry, commodity sourcing, and accounts payable, are "mapped" or documented and then redesigned (see Schneier et al., 1992; Kaplan and Murdock, 1991; Hammer, 1990). Focusing on process-based approaches to change instead of solely on outcomes has the advantage of leading to a fundamental rethinking of how work is performed (see Figure 25–8). Order-of-magnitude process performance improvements are possible when work processes are zero-based, that is, each step is scrutinized and questioned: Is this step absolutely necessary? Must it be performed inside the organization (or outsourced)? Where in the organization should it be performed? How can it be redesigned to be performed with maximum efficiency?

Work process-based approaches to culture change. Based on studies (e.g., Hammer, 1990; Schneier et al., 1992) of successful work redesign initiatives, the following results are consistently found:

• Accountability for improvement is given to an appointed "process owner."

FIGURE 25–6

How the Natural Work Team Operates to Change Culture (Manufacturing Illustration)

Responsibilities	Authorities
1. Working with suppliers and customers to establish or clarify quality standards. 2. Forecasting and recommending overtime hours, after pursuing all other reasonable alternatives (Team Leader approves overtime). 3. Determining what must be produced daily to meet scheduled requirements. 4. Communicating forward to the customer and backward to the supplier on service, delivery and quality issues. 5. Reporting and visually displaying performance against standards for Quality, Service, and Productivity. 6. Establishing housekeeping standards and identifying/resolving safety, housekeeping, and ergonomic problems. 7. Cross training, operator training, job rotation, and role assignment. 8. Establishing methods and techniques to meet quality standards and solving quality problems. 9. Contributing to the reduction of scrap and rework through maintaining tools and equipment, monitoring incoming materials, and implementing improvement projects. 10. Continuously reducing the costs within the area of control, such as labor and material, indirect labor (handling, setup), indirect materials (oils, gloves, tools, etc.), scrap/rework, and overtime hours. 11. Communicating on an as-needed basis across customer-supplier teams, shifts, and team leaders.	1. Stop production if the product is not conforming to the established quality standards. 2. Prioritize and take actions to reduce backlogs. 3. Request parts from internal suppliers. 4. Challenge designs, systems, and practices that prevent attainment of goals. 5. Shut equipment or processes down if they are not conforming to safety standards. 6. Request support and information needed for meeting responsibilities. 7. Recommend and assist in implementing plant floor layout changes. 8. Conduct internal customer-supplier visits. 9. Evaluate the performance of their processes and their suppliers.

FIGURE 25–7
The New Role of the Foreman/Supervisor

Cultural characteristics	Traditional culture	Self-directed team culture
Customer	Boss	Customers/team members
Focus	Internal	External
Career	Functional	Cross-functional
Structure	Vertical	Horizontal
Leadership	Hierarchical	Process
Managing	People	Information/resources
Rewards	Individual	Team
Competitive focus	Internal	External
Work process	Transactions	Relationships
Goals	Winning	Aligning
Coordination	Low	High
Loyalty/commitment	Boss	Team/unit/organization
Measurement	Individual	Team
Evaluator	Boss	Customers/team/members

- Process mapping is used to document current work flow, decisions, and process performance.
- Cross-functional, cross-level, and in some cases cross-business unit teams generate data, redesign processes, and implement solutions.
- Internal and external customers and suppliers, as well as the people operating the process, participate in all phases of the initiative.
- A top leader becomes the process redesign "champion" and sponsors the work, reorders priorities of team members, secures resources, sets challenging and concrete goals, and rewards results.
- Systems (e.g., performance measurement) are aligned with the redesign to facilitate implementation.

Thus the culture change has been driven by a change in the way work is done. Eastman Kodak has successfully redesigned work processes in its black-and-white film manufacturing. The manufacturing employees and managers (called "zebras") reside not in functional departments but in "flows"—streams of work activity, such as production of film for a specific Kodak division— and operate in self-directed teams. The "zebras" have cut the time to fill an order in half and have cut costs to beat their budgets by 15 percent (Stewart, 1992). Xerox, Texas Instruments, General Electric,

FIGURE 25–8

Focus on Work Processes versus Solely on Performance Outcomes for Lasting Culture Change

What are examples of work processes?	How are work processes identified?	How are work processes approved?
1. New product development	1. Identify outputs and ask how they are obtained.	1. **Process identification and prioritization:** listing of processes and their purposes; prioritizaton as to what to work on.
2. Budgeting	2. Identify goals or objectives and ask how they are met.	
3. Sourcing raw materials		2. **Process "mapping":** documentation of how process is performed now.
4. Planning for increased market share	3. Identify performance measures (individual, team, unit, organizational) and ask how they are evaluated.	3. **Process analysis:** assessment of value (benefits minus costs), based on customer input.
5. Order processing	4. Identify internal or external customers and ask how they are satisfied.	
6. Goal setting		4. **Process benchmarking:** identification of "world-class" or "best-in-class" processes, based on assessment of "best practices" inside or outside the organization.
7. Collective bargaining	5. Identify financial, managerial, people, logistical, legal, etc. problems and ask how they can be solved.	
8. Manufacturing		5. **Gap analysis:** identification of gap between current process and customer expectations and/or world class processes.
9. Issuing payroll checks	6. Identify decisions and ask how they are made.	
10. Developing an advertising campaign	7. Look at critical success factors—what it takes for a person, unit, team, or organization to succeed—and ask how the person, unit, team, or organization is impacted.	6. **Process redesign:** revision/improvement and action planning to implement new design.
11. Paying vendors		7. **Implementation.**
12. Distributing products		8. **Continuous improvement.**

FIGURE 25–9

Process-Based Structure in a Manufacturing Business

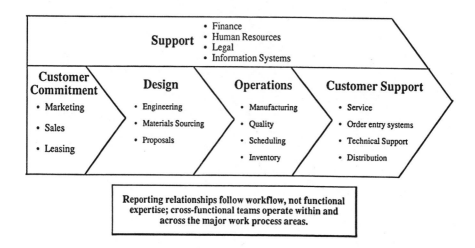

Deere, Oryx Energy, Corning, 3M, Boeing, Ford Motor, Colgate-Palmolive, and numerous other companies, large and small, have reported positive results with work process redesign.

Process-based organization design. The process-based structure for Southern Company's manufacturing business is illustrated in Figure 25–9. Compared with a functional structure, fewer units are needed, once the basic work processes that add value are identified and improved. As Southern moved to a process-oriented structure, implications for performance measures, career paths, and job design were evident. For example, horizontal developmental career moves became important in building broad skills, since functional boundaries weakened. Since those who design the product now work in teams with those who manufacture it, both engineering and manufacturing expertise of team members are valued in deciding who to promote. The mandate to gain new experience and skills necessary to make the process-driven structure work was resisted by many workers, however, until promotion criteria were changed to include the new skill set.

The doing, thinking, learning, and leading organization structure. Many companies alter job design to broaden accountability and discretion, increase spans of control, remove supervisory layers, overlay "networks" within their hierarchies to focus effort on results (Charan, 1990), "rightsize" the work force or break functional walls through process-based work designs to utilize structure effectively in facilitating change. All of these design tools lead to a fundamentally new

FIGURE 25–10
Moving to the Thinking, Leading, and Learning Organization

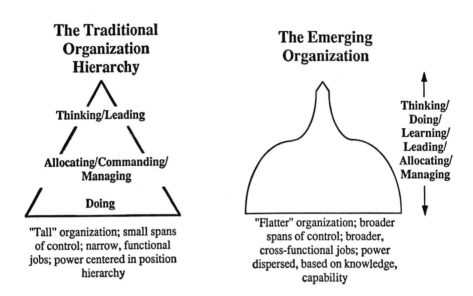

The Traditional Organization Hierarchy

Thinking/Leading

Allocating/Commanding/Managing

Doing

"Tall" organization; small spans of control; narrow, functional jobs; power centered in position hierarchy

The Emerging Organization

Thinking/
Doing/
Learning/
Leading/
Allocating/
Managing

"Flatter" organization; broader spans of control; broader, cross-functional jobs; power dispersed, based on knowledge, capability

organization structure. However, the new organization designs that facilitate culture change are more than a new set of boxes on the company's organization chart. Organization design itself can be an initiator and sustainer of culture change. Nadler's (1992) notion of "organization architecture" captures this broader view of structure:

> Architecture therefore includes the formal structure, the design of work practices, the nature of the informal organization or operating style, and the processes for selection, socialization, and development of people. . . . organization architecture can be a source of competitive advantage to the degree that it motivates, facilitates, or enables individuals and groups to interact more effectively with customers, the work, and each other. (p. 4)

In this emerging view of organization design, the traditional hierarchical pyramid will probably be drastically altered. The key organizational tasks of doing, thinking, learning, and leading no longer are hierarchically based, rather they are pervasive and operate at all levels of the organization (Figure 25–10).

Competitive companies are aligning their formal and informal structures—how they organize tasks, jobs, and people, as well as the patterns of their relationships—to capitalize on the capability of the entire work force from top to bottom. As winning in the marketplace requires culture change, everyone must do, think, learn, and lead.

The challenge of organization structure is to ensure and reinforce change. The goal is to design an organization that both requires and allows *everyone* to lead, to have enough discretion and accountability to contribute to its success.

CULTURE CHANGE AND PEOPLE SYSTEMS CHANGE

Three "people" systems—performance measurement/management, career development/internal selection, and compensation/rewards—have particular impact on implementing culture change. These three are examined here because their typical characteristics and operation are impediments to lasting culture change (see Ulrich and Lake, 1990).

Performance Measurement and Management (PMM)

In order to support a culture change initiative, several aspects of measuring and managing performance (PMM) deserve attention (see Schneier et al., 1991):

- Identification of the outcomes that truly drive strategy execution and enunciation of the measures that describe them.
- Identification of the behaviors required both to operate in the desired culture and to produce the strategy-driving outcomes.
- Incorporation of the desired behaviors into a performance evaluation/appraisal and development system.
- Building of a performance management process that enhances managers' skills and holds managers accountable for the continued measurement, management, development, and rewarding of performance, not just the annual rating of performance.
- The linkage of performance to consequences.
- Development of culture change metrics or benchmarks against which to evaluate the progress of a team, unit, and/or the entire organization.

Let us consider the Western and Southern Companies' PMM efforts. Western Company, despite directives from its leader to change, failed to translate its organizational change agenda into an individual change agenda. The change effort stalled as middle management tired of "pronouncements," memos, and training courses. No one spelled out *what* they needed to do differently as a result of the new culture, and *why* they should behave differently.

The Southern Company took a different approach by using systems levers for culture change at the outset of the change initiative. It addressed all of the aspects of PMM just cited.

Southern examined its business strategy to ascertain its business-level critical success factors (see Figure 25–11). Next, it identified and communicated a set of individual success factors—the behaviors it expected of its people in order to execute strategy and shape the desired culture (see Figure 25–11). Managers were appraised against this new behavioral "screen" and incentive pay and promotions were made contingent on both behavior and results. A new process for managing performance was installed (see Figure 25–12), stressing ongoing management, assessment, and development of performance. Only after the linkage between their effectiveness at performance management and their incentive pay was made clear did many managers begin to take the performance management cycle seriously. Demand for training shot up quickly. Finally, at the organization level, progress toward culture change, not just financial performance, was tracked at Southern.

If individual behavior is being managed effectively, movement toward the desired culture should be evident. A set of benchmarks or standards for such outcomes as productivity, customer satisfaction, candor in communications, decision-making speed, and innovation was developed against which to assess change. Discussions at Southern Company Management Committee meetings addressed the benchmarks, and people at all levels provided input. The CEO continually probed for whether anything in the organization was truly different and made his judgments only after considering the baseline, the targets, and the benchmarks.

Western's PMM system, in contrast, was not aligned with the desired culture. Performance measures rewarded people for pointing out fault but not for coaching; for short-term cost cutting but not for increasing quality; and for extra effort to fix others' mistakes but not for preventing them. Lasting culture change was thwarted at Western partly because the hunt for scapegoats did not build the self-confidence required to innovate in product development or improve quality. Products that offered no distinctive value or higher quality than those of the competition hurt Western's market share and divided profit margins. Western's PMM system seemed to reward enormous effort for "doing it right the second time," a philosophy that hardly cuts costs or increases productivity!

Compensation and Rewards

Corporate culture is defined, in large part, by how individuals actually behave (see, e.g., Schein, 1985). At many companies, for example, there are no significant *negative* consequences, such as denial of promotions or pay increases, for failure to communicate candidly with subordinates or empower subordinates to take the initiative in solving problems. These are not particularly "open" or "participative" cultures, yet these very words may appear in the companies' value statements. At still other companies, too few *positive* consequences are provided to those who do behave in a manner consistent with the desired culture. The people who help deliver short-term

FIGURE 25-11

Performance Measurement and Management (PMM) in a Manufacturing Business, The Southern Company

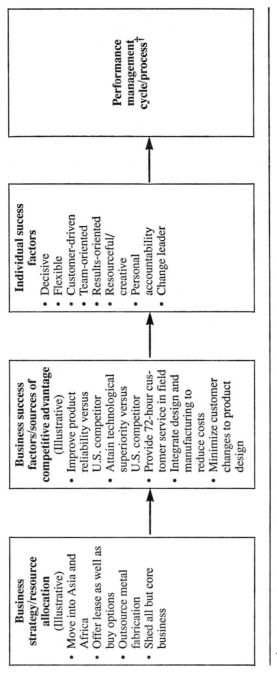

†Specific behavioral illustrations were developed and communicated for each. See Figure 25–12.

FIGURE 25–12
The Performance Measurement and Management Cycle

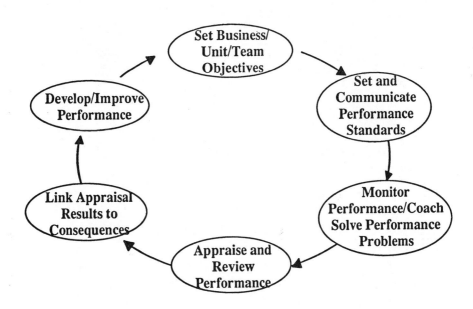

earnings are typically rewarded, but what rewards are offered to those who are the most flexible and participative people or the best coaches?

The net effect of the prevailing reward system in many businesses that are attempting to change is that their culture does not punish, and often rewards, the behaviors that entrench bureaucracy, such as maintaining and enlarging staffs. For example, most "merit pay" budgets are limited, in times of low inflation, to primarily cost-of-living increases, and most workers receive essentially the same base salary increases. The "line of sight" between performance and rewards hence is strained and motivation is dampened. Merit pay becomes pay for not failing, rather than pay for excellence.

How Southern Company Changed Compensation and Rewards

Southern Company had a compensation/reward system that was divergent with its business strategy and its desired culture. Rewards driving status quo behaviors had to change if the culture was to change. Characteristics of Southern's compensation and reward system included the following:

- Employees paid at higher than market rates.

FIGURE 25–13

Job Evaluation Factors and Weightings Can Block Culture Change

(One Company's Actual Point-Factor System)

Factor	Number of points
Administration*	680
Education and experience	550
Decision making	500
Creative requirements	200
Analytical requirement	185
Relations with others	150

* Size of budget, number of subordinates.

- Job evaluation that reinforced empire building since the highest pay went to the managers of the largest staffs (Figure 25–13).
- Merit pay increases differentiated very little between outstanding and average performers.
- Rewards were provided largely for effort, not for innovation or results that drove business objectives.
- Rewards were allocated subjectively, inconsistently, and secretly.
- Recognition, highly valued by employees according to survey, was seldom used.

After a team of line and staff managers carried out a careful study, they made several recommendations to make Southern's compensation and reward system into a lever for change (see Figure 25–14). Rewards—both financial and nonfinancial—became more performance-based. Although the new system was "budget neutral" (i.e., no additional money spent on compensation compared with prior years), it used the compensation dollars more effectively, directing more money to those people who both met or exceeded business objectives and implemented desired cultural changes. Southern's management came to regard its compensation and reward system as a powerful determinant of behavior—a precondition rather than an afterthought to implement culture change.

CULTURE CHANGE AND SKILLS CHANGE

As noted in the culture change road map (Figure 25–2), skills represent a key lever for change. Changes in skills required to initiate and sustain culture change have been noted throughout this discussion. New skills are required for these purposes:

- Operate in a team-based culture (see Figures 25–6 and 25–7).
- Execute critical success factors (CSFs) (see Figure 25–11).

FIGURE 25-14

Using the Compensation/Rewards System to Drive Culture Change

From		To
Job evaluation factors emphasizing bureaucracy	→	Factors emphasizing strategy execution and culture change
Little linkage between pay and performance	→	Responsibility to keep solid performers merely "whole" (i.e., cost-of-living and market-mandated increases) and significantly reward top performers
Little relationship to market pay rates	→	Strong relationship to market pay rates
Supervisor/peer recognition seldom used	→	Spot awards emphasized; small customer (internal/external) awards can be given by anyone to anyone at anytime
Awards perceived as inequitable, inconsistent, secret	→	Criteria communicated (i.e., results not just efforts, count), administered consistently; visible heroes made of recipients
Merit increase budget too small to keep up with market, Consumer Price Index and reward performance adequately	→	Sizable lump sum awards offered in addition to base, but only for top performers

FIGURE 25–15

Significant Developmental Opportunities: * *A Stimulus for Culture Change*

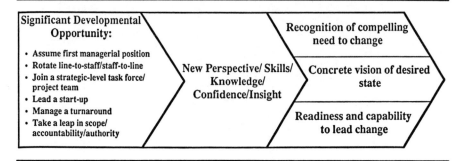

* After McCall et al. (1988)

- Successfully implement a PMM system (see Figure 25–12).
- Operate in a process-based organization design, e.g., distribution and technical support capability in "Customer Support" and engineering and proposal capability in "Design" (see Figure 25–9).

Many organizations undergoing culture change find their managers weak at such critical skills as leading change, communication, and coaching, (see, e.g., Kanter et al., 1992; Beer et al., 1991). How do companies build the skills and the confidence necessary to embrace change? Classroom training alone is inadequate (see Figure 25–5). Those opportunities frequently cited as critical to developing managers (see Figure 25–15) are particularly effective culture change stimulators, providing new perspectives, new relationships, and new challenges.

In order to sustain culture change, talent must be fully developed and then mobilized where it can have the most impact. Southern found that developmental activities, not merely training, needed to be examined because opportunities for growth capability were being squandered. Noteworthy characteristics of the career management system that facilitated culture change at Southern included the following:

- Recognition that rightsizing and de-layering resulted in far fewer opportunities for vertical movement within functions.
- Career "bands" containing fewer position levels and broader job scope and responsibility resulted in fewer hierarchical levels.
- An emphasis on horizontal movement—across functions, business units, countries—more effectively utilized talent and maximized developmental opportunities within career paths.
- Value-added and competency-based distinctions, rather than status-based or seniority-based differences, were made between and among steps on career paths.

- Managers were held accountable for providing talent for the good of the business.

As evidence of the "lead variable" nature of systems in driving culture change at Southern, the company cut 14 career bands to 5 (e.g., Leadership, Technical). Each band had descriptions of required knowledge, associated abilities, and competencies, and the formal training and education required. Career development was working at Southern as a culture change tool.

CULTURE CHANGE: WHAT WE KNOW WORKS

Almost every CEO today talks about the need for change. Far fewer actually initiate significant change and only a very small number actually make change last. Changing culture—the fundamental behaviors and beliefs—within a large corporation is a long-term and daunting task. The analysis by Kotter and Heskett (1992) of 10 companies showed that even though it was the CEO's primary goal, culture change took an average of 6.5 years. Recent studies of successful culture change (e.g., Ulrich and Lake, 1990; Beer et al., 1991; Kanter et al., 1992; Bolman and Deal, 1981; Nadler, 1992; Schaffer and Thomson 1992; Kotter and Heskett, 1992; Waterman, 1987; Senge, 1990) point to a consistent set of necessary conditions:

- Heavily involved leaders.
- Compelling business reasons to improve that are communicated effectively.
- Broad participation and collaboration in diagnosis of problems, design of solutions and implementation.
- "Over" - communication to all impacted parties.
- Reduction of functional and hierarchical boundaries.
- Clarity of vision of the desired culture and its translation to specific expected behaviors and outcomes.
- Adequate skills within a critical mass of people to lead change.
- Structures and systems that reinforce desired behavior.
- Elimination of low-value work and/or redesign or improvement of work processes.
- Deliberate publicizing of early successes.
- Tenacity, passion, and persistence, along with behavioral consistency by leaders at all levels.
- Increased discretion and autonomy.
- Bias toward action, measurement, and results.
- Team-based structures and problem-solving.

FIGURE 25–16
Initiating Culture Change: What Successful Executives Did First to Start and Sustain Culture Change

1. Listen to employees, customers, suppliers, unions, managers, communities, shareholders; identify, for example, problems, expectations, company strengths, performance, and potential of key managers.
2. Communicate current and likely future business conditions candidly and face-to-face; help everyone understand how their job impacts company financial performance.
3. Develop a few key strategic directions, state them succinctly in simple, clear language, and provide examples of what behaviors must change to implement strategy.
4. Answer the question: What kind of place do I/we want/need this to be? A few key values will emerge from the discussion and the answers. Communicate these values.
5. Make a few visible (surprising) selection/promotion/succession/termination decisions based specifically on criteria directly derived from the values, versus historically used criteria. Tell people why the likely candidates did not prevail.
6. Review (and direct subordinates to review) every one-over-one and one-over-two reporting relationship. In almost all cases, eliminate these layers of management.
7. Initiate action to remove perennially poor performers on your own staff from their jobs, do so fairly and swiftly, and instruct each of your subordinates to do the same.
8. Ask a few small teams of operating-level people directly involved in the work to solve longstanding problems (e.g., poor information flow, outdated tools/technology, skill deficiencies) hindering performance in their jobs; give them the authority needed to be effective.
9. Set order-of-magnitude—not 5% or 10%, but 30–50%—performance improvement goals for the entire organization in such areas as cycle time, cost reduction, quality, and new customers. State what the rewards will be for achievement (make them order-of-magnitude increases too); put one team in charge of each initiative.
10. Identify those few critical skills (leadership and technical) required to execute strategy and either develop them quickly or "buy" them to ensure they are in abundant supply.

Source: Based on Craig Eric Schneier Associates research, 1990–1992, involving 31 *Fortune* 500 industrial, service, and financial companies; most frequently cited actions.

- Customer focus.
- Learning from others, inside and outside, and sharing and applying newly gained knowledge.

Numerous executives in companies undergoing major change indicate that early results are critical. Credibility and momentum are fragile and easily damaged at the outset. If the culture change effort is perceived as an event or a "program," rather than a process that arrives at specific outcomes, it will fail. People simply do not take most change or improvement programs seriously unless they see top executives change their behavior. In fact, many executives suffer from low credibility because their rhetoric is not matched by their actions. Figure 25–16 provides an activity road map that was constructed as a result of work with executives who were initiating and leading culture change efforts. The tasks listed in Figure 25–16 are consistent with the keys to effective change synthesized from prior studies and noted earlier.

CONCLUSION

The cultural change initiative at Western met many of the conditions necessary for success: top management involvement, a clear, shared vision, ample resources, and a long time frame, among others. Yet these conditions did not lead to cultural change at Western. We have argued, via examples from the Southern Company and others, that lasting culture change requires simultaneous changes in structure, systems, and skills. Vision is necessary but not sufficient; mechanisms that govern individual behavior must be directly addressed.

Changes in such fundamental organizational characteristics as job design, performance measurement, and compensation practices are not merely maintaining and sustaining forces for change, but initiating forces as well. When the power of compelling need, shared vision, and top management involvement team up with changes in structures, systems, and skills, individual beliefs and behavior change. Only then is cultural change truly underway and moving from a one-time event to a permanent way of life.

REFERENCES

Beer, M.; R. Eisenstat; and B. Spector. *The Critical Path to Corporate Renewal.* Cambridge, MA: Harvard Business School Press, 1991.

Bennett, A. "Downsizing Doesn't Necessarily Bring an Upswing in Corporate Profitability." *Wall Street Journal,* June 6, 1991.

Bolman, L. G.; and T. E. Deal. *Reframing Organizations.* San Francisco: Jossey-Bass, 1991.

Charan, R. "How Networks Reshape Organizations for Results." *Harvard Business Review,* September–October 1991, pp. 104–15.

Filipowski, D. "The New Employee Loyalty." *Personnel Journal,* September 1992, p. 38.

Forbis, J.; and W. Adams. "Corporate Victims of the Eighties." *Across the Board,* December 1991, pp. 15–21.

Fortune. "How Companies Handle Layoffs." *Fortune,* April 8, 1991, p. 39.

Hammer, M. "Reengineering Work: Don't Automate, Obliterate." *Harvard Business Review,* July-August, 1990, pp. 104–12.

Irvin, R. A.; and E. G. Michaels. "Core Skills: Doing the Right Things Right." *The McKinsey Quarterly,* Summer 1989, pp. 4–19.

Kanter, R. M. "Transcending Business Boundaries: 12,000 World Managers View Change." *Harvard Business Review,* May–June 1991, pp. 151–65.

Kanter, R. M.; B. A. Stein; and T. D. Jick. *The Challenge of Organization Change.* New York: Free Press, 1992.

Kaplan, R. B; and L. Murdock. "Core Process Redesign." *The McKinsey Quarterly,* Spring 1991, pp. 27–43.

Kotter, J. P.; and J. L. Heskett. *Corporate Culture and Performance.* New York: Free Press, 1992.

McCall, M. W.; M. M. Lombardo; and A. M. Morrison. *The Lessons of Experience.* Lexington, MA: Lexington Books, 1988.

Nadler, D. A., and associates. "Organization Architecture: A Metaphor for Change." In *Organizational Architecture.* Eds. D. A. Nadler and associates. San Francisco: Jossey-Bass, 1992.

Ostroff, F.; and D. Smith. "The Horizontal Organization." *The McKinsey Quarterly,* 1992, pp. 148–68.

Prahalad, C. K.; and G. Hamel. "The Core Competencies of the Corporation." *Harvard Business Review* 68, no. 3, pp. 79–91.

Schaffer, R. J.; and H. A. Thomson. "Successful Change Programs Begin with Results." *Harvard Business Review,* January–February 1992, pp. 80–89.

Schein, E. H. *Organization Culture and Leadership.* San Francisco: Jossey-Bass, 1985.

Schneier, C. E.; D. G. Shaw; and R. W. Beatty. "Companies' Attempts to Improve Performance While Containing Costs: Quick Fix versus Lasting Change." *Human Resource Planning,* 15, no. 3, 1992. pp. 1–25.

Schneier, C. E.; D. G. Shaw; and R. W. Beatty. "Performance Measurement and Management: A Tool for Strategy Execution." *Human Resource Management* 30, no. 3 (1991), pp. 279–301.

Senge, P. M. *The Fifth Discipline.* New York: Doubleday, 1990.

Stalk, G.; P. Evans; and L. Shulman. "Competing on Capabilities: The New Rules of Corporate Strategy." *Harvard Business Review,* 69, no. 2 (1992), pp. 57–69.

Tregue, B. *Vision in Action.* New York: Simon & Schuster, 1989.

Ulrich, D.; and D. Lake. *Organizational Capability.* New York: Wiley, 1990.

Waterman, R. H. *The Renewal Factor.* Toronto: Bantam, 1987.

Chapter Twenty-Six

The People Factor

Terry L. Bowman

L ike an actor, politician, or sports star, the good corporate executive needs two things: The Opportunity (the managerial proxy for the spotlight) and The Execution (proxy for performance). Human Resource Planning is the art of aligning Opportunity with Execution while "casting" the right or the best individuals to handle the "roles" necessary for achieving what the plan is aimed at. The plans that fall short usually don't identify the human resource specifics—and the right people—needed for proper execution.

No matter how elaborate and well-researched the scenarios, many plan architects think results somehow will be delivered by unnamed or unidentified people who really haven't been cut in on the plan. This assumption asks for disaster. When the activities of the organization are changed, the behavior of its people must be changed accordingly. Only people—with their values, skills and beliefs—actually change results. The real trick in human resource planning is to align the skills, competencies, values, and change readiness potential continuously with the requirements of the business situation and make them an integral part of the organization's change plan.

Too many firms historically have approached Human Resource Planning as a numbers game—as though they were ordering a commodity, as though their "living, breathing resources" were all interchangeable parts or grains of rice, as though all needed skills were assumed to be on hand when required. A common way of treating the human element in the traditional planning process is to say, "We will need twenty (20) new marketing managers; ten (10) new sales people in the Midwest territory; five (5) new employees in accounting, and 50 additional people in the factory...." Or a company will play the human element in "generics," by creating planning based on activity (Production Managers, General Accountants, etc.), or on rank (10 level 4s, 18 level 5s, etc.)—without establishing priorities or specific skill requirements for the new job.

Conversely, companies often concentrate on the latest requirements dictated by a new plan but don't weed out the jobs, skills, or individuals that may no longer be required and the positions that have been outdated or changed by new business demands. Planning must face not only the addition of numbers, but *subtraction* and *substitution* as well.

Our analysis of many organizations and outplaced individuals frequently reveals inadequate knowledge of talent and potential already in place, little or no career planning, inappropriate position assignments, and job stagnation or frustration. We attribute these problems to breakdowns in management development and planning, and *inadequate information about people*. Many organizations could have achieved greater results had the *existing* human potential been recognized and appropriate action taken.

This chapter will focus on identifying the existing strengths of an organization and the development of opportunities for establishing the interventions required to move the business forward, in line with a new strategy and a new vision.

THINK HORIZONTALLY—NOT VERTICALLY

Much of the weakness in human resource plans can be blamed on history, the relative position of the human resource (HR) executives in the organization, and the absence (or the poor understanding) of proper HR tools. Typical flaws within these categories include the following:

History

The rate of change and the understanding of existing corporate *culture* are not considered relevant to the development and execution of business strategies in many organizations or in many planning processes.

Growth in the economy and in specific industries has made it easy over time to regard additions to staff and pay increases as the most relevant issues in human resource planning. However, the rate of change within the social, political, and business environments of the past few years has made a significant impact on personnel requirements and demanded a shift in thinking. The current economic demands and the requirements demanded by competition in a global marketplace have raised corporate awareness of the need for people's skills and made effective human resource planning a mandatory requirement among surviving businesses.

Human Resource Management

Human resource executives haven't been considered part of the "strategy group" in many organizations and have been relegated to specialist roles that often focus on simply meeting regulations and compliance. Or they are troubleshooters that are called in *after* a problem is discovered. Human resource executives themselves have not taken positions of influence and leadership that enable them to impact strategy.

The approaches to managing and to traditional organizational boundaries are changing. Human resource planning at many firms is no longer a function of simply filling available holes, but of identifying individuals with the skills to define what needs to be done and then to get it done.

HR Tools Have Been Absent or Focused Incorrectly

The ways tools are used don't promote consensus or actually inhibit comparability of people. The inability to differentiate among individuals, except through cumbersome and time-consuming processes that establish or encourage adversarial roles, contributes to poor or uninformed decisions. Government regulations and requirements and a real desire to be fair and consistent often preclude or hamper key decisions that discriminate among specific positions and individuals.

Planning requirements for the 1990s and beyond demand a *horizontal* approach that identifies the following:

The existing "bench strength" of the organization.

Both current and new job requirements.

Clarity of new demands so they can be weighed against current strengths and weaknesses, that is, what is needed versus what exists.

That is, a framework (Gateway) is needed to help identify and reconcile the strategies, culture, skills, and required interventions necessary to identify, hire, develop, and energize the best people into the positions where their impact will be greatest.

Vertical systems (Figure 26–1), such as most performance appraisal schemes, compensation techniques, and reward systems, as well as approaches to training and even to promotions, do not permit managers to compare or differentiate performance and potential of individuals throughout the organization. This fact often has a negative impact on identifying, advancing, and rewarding the best individuals. The implication of this approach, shown in Figure 26–2, is that the distribution curves of performance run vertically along each function or department. In fact, that is not the case. The organization of the 1990s needs to identify the skilled resources at each level of an organization—that is, horizontally–regardless of where the level is located.

The important question has always been how to identify the key jobs and activities that are required by the company and that will directly impact the business plan. But a more important question might be: How can the firm identify or build a consensus on *the key players* that could best fill the important positions demanded by the plan?

ALIGNMENT OF WHAT <u>SHOULD</u> BE WITH WHAT <u>IS</u>!

The human resource planning process should resemble a subset of the traditional business planning process that focuses on four priorities:

- Alignment of business strategy and the corporate culture.
- Identification and prioritization of key activities, actions, skills, and behaviors needed to to carry out the plan.

FIGURE 26–1
Vertical Systems

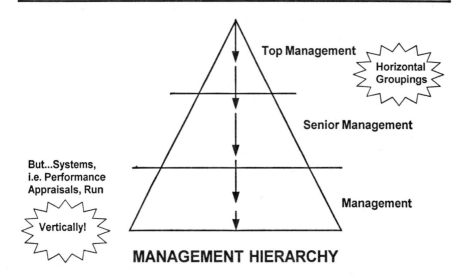

MANAGEMENT HIERARCHY

- Designation of the bench strength of the organization so as to build a knowledge base, that is, identify the best of the best, and to position the best-fit individuals into roles where they can impact the business positively.

- Determination of the interventions, moves, changes, and rewards necessary to promote achievement and reinforcement of the plan objectives.

In any planning process leadership, vision, and communication are critical elements to success. Human resource planning, however, requires the matching of real skills to the job demands of the business strategy. Thus, the strategy, vision, and culture of an organization must be properly aligned and the conflicts between current thinking and behavior and the new demands must be minimized. Real change can take place only when the basic values and behaviors of people are changed in concert.

At many companies, however, this fine tuning is difficult to accomplish because of these barriers:

- Companies historically have lacked the tools to think horizontally about human resources. HR plans are consigned to single groups that think vertically. Human resource planning for the 1990s must become a *horizontal* activity, must be companywide in scope, and must provide for comparability and differentiation among positions and individuals.

- The responsibility to plan for people often is left to human resource professionals who lack the strength of position and "visibility" in the form of needs and avail-

FIGURE 26–2
Implied Distribution of Management Strength

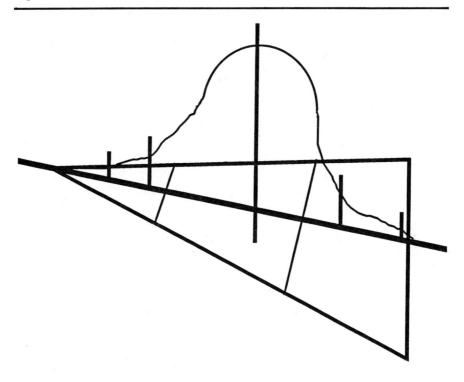

able skills. Modern human resource planning instead must be structured so that all levels of management have defined responsibilities for guiding the development of subordinates within the vision and culture to be put in place.

• We are often victims of our own culture. Culture is the accepted values and behaviors of the organization, but it also homogenizes and conditions the manner in which an organization's people act and think. Human resource planning of today must develop and utilize tools that clearly identify the relevant cultural issues and reconcile them to strategy, while identifying and minimizing cultural dissonance. The skills of an organization's human resources and the beliefs and values can both *help* and *hinder* the planned strategy. Understanding and managing these conflicts, while positioning the best people where they can most benefit the organization, is critical.

A number of checkpoints must be developed to help identify the human strengths and weaknesses of the organization with respect to what is needed to make the business plan work.

The right alignment of human resources with the business plan can be achieved through these 1990s-style approaches:

Establishment of a "Gateway"—Create a common framework of what exists (skills, competencies, culture, etc.).

Creation of a map—Identify the shortfall between what is in place and what is needed.

Interventions—Determine the actions needed to close the gap.

Communications—Let everyone know what is being done and why it is being done and clarify the new requirements.

As the firm identifies its strengths and weaknesses, the skills of its people must be honestly evaluated, not in the aggregate but by function, activity, and individual. Additionally, the firm must establish a level playing field, free from individual prejudices and functional and personality biases. In other words, it is valuable to build, where possible, a consensus of priorities, positions, and individuals from both "current performance" and "potential" viewpoints. This consensus should transcend functional, departmental, and location boundaries. Who are the key individuals? In what capacities can they deliver the objectives of the plan? How can they preserve or enhance the strengths and values of the business? Traditional "vertical" processes alone cannot answer these questions.

A NEW APPROACH

Culture, as stated earlier, will play a final role in the execution of the business plan, and it must be assessed in identifying possible organization conflicts or inhibitors of the plan. Culture basically consists of the behaviors, values, and beliefs that are inherent parts of the organization's ability to act as the strategy requires.

Let us assume a hypothetical company with a strong culture. It has been internally focused on a single successful product and has built an environment of conformity and introspection. Suddenly, it realizes it must become more competitive and more customer oriented, improve its delivery of service, and develop new products to counter its competition in a newly energized market.

However, the existence of the knowledge that significant change is needed, even if there is a well-conceived plan to alter the focus of the business, is not sufficient unless the firm changes the specific behaviors and values of the employees. Ultimately, identifying and then rewarding the new behaviors, skills, and values that the strategy may demand are required.

Therefore, the ability to identify key positions and individuals as well as skills—leadership, communication, and such—requires a knowledge of current bench strength, the tools for comparing individuals, and the tools for position planning and development. Finally, a process for identifying opportunities for hiring, moving, and possibly terminating individuals—the interventions—should be created.

How does one approach these often confusing demands quickly, fairly, and consistently? Three levels of human resource planning should be considered in carrying out the cultural function of change management.

FIGURE 26–3
Alignment

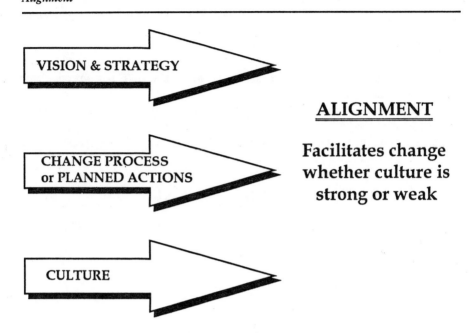

VISION & STRATEGY

CHANGE PROCESS
or PLANNED ACTIONS

CULTURE

ALIGNMENT

**Facilitates change
whether culture is
strong or weak**

1. The first level includes the understanding and identification of issues affecting culture and the change process. If a firm is to be successful in the delivery of its plan—particularly a long-term strategy—it is critical to ensure that the organization's strategy, culture and change processes or demands (requirements), are in alignment, as shown in Figure 26–3.

If a company has built a reputation (and culture) around free spending, first-class air travel, large offices, big expense accounts, and little control or accountability, it will have trouble moving to a cost-conscious, tightly controlled system with monitored budgets and emphasis on cost reduction. The transition will be long and difficult without a clear understanding of the dynamics of people's behavior and attitudes and the values that employees *believe* have been important. Identifying, understanding, and eventually changing a firm's culture should be part of a good human resource plan.

2. The second and parallel level involves identifying the actions, skills, and priorities that will contribute to delivery of expected results. Numbers and costs alone will not help meet the objectives in a good business plan or strategy.

If the strategy calls for improvements in *product quality* and *customer service* as the ways to increase profitability and widen market share, very specific actions and responsibilities must be identified. These could range from reducing the number of levels within the organization from eight to four to decentralizing some functions while centralizing certain controls and responsibilities. These actions also may call for eliminating or replacing specific activities and positions and simultaneously investing in technologies and education and training, reducing spans of control, or altering employee selection practices and promotion criteria.

3. The third level of human resource planning deals with understanding the bench strength of *what* and *who* the organization has to work with. If our objective is to "finish first," then we know *what* we need to do.

Whether our objective is realistic or can be made realistic is a function of knowing what talents are in-house and how to get them into positions where they can make meaningful contributions to the task(s) at hand. We need to get the best people into the best roles for the mutual benefit of all concerned.

FINDING THE BEST OF THE BEST

The key to the people retention process involves answering these questions:

- Who can, should or could do the identified tasks best?
- Who can we move?
- Who can we replace?
- Who can we lose?
- Who should be trained?

Alternative approaches to getting the answers have included the following:

Management reviews. These are characterized by lengthy debates, strongly adversarial roles, and long hours, but rarely consensus.

Development plans. These programs are idealistic but unrealistic and often unrelated to the organization's needs. They seldom identify priorities or the means to execute them.

Performance appraisals. These systems do not discriminate among individuals, are often tainted with halo effect, and seldom meet with consensus or organizational acceptance.

Additionally, these processes are often a burden to management. The roles often are not clear or meaningful and there is usually a failure on the part of the person being evaluated to identify with the process. These evaluation systems also can lead to poor decisions such as promotions of the wrong individuals or inadequate rewards for the right people.

Better decisions are possible if an alternative system is used, such as a process based on a systematic collection and evaluation of opinions from qualified observers rather than reliance on one person's judgment or on the narrow vision brought about by the vertical approach to human resource systems.

FIGURE 26–4
Manager Grid

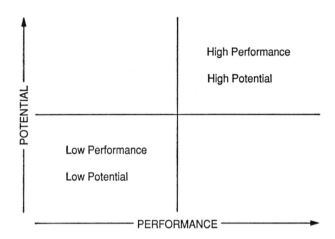

Similarly, if we could quantify this opinion and knowledge of each individual, we could build a graphic and statistically valid representation of each individual's relative ranking within any given group. And if we can define "potential" within the context of the organization or group and ask the same group of evaluators to identify those individuals that meet the criteria for potential, we would have both a quantitative evaluation of performance and a list of those individuals that have potential as defined by the organization. It is possible to represent both performance and potential on one graphic output—a standard distribution chart (or quadrants) such as Figure 26–4 showing "high performance/high potential" to "low performance/low potential" of each individual within the group.

This simple approach of utilizing a ranking technique and a systematic process of collecting and assigning scores would provide a unique and useful view of an organization's management strength. If we then forced a normal distribution curve over each group, we would differentiate among a number of similar individuals at any level of an organization. Supervisors and/or human resource executives then would have a set of distribution charts about each group of individuals ranked, showing which ones are in the top 10 percent, 20 percent, and such, or in the lower 10 percent, 20 percent, and so on, as shown in Figure 26–5.

From this "Gateway," a number of interventions can be made or questions asked. Since this is a consensus of qualified individuals who were selected because they had "line of sight" or working knowledge about the individuals in each group, this

FIGURE 26–5

Performance/Potential (Group: Unit Directors)

	Performance				
	1	*2*	*3*	*4*	*5*
Meets potential definition	Hopkins, M. Deese, C.	Warner, C. Strauss, R.	Salazar, P.		
Does not meet potential definition		Kogan Dein, N.	Magluilo, J. Alexovich, D. Janke, H. Landahl, J. Lesnick, M.	Reemer, A. Jones Jr., J. Beaver, L.	Sloan, M. Olk, G.
Number	2	3	6	3	2
Percentile	12.5%	18.7%	37.6%	18.7%	12.5%

FIGURE 26–6

Implied Interventions at Any "Level" of Management

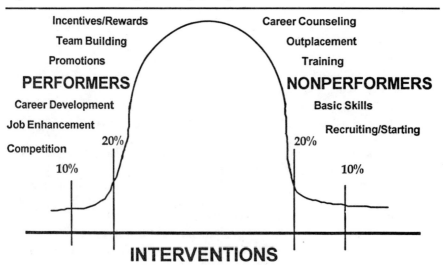

consensus is really about *how* the individual managers are seen by the people that work with them and who are affected by their work.

Once the ranking takes place and the data base is constructed, we can then compare how an individual's latest performance appraisals rate them. Individuals that are at either extreme, the lower percentiles or upper percentiles, for example, should have performance appraisals that closely match their group evaluation. Many comparisons will not agree with the group evaluation, while some other comparisons will reflect a totally different view of an individual's performance. However, this appraisal provides data to challenge or support the other information about each individual that may exist from the vertical, one-on-one system. Most importantly, it allows a firm to manage the exceptions. If there is a consensus about key individuals in the top percentiles, one could ask whether they are in jobs that are key to the firm's future plans, or whether the organization is doing enough to retain those individuals. The consensus extends the perceived value of an individual beyond the opinion or judgment of a single supervisor, while establishing a distinction between good and not so good performers, at each level across functional boundaries or departments, as shown in Figure 26–6.

Similarly, questions should be asked about individuals appearing in the lower percentiles of each ranking, such as these:

- Are these people in need of help—additional education, training, or other interventions?
- Are they in need of counseling or help in finding another job?
- Should they be replaced?
- How does his or her own supervisor view them compared with the views of other managers or "rankers"?

By managing the exceptions and utilizing other available data, the organization has a *fair* and consistent basis for establishing promotion, substitution and/or possible dismissal plans. When used with other information, these data help identify the individuals that would benefit from programs of education and training while establishing a basis and priority list for employee moves and career and development changes.

The results help clarify the true bench strength of diverse companies and organizations. In downsizings or mergers, the system provides a *fair* and *consistent* approach to understanding and identifying the performance and potential of individuals within any organization. This approach also provides the comparability for a fair and *consistent* approach to differentiate among individuals horizontally at any given level of an organization. Most importantly, it establishes an inventory of bench strengths at each critical level—thereby building an important "Gateway" for job and succession planning, education, and comparative programs.

Chapter Twenty-Seven

The Key to Corporate Survival: Change Begins and Ends with People

Marti Smye
Robert Cooke

In the business climate of the 1990s, organizational change is a fact of life that is reflected in the headlines, with almost daily news of companies restructuring, laying off, developing new strategies, merging, or acquiring and divesting. Merger and acquisition (M&A) trends alone bespeak the frenetic pace. Between 1988 and 1992, at a time when M&A activity was slipping from earlier years, there were more than 13,000 deals involving a U.S. dollar value of more than $800 billion. With the odds favoring an even swifter pace of change as we advance through the 1990s, most organizations recognize that their survival depends upon excelling in the management of change.

Unfortunately the change management report card for many businesses shows a solid A for effort but a borderline grade for execution. Despite great expectations, incisive strategic plans, bright minds to master the process, and impressive levels of activity, many major initiatives neither live up to their advance billings nor deliver promised payoffs. Change objectives seem to dissolve, leading to lost strategic vision, a high price tag—essentially, wasted money—for lackluster results, and high blood pressure in the executive suite.

In the merger area, for example, many acquisitions don't live up to business expectations or are outright failures. And what about new business strategies? Why do these fail? A study by McKinsey & Company into failures to shift strategic gears successfully found the following:

- 40 percent of the firms failed because they lacked the capability to execute the strategy.
- 35 percent of firms failed because the organization was not "change ready" or committed.
- Only 17 percent of the failures were attributable to poor strategy.

So there is a very human answer to why strategies derail. They depend on *people* for successful execution, and massive change creates fear in most people. Fear is inherently human and is the enemy of change. To achieve change, we must first conquer people's fear of it.

We have all gone through change in our lives, both personally and professionally. On a grander scale, one might be excused for thinking that our species would be used to it. We have evolved from Neanderthal to Nintendo. We used to go outside to sniff the wind, now we access satellite weather maps. Yet despite our collective history and experience of massive change, it still does not come easily to us. Each new change brings with it fresh fears that undermine our confidence: Will I be successful? Will my security be threatened? Do I want this new thing?

The fear of changing the status quo repeatedly surfaces during times of organizational change. When contemplating new strategies and significant organizational shifts, CEOs have the opportunity to ensure that their organizations do in fact reach their strategic objectives, instead of merely holding the false belief that they have. Good human resource management may mean having the right people in the right place at the right time, but it also requires much more.

When we initiate change, we must not rely on education or communication alone to gain commitment. Observable positive change becomes possible only when people are able to make an intellectual and emotional commitment to modifying their ideas and beliefs. Total organizational commitment, from boardroom to shop floor, is like a dance in motion, everyone moving to the same rhythm. The successful change implementor is the choreographer of the dance.

Most companies have good ideas but fall far short in the execution. How can organizations ensure survival in the 1990s by avoiding the people-related pitfalls of implementing change? To understand the processes underlying change, we use what we call **The Change Triangle** (see Fig. 27–1). This model helps to identify key issues in any organization's change strategy. It operates at three levels: organization; groups; and individuals. Change must be successfully implemented at every one of these three levels, or else the organization's new strategy is doomed to failure. And people issues such as commitment, teamwork, and skills lie at the heart of each of these three levels. Below, we examine each one in turn and demonstrate the importance of addressing all three.

FIGURE 27–1
The Change Triangle

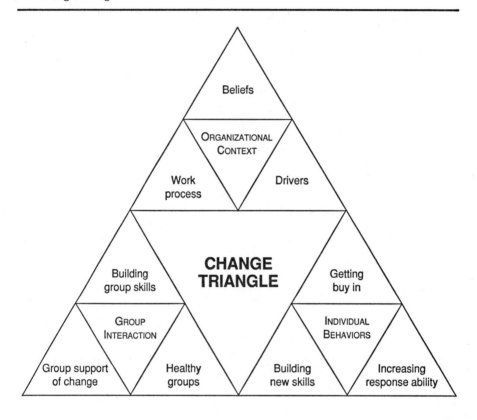

HOW TO IMPLEMENT CHANGE SUCCESSFULLY AT THE ORGANIZATIONAL LEVEL

In every organization, there are three areas to master.

Beliefs

An organization's belief system involves vision and values; business purpose and strategy; its notions about its strengths and weaknesses; and its attitudes of who matters, and how much. If you understand your company's belief system, you can mobilize it and turn the organization in new and daring directions.

One of our clients tried and won. This company thought it was successful, for it consistently achieved 15 percent return on sales. The staff knew that they were doing a good job. A mantra for success was established: "Success equals 15 percent." One day, the world tilted. The shareholders asked for a 20 percent return. Overnight, high achievers became underachievers. Challenged and motivated, the personnel were eager to reestablish their self-image of success. They were supported in the discovery of new ways of working and achieved the extra 5 percent.

The lesson? Challenging belief systems can set an organization into motion and produce results. Changing accepted beliefs often meets resistance, which must be recognized and addressed. But a well-defined organizational vision can obviate the need for crisis management and facilitate a smooth transition. If your organization's present belief system is not working or is out of date, alter it. Rewrite the way your employees see the company.

Performance Drivers

These are the forces that shape people's actions. If your performance drivers are not consistent with your belief system, successful organizational change will not be possible. What are performance drivers? They include goals (e.g., sales, profits, returns), key results, reporting systems, and reward systems. If you have a new vision, or change direction, without changing performance drivers, the effect is similar to sending employees the wrong way down a one-way street. You can count on collisions and confusion. Properly aligned performance drivers steer and motivate people to behave in ways that will lead to organization and personal success.

One company wanted to improve cash flow by getting customer accounts paid faster. The sales force, however, was not committed to this goal because it received a set commission regardless of when bills were paid. Performance was driven by that system. Management took action to redesign the commission system to increase the rewards that salespeople received for promptly paid accounts. The result: the sales force put effort into expediting payments, receivables flowed in more swiftly, and cash flow blossomed.

Work Processes

This element represents another important area of opportunity when developing an organizational context for change. The management style of the 1980s was vertical. Departments worked independently to achieve narrowly defined goals. Convention dictated a functional parochialism. Sales focused on sales numbers, manufacturing pursued cost and output improvements, the finance department kept score, and the company assumed that these discrete activities would somehow add up to ever-improving performance. In the 1980s we learned that our customer has little interest in how an organization functions—or its bottom line for that matter. What they want is better value through improved products and service levels.

The weaknesses of the traditional, 1980s-style organization are easy to enumerate:

- Responds slowly.
- Smothers individual talent.

- Promotes duplication.
- Defeats cross-functional cooperation.
- Is deaf to the customer.

When we allow functional silos to dominate, we fail to realize that value is the result of functional integration and collaboration. Take a visit to the hospital as an example. When you go to the hospital for surgery, each professional has a vertical specialty. The anesthetist puts you to sleep, the surgeon operates, the nurse handles the tools, and the administration gives you the bill. However, you do expect the specialists to coordinate themselves and remove your gall bladder *after* you are unconscious. Customers expect the same coordination of efforts. We need to recognize that important work flows horizontally across the organization. Not every function participates in every process; the ones involved are those that add value as measured by the customer. Alignment of work processes and strategy offers a better chance for success.

Phase I Survival Tip

There are three tasks to make the organization ready for change:

1. Mobilize basic beliefs to realize the new vision.
2. Install performance drivers so that people will do the right things.
3. Ensure that work is integrated; each task should add stakeholder value and not duplicate efforts.

THE IMPORTANCE OF GROUPS
TO SUCCESSFUL CHANGE IMPLEMENTATION

No business is all machinery. It is run by human beings. As we have already seen, departments must link their work processes to serve the customer. This new work environment emphasizes employee interaction—how we regard each other and how we work together. Synergy, that process of making the whole greater than the sum of the parts, is essential. To achieve synergy, we must address the following three areas.

Building Group Skills

It is natural to feel that we work best with those people we know. When we begin to work with others from outside our circle it creates tension. They don't speak our language. They have different priorities. We often don't understand each other's jobs. It's important, then, to take action to enable heterogeneous groups to function effectively.

Organizations that establish the following skills boost the performance of their cross-functional teams:

- Common problem-solving methods.
- New communication skills.
- Ability to grant and show trust.
- Dealing with diversity.
- Team skills.

New skills are not enough, however, and that fact takes us to another key area.

Healthy Group Systems

Many of us have grown up thinking of the individual job as the basic building block of the organization. As we move through the 1990s the team unit is surfacing as the underpinning of the organization. Many star individual performers find this new reality disconcerting. The organization is also at risk if group work turns into "groupthink" and fails to move beyond the least common denominator.

Healthy groups are systems that are characterized by a clarity of purpose, innovation, healthy discourse, and crisp decision making. Healthy groups depend on leveling barriers and eliminating stereotypes. Mutual respect and understanding allow room for growth and create an environment where accomplishment of the impossible may just be possible.

A major client recently had a breakthrough in this area. This firm, a major consumer products company, devised a new strategy that depended upon regional business teams. A quick start to this new team approach was crucial. All of the teams worked together from the start. They jointly hammered out their goals and the tactics that would lead to success. Included in these plans were steps to improve their team effectiveness continuously. They cleared pathways for each other to make rapid change happen.

Group Support of Change

Astute leaders of major change recognize that the group is an important medium for individual change. People find change easier when they are part of a group that is moving in a common direction. We see many examples of this in our daily lives. We join diet groups in order to lose weight. We work out with others at the gym and share our fitness pains and gains.

Groups provide a particularly powerful forum for dealing with the emotional challenges of change. Feelings of fear, anomie, and confusion are common when work lives are thrown into flux. We encourage leaders to establish transitional support groups to make it easier for employees to bring these feelings into the open. Properly structured group processes help individuals to break out of the victim mindset. Participants discover that they can help each other to become the masters of their destinies. In sum, they are empowered by the energy of the group.

Phase II Survival Tip

There are three requirements for effective change among groups:

1. Build the hard skills required for group interaction.
2. Understand and foster the characteristics for healthy group systems.
3. Create momentum by gaining group support for change.

THE KEY TO SUCCESSFUL CHANGE: THE INDIVIDUAL

Individual behaviors are the litmus test for meeting change objectives. The following three areas influence individual behavior.

Gaining Buy-In

There can be no change until individual employee buy-in is achieved. As an illustration, imagine a situation in which you are pressured to provide a yes or no answer. You are not ready to answer, but you have no choice, you must respond. Now step back. How are you feeling? It is likely that you would resist, and most likely that, whatever the question, you said *no*.

People often respond negatively if they are pressured to commit before they are ready to do so. Resistance is our way of buying time so that we can work through the implications of change. Most of us have an internal time clock that signals us when we are ready for change. The time required varies, depending upon our current level of investment in the status quo and other events in our lives. We noted earlier that fear and denial are natural reactions to change. Accepting this is crucial when effecting a new corporate strategy.

Gaining buy-in is a process that happens in stages. Communication efforts often are concluding when the commitment building process is just starting. We advise clients that *understanding change means that people know what is supposed to happen; getting buy-in means they believe it needs to happen.*To help people through change, we need to make a good case. We must also remember that the individual's perspective on the business affects how the case should be presented. Consider these examples:

- For executives, the case for change should demonstrate the **strategic merits.**
- For managers, the **operational implications** of the change will be a key area of interest.
- For the front line, communicate how the changes will affect **day-to-day job satisfaction and security.**

Increasing Response Ability

Managers often bemoan the fact that employees aren't doing the new things they are supposed to do, that they are not being responsible.

To translate buy-in into action, people need to be able to respond. We call this *increasing response ability,* and it is the manager's job to make this happen. When employees' behavior is not meeting expectations we ask managers to take accountability. We encourage them to consider these possible reasons:

- They don't know what is expected of them.
- They lack the skill.
- They think something else is more important.
- There is no reward.
- They think they are behaving correctly, but they aren't.
- There are obstacles in the way.

By focusing on response ability, managers can improve their employees' capacity to cope with change.

Building New Skills

In order to execute change it is essential to build new skills, which requires training. Managers must also coach and counsel the employees in their spheres of activity. Assimilating new skills also requires employees to be courageous. When new skills are required, the natural first response is to feel awkward and uncomfortable. Anyone forced to write with the wrong hand because of an injury knows the feeling. While we are learning new skills, it is difficult to accept mistakes, yet temporary failures are a normal part of learning.

Organizations must recognize this dichotomy and assist people to move past the discomfort and on to a new skill level. This requires allowing people to err for a while. Let them explore new avenues of personal ability. There are many benefits to the organization in this approach. The more skills an employee can muster, the more they can contribute to the firm.

Phase III Survival Tip

One can influence individual behavior with these strategies:

1. Gain individual buy-in by making the case for change.
2. Take accountability for increasing the "Response Ability" of your employees.
3. Build new skills and allow time for learning adjustments.

CONCLUSION

In this age of science, many CEOs would like to believe that if they could only find the right system, the right technology, or the right design, their strategic objectives will fall easily into place. Unfortunately, the only power that drives any technology is in the minds and the hands of the people charged with using it. Therefore, if the organization is to survive and to thrive, three main people-related areas must be addressed in any change execution strategy: organization, groups, and individuals. Weaknesses in any one area will serve to stall or sabotage the entire strategy. In effectively implementing change, we must remember the following:

1. Stronger organizational context means beliefs, drivers, and work processes are aligned to create the environment for change.
2. Group skills, healthy group systems, and group support ensure that people are working together for change.
3. Gaining buy-in, increasing response ability, and building new skills translate the organization's intentions into actions.

Every business has the capacity to become a winner during times of massive change. Stress affects every organization differently, and there is no set formula that will work in every instance. But if we put the right elements in place we will ensure that we achieve our goals and maybe even our dreams.

Chapter Twenty-Eight

Human Resource Planning and Change

Dave Ulrich

T raditionally, human resource planning (HRP) models have been the antithesis of change. HRP implied bureaucratic, static, process-rich but results-poor, staff-driven efforts to quantify how many people with what types of skills would be needed to help an organization succeed. HR planners would develop a language of their own around Markov chains, distinctive competencies, and environmental scanning. More extraneous to the business and less central to business processes, HRP often existed in naive isolation. Reports became longer; HRP processes became more complex; and relevance to business became less important than well-crafted and well-documented narratives. HRP not only failed to support change—it also encouraged planning rigor, which impeded change.

However, at the very time many HRP models were becoming the antithesis of change, the need for building an organization's capacity for change was increasing (Kanter et al., 1992). Innovative ideas often led to exciting programs that began with great acclaim but ended with quiet bookshelf funerals. The ability to translate ideas into sustainable policies and actions required more than hope; it required increased rigor and discipline. Ideas with impact required institutional mechanisms that would move ideas from initiatives into ongoing business processes. Change initiatives needed what HRP *should* provide. When HRP models became intellectual road maps for change and not bureaucratic impediments to change, a synthesis between HRP and change might develop.

The question addressed in this chapter is simple: How can HRP processes be used to leverage change? This question will be answered by (1) reviewing the rationale for HRP, (2) suggesting a framework that provides an overview for HRP, (3) identifying HR choices that will help accomplish change, and (4) giving examples of how the HRP process applies to a series of change initiatives. The analysis will demonstrate how HRP models can be used to drive, sustain, and encourage change.

RATIONALE FOR HUMAN RESOURCE PLANNING

Definition of Human Resource Planning

Human resource planning represents the *processes* used to link business strategy with human resource practices in ways that sustain competitive advantage (Ulrich, 1987; Walker, 1992). This is a broader definition and concept of HRP than taken by some authors (Alpander, 1980; Nkomo, 1987) who focus more on HRP as labor power planning models. But in the broadest definition, HRP becomes the process of executing human resource management strategy (Fombrun et al., 1984) with emphasis on four factors.

First, the end, or result, of effective HRP efforts must be building *competitive advantage*. Competitive advantage simply means that the organization is able to differentiate itself appropriately in the eyes of customers (Ulrich and Lake, 1990).

Second, to add value to customers and to be competitive, business strategies (stated in terms of strategic intent, missions, visions, product niches, services provided, financial results, or core competencies) must be both appropriate and implemented. HRP helps ensure the appropriateness of a business strategy by making sure that what happens inside a firm adds value to that which happens outside the firm. For example, when Harley-Davidson began its Harley Owners Group (HOG), the intent was to build a communications forum that enabled Harley owners—the firm's customer base—to share information and establish a unique identity. The internal program for improved customer communication (HOG produces newsletters, holds rallies, and participates actively in social events such as the Muscular Dystrophy Marathon) adds value to the external marketplace (Harley customers). HRP also helps ensure that business strategies are implemented. A critical assumption of all strategy implementation work is that executives implement business strategies by building a responsive organizational infrastructure (Galbraith, 1977; Nadler and Gerstein, 1992). Organizational infrastructure derives from HR practices.

Third, HR practices represent institutional routines and policies to shape employee behavior. A commonly accepted typology of HR practices (Tsui and Milkovich, 1985; Ulrich and Lake, 1990) includes work on staffing, development, appraisal, rewards, organization design, and communications. The deliverable of an effective HRP is to align these HR practices with business strategy to ensure customer value.

Finally, effective HRP must focus on the *process* of linking strategy and HR, not the *outcome* of that relationship. Some HRP efforts have focused on end states, which often take the form of documents that detail how to obtain and secure talent. A process-focused view of HRP centers on questions that must be answered and actions that must be taken by laying out a conceptual road map of the choices that can be made in response to each question.

Why HRP Matters

Because HRP is linked to competitiveness, corporate executives should dedicate more time to HRP efforts. Five reasons for HRP's contribution to competitiveness may be articulated.

Resource dependence.   In its simplest form, resource dependence theory argues that organizations will be competitive if they secure scarce resources better than their competitors. Because of changing demographics such as work force diversity, feminization of the work force, age of the work force, and lifestyle of the work force (Coates et al., 1991), work force *competence* is rapidly becoming the most scarce organizational resource. Core competence (as articulated by Prahalad and Hamel, 1990) must be more than technical architecture; it must include the knowledge, skills, and abilities of the work force. As resources with competence in the work force have become increasingly scarce, their importance has escalated.

Finding, securing, and stabilizing work force competencies become a competitive advantage because a firm with greater work force competence can better anticipate and meet customer requirements. HRP should help secure work force competence by establishing HR practices that attract, retain, and motivate competent employees. When Motorola considered entering the cellular telephone business, the company learned that its work force competence was a significant barrier. To design and manufacture telephones that met the stringent quality requirements, employees had to have the competence to deliver six sigma quality in all operational activities. Delivering quality required some basic reading, statistical, and process skills. Motorola invested heavily in employee training so that it could establish a work force with sufficient competence to deliver the desired product.

Contingency.   Contingency theory argues that fit occurs when internal organization practices are aligned between each other and with external conditions (Drazin and Van de Ven, 1985). The application of contingency theory comes through strategy implementation, which occurs when there is a fit between a firm's business strategy and customer expectations. As Schlessinger and Heskett (1991) argue, customer expectations for better service have gone up. Businesses that are able to provide more service are most likely to meet these expectations, differentiate themselves, and be competitive.

HRP may help highlight which HR practices can lead to service guarantees (Hart, 1988). So as to ensure delivery of service, staffing, training, and rewards programs need to be focused on employee commitment to service. Part of Wal-Mart's success is attributed to the unique and high-quality service rendered by its employees. The practices of the discount chain in staffing (hiring mature employees), compensation (requiring all Wal-Mart employees to own stock), and communication (constantly emphasizing customer service) have increased employee commitment to service. At Wal-Mart, HR practices help align the service component of both the business strategy and customer expectations. Although not formally called HRP at Wal-Mart, HRP exists. It affects competitiveness by ensuring that business strategies fit with customer expectations (Walton and Huey, 1991).

Transaction costs.   The primary concept behind transaction costs (Barney and Ouchi, 1986) is efficiency. When firms can govern their transactions or exchanges more efficiently, they are likely to be more competitive. HRP has implications for reducing transaction costs within a firm. Cascio (1987) has estimated that 55 percent of the *Fortune* 500 costs are directly or indirectly related to labor costs. When HR practices can be applied to reduce or more effectively manage these costs, firm efficiency increases. In practical terms, transaction cost efficiency is directly linked to firm productivity. When fewer employees can produce the same or more output, transaction costs are reduced and productivity is increased.

HRP may focus on HR practices that enable firms to do more with less. By better training employees, by hiring more competent employees, by implementing pay-for-performance programs, or by better communicating with employees, worker productivity increases. At General Electric, management initiatives, which included what traditionally would be considered HR programs, increased productivity dramatically. The productivity gains helped ensure General Electric's competitiveness because the company was able to outperform the competitors on speed (it could respond faster to customer demands), simplicity (it had less bureaucracy to thwart decision making), and self-confidence (its employees were empowered to make decisions).

Cognitive consensus.   The primary concept from a cognitive perspective is that organizations with shared values or mind-sets will be more likely to compete because employees share expectations, norms, and commitments. When employees share expectations, the cost of governing employee behavior is reduced because employees form organizations much like clans, where control costs are significantly reduced (Ouchi, 1980). When employees have a shared mind-set or cognition, they are able to focus attention, develop greater commitment, and develop a culture that affects competitiveness. Brockbank and Ulrich (1992) have argued that shared mind-sets come primarily from HR practices. HR practices provide information to employees and shape their behavior in ways that engender a shared mind-set. As Yeung, Ulrich, and Brockbank (1992) have found, a shared mind-set (or cognitive consensus) correlates positively with firm competitiveness. Kotter and Heskett's (1992) work also documents that a firm's culture correlates with business performance.

By effectively specifying and deploying HR practices that provide information and shape behavior, HRP becomes a means of building a shared mind-set within a company. Ulrich (1992) has argued that shared mind-set has been a missing ingredient in many HRP models. Shared mind-set becomes a summary of mission, vision, and values by addressing the simple question: "What do we want to be known for by our customers?" The answer to this question becomes the foundation for an HRP process. When Eastman Kodak focused on its HRP efforts, it gave special attention to shared mind-set (Boroski, 1990; Boroski and Davis, 1992). Kodak wanted to ensure that its strategic intent led to a focused organization. The senior executives spent time figuring out the shared mind-set they wanted in the organization and then worked to align HR practices with that mind-set. HRP, by helping create a shared mind-set, leads to competitiveness because employees and customers share a common aspiration and image.

Change.   The goal of all change models is to move an organization from point A to point B (Tichy, 1983; Kanter, Stein, and Jick, 1992). The need for change comes as conditions external to organizations (e.g., technology, information, globalization, customer demands) shift. Organizations then must be able to change quickly to adapt and compete. Organizations that don't rearrange infrastructures in environments of rapid change fail to adapt, and they lose competitiveness.

In the computer industry, the environment of the mid-1970s demanded large, complex suppliers to meet the needs of large, complex customers because most buyers of computer equipment were large firms. However, as the competitive environment for computers changed and buyers became more dispersed, computer suppliers that continued to focus primarily on serving large users became somewhat outdated. They were not able to respond to the more decentralized purchasing decisions, the use of localized networks, and the emergence of the personal computer market. IBM, in an effort to increase its ability to respond, changed its organization from a centralized, bureaucratic, functional structure to a federation of business units in which more decisions could be made at the lowest level to serve local customer needs. The organization had to get in line with changing environmental conditions.

The key success factors for change lie within an organization's boundaries. Individuals and processes may be either barriers to change or supporters of change. Individuals can become calcified in traditional work patterns because management processes become comfortable and people do not want to endure the discomfort of change. Strong HR practices that actually encourage change can counter such inflexibility.

In brief, HRP matters. It builds competitiveness through reducing resource dependence, aligning business strategy and environment, reducing transaction costs, increasing shared mind-set, and improving the capacity for change. As these issues are managed, organizations increase their abilities to find unique ways to add value for customers and to sustain peak competitiveness.

Approaches to HRP

HRP efforts may be classified by who owns or champions the HRP effort (see Figure 28–1).

Cell 1 represents companies that consider HRP irrelevant. These companies may fail to do either strategic planning or HR planning, but they may be successful through excellent products, managerial insight, or luck.

FIGURE 28-1

Classification of Human Resource Planning Efforts

Responsibility by Human Resource Professionals	Responsibility by Line Managers	
	Low	High
High	2*— Isolated	4—Integrated
Low	1— Irrelevant	3—Afterthought

*Cell number

Cell 2 represents HRP efforts in which HR professionals own the planning process. They have an HRP time line that may or may not fit with the business planning cycle. HR professionals meet, do environmental scanning, and identify the HR priorities for the corporation, taking advantage of their unique competence not only to identify priorities but also to design and implement practices to accomplish priority goals. The disadvantages of such isolated efforts are that HR professionals often are not considered part of the management team and they may lack the in-house political leverage to make HR priorities happen. HR plans can become SPOTS (strategic plans on top shelf) rather than working guides for action (Brockbank and Ulrich, 1991). Isolated HRP efforts may be elegant but their products are likely to become corporate fodder, more likely to fill file cabinets than fulfill strategic aims.

Cell 3 represents HRP efforts in settings where business planning becomes a dominant process and HR issues are an afterthought to the process. Business planning may include assessments of strengths, weaknesses, opportunities and threats, core competencies, product or service priorities, and key success factors. The results often are statements of mission, vision, values, strategic priorities, strategic measures, and strategic frameworks.

The challenge presented to Cell 3 companies is that strategic planning may lead to great expectations, but failed exploitations. Just as plans can end up as bureaucratic fodder, so can mission/vision/value statements. When they don't influence action and are changed before being fully implemented, they engender more cynicism than commitment. Managers who only consider HRP as an afterthought fail to recognize how organizational capability can be a critical source of competitiveness (Ulrich and Lake, 1990). So much time is spent on business and strategic planning that the managers deny the requisite equal commitment to the organizational processes needed to institutionalize strategy. HR plans that are afterthoughts are doomed to failure.

Cell 4 represents an integrated approach to HRP followed by firms that use teams of line managers and HR professionals to work together in forming strategic and HR plans. The combined planning team commits resources collectively to make sure that both plans are actionable and are consolidated into a single program that highlights both business priorities and the HR priorities needed to accomplish the business goals.

The challenge in ensuring that integrated HR plans are put into action is to have a framework or model that identifies the process for doing human resource planning and identifies choices for making HRP effective.

FRAMEWORK FOR HRP

A successful model lays out a process for doing HRP, by providing an intellectual road map, and identifies choices for aligning HR practices with business strategy. An architecture for HRP is presented in Figure 28–2 that describes how organizations can build an infrastructure to support business decisions (Nadler et al., 1992; Howard, 1992). The architecture metaphor focuses on four pillars, or supports, that must be in place so as to execute a business strategy.

- The *competence* pillar ensures that the organization has the knowledge, skills, and ability to carry out a business strategy.
- The *consequence* pillar ensures that the organization develops processes to demonstrate what will happen to individuals for meeting or missing business objectives.
- The *governance* pillar ensures that the organization institutes structures and communication routines to shape employee behavior.
- The *capacity for change* pillar ensures that processes exist for adapting and transforming the organization.

The organization that assembles competence, consequence, governance, and capacity for change will have the capability to translate business strategies into mind-sets and subsequently into actions. Business strategies do not become fodder, but courses of commitment.

The four pillars provide a framework that contains choices for translating strategy into action. Identifying and executing choices in each of the four pillars ensure a stable base on which to build an implementation strategy. Conversely, if all attention and resources are misallocated to just one pillar an unstable foundation is created.

An example is the company that worked hard to establish a global strategy and to create an organizational structure (governance pillar) to deal with global business requirements. The firm assumed that it had not only created the appropriate strategy but had also done what was required to carry it out. The management was wrong. The strategy failed because structure alone could not support the global strategy. The firm also needed to build competencies to deal with global issues, to design performance management systems (governance pillar) with global application, and to create a change process that would move it from domestic to global player. Working with only the organization pillar of the architecture led to a false sense of security. Choices in one pillar may affect choices in others. And there must be alignment among the pillars.

FIGURE 28–2

Architecture for Human Resource Planning Initiatives

Strategic intent: What are we trying to accomplish?
  ** strategy: business focus/drivers
    ** customers: what markets are we trying to serve
    ** numbers (measures of succes)
Mind-set: What we want to be known for by our customers

Competence Pillar	*Consequence Pillar*	*Governance Pillar*	*Capacity for Change Pillar*
What are the competencies we require to accomplish our strategy?	What are the standards and consequences required to accomplish our strategy?	What is the organization we need to accomplish our strategy?	How able are we to manage the process of change to accomplish our strategy?
Staffing	**Appraisal**	**Organization Design**	**Change Initiatives**
Who is hired into the organization? Who is promoted through the organization? Who is outplaced from the organization?	What are the performance standards for individuals, groups, and departments within the organization? What are the mechanisms for giving feedback to employees about their performance against standards? What are the processes used to ensure accurate, meaningful, and effective appraisals?	What should be the shape of the organization, e.g., how many levels, what roles, what reporting relationships, what division of labor, etc.? How do we remove vertical, horizontal, and external boundaries?	What types of initiatives should we offer to ensure that our management processes (e.g., quality, reengineering, etc.) work well?
Development	**Rewards**	**Communication**	**Change Processes**
Given our business environment and business strategy, what training should be offered? Given our business environment and business strategy, what alternatives to development should be offered?	What are the financial and non-financial consequences of meeting standards? How will the reward system ensure that individuals are motivated in appropriate directions?	What information should be shared in the organization? Who should share and receive information? What mechanisms should be used for information sharing?	What are the critical processes for making change happen? **Leveraging Change Lessons** How can we share ideas and learning across organizational boundaries?

Leadership

When executives use the four pillars as a guide to their HRP efforts, they are able to offer an integrated human resources approach that specifies the choices that must be made in each of the four pillars to activate strategy. As business strategies shift to fit changing business conditions, integrated HR practices can be designed and delivered to ensure competence, consequence, governance, and capacity for change.

HR CHOICES TO ACCOMPLISH CHANGE

The four pillars identify what organizations must do to ensure that strategies are executed and where managers should focus attention to carry the business plans into action. The questions in the pillars of Figure 28–2 summarize the HR practices and choices that may be used to support each one. An effective human resource plan generates alternatives for each pillar based on the best available practices. The alternatives are then prioritized so that critical HR initiatives are established for the organization.

Competence Pillar

The competence pillar focuses on ensuring that the organization has the knowledge, skills, and abilities to deliver the business strategy. Two steps exist for building competence in an organization. First, an audit of available and required competence ascertains what competencies the company needs to carry out a strategy, but doesn't have. Competence audits generally are done by a joint line/HR planning team, which examines the business strategy and projects the knowledge, skills, and abilities necessary to fulfill it. Second, tactics for acquiring competencies must be articulated, whether they are to be bought or built.

Buying competence comes from staffing practices that bring in, move up, or move out employees. In some ways, staffing is the most obvious and the easiest way to build competence. When Stanley Gault became chairman of Rubbermaid, he replaced people in 160 of 161 key positions; when Larry Bossidy became chairman of Allied Signal, he put new people in half of the 120 key positions. In both cases, these executives enhanced competence through staffing. Targeted selection, succession planning, and outplacement are examples of HR initiatives that buy competence for the organization.

However, the extensive replacement of employees may not be reasonable or feasible. At these times, building competencies internally may complement buying competencies. Building competencies occurs through training and development initiatives. Some companies like General Electric, Motorola, and IBM have committed enormous resources to ongoing education programs. Executives at these companies recognize that their primary competitive assets are the knowledge and competence of employees. Training innovations such as action learning, team participation, and project-focused training have begun to illustrate how training can be used to ensure competitiveness. In addition to formal training, competencies may be developed through job assignments, task force work, coaching, mentoring, and other development experiences.

The net effect of the competence pillar is that employees in the organization have the knowledge, skills, and abilities to put a business strategy into action.

Consequence Pillar

The consequence pillar focuses on how performance management systems ensure that standards and rewards align with business strategy. Strategies without consequences are like chronic procrastinators who always intend to get the work done but just never get to it. Many strategies are founded on noble intents but backed with idle deeds. The consequence pillar assumes that employees do what they are rewarded for and are rewarded for accomplishments that can be measured.

Building competence begins with clear measures, standards, and expectations. Without clear expectations for performance, employee behavior will randomly hit or miss strategic goals. Effective standards ensure the following:

- Employee behaviors are tied to business strategies. Some behaviors may be "nice to do," but they may not correlate to business success. For example, first downs in football, a standard often reported as part of the summary statistics of a game, have no correlation with winning or losing the game. Many companies have "first down" standards, which are easy to measure but do not tie well to business strategy.

- Employees feel a commitment to the standard. Sometimes, imposed standards may evoke compliance rather than commitment. An effective standard involves those who are affected by it at the time of its creation.

- Desired results are obtainable and within the control of the employee who must attain the results. Setting unrealistic expectations in the spirit of "stretch" goals may create more cynicism than commitment. Standards need to stretch but not break commitments.

- Specific behaviors and outcomes are defined. Vague standards do not elicit commitment, only hopes. Vague standards are those that cannot be operationally determined or audited. Specific standards are precise and crafted around behaviors (what needs to be done), outcomes (how we will see the result), deadlines, and accountabilities.

The content of the standards (what is measured) as well as the process for setting the standards (how standards are set) are equally critical to development of effective standards.

Meeting as well as missing standards should lead to consequences, which often are translated in the business world to financial and nonfinancial outcomes. Financial outcomes include money and economic gain. Increasingly, "at risk" reward systems tie accomplishment of standards to financial results through gain-sharing, pay-for-performance, or profit-sharing techniques. To accomplish a business strategy, a human resources plan should specify how rewards are tied to meeting business goals. The consequence pillar ensures that both positive and negative consequences occur based on the extent to which strategies are executed.

Governance Pillar

The governance pillar focuses on choices—about organization structure, decision making, and communication—that determine how an organization will govern its people and processes. Organization choices can be made about reporting relationships, accountabilities, uses of intrafunctional and cross-functional teams, and how organizations ensure that resources within an organization flow effectively and efficiently through to satisfy customer requirements. Executives develop and refine organizational structure to ensure that the organization can pull together a network of resources to meet customer needs.

Decision-making choices also set a governance tone within an organization. Empowerment, involvement, participative management, or quality circle initiatives shift decision making from the top to the bottom. The sharing of knowledge, power, information, and rewards through all levels shifts the locus of decision making and sets a tone for governance.

Communication choices center on what information to share, who will share information, who should receive information, and how to share information.

Collectively, organization, decision-making, and communication choices ensure that a culture is set for governing employee behavior and attitudes. This governance process institutionalizes values, norms, and paradigms within organizations.

Capacity for Change Pillar

The capacity for change pillar focuses on how organizations make changes happen. This pillar includes choices on change initiatives that direct people's energy to change management. Change initiatives may include process mapping, quality, reengineering, or other programs that promote change in the company. Choices in the capacity for change pillar ensure that these initiatives are thoughtfully defined and appropriately sponsored.

In addition, the processes necessary to move strategy to action can be identified. Many models of change have identified critical processes for managing change, including the following:*

- Having a sponsor of change who "owns" and leads the change initiative.
- Creating a shared need among those who are affected by the change.
- Shaping a vision of the desired outcome from the change.

---

*These processes have been identified in work with General Electric and a design team including Steve Kerr, Craig Schneier, Jon Biel, Ron Gager, and Mary Anne Devanna (outsiders to GE) and Jacquie Vierling, Cathy Friarson, and Amy Howard (GE employees).

- Mobilizing commitment to the change by key stakeholders who will have to be involved in accomplishing the change.

- Using the tools in the other pillars (competence, consequence, and governance) to make sure that the change is built into the infrastructure of the organization.

- Monitoring progress on the change through benchmarks, milestones, and experiments that demonstrate progress.

- Making change endure through implementation plans, follow-through, and ongoing commitments.

Finally, the capacity for change pillar encourages a commitment to ongoing learning throughout the organization. Learning implies that ideas generated in one area of the organization are shared across boundaries. Boundaries may include levels in the hierarchy (ideas are shared up and down the organization), functions in the organization (ideas are shared across functions), businesses (ideas are shared across business units), and geographies (ideas are shared across national borders). Sharing ideas implies a learning process that helps organizations continually renew themselves.

In the capacity for change pillar, choices on change initiative, change processes, and learning processes help create an organization's ability to make change happen quicker.

APPLICATION OF THE HRP FRAMEWORK TO BUSINESS CHANGE

HRP processes work to ensure that choices are made in each of the four pillars to translate strategic plans into actions. When choices are made in each pillar, major strategic initiatives can be translated into organizational attributes, programs, and processes. Some examples of questions raised by each pillar as they relate to commonly targeted business strategies include the following:

Competence

- To what extent do we have the competence to accomplish the globalization, market growth, cost reduction, or other strategy?

- To increase competence, what staffing and/or development initiatives can be implemented?

Consequence

- To what extent does the global, market growth, cost reduction, or other strategy connect to positive or negative consequences for employees?

- To ensure these positive consequences, what can be done to set better standards and to ensure that rewards are linked to strategies?

Governance

- To what extent do the governance processes match the strategic requirements of globalization, market growth, cost reduction, or other strategy?
- How can we improve our organization, decision making, and communication efforts so they are aligned with our business strategy?

Capacity for change

- To what extent do we have a commitment to change to accomplish a global, market growth, cost reduction, or other strategy?
- What change initiatives, change processes, and change learning techniques can be effected to accomplish global, market growth, cost reduction, or other strategies?

The HRP framework in Figure 28–2 provides an intellectual road map for making informed choices about how to accomplish business strategies. Once key choices are identified and programs initiated consistent with the choices, strategies are more likely to produce results.

HRP: CONCLUSIONS FOR A SYNTHESIS

Traditional HRP models are the antithesis of change. The framework provided in this chapter attempts to create a synthesis of HRP and business strategy to make change happen. The synthesis occurs at multiple levels:

- Between business strategy and HRP to translate market-driven positions into organizational capabilities.
- Between line managers responsible for business results and HR professionals who design and deliver HR programs.
- Between change initiatives with novel ideas and management commitments that move the ideas into results.
- Between strategic plans and operational tactics to accomplish the plans.

These syntheses occur because HRP frameworks are road maps that guide decisions rather than policy manuals that edit behavior. The four-pillar model in Figure 28–2 orders and frames questions that, when addressed, ensure that HRP processes encourage change.

This chapter deals with a basic question: How can HRP processes be used to leverage change? The answer lies in (1) an increased commitment to HRP because it is central to competitiveness, (2) a framework for HRP that identifies critical choices and initiatives for human resources, (3) an awareness of the choices for ensuring that HR issues are focused on changing business strategies, and (4) the application of the framework to building the internal organization to respond to business needs. In brief, the question-focused, process-driven HRP framework offered in this chapter leads to a synthesis of business strategy and human resources.

REFERENCES

Alpander, G. G. "Human Resource Planning in U.S. Corporations." *California Management Review* 22, no. 3 (1980), pp. 24–32.

Barney, J. B.; and W. G. Ouchi (eds.). *Organizational Economics*. San Francisco: Jossey-Bass, 1986.

Boroski, J. "Putting It Together: HR Planning in 3D Eastman Kodak." *Human Resource Planning* 13, no. 1, 1990, pp. 45–57.

Boroski, J.; and G. Davis. "Human Resource Planning at Eastman Kodak." *Human Resource Management* 31, no. 1/2, pp. 81–95.

Brockbank, J. W.; and D. Ulrich. "Avoiding SPOTS: Creating Strategic Unity." In *Handbook of Business Strategy 1990*. Ed. H. Glass. New York: Gorham, Lambert, 1991.

Brockbank, W.; and D. Ulrich. "Institutional Antecedents of Shared Organizational Cognitions." Unpublished Manuscript. Ann Arbor: University of Michigan, 1992.

Cascio, W. F. *Costing Human Resources: The Financial Impact of Behavior in Organizations*. New York: Van Nostrand Reinhold, 1987.

Coates, J. F.; J. Jarratt; and J. Mahaffie. *Future Work*. San Francisco: Jossey-Bass, 1991.

Drazin, R.; and A. Van de Ven. "Alternative Forms of Fit in Contingency Theory." *Administrative Science Quarterly* 30 (1985), pp. 514–39.

Fombrun, C.; N. M. Tichy; and M. A. Devanna. *Strategic Human Resource Management*. New York: John Wiley, 1984.

Galbraith, J. *Organization Design*. Reading, MA: Addison-Wesley, 1977.

Hart, C. "The Power of Unconditional Service Guarantees." *Harvard Business Review,* July–August 1988, pp. 54–62.

Howard, R. "The CEO as Organizational Architect: An Interview with Xerox's Paul Allaire." *Harvard Business Review,* September–October 1992, pp. 106–23.

Kanter, R.; B. Stein; and T. Jick. *The Challenge of Organizational Change: How Companies Experience It and Leaders Guide It*. New York: Free Press, 1992.

Kotter, J.; and J. Heskett. *Culture and Performance*. New York: Free Press, 1992.

Nadler, D. A.; M. S. Gerstein; Robert Shaw and Associates. *Organizational Architecture: Designs for Changing Organizations*. San Francisco: Jossey-Bass, 1992.

Nkomo, S. M. "Human Resource Planning and Organization Competitiveness: An Exploratory Analysis." *Strategic Management Journal* 8, no. 4, 1987, pp. 387–92.

Ouchi, W. G. "Markets, Bureaucracies, and Clans." *Administrative Science Quarterly* 25, no. 1, 1980, pp. 129–41.

Prahalad, C. K.; and G. Hamel. "The Core Competence of the Corporation." *Harvard Business Review,* May–June 1990, pp. 79–91.

Schlesinger, L.; and J. Heskitt. "The Service-Driven Service Company." *Harvard Business Review,* September–October, 1991, pp. 71–82.

Tichy, N. *Managing Strategic Change: Technical, Political, and Cultural Dynamics.* New York: John Wiley, 1983.

Tsui, A.; and G. Milkovich. "Dimensions of Personnel Department Activities." Paper presented at Academy of Management, 1985.

Ulrich, D. "Strategic and Human Resource Planning: Linking Customers and Employees." *Human Resource Planning* 15, no. 2, 1992, pp. 47–62.

Ulrich, D. O.; and D. Lake. *Organizational Capability: Competing from the Inside/Out.* New York: Wiley, 1990.

Ulrich, D. "Strategic Human Resource Planning: Why and How?" *Human Resource Planning* 10, no. 1, 1987, pp. 25–37.

Walker, J. W. *Human Resource Planning.* New York: McGraw-Hill, 1992.

Walton, S.; and J. Huey. *Sam Walton: Made in America.* New York: Doubleday, 1992.

Yeung, A.; D. Ulrich; and W. Brockbank. *Cognitive Consensuality and Organizational Performance: An Empirical Assessment.* Working paper, University of Michigan, School of Business, 1992.

Chapter Twenty-Nine

The Ethics of Change

Keith T. Darcy

E *thics* comes from the Greek word *ethos,* meaning "the character peculiar to a specific people, culture, or group." Alternatively, the word *moral* comes from the Latin *mores,* meaning "the customs and accepted traditions" of a people. Indeed, culture is generally acknowledged as the collective values of any community of people that are passed from one generation to another. It consists of the customary beliefs, social norms, and values of a group.

Unfortunately, given the velocity of change today, our customary beliefs are no longer customary. We are in the eye of a global cyclone. Change is everywhere, from the former Soviet Union to Hong Kong, from the Eastern bloc nations to the Middle East, from Berlin to Soweto, from the fall of communism to the dismantling of apartheid. In an era of such constant volatility, it is essential that ethics, values, and culture be continually reassessed to determine if they must be altered to meet newly emerging conditions or, at the minimum, if they are consistent with the changes.

Change in the business environment is no less profound. It includes globalization with its varying and sometimes contradictory cultural standards and practices, intense cross-border competition, frenzied merger, acquisition, and divestiture activity, corporate consolidations and work force reductions, rapidly shifting work force demographics, and a schizophrenic process of deregulation and reregulation by federal, state, local, and host governments. Taken together, these represent complicated and threatening changes to the environment in which business operates.

The pressures to assess and align ethics are especially pronounced in the conduct of business. Adherence to an appropriate standard of conduct may, indeed, be a primary factor in the success of the changing organization, a welcome dash of consistency and trust in an era when everyone is being forced to manage change. The customer that doesn't have to stop to ask about its supplier's ability to deliver quality goods in timely fashion and at the right price is a customer with confidence to order at the very time it too is beset with myriad change management issues. It is one less issue to worry about. In a real sense, ethics provide a framework for fruitful dealings with customers and other stakeholders, and the efficacy of the organization's culture and value system may be measured by how well the company interacts with its external associates.

For managers it is becoming increasingly difficult to operate in today's wilderness with yesterday's compasses and tools. As sophisticated as yesterday's strategic operating plans may be, they can be rendered useless by such rapid change. Often the ink isn't dry before new plans must be drafted. The velocity of external change requires constant management attention to assess market attractiveness, the company's competitive position, and the internal capabilities of the organization to meet these new conditions.

Without question, change is a destabilizing influence on the environment in which business operates. It represents a powerful threat to organizations and individuals, causing not only uncertainty but also fear. Ayn Rand once said, "Anxiety resides in the place between reality and illusion." Stated differently, fear exists between the world of "shoulds" and "oughts" and what really is. Many executives are caught up in this place of anxiety. Their world is changing so rapidly that they sometimes deny the changes are taking place, clutching to the world of "shoulds" and "oughts" and playing all this out in constant, unexpressed fear while waiting for the unlikely return of the "good old days."

Alvin Toffler defined the title of his best-selling book, *Future Shock*, as "disorientation due to premature accelerated change." Indeed, today's executive is disoriented. The present isn't what was, and the future is unpredictable. Toffler defines culture shock as "a sense of confusion and uncertainty, sometimes accompanied with feelings of anxiety, that may affect people exposed to change without adequate preparation." Without question, much of America's business is suffering from culture shock.

Paralysis permeates the shocked organization. Managers whose primary function is to plan, organize, and control treat change as an unwelcome stranger. Change, however, is here to stay. The short-term survival and long-term success of today's corporation depend heavily upon being responsive to the changing conditions posed by its operating environment. Executives must learn how to anticipate, cope with, and implement change.

As changes continue to sweep through our lives and pervade the business environment, a thorough understanding of ethics and values has become paramount for effective corporate leadership. Leadership derives from trust, and trust is built on a common understanding between people. As our common understanding becomes increasingly uncommon, ethics is the language that realigns corporate leaders with their employees, customers, shareholders, suppliers, and neighbors in the communities served by the organization. Ethics, therefore, is not just a personal matter; it is interpersonal.

Corporations have complex involvements with other people, groups, and organizations that have a stake in their decisions. Linking the needs of the business and the needs of its various stakeholders is a primary challenge for today's leaders. Developing a sense of shared values—a set of beliefs against which all business decisions can be measured and tested—is increasingly the basis on which long-term strategies and their successful implementation are built.

Values enable an organization to absorb change. Given the velocity of change in the 1990s, the failure of corporate leadership to align ethics and values with business strategies and operating plans bears potentially heavy costs and can result in many lost opportunities. The value systems of institutions that fail to change often become riddled with hypocrisy or undermined by criticism and, in many cases, are simply abandoned. Adapting organizational values to current conditions may be hard but the price of standing pat is steep. There are simply too many areas where the company is vulnerable to a breakdown in ethics that threatens a costly backlash among stakeholders, including customers.

Anyone who has spent five minutes in an executive suite knows that a strategy that is incompatible with a firm's culture and organizational values is difficult and perhaps impossible to achieve. Successful implementation of strategy requires not only the physical and intellectual commitment of people but also their emotional and spiritual commitment. This match-up is especially critical in time of change. If people are being asked to alter their behaviors in line with a new strategy, are they also being given the right message as to how they are to act ethically?

The stress and anxiety involved in change often create an environment for wrongful behavior that unfortunately may be pursued unwittingly. People who are excessively loyal may cut corners in the belief they are "helping the company" at a time when it needs extraordinary help. Managers who normally would be the soul of propriety wink at poor business practices or infractions of the law while deceiving themselves into believing that their actions really aren't wrong and that the company wants them to do whatever it takes to get the job done. Blunders linked to excess loyalty are common—Salomon Brothers' abuses in cornering Treasury bill auctions, Dow Corning's data manipulation to minimize dangers of silicone implants, and General Electric's irregularities in calculating costs of government contracts being among the primary examples.

Telecommunications technology has virtually eliminated the communications "float" that once acted to cushion the company and its stakeholders from the shock of awareness and change. Information is universally and instantaneously available. As a result, corporations are increasingly subject to criticism by the media, competitors, regulators, social commentators, and the public. As society becomes more informed, the information dispensed by companies and other organizations must be truthful. Unfortunately, this demand is not being met. Gaps are emerging in our common understanding of what constitutes fact and truth, and misalignment of values has become increasingly visible. Contradictions have developed to breed credibility gaps between groups that question the essence of relationships, and they threaten to damage the trust that should govern intergroup behavior.

Among the factors that have been driving wedges between groups are the following:

- Employees and shareholders are questioning corporate leaders about their commitment to affirmative action in companies whose boards and top managements continue to be dominated by white males.

- Layoffs, pay freezes, and plant closings and downsizings, at the very time the compensation gap between top management and the rank and file widens, alienate employees rather than nurture loyalty and dedication.

- Communities in which companies operate, as well as their employees and consumers in general, are becoming increasingly concerned about the environmental impact of business operations, not just locally, but nationally and globally as well.

- The Senate hearings on the nomination of Clarence Thomas to the U.S. Supreme Court and the trial of the Los Angeles policemen accused of beating Rodney King have raised the consciousness of society about sexual harassment and racial discrimination.

The instantaneous and globally abundant flow of information has fundamentally altered not only the way we do business but also the way we interact with each other as individuals and organizations. Information requires truth, and truth *demands* freedom. In short, there isn't any place to hide anymore. The alignment of values between an organization and *all* of its stakeholders is imperative for success in the 21st century.

In the midst of this sea change, employees are increasingly saying that they want to be identified with a company that stands for something. They want to work for a company that has a vision about what it is doing. They want to take pride in what they produce. They want to admire the people they work with. As a response, leaders must develop a culture in which employees are encouraged to discuss their day-to-day dilemmas openly. Lines of communication must be opened to gain the trust of people inside and outside the firm. Today's leader must create an organizational culture in which ideas come together without generating fear among people. Such leaders are committed to problem finding, not just problem solving. They embrace error, even failure, because mistakes teach more than success does. They encourage healthy dissent and reward those brave enough to say no. They unleash other people's creativity and talents and foster the release of human potential.

The payoff is even more significant. This trust, once developed, will extend to customers, regulators, and the public, while developing a renewed sense of pride, dedication, and loyalty to the company among employees.

First, the starting point for all of this is the words and actions of top management. The most crucial ingredient is a chief executive officer who actively projects a strong ethical concern for the various stakeholders and is willing to encourage widespread discussion on how to align the company's business objectives with its own and its stakeholders' systems of values. This should lead to a comprehensive understanding of key ethical principles within the company. However, words that cannot be put into action, or actions that cannot be spoken about, are equally dangerous disincentives to corporate moral development. Top management is required to "walk the talk" and to set the moral standard for its organization. Corporate leaders must be prepared to address critical and social business issues openly. As Dante once wrote, "The hottest places in hell are reserved for those who in times of great moral crisis maintain their neutrality."

Next, companies must integrate strong ethical standards into their corporate culture and business objectives. Corporate culture exerts a powerful influence on the behavior of employees. In many companies, especially larger ones, there are multiple cultures, which often vary by geography and product lines. Thus, various levels and degrees of culture must be dealt with. Executives must be attuned not only to the "formal organization," comprised of published policies and procedures, but also to the "informal organization" that is the silent, less visible way of "getting things done."

Third, companies must open up corporate values to a broad definition of cultural standards. A company is made up of people from various cultures and backgrounds, each of whom brings particular strengths in their diversity. While setting appropriate standards of expected behavior, executives must also listen for the cultural differences being introduced in a demographically changing work force and honor and value those differences.

Last, it is imperative that companies take appropriate action to build ethical safeguards into the company. A fully integrated, comprehensive process begins with a code of ethics. The words themselves, however, are in many cases less important than how they are developed, implemented, and understood in the firm. Employees need guidance on how to handle day-to-day dilemmas. Employee grievance processes are an important expression of how a company values dissent and opens communications. Having the right performance goals and incentive systems helps reinforce the desired behavioral objectives. Periodic ethics audits are an effective way of taking the pulse of the organization to identify where values are aligned and where there are gaps.

New legal changes make it increasingly dangerous to avoid integration of values into a corporation's business plans. One example is the United States Sentencing Commission's new guidelines to federal prosecutors and courts that have fundamentally altered the scope and definition of management and corporate responsibility. Because the most significant government campaign ever waged against white-collar crime has been underway in the 1990s, top executives and others responsible for the management and policy making of the company may now be subject to substantial personal risks—including fines and/or jail sentences—where there have been legal violations by their employees in the conduct of business. Willful ignorance is no longer a defense.

Companies, their officers, and their directors may be held criminally liable for the behavior of their employees, even though an employee may have acted contrary to explicit instructions. In such instances, mandatory fines—up to $290 million in the Salomon Brothers' case—may be levied against the company for taking inadequate steps to prevent and detect illegal behavior. Senior executives and board members who ignore these guidelines do so at their own peril.

These guidelines place responsibility for corporate values and employee behavior squarely on the corporation and its leaders. They deliberately take a strong "carrot and stick" approach using both severe economic and personal threats. But the commission also specifies where risks can be substantially reduced. A comprehensive program for communicating values and defining clear behavioral expectations throughout the firm, coupled with appropriate reinforcement mechanisms such as auditing procedures, performance goals, incentive systems, organizational structures, and effective education and communication, can meet the commission's defined standard of "effective compliance."

It takes the entire history of the company to develop and build stakeholder trust. It takes only one article in *The Wall Street Journal* or on the six o'clock news to destroy it. In effect, there now exists a new legal definition for leadership and corporate responsibility. The failure of industry to respond to this partnership offer by the government can only lead to increased regulation.

A company is defined as "a community of people with common interests and shared values banded together to achieve a common goal." Business is expected to adhere to the same ethical standards and shared values applied elsewhere by its stakeholders. The failure to do so easily exposes the gaps, especially in an age of information. The larger the gap between what business does and what stakeholders expect, the bigger the risk to a company. Business ethics is not a special set of rules different from ethics in general and applicable only to business. Alignment of values is crucial for success.

The winds of change are blowing rapidly through our host company's environment. A company and its stakeholders, taken together, are an interactive system. They are each integral to one another. Survival of a person or a company depends on its capacity to adapt to changes posed by the environment. Companies most likely to succeed in this environment of change will have not only the technical competence required for service and production in meeting customer needs but also an awareness of broad social changes and how their company's ethical performance compares to society's values and expectations. Harnessing the collective human and moral capital of the firm is the great challenge of today's leader.

Change will forever dominate our lives. Instantaneous and globally abundant information along with a growing human consciousness ensure it. Leadership dedicated to enlarging human understanding and improving the broadly defined human neighborhood provides stability in our relationships with one another and in our business strategies in an otherwise chaotic and perpetually changing environment.

Structure of The Change Management Handbook

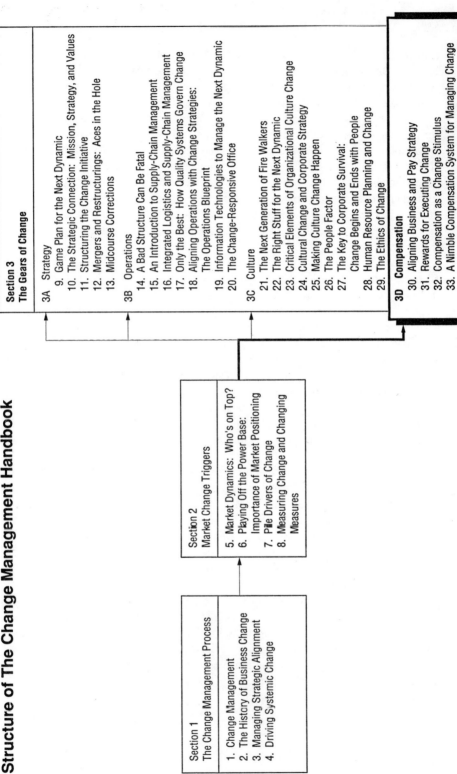

Section 1
The Change Management Process

1. Change Management
2. The History of Business Change
3. Managing Strategic Alignment
4. Driving Systemic Change

Section 2
Market Change Triggers

5. Market Dynamics: Who's on Top?
6. Playing Off the Power Base: Importance of Market Positioning
7. Pie Drivers of Change
8. Measuring Change and Changing Measures

Section 3
The Gears of Change

3A   Strategy

9. Game Plan for the Next Dynamic
10. The Strategic Connection: Mission, Strategy, and Values
11. Structuring the Change Initiative
12. Mergers and Restructurings: Aces in the Hole
13. Midcourse Corrections

3B   Operations

14. A Bad Structure Can Be Fatal
15. An Introduction to Supply-Chain Management
16. Integrated Logistics and Supply-Chain Management
17. Only the Best: How Quality Systems Govern Change
18. Aligning Operations with Change Strategies: The Operations Blueprint
19. Information Technologies to Manage the Next Dynamic
20. The Change-Responsive Office

3C   Culture

21. The Next Generation of Fire Walkers
22. The Right Stuff for the Next Dynamic
23. Critical Elements of Organizational Culture Change
24. Cultural Change and Corporate Strategy
25. Making Culture Change Happen
26. The People Factor
27. The Key to Corporate Survival: Change Begins and Ends with People
28. Human Resource Planning and Change
29. The Ethics of Change

3D   Compensation

30. Aligning Business and Pay Strategy
31. Rewards for Executing Change
32. Compensation as a Change Stimulus
33. A Nimble Compensation System for Managing Change
34. Using Executive Compensation to Promote Change

D

COMPENSATION

N one of the foregoing elements of alignment will come together unless the people being asked to forge the links are properly recognized. That is done through the compensation system that provides the rewards for performance. In the contexts of change management and alignment, these rewards are made for improving performance while helping execute change, for buying into specific changes and change orientation on a continual basis, and for helping the firm get ahead of change.

For openers, there must be complete acceptance of the inextricable connection between a company's strategy and the way it pays employees (Berger, Chapter 30). At many firms, this interconnection is elusive, and performance suffers. Often, the managers are at a loss to explain the misfires. Some of these firms pay well and get poor results, others pay poorly and achieve better results than they have a right to obtain, whereas still others have discriminatory systems that may reward the paperpushers while shortchanging the people who work most closely with the customers.

These organizations are totally misaligned (even if their cultures, operations, and strategies are in sync). They may pay lip service to rewards for performance but they don't practice it in fact. The firm that maintains a flawed pay system in supposedly routine times will be ill prepared to meet change. It will be unable to determine how far out of line its pay system is and, therefore, will be unable to use it as a viable instrument of change.

There are, however, many ways in which to get the pay gear into alignment with other internal factors. The correct pay system will indeed be structured to provide incentives for commitment to change and to the actual carrying out of practices that revitalize the company and sustain the right relationships with customers (McNutt and Spiegel, Chapter 31). This is the purest manifestation of pay for performance. In a parallel approach, the compensation system should be far-reaching enough to serve as a stimulus to change, to provide real rewards for people whose actions represent clear-cut buy-in to the concept of orientation toward continual change (Giblin, Chapter 32).

In perhaps the biggest conceptual shake-up, the work force may have to be totally revamped in order to eliminate the traditional structure of job slots and replace them with the idea of assignments for people (Wolf, Chapter 33). How would this work? People would be hired by firms for their skills and commitments but not assigned to specific organizational positions. Instead, they would be shifted from post to post as needed—or wherever their talents can best be employed. This flexibility is perhaps the greatest testament to change management. It creates a policy of moving people, not willy-nilly but with some rationale, relatively often. The keys are that the movement would be expected; that structural barriers to shifting people when change demands it would be demolished; and that traditional concepts of linking pay to a single job would be discarded for a compensation system that stresses flexibility and nimbleness. People would be compensated for how quickly they adjust and how well they fulfill new assignments–which invariably will be equated with their accomplishments in managing change. Understanding these new concepts requires an overview of how executive pay has been used to promote change (Pennings, Chapter 34).

Chapter Thirty

Aligning Business and Pay Strategy

Lance A. Berger

I f Franklin Roosevelt were alive today, he might counsel millions of Americans that the only thing certain is uncertainty itself—and that those who learn how to manage change will gain a competitive edge on the future.

But gaining this edge is not an easy task. We live in an era of slow global economic growth, wildly fluctuating currency rates and stock market prices, worldwide competition, constantly differentiating labor markets, rapid technology development and transfer, and the twin phenomena of industrial consolidation and the explosive emergence of the small-business sector.

Several barriers inhibit our capacity to deal with these potent forces of change:

An inability to recognize fully the scope of change.

A lack of the skills needed to manage change.

Cultural characteristics that cause people to resist change.

Absence of a framework within which change can be managed.

A common contributor to each of these barriers is the company's system for compensating employees and managers. Although change is demanded of key personnel, the methods by which they are compensated for performing new skills don't change, and many fear that if they don't get change right, their jobs, careers, and livelihoods are in jeopardy. A program for paying people to lead change would go a long way toward knocking over the barriers.

Furthermore, the combination of external forces and internal barriers has exacerbated employee anxieties over their company's ability to compete successfully. And that anxiety may include fears over the safety of their jobs. To manage strategically in a world of uncertainty is literally "risky business." As Robert Szakoni suggests, effective strategic planning is problematic when knowledge of the future is difficult and forecasting techniques lack credibility.[1]

How then can we develop a relationship between pay strategy and business strategy, particularly when the basis for the business strategy itself may be uncertain? We propose creating a "framework for choice" that can help companies find, as Milkovich suggests, "the best fit between an organization's strategy and its compensation programs.[2] This framework provides the guidelines for changing pay programs when a company's business situation changes.

OUT OF THE SCIENTIFIC REALM

Few studies have empirically derived relationships between pay decisions, strategy, and business performance. What few attempts have been made inevitably have fallen short because of an inability either to refine or to control enough variables in enough business units to meet rigorous statistical tests.

It is the author's belief that pursuit of definitive empirical linkages will be like the search for the Holy Grail. Let's leave that exploration to the academicians and try a different approach that treats both strategic planning and compensation as disciplines rather than sciences. Such an approach permits us to deal efficiently with the process of change, by allowing us to suggest that practitioners should move through a series of structured situational analyses that help produce an integrated series of informed choices. Ultimately, this process will lead to the right pay strategy within the context of the changing organization.

The proposed framework is flexible and capable of addressing compensation strategies each time a company changes its business strategy. As we move toward new compensation programs, we need simply to remember the following:

- Organizations with different business, organization, and human resource strategies will require different pay strategies.
- Pay strategies must be sensitive to, and adjusted in accordance with, changes in business strategy.
- The only pay strategies that will succeed are those based on affordability levels specified in strategic and operating plans and distributed in accordance with the values of the institution and the demands of its external environment.

Figure 30–1 graphically illustrates the alignment relationship between a company's compensation strategy and its business strategy, organization design, human resource strategy, and culture. Although the details contained in each cell will vary with a particular company's business situation and industry, the model holds that once classified, a business must ensure that its management processes are synchronized in order to be successful. Furthermore, it must develop comprehensive realignment plans once a change trigger causes it to protect its business classification or move between classifications. Each action requires repositioning of activity within a cell.

FIGURE 30–1

Alignment Model

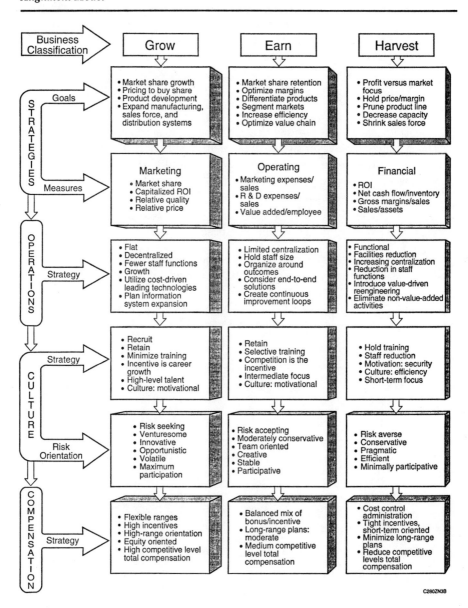

Business Classification	Grow	Earn	Harvest
STRATEGIES — Goals	• Market share growth • Pricing to buy share • Product development • Expand manufacturing, sales force, and distribution systems	• Market share retention • Optimize margins • Differentiate products • Segment markets • Increase efficiency • Optimize value chain	• Profit versus market focus • Hold price/margin • Prune product line • Decrease capacity • Shrink sales force
STRATEGIES — Measures	**Marketing** • Market share • Capitalized ROI • Relative quality • Relative price	**Operating** • Marketing expenses/ sales • R & D expenses/ sales • Value added/employee	**Financial** • ROI • Net cash flow/inventory • Gross margins/sales • Sales/assets
OPERATIONS — Strategy	• Flat • Decentralized • Fewer staff functions • Growth • Utilize cost-driven leading technologies • Plan information system expansion	• Limited centralization • Hold staff size • Organize around outcomes • Consider end-to-end solutions • Create continuous improvement loops	• Functional • Facilities reduction • Increasing centralization • Reduction in staff functions • Introduce value-driven reengineering • Eliminate non-value-added activities
CULTURE — Strategy	• Recruit • Retain • Minimize training • Incentive is career growth • High-level talent • Culture: motivational	• Retain • Selective training • Competition is the incentive • Intermediate focus • Culture: motivational	• Hold training • Staff reduction • Motivation: security • Culture: efficiency • Short-term focus
CULTURE — Risk Orientation	• Risk seeking • Venturesome • Innovative • Opportunistic • Volatile • Maximum participation	• Risk accepting • Moderately conservative • Team oriented • Creative • Stable • Participative	• Risk averse • Conservative • Pragmatic • Efficient • Minimally participative
COMPENSATION — Strategy	• Flexible ranges • High incentives • High-range orientation • Equity oriented • High competitive level total compensation	• Balanced mix of bonus/incentive • Long-range plans: moderate • Medium competitive level total compensation	• Cost control administration • Tight incentives, short-term oriented • Minimize long-range plans • Reduce competitive levels total compensation

C280ZN3B

LINKING PROCESS TO STRATEGY

This chapter will present the "framework for choice" by linking results (objectives) of three key strategies—business, organization, and culture/human resource planning—to the three key elements of pay strategy. In short, it will show how to utilize the situational analysis described in Figure 30–1.

The three elements are these:

Pay market—the source of recruitment for each employee or group of employees in a defined work unit.

Competitive level—the targeted level (base salary, total compensation) in defined compensation surveys for an employee group of a business unit. This level affects costs directly by defining affordable levels as well as by having an impact on employee turnover rates. It is typically expressed as a percentile, for example, 50th percentile of the pay market.

Mix—the components and their representation, expressed as a percentage of total employee pay (base salary, variable pay, benefits).

Figure 30–2 illustrates the relationship graphically and suggests that the key implications of the three key processes must be clearly identified and reconciled into a final pay strategy.

In the next sections we provide the reader with a series of exercises designed to complete each section of the Pay Strategy Decision Matrix.

Exercise I

BUSINESS PLANNING

Objective

To identify and measure the performance of business units against their own strategies by establishing the following:

- The competitive compensation levels that a unit can afford.
- The mix of compensation that would be most appropriate for reinforcing behavior that supports defined business strategies.

The specific steps the reader will follow include these:

- Strategic business unit (SBU) identification.
- Classification of business unit (stage of growth/competitiveness/market attractiveness).
- Classification of business unit strategy.
- Classification of business measures associated with strategy.
- Evaluation of business performance.

FIGURE 30–2

Pay Strategy Decision Matrix

	Elements of Pay Strategy		
Management Plans	Pay Market(s)	Competitive Level	Mix
Business			
Organization			
Culture			
(Human Resources)			
Final Strategy			

The following matrix decisions will be made:

- The affordable competitive level.
- The mix based on business classification.

For the purpose of this exercise, we will use the planning model developed by Cassano[3]—but any business unit classification model may be substituted.

Classifying the business, establishing the measure of strategy, and determining performance

1. In Figure 30–3 rank each business unit according to market attractiveness and competitive strength, and define current and new principal objectives (grow, earn, harvest).

2. Next, identify the principal measures of how strategic objectives will be attained. Figure 30–3 suggests that each strategy will be dominated by a different primary measure. These measures later will be used as the basis of performance assessment.

3. Finally, determine the current strategy for each business objective and its financial measurements. Figure 30–4 classifies strategies according to business objectives. There will be obvious implications for operations and human resource strategies in each area (i.e., growth leads to hiring, enhancement suggests downsizing, etc.).

If strategies you are following (grow, earn, harvest) do not align themselves with the strategic objective, you must go back and reconcile the two.

Figure 30–5 illustrates the principles previously outlined for a diversified company. Each business unit is identified and classified. Measures and performance evaluations are derived from respective strategies, and preliminary compensation practice components are selected. The reader can determine the suggested elements of pay strategy for each of three business units with three different business objectives based on data presented. One must be particularly sensitive to changes occurring when a company changes its business classification, for example, from Grow to Earn or from Earn to Harvest. The pay strategy components are preliminary

FIGURE 30–3
Business Classification

Competitive Strength (Your current position and market share)	Market attractiveness (Growth: your customer base)		
	High (15% above industry average)	Medium (5%–15% above industry average)	Low (5% below industry average)
High (Rank 1–3) Market share + 15%	GROW • Market measures		
Medium (Rank 4–9) Market share 5%–15%		EARN • Operating measures	
Low (Rank below 10) Market share Below 5%			ENHANCE • Financial measures

FIGURE 30–4
*Business Strategies**

Grow	Earn	Harvest
• Market share growth	• Maintain market share	• Forgo market share for profits
• Price to buy market share	• Optimize margins	• Hold prices and margins
• Develop new products	• Differentiate products	• Prune product lines
• Expand manufacturing, sales force and distribution systems	• Segment markets	• Decrease capacity
	• Optimize value chain	• Shrink work force

*Figure 30–4 outlines the strategies with each business classification in Figure 30–3.

and based on data collected during this exercise. The reader will note that the business classi-fication for each unit suggests a particular mix of compensation based on the broad guidelines shown in the Alignment Model (Figure 30–1). For example, growth companies like unit **A** have a higher incentive base pay. Additionally, performance levels suggested that the **B** and **C** companies will be able to afford to pay higher competitive pay levels. Most likely those high-er levels will be generated by incentives paid for above-target-level performance.

FIGURE 30–5
Business Planning Exercise

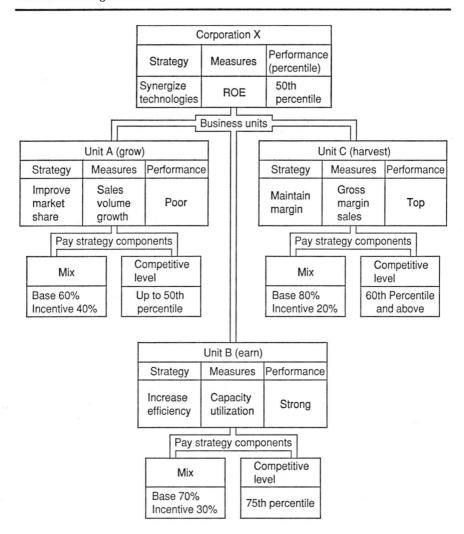

Corporation X

Strategy	Measures	Performance (percentile)
Synergize technologies	ROE	50th percentile

Business units

Unit A (grow)

Strategy	Measures	Performance
Improve market share	Sales volume growth	Poor

Pay strategy components

Mix	Competitive level
Base 60% Incentive 40%	Up to 50th percentile

Unit C (harvest)

Strategy	Measures	Performance
Maintain margin	Gross margin sales	Top

Pay strategy components

Mix	Competitive level
Base 80% Incentive 20%	60th Percentile and above

Unit B (earn)

Strategy	Measures	Performance
Increase efficiency	Capacity utilization	Strong

Pay strategy components

Mix	Competitive level
Base 70% Incentive 30%	75th percentile

Note: Mix refers to ratio
of pay component
to the total pay.

Competitive level
refers to a percentile
in a chosen pay market.

FIGURE 30–6
Comparison of Staff Costs

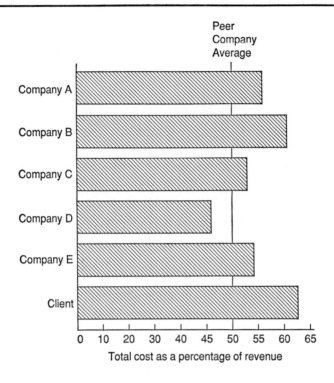

Exercise II

ORGANIZATION PLANNING

The next exercise focuses on utilizing an assessment of operations as input to pay strategy.

Objective

To determine the effectiveness of the organization structure and its associated competitive level of human resource costs—specifically, to show the following:

- How the competitive level of human resource costs (HURCOS) is related to an affordable competitive level.
- How the characteristics of the organization design relate to the mix of compensation.

FIGURE 30–7
*Organization Design Criteria**

Organization Design Elements	Weight: High—3 Medium—2 Low—1	*Comparison with Competitors*		
Number of management levels		High 1	Medium 2	Low 3
Spans of control		Narrow 1	Medium 2	Wide 3
Culture characteristics		Risk-averse 1	Risk-accepting 2	Risk-oriented 3
Decision-making process		Long 1	Medium 2	Short 3

*Variable Compensation
    Total Score

High	10–12
Medium	7–9
Low	1–6

The specific activities that the reader will follow are these:

- A competitive payroll analysis (relating payroll as a percentage of key business measures defined in business planning activity).
- An assessment of organization design.

Figure 30–6 illustrates how a business unit's weak competitive human resource cost posture can suggest a lower affordable base (fixed) compensation program. High fixed staff costs are also a potential change trigger since they can destabilize companies, particularly those in Earn or Harvest modes.

Organization Design Assessment

Figure 30–7 is an organization design assessment exercise that can help one determine what the mix of compensation components should be. The structural characteristics of an organization have implications for the amount of personal authority permitted. Similarly, the cultural characteristics of the work force can indicate how capable employees are of taking risk. Figure 30–7 is a useful exercise that can classify the risk-sharing orientation of an organization design based on key organizational characteristics. The higher the total score, the more capacity for risk in the organization. The greater the risk, the greater the potential for variable compensation, that is, a higher performance orientation.

FIGURE 30–8

Organization Planning Exercise

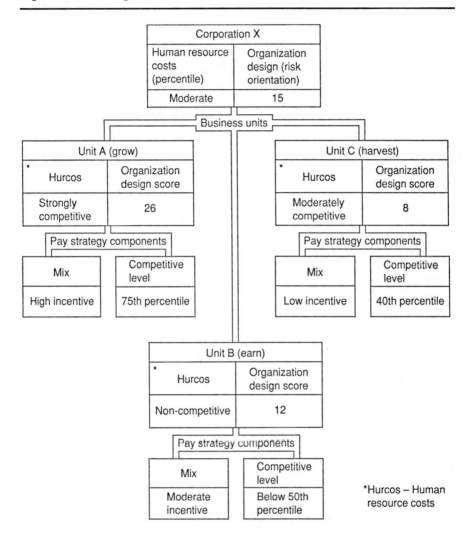

Figure 30–8 summarizes how the same three business units look after the organization planning exercise and the implications for pay strategy of this exercise.

Unit A has human resource costs that are strongly competitive and a risk-seeking culture. This organization can afford a high competitive level of total pay but should reach that level through high incentive-driven pay.

Unit B has noncompetitive human resource costs and is risk accepting. This suggests that competitive pay levels for total compensation must be lower because of these costs. Additionally, the culture will accept only a moderate level of incentive pay. The total pay package must be below the 50th percentile of the company's pay market until human resource costs are reduced.

Unit C has moderately competitive human resource costs and has a risk-averse culture. The culture will tolerate only smaller incentives, and human resource costs can be controlled by a lower competitive level (assuming key person turnover can be selectively handled).

Exercise III

CULTURE/HUMAN RESOURCE PLANNING

Objective

To identify appropriate external job market characteristics and internal work force requirements through the following:

- Definition of specific compensation elements appropriate to the marketplace.
- Establishment of the competitive level appropriate to the marketplace.
- Determination of the mix of compensation appropriate to the company's management style.

These are the specific activities the reader will follow:

- Identifying competitors for talent, and measuring their pay levels.
- Determining the general level of work force skill required to perform jobs and the level of training provided by the unit.
- Classifying the general level of market activity applicable to the unit (turnover rate/recruitment time).

The steps below describe a series of processes that help determine the characteristics of your pay markets.

Job market competitor analysis

- Identify each employee group in each strategic business unit (SBU) (see Figure 30–9).
- List all of the companies that have served as primary sources of recruitment for each employee group in the SBU.
- Classify these competitors into one of the following categories by selecting the appropriate one(s).

Geographical	Industry
Technological/Functional	Internal (within your company)
Combination (Specify)	Other

FIGURE 30–9
Employee Groups

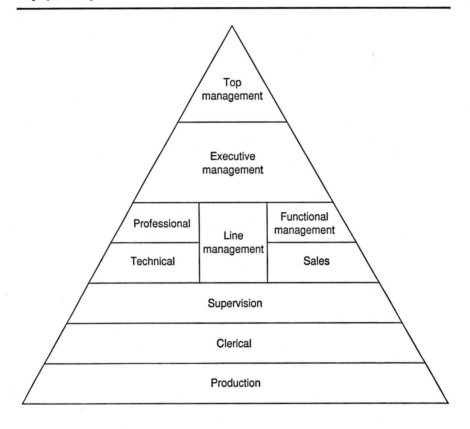

- Establish the cash compensation characteristics for each market. For example, compare the median in each pay component of each pay market against one another and against a composite national norm.

Next, using Figure 30–10, classify talent utilization for each employee group in a business unit. This will suggest an appropriate competitive level for each group. For each job classification you can determine competitive level by completing Figure 30–10.

At this point, you are ready to classify the risk or exposure for each employee group. Using industrial, functional, or geographical breakdowns, or other appropriate norms, classify the turnover rate and the time required to fill openings on the grid and link these to competitive levels in Figure 30–11.

Figure 30–12 tracks the three business units through the organization culture exercise and illustrates suggested strategies.

Unit A is located in a high-pay market. It is a highly risk-oriented environment and has a high level of talent requirement; it also is in a heavy recruitment mode. The pay market study reflects a 60/40 base/incentive mix, and since the company is growing faster than its competitors it must pay at a high competitive level in total compensation.

FIGURE 30–10

*Talent Utilization Analysis (Pay Market Competitive Levels)**

	Level of Skill Required		
Training Budget	*High*	*Medium*	*Low*
High	High	Medium	Medium
Medium	High	Medium	Low
Low	High	Low	Low

*	High	Medium	Low
	75th percentile and over	50th up to 75th percentile	Below 50th percentile

FIGURE 30–11

*Job Market Risk Classification (Pay Market Competitive Levels)**

	Turnover Rate		
Recruitment Time	*High*	*Medium*	*Low*
Long	High	High	Medium
Medium	High	Medium	Low
Short	High	Low	Low

*	High	Medium	Low
	75th percentile and over	50th up to 75th percentile	Below 50th percentile

Unit B is located in a low-pay market, requires low talent levels, has little turnover risk, and is encouraging some turnover. The pay market study reveals a 75/25 base/incentive mix, and the company can achieve cost control by targeting total compensation to the 50th percentile of its chosen market; high pay levels would be generated by exceeding incentive targets.

Unit C operates in a moderately competitive pay market, has medium talent levels, and has no unusual turnover risk; it is counting on significant turnover. The pay market study reflects an 80/20 base/incentive ratio. To conserve costs and encourage more turnover, the competitive level is lowered. Strong performance could fund competitive pay above the 40th percentile.

Figure 30–13 is designed as a work sheet as well as an example that will enable the reader to consolidate the implications from each of the three key exercises, to compare each employee group between businesses, and to create the best combination of compensation strategies for the enterprise.

The final strategy recommendation is derived from inputs from all three exercises.

Compensation for unit A was based on its Boston high-tech pay market. On the basis of the capacity of its work force to tolerate risk and the high potential for turnover, management decided to emphasize a strong pay-for-performance culture with high competitive pay levels driven by high levels of variable pay (risk sharing).

FIGURE 30–12

Human Resources Planning Exercise

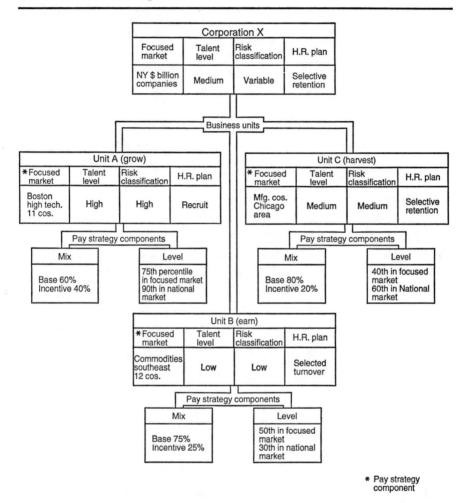

Unit B selected a pay strategy based on a commodities pay market, a lower risk orientation, and a weak talent group. It emphasized a moderate incentive with strong "upside" potential to provide a strong performing group the opportunity to fund higher competitive levels.

Unit C was in a relatively expensive pay market, demonstrating good performance but essentially in a self-liquidating mode. It chose to introduce a higher mix of base/incentive pay than market to keep costs down and reduce company risk. It was not concerned with the impact of higher incentives on the risk-averse culture since it was in a staff reduction mode. The combination of strong performance and higher incentives did fund a competitive level in excess of the 50th percentile.

FIGURE 30–13
Business Unit Portfolio

Unit	Business Exercise		Organization Exercise		Culture/H.R. Exercise			Strategy Recommendation		
	Mix*	Level†	Mix	Level	Pay Market	Mix	Level	Pay Market	Mix	Level
A (Grow)	60/40	<50th	High incentive	75th	Boston high-tech companies	60/40	75th	Boston high-tech companies	50/50	75th
B (Earn)	70/30	75th	Moderate incentive	<50th	Commodities companies	75/25	50th	Commodities companies	70/30	50th
C (Harvest)	80/20	60th	Low incentive	40th	Chicago manufacturing companies	80/20	40th	Chicago manufacturing companies	75/25	40th

*Mix is percentile of total pay represented by base and incentive portions.

†Level is competitive level for total compensation expressed as a percentile of targeted pay market.

Managing compensation in uncertain times is clearly a risky but essential activity. The framework presented here should be applied to both current and future management plans. It will provide a useful framework of choice, thereby reducing uncertainty in the development of pay strategy. It will accomplish this by providing a set of guidelines covering when to change reward strategies and what types of reward strategies to shift to. The framework will also help organizations respond with more flexibility to the increasingly divergent compensation and motivational needs of a rapidly segmenting work force. With the dissipation of the traditional employment contract and its associated entitlement mentality, employers can no longer rely on one-size-fits-all approaches to reward management.

Nimble organizations anticipate and respond early to change triggers affecting their business classification and change their compensation programs accordingly. They must develop and implement customized approaches, such as those that have been discussed in this chapter, to address the widely varying needs and value structures that can be found *within* the employee groups of a given organization or business unit. In all cases, these new approaches will be performance oriented, but the way performance is defined, measured, and leveraged for different worker populations will differ significantly.

The challenge for future change managers, then, will be to find efficient means of first creating and then delivering compensation packages that include the proper mix of incentives and performance measures for *each* business segment. The framework for choice provides the scaffolding around which the proper compensation structure can be built. With enough care and precision, employee compensation can be aligned with both the overall strategy of the organization and the many particular requirements of its units and its people.

Armed with a flexible business-driven pay strategy of this sort, organizations should have no reason to be fearful about the future, no matter what change it might bring. Instead, they can meet the future head-on, with all the confidence of another famous Roosevelt—Theodore—who said, "Business has to prosper before anybody can get any benefit from it." Business-driven compensation strategies will help companies prosper.

NOTES

1. R. Szakoni, "Long Range Planning: Its Role in Challenging Current Company Operations," *Handbook of Business Strategy 1987/1988 Yearbook* (Boston, MA: Warren, Gorham and Lamont), Chap. 7, pp. 1–19.

2. G. Milkovich, "A Strategic Perspective in Compensation Management," Center for Advanced Human Resource Studies, Cornell University, 1988.

3. J. S. Cassano, "The Links between Corporate Strategy, Organization and Performance," *Handbook of Business Strategy 1987/1988 Yearbook* (Boston, MA: Warren, Gorham and Lamont), Chap. 3, pp. 1–12.

Chapter Thirty-One

Rewards for Executing Change

Robert P. McNutt
Bruce I. Spiegel

INTRODUCTION

F ew single compensation programs have received the widespread attention given the "Achievement Sharing" variable pay plan implemented by the Fibers Sector of Du Pont Company in 1989. Du Pont replaced a traditional merit-based pay system for its 20,000 Fibers unit employees with a plan that put a portion of future pay increases at risk, but promised potentially higher pay overall based on the Sector's financial performance. The *Wall Street Journal* described the concept as "one of the most extensive and innovative ever tried at a major U.S. corporation."

From the moment it was announced, the Du Pont plan was watched closely and expectantly, not only by the human resources community but also by chief executives who recognized that it represented a major strategic and cultural departure for one of the world's largest and most tradition-bound organizations.

Less than two years later the Achievement Sharing plan was discontinued after it became clear that employees were not so willing as they had originally indicated to accept the program's inherent downside risks. Widespread doubts began to be expressed about the overall viability of variable pay, largely on the basis of the discontinuation of the Du Pont program.

A strong case can be made, however, that the Du Pont Fibers pay plan can be used as an example of how to implement managed change in the compensation arena. In fact, there are four key reasons why the effort can still be deemed a least partially successful:

• Although the plan itself may have been suspended, the process that was used to create and implement the Achievement Sharing program stands as a useful model for how efforts to institute new compensation programs must be aligned from the start with broader strategic initiatives.

- Even with the decision to disband the new pay plan (at least temporarily), Du Pont made major strides toward introducing important new operating philosophies—most specifically the concepts of large-group incentives and shared risk—into its corporate culture.
- Du Pont's timely decision to "pull the plug" on the Achievement Sharing plan showed that the change management process was working properly, in that the "Alignment Team"—which included senior executives as "Chief Alignment Officers"—was able to read signals clearly and promptly and thus did not follow the new initiative doggedly, blindly—and perhaps catastrophically—down the wrong path.
- Finally, the process legitimized the role of an "Advisory Group"—a cross-functional, standing committee of line management and other employees that reports to the "Chief Alignment Officer(s)"—which was formed for the following purposes:

  - To provide historical perspective on the organization's culture and compensation strategy and practices.
  - To review program design and administrative guidelines as the compensation program is being developed.
  - To offer input and recommendations concerning employee involvement and communication needs.
  - To provide feedback on employee involvement and communication processes, training and materials.
  - To monitor and evaluate success once the programs are implemented.

This chapter first explores an iterative process to align compensation programs properly with fundamental changes in strategy, structure, and management processes. These changes are stimulated by (1) increasing global competition and other economic pressures; (2) a change in control as a result of a merger, acquisition, internal reorganization, rightsizing, or other major organization alignment; (3) changing employee, shareholder, and customer expectations; (4) changing technology; and (5) shifting corporate culture and values. We then show how Du Pont followed this process and how, given the benefit of hindsight gained from the experience, a company can improve the effectiveness of future compensation initiatives.

An overview of the various phases of this process is depicted in Figure 31–1. As you review the steps in each of the phases, think of them as a continuous flow. When the steps in Phase 4 are completed, we begin again at Phase 1. If Chief Alignment Officers were to wait for a "trigger" to initiate the process, new compensation initiatives would lag and, hence, not support the broader changes. For the most part, this process retraces the steps companies use initially to assess the readiness of their organizations for new compensation initiatives and for aligning compensation systems with the evolving culture and business strategies. Too often, the process applied to developing and implementing compensation programs is allowed to lapse after the program is operational. The remainder of this chapter illustrates the process in more detail.

FIGURE 31–1

Alignment: A Continuous Process

Phase 1: Background Review	Phase 2: Subjective Assessment	Phase 3: Measurement	Phase 4: Realignment

• Review objectives, priorities, and status of the broader changes
• Review the intent and design characteristics/ assumptions of the compensation system
  • What is/was
  • What were the performance expectations
	• Review applicable employee survey results
	• Conduct Advisory Group working sessions
	• Interview selected management
	• Conduct focus groups
	• Administer written survey
		• Examine various financial measures
		• Measure productivity improvement
		• Identify trends in customer-driven success factors
			• Define and refine compensation alternatives
			• Hold Management Group workshops to review alternatives
			• Hold employee focus groups
			• Select and finalize modified plan design

PHASE 1: BACKGROUND REVIEW

Before we can evaluate the effectiveness (alignment) of reward systems, we must first understand the imperative for the broader change process along with strategic choices that were made, objectives to be achieved by such change, and barriers that had to be overcome. Phase 1 builds the foundation for discovering the barriers and opportunities in the current environment and validating that the compensation program objectives and philosophy support the evolving culture. It assumes that the environment is evolving—that progress is being made—and that the compensation program will evolve also.

This phase involves holding a meeting or series of meetings for these purposes:

- Develop insights into the current environment and implications on pay.
- Help develop the approach and discussion guide for selected management interviews.
- Help develop the approach and discussion guide for selected focus group discussions to gain employee perspectives on the barriers and opportunities.

Ideally, the content and context for these meetings are that they will not be a substitute for ongoing tracking and feedback.

Step 1. Review the Organization Change Process

The first step in the process is to review the status of the broader organization change process that led to the need for change, and the objectives, priorities and status of the broad change process. It begins with a comparison of current internal business conditions to previous conditions, based on such elements as these:

- Business strategy and objectives.
- New technology and processes.
- Organization restructuring (rightsizing, de-layering, etc.).
- Organization culture.
- Human resources policies, programs, and practices.
- Employee involvement programs.
- Deficiencies in skills and overcapacity.
- Both barriers to and facilitators of change.

This step also needs to take into account current versus previous external pressures, such as these:

- Industry overcapacity or undercapacity.
- Customer requirements (e.g., just-in-time delivery).
- Overall competitiveness based on product, price, quality, delivery, and so on.
- Regulatory environment.

Competitive benchmarking is a useful way to compare a company's performance on critical success factors with those of "best in class" companies and establish targets and the steps necessary to reach the targets.

Much of what follows is internally focused, yet performance expectations typically are based on external customer expectations and impact by external forces.

Step 2. Review the Intent and Design of the Compensation System

Before implementing a new program, the organization asks a series of basic questions related to the environmental context (see Step 1) and then to the "fit" of current programs and possible future programs with business strategy, current and desired culture, and the employee climate.

In this step, the Advisory Group asks *the same* questions to produce a "snapshot" of the state of the employee involvement processes, including compensation and other reward systems. Also the group identifies indications of success or need for change. In other words, the Advisory Group identifies the current context and what the Compensation Program was supposed to accomplish in order to develop a broad sense of how it is succeeding.

Key issues include (but are not limited to) the following:

- Degree of involvement and participation.
- Barriers to work force effectiveness.
- Communications.
- Training availability and motivation.
- Appropriateness of performance measure.
- Opportunities for improvement.
- Meaningfulness of rewards.
- Perceptions of cost savings, productivity gains, and quality improvements.

Of course, it is presumed that all of the items to be covered were identified during the original program development.

Finally, the Advisory Group subjectively concludes whether the compensation system appears to be fulfilling stated work force objectives and priorities. This step is more than just a summary review; it would typically involve a subjective rating of progress, an identification of the place at which the process is, and the barriers that may exist.

Figure 31–2 helps to illustrate how a compensation system might be aligned with a business strategy. In this example, the Advisory Group would assess the degree to which compensation objectives have been met.

PHASE 2: SUBJECTIVE ASSESSMENT

The first phase builds the foundation for the review and provides a sense of the general conditions that exist. In this phase, we begin a systematic process for exploring the key areas that determine the success of compensation and other reward programs.

Phase 2 provides essential information from an employee perspective that impacts on the success of the program, and it potentially provides indicators of why the program is or is not working. The information is in these categories:

- *Culture*—Customer service orientation, employee relations climate, trust and confidence in management, and company's willingness to share information.
- *Opportunity*—For improving customer service, productivity, safety, and quality and for reducing cost.
- *Operation*—Availability of performance data and standards, management information systems, accounting and budgeting systems, facilities and equipment.
- *Employees*—Demographics, interest in job security, and receptiveness to change.
- *Management practices*—Management style, communication practices, employee involvement practices, and management and employee training.

FIGURE 31–2

Develop a Compensation System Aligned with Business Strategy

Strategic Context	Compensation System Objectives
Creation of focused modern plants	Pay program needs to reflect the fact that the company will be a different organization, with different machines, skills/jobs, and employee profile than today
Fluid organization	Pay program must be flexible and resilient; cannot be difficult to administer; must be adaptable *or* designed to be short-lived (and communicated as such)
Drastic improvement in cost, quality, safety, and service	Pay program must provide motivation/reward for incremental achievement of stated goals
Organization of accountable and creative teams	Pay program must reinforce team achievement (dependent on teams first being clearly defined, trained, and monitored)
Team success dependent on **individual** high performance	Pay program must encourage, support, and reward high individual performance appropriately; team and individual performance need to be linked
Flexible, multiskilled employees fully accountable for a coherent product line	Pay program must "stretch"/evolve to recognize levels of skill and accountability
Development of people through education, training, and experience to meet business requirements and provide growth opportunities	Pay program must provide clear progression that reflects acquisition of knowledge and recognizes experience
Empowerment of employees with training and authority to make use of state-of-the-art equipment and processes	Pay programs must recognize differing levels of sophistication, recognizing skills acquisition

This information can come from informal observations, as well as one or more of the following formal sources:

- The "Advisory Group."
- A general employee survey conducted within six months of the evaluation.
- Management interviews.
- Employee focus groups.
- A targeted written survey.

Step 1. Review Any Available Employee Survey Results

A recent employee survey may provide relevant information on employee perceptions of pay equity and competitiveness, performance appraisal, pay communications, and the recognition and rewarding of performance. Yet, more specific information is typically needed to assess and refine a compensation approach than most climate surveys provide. If the survey has been specifically designed to capture necessary information, all that may be needed is a review of employee survey results to identify issues. If not, the review will show the areas that need to be further researched through focus groups and/or a targeted survey.

Step 2. Advisory Group Working Sessions

As mentioned earlier, one success factor for compensation program effectiveness is the ongoing role of some advisory body consisting of line management and selected other employees who participate in program design, implementation, evaluation, and refinement. The Advisory Group usually represents the major constituencies in the organization—department, division, function, and so on. It is not a policy-setting body, but it provides substantial input and recommendations for review and final approval by senior management.

In monitoring and evaluating program effectiveness, the Advisory Group's continuing role is this:

- Define the time period for measuring effectiveness.
- Establish, document, and update objective and subjective success measures.
- Monitor those measures through appropriate mechanisms, having determined up-front what those mechanisms will be.
- Develop recommendations based on the outcome of the evaluation.
- Facilitate the implementation of any changes.

The Advisory Group recommends the extent of, and the method for, gathering employee perceptions of the compensation program in the broader business context.

Step 3. Management Interviews

One of the communication channels that may be appropriate is interviews with selected managers, both at senior management and middle management levels. Such interviews focus on the issues outlined earlier, with the goal of determining qualitatively if the compensation program is furthering or hindering achievement of the specific goals it was designed to support, while soliciting ideas for change.

Step 4. Focus Groups

Direct group discussions with employees are invaluable ways to gain insight quickly into what employees feel about certain issues and why they feel that way. They also provide a venue for drawing out employees' recommendations for change and improvement. When a compensation program is being evaluated, they provide information that is easier to glean than through a written survey.

The focus groups need not be created especially for this purpose. Work teams, Total Quality Management (TQM) teams, or other groups of approximately 12 employees can be convened to focus on the relevant compensation issues. The key is to involve employees directly in the evaluation process. Failing to do so and judging program effectiveness only on "objective" measures like customer satisfaction, on-time deliveries, and so on, not only may contradict a commitment to employee involvement but also can leave a time bomb of employee concern ticking until it explodes. Deep dissatisfaction can be building, even while all appears to be going well on the surface.

Step 5. Administer Written Survey

By itself, a written survey will not provide the richness of understanding needed to appreciate employee perspectives and suggestions fully. However, it can be a useful tool in at least two cases: when there is a need or desire to enable all employees (or more than can be included in focus groups) in the input process, and when there is a need for quantitative data. If a written survey is conducted, it often is followed by focus groups.

To measure the factors that might influence the success of a new compensation system, we take a "Readiness Inventory." The inventory provides an indication of the extent that an organization's culture is open to a new approach. A written survey is used to build the "Readiness Inventory." When compared with the results of the previous surveys, the results provide insight into the effectiveness of the change process, the reward systems, and possible program refinements.

PHASE 3: MEASUREMENT

Traditional performance measures have focused on cost, that is, labor, materials (yield), and overhead. In Phase 3, we assess a broader set of financial measures and examine the impact of cycle time including delivery, throughput, and flexibility. And we assess performance against measures of quality and customer perceptions.

In other words we recognize the relative importance and interdependence of multiple measures. And we place measurement in a more appropriate perspective as an indicator rather than an absolute determinant.

Step 1. Examine Various Financial Measures

As indicated in the preface to Phase 3, financial data, namely, those related to cost and profitability, traditionally have been accepted as reasonable measures of the payback of an investment by the business. Further, the payback often is equated with "value."

Obviously, making and measuring profits represent a business necessity. Yet there are numerous cases in which short-term profits have been made at the expense of the long-term viability of the organization. Moreover, profits can be earned regardless of the levels of productivity and quality.

Conversely, an organization that is investing for future growth, buying market share and the like, may not be profitable in the short run. Hence, there is also a need to balance various financial objectives and measures.

Finally, it is important to note that financial measures are indicators of the effectiveness of a number of change initiatives. Therefore, it is very difficult, if not impossible, to isolate the "value" of any specific program in financial terms.

Step 2. Measure Productivity Improvement

Similarly, change initiatives that result in greater output with the same amount or less labor input (hours) generally lead to higher profitability. Yet this profitability depends on the relative importance of labor as an input and the way in which outputs are measured. For example, if we measure only output that meets customer quality requirements when shipped, we have a truer measure of the value of increased productivity to the company.

Numerous plans are narrowly focused on a single dimension of productivity. Therefore, they are vulnerable to providing incentives to employees without returning a payback to the organization. In such cases, we can recognize when value is not being received more easily than we can isolate value received.

Step 3. Identify Trends in Customer-Driven Success Factors

We long have recognized the importance of price and product competitiveness in achieving business success. More recently, as we looked at product competitiveness, we began to understand the significance of quality, delivery, and service as related to product and price. Yet most compensation systems currently do not provide incentives for increased customer satisfaction as measured by these important parameters.

We should measure customer perceptions in much the same way as we measure employee satisfaction—and this trend is starting to take place. Moreover, we should identify and reward improvements in customer-driven success factors and accept these factors as indicators of long-term business success. But we should balance these "soft" measures with financial and productivity measures.

In conclusion, measurement is important. Yet we need to keep it in perspective as an all-encompassing determinant of the relative effectiveness and paybacks of the compensation system to the organization.

PHASE 4: REALIGNMENT

Realigning and revising are inherent in the concept of measuring. If the organization is dynamic, the compensation system must be also. What's not working needs to be fixed. New barriers and opportunities can arise. The key is to look at compensation as dynamic, not static, and to expect it to evolve. It also should be communicated to employees as a system that will change over time.

Step 1. Compensation Alternatives

In this step, the Advisory Group would determine and evaluate alternatives to the current compensation system approach. The activities include the following:

- Developing pros and cons, including the impact on organization environment and characteristics, compensation philosophy, business strategies and objectives, human resources values and programs, performance and productivity programs, and communications.
- Determining programs flexible enough to fit changing business needs.
- Determining employee relations and business risks.
- Determining needs for additional resources and support systems.
- Testing against basic principles.
- Determining costs and benefits.
- Evaluating the impact on long-term and short-term balance.
- Determining the relationship to other compensation programs.

Step 2. Management Group Workshops

Once the alternatives are clear, it's time for a "reality check." In Management Group workshops, key managers have the opportunity to review and comment on possible alternatives. Like the other review sessions, these workshops are probably best conducted by the Advisory Group members. By holding these review sessions, a company will be better able to gauge potential reactions to the alternatives, as well as to test how easy they are to comprehend and what kind of training and communication will be needed to make them work. They also provide another check on the viability of the alternatives.

Step 3. Employee Focus Group

Next, selected employees should have a chance to examine the alternatives and share their opinions on the desirability of any single approach, how well it would be likely to work, and what it would take to make it work. A company could reconvene the groups that met in Phase 2 or select a different array of employees. Using different employees broadens the sense of participation. Using the same employees provides an opportunity to see if the alternatives address their concerns and expectations.

Step 4. Modified Plan Design

Once the alternatives have been discussed and narrowed, the next step would be to select the plan design that is most desirable, model the modified plan design, and calculate its financial implications. A company also will need to identify key transition issues at this time and recommend steps for bridging present and future plans that are as fair as possible.

CONCLUSION

The outlines of the generic program to align compensation systems with other elements of a company, especially when the firm is in transition, may be varied as the company-specific case demands. The form, of course, is important to ensure that the compensation system eventually adopted or revamped is viable. But what is most important is the recognition that changing the compensation cannot be done in isolation. Any company taking that approach is likely to find that the anticipated payoffs from realigning a compensation system won't be realized.

Case: Variable Pay in the Fibers Sector of E.I. du Pont de Nemours and Company, Inc.

BACKGROUND REVIEW

Broader Changes

Du Pont Fibers, one of the largest business segments for the Du Pont Company and its largest Sector, has undergone dramatic changes over the last several years. It has trimmed its work force from 27,000 to 20,000 and moved from a traditional pyramid-style management structure to a more self-directed work force that reduces the layers of management and encourages greater teamwork at all levels. Over the same time span, it has sharply increased its sales—from $4 billion to almost $6 billion—and more than doubled its earnings—from $250 million to more than $500 million.

Compensation System

Like many companies, Du Pont Fibers has relied on a traditional merit pay system for its exempt employees and a local pay reference system for nonexempt employees. Salaried compensation was determined based on average compensation for similar job titles on a national scale. Hourly workers received pay consistent with local standards.

Some managers in the Sector felt that these traditional compensation approaches were no longer effective for an organization that had changed. Also at issue was a feeling among managers that existing compensation structures did not effectively reward and encourage a work force that was contributing at a higher level than ever before.

In the late 1980s, a representative study team was assembled to look at designing a compensation program that would link pay with business success.

Original Intent

The intent of the variable pay program was to accomplish the following:

• *Enhance employees' sense of being stakeholders* by giving them all a personal stake in the business. It also was designed to support and reinforce behavior consistent with the new culture in Fibers, which valued business success.

- *Increase interest/awareness in business performance* by providing an opportunity to understand the business and contribute ideas for continuous improvement.

- *Reinforce competitive reality versus entitlement* as related to compensation. Compensation would no longer be an entitlement but a shared destiny reflecting the success of the business.

- *Support the Vision 2000 in the Fibers Sector,* which represented a 4 percent per year real growth in earnings.

- *Create a win/win environment* for both the employees and the business.

An Innovative Approach

On January 1, 1989, Du Pont Fibers implemented Achievement Sharing, a new variable compensation program for its employees that the *Wall Street Journal* described as "one of the most extensive and innovative ever tried at a major U.S. corporation."

The program had several unique features that were a radical change for the organization:

- *It was a large-group incentive.* Conventional wisdom has always been that incentive pay schemes must be pegged to the smallest possible business unit in order for the benefits of participation to be clear to employees.

- *It linked pay to the business success of the organization* rather than to individual or small unit performance.

- *It represented a departure from the corporate compensation program.* It grew out of, reflected, and built on the culture of the organization/business sector.

- *It did not involve a salary freeze, "give back," pay cut, or other measure that affected current salary.* Instead, it put at risk a portion of **future pay increases,** with the potential payback of a variable annual bonus if the Sector's profit goals were met or exceeded, and with the potential loss of that bonus if profits were to fall below 80 percent of goal.

Design Summary

Achievement Sharing put a portion of future pay increases at risk in exchange for potentially higher pay based on the Sector's financial performance. When the Fibers Sector met its annual earnings objective, participating employees would receive an amount greater than what was placed at risk. If Fibers failed to meet its annual earnings objective, participating employees would get part or none of the pay placed at risk for that year. In this way, employees shared the rewards for financial success, as well as the consequences of unsuccessful performance.

After a transition period, the target payout for the program was 6 percent; base pay would be 94 percent of what it would have been in the rest of Du Pont for comparable positions. Yet, when Fibers achieved earnings growth at 4 percent a year above its earnings objective in any given year, employees would get an additional 12 percent (of base pay).

Subjective Assessment: Employee Survey

When approximately 2,000 employees were asked in 1990 how they felt about the program, they felt the program was effective in these respects:

- It provided an opportunity for financial gain when business success was achieved.

- It increased awareness of cost/earnings and business information.

- It provided a vehicle/forum for employee feedback—it became a conscience for leadership behavior. Employees spoke up as to things that should or should not be done to improve business performance.

- There was increased value in being a stakeholder, as there was a shared destiny around the success of the business.

- It supported teamwork as an integral part of the new and emerging culture.

MEASUREMENT

From the time the program gained Executive Committee approval to the end of its life, there was never any attempt to quantify objective financial measures of program effectiveness. Rather management felt that the original interest as discussed earlier, combined with the fact that the program supported the culture that Fibers was trying to create, was success enough. Overall success was to be measured by the program being supportive of earnings growth and continuous improvement. Other initiatives such as Quality Leadership and Empowered Learning Teams were the drivers of a culture change, while the new pay program reinforced and supported change.

Even with the discontinuance of Achievement Sharing as will be discussed next, the participants felt that the program was well thought out and that it was approached as a test or experiment that would be evaluated by employees rather than a pay plan put in place by management edict.

REALIGNMENT

Define and Refine Compensation Alternatives

At the beginning of the Achievement Sharing program, Du Pont told participants that the company would be asking for their input as to what changes might be made to enhance the program over time.

In the Du Pont environment, employees are encouraged to express their individual desires and choice. In the 1990 employee survey, employees indicated that they wanted individual choice regarding the amount of pay-at-risk.

Du Pont began moving down the road of offering individual choice around the amount of pay-at-risk. However, it soon became apparent that adding individual choice to the Achievement Sharing program would require the program legally to be treated as an investment opportunity in the eyes of the Securities and Exchange

Commission and would require public disclosure of detailed business sector information. The company was more than willing to provide such information to its employees so they could make the proper choice, but public disclosure of this information would give an advantage to its competitors.

Thus, the company was faced with the decision of continuing the program as it was originally designed without individual choice or discontinuing the program altogether. Individual choice was very important in the eyes of employees, so the company chose to discontinue the Achievement Sharing program.

The inability to offer individual choice as to amount of pay-at-risk was the major reason for discontinuance. If the Fibers Sector had had very attractive earnings for 1990, they might have continued the program without individual choice. Maybe over time or in the future, employee choice as to amount of pay-at-risk will be accomplished.

*****

Some of the key lessons that Fibers experienced with the Achievement Sharing program that can be important in the development and measurement of program effectiveness in the future are these:

- Employees want to participate and share in the success of a business.

- Employee involvement in compensation change is critical.

- Individual employee choice is important in many new HR initiatives that value individual uniqueness (e.g., flexible benefits, work practices, career pathways).

- Variable pay programs with pay-at-risk should honor individual choice as to amount of pay-at-risk.

The basic premise of the Achievement Sharing program was to give employees a stake in the business. That concept is as important today as when the program began, and it will be increasingly important.

The idea of linking pay to business success is important. As we approach the year 2000, most successful global companies will in some fashion link pay to business success. It may not be exactly the same way Du Pont did it, but the concept of variable pay will not go away.

Chapter Thirty-Two

Compensation as a Change Stimulus

Edward J. Giblin

M ore than 30 years ago, Frederick Herzberg announced to the world that salary was a dissatisfier or hygiene factor. In his model hygiene factors did not motivate people. Rather, the satisfiers, or motivators, were factors such as achievement, recognition, and responsibility.[1]

Herzberg specifically referred to wages and salaries, and not to incentive forms of pay. He also astutely noted that failures to administer wage and salary programs effectively contributed to employee dissatisfaction with them. These caveats largely went unnoticed; the message that came through was that pay did not motivate employees. If properly handled, pay has a neutral effect; if poorly handled, it becomes a dissatisfier.

As the answer to motivating people appeared to lie elsewhere, the concept of pay was relegated to an intellectual backwater in universities.[2] In the corporate sphere, pay programs were turned over to midlevel staff who, along with their consultants, devised elaborate systems for administering pay.

All of this had dire consequences for corporate pay systems. In particular, the relationship between pay and individual, group, and business performance had been neatly severed.

CORPORATE ENTITLEMENTS

In order to determine which pay systems can promote and reinforce organizational change, it is necessary to begin with a brief review of current corporate compensation practices.

For the vast majority of workers in U.S. business and industry, as well as for virtually all employees in government and not-for-profit organizations, wages or salaries represent all of their direct pay. In addition, most workers receive forms of indirect pay, such as medical coverage and retirement income. Indirect pay has become an increasingly large and expensive portion of what is referred to as the employee's total pay package.

Recently it has become a second national pastime to vilify the compensation packages of top executives. However, the vast bulk of a corporation's pay costs result from its wage, salary, and benefit programs, not from executive and other incentive pay programs. As financial resources to meet pay costs are not infinite, and as most of the cost is consumed by wage and salary and benefit programs, this criticism poses a dilemma for the executive who wants to use the pay system to promote and reinforce organizational change. The base direct and indirect pay system does not facilitate this end but consumes most of the resources available to pay people. In fact, the pay system represents yet another impediment to promoting and reinforcing change. Why is this so?

Quite simply, base pay programs are not designed to facilitate and reinforce organizational change. Nor are they designed to motivate employees, or to link individual and group efforts to company goals and strategies. In brief, these programs are not designed to be proactively managed to achieve business results.

A major axiom of pay practice is this: Pay for the position not the person. Because the focus is on job positions, as opposed to people and their performance, this leads to an administratively driven pay program. The goals of these programs are to ensure external competitiveness and internal equity among job positions. In reality, external competitiveness amounts to copying what other companies do.

The problem is that, whereas a company can achieve competitive pay levels and internal equity, they have nothing at all to do with the performance of individuals, groups, or the company. It is simply a system for dividing the corporate spoils, but it does nothing to increase them.[3]

Each year corporations develop budgets for salary increases. Although the United States has been in a serious recession for most of the 1989–92 period, with high unemployment and poor corporate profits, corporate salary budgets have gone up 5 to 6 percent in each of these years. Base pay programs are unrelated to economic circumstances or business performance.

These are entitlement programs that simply go up each year at a rate slightly higher than changes in the Consumer Price Index (CPI), the most widely accepted measure of the inflation rate. In the competitive marketplace revenues and profits may decline but employees expect, and are given, pay increases. Similarly, indirect pay programs are unrelated to business performance. A defined benefit (pension) program means just that: A specified benefit is to be funded, and provided at retirement, irrespective of individual, group, or company performance.

It must be acknowledged that most base pay programs also claim to promote a pay-for-performance culture. This is supposedly achieved by means of the annual merit increase component of the base pay program. In theory, employees accorded better performance appraisal ratings receive larger merit increases. In practice, the results differ little from giving employees cost-of-living adjustments.[4]

This summary is not intended to suggest that most corporations have no incentive forms of compensation. Rather, it suggests that wage or salary is the primary source of compensation for most employees and that base pay programs contribute little to business results.

Corporations do provide incentives, but they have largely been for executive and sales positions; at the other extreme, there are individual productivity incentives for the blue-collar work force. There is too much wrong with all of these programs to discuss here. The point is that most employees in most corporations are not covered by performance-based incentive programs. Even if they were, most incentive programs in common use have absolutely nothing to do with promoting and reinforcing organizational change.

COMPENSATION SYSTEMS FOR REINFORCING ORGANIZATIONAL CHANGE

At present, compensation practice in the United States is going through its first major change since it became a formal discipline. Alternative compensation programs, also referred to as *new wave compensation,* are coming to the fore. Such programs include various forms of gain sharing, team incentives, variable pay and pay-at-risk, and the extension of programs formerly provided only to executives—such as stock options and bonuses—to lower levels of the ranks. Employee stock option plans (ESOPs), a form of corporate ownership, also have significant implications for pay practices.

Unlike conventional base pay programs, the new wave programs can be very powerful tools for organizational change. However, as is true of most powerful tools, new compensation programs must be used carefully. Although these programs hold much promise, they can have unintended negative consequences for the organization. Two examples make the point.

In 1991, the venerable investment banking house of Salomon Brothers was rocked by a scandal, resulting from engaging in improper practices in the government bond market. For a time, it looked as if the firm might not survive. Those close to the situation attributed a good part of the blame to a compensation program that relied heavily on bonuses for performance, creating a climate of greed and irresponsible behavior.

On a less dramatic basis, the author has a financial services client that extended bonuses to all employees, nearly 3,000 people. The intentions were noble enough, to link employees to the company's success and provide a modest variable element to their pay package. The results to date have been abysmal, alienating much of the work force.

The problem was implementation. The company did a poor job of communicating the program and did not train employees and managers in performance management techniques that were essential to the program's success. This young, dynamic company also lacked the depth of management expertise required to bring off such a large-scale, complex effort.

LESSONS TO BE LEARNED

There has been sufficient experience with alternative compensation programs to draw some lessons for executives contemplating their introduction.

LESSON 1: ESTABLISH BROAD OBJECTIVES FOR THE PROGRAM THAT RELATE TO ORGANIZATION AND CULTURE CHANGE.

These programs traditionally have been implemented with a specific, often narrow objective in mind: A gain-sharing program to motivate employees to increase productivity is one example. Many practitioners, in fact, recommend narrow, single measures of performance for such programs.

However, these programs have had mixed success in motivating employees to achieve narrow performance objectives. Even if there is an improvement in a single measure of performance, it doesn't necessarily promote or reinforce organizational change. Installing a more efficient piece of plant equipment should improve productivity, but it does not change organizational behavior and culture.

Achieving and reinforcing organizational change must invariably go beyond motivating employees to improve one narrow measure of performance. In fact, a narrow mechanical focus seems to detract from the intrinsic value of new wave compensation.

New wave programs will create and reinforce constructive organizational and cultural change when they help achieve the following:

- Create a *shared-fate environment,* that is, an environment in which employees understand, accept, and commit to the values and goals of the organization. The program then acts as a motivator or reinforcer when the company succeeds and employees share financially in that success.
- Make direct and indirect pay more of a variable than a fixed cost, and place some amount of pay at risk, specifically based on achievement of real performance goals.
- Broaden the concept of measurement on which the variable component of pay is based. Narrow measures of success, be they increasing shareholder value for executives or increasing productivity for blue-collar workers, will not, in and of themselves, result in constructive organizational change.

LESSON 2: THE NEW COMPENSATION PROGRAM MUST BE FULLY INTEGRATED WITH THE OVERALL CHANGE MANAGEMENT STRATEGY.

The new compensation program is not alone going to create or reinforce organizational change. To do so, it must be fully integrated into the overall change management strategy of the firm. In fact, the success of new wave compensation largely depends on changes in organizational climate and culture. For example, team incentive programs won't improve team performance just because a new compensation formula is developed. People need to learn to work as a team, and one team must be properly integrated with other teams on which it depends for the formula to be effective. The compensation element reinforces these changes; but absent organizational and attitudinal changes, compensation cannot achieve the desired purpose.

LESSON 3: DON'T ASSUME THESE NEW COMPENSATION PROGRAMS WILL BE EFFECTIVE IN YOUR COMPANY.

Although the new compensation programs can help bring about change as well as reinforce it, there is no evidence to suggest that they create miracles. In the wrong organizational climate and culture they are very likely to fail.

A good starting point is a diagnostic study of climate and culture to determine if the organization is ready to launch a new wave program. A company with multiple layers of management, centralized decision making, directive and punitive supervisory leadership, and poor communications processes is not a prime candidate for a new wave compensation program.

To return to Lesson 2, the new compensation program must be linked to the overall change management strategy. A concerted effort can be made to create a climate and culture that are more conducive to a new wave compensation program. The new compensation program, when properly positioned, will help to facilitate and reinforce the overall change effort. In brief, the change management and new wave compensation program must be fully aligned.

LESSON 4: NEW WAVE COMPENSATION PROGRAMS WILL NOT SUCCEED WHEN THEY ARE IMPOSED ON THE ORGANIZATION.

Organization development professionals have long been aware of the need to involve people in the change process. Yet, compensation programs usually have been imposed on organizations. Thus, there is an inherent tendency to try to impose new wave compensation programs on organizations. The problem is that these programs are not administrative systems but involve, in fact require, changes in organization climate and culture. They cannot successfully be imposed on the organization without proper conditioning.

It is essential to involve employees in both the design and implementation of new wave programs. Ensuring that the new compensation program is fully integrated with the change management strategy is a key method promoting widespread employee involvement.

Of course, when the target work force belongs to a union, it will be impossible simply to impose these programs without consultation, involvement, and changes in analogous areas.

LESSON 5: BE PREPARED TO ACCEPT THE INTENDED CONSEQUENCES OF THE PROGRAM.

It may seem paradoxical, but managing the ripple effects has been a real problem for many corporations changing pay systems. Ironically, even the intended results of these programs often are greater than management bargained for.

The management of an oil company, for example, was concerned about the high pay of the oil company's truckdrivers and the high costs of delivering oil. To attack both problems, they convinced the drivers to forgo their hourly wages and to be paid solely on the basis of an innovative productivity plan. If all worked out, the drivers were told, they could substantially increase their incomes.

It did work out. Productivity skyrocketed and there was a dramatic decline in delivery costs. The drivers evolved into self-directed work teams, allowing management to eliminate most supervisory employees at their terminals and further reduce costs. The program was terminated.

Why on earth would a resoundingly successful program be scrapped? Because the drivers' pay surged from about $35,000 on average to more than $80,000. Although the company was reaping overwhelming benefits from the program, a top executive remarked: "We can't have drivers making over $80,000!"

Du Pont Company's basic, and much publicized, pay-at-risk program also was terminated. For two years workers gained through improvements in their division's results. However, in the third year it looked as if pay-at-risk would result in decreased wages. Both an upswing and downswing, when linked to business results, are the intended consequences of a pay-at-risk program.

Du Pont has argued that the program was terminated for different reasons. But most interested observers felt that the big chemical company could not cope with the success of its own program.[5] It was successful, because pay should go down, as well as up, in pay-at-risk programs.

KEY CONCEPTS

Four key concepts determine the capability of the new programs to promote and reinforce organizational change:

1. Variable pay.
2. Pay-at-risk.
3. Employee control.
4. Group-centered.

All of the programs to be discussed have a variable pay element, that is, some component of pay isn't fixed, but varies with some measure or measures of performance. For example, a gain-sharing or team incentive award is a variable, as is an employee bonus.

Most variable pay is an addition to a fixed pay base that is often set at a competitive level, that is, it is similar to what is paid to employees of comparable or competing companies. This feature reduces the power of variable pay to influence organizational change. In general, the greater the variable component in relation to the fixed component, the greater the power of the variable component to influence change. This last point brings us to a closely related concept, pay-at-risk. In this approach, the fixed component of pay is set below the competitive (or market) level, thereby automatically increasing the variable component of pay. In fact, achieving the full effect of variable pay *requires* that some pay be put at risk.

That is perhaps the most difficult and controversial concept of new wave pay programs. Du Pont's failure to maintain a pay-at-risk program because of a one-year decline is an example of the problem. As a result, most variable pay programs avoid pay-at-risk. Employees, in fact, find it threatening and unions almost always resist it.

This response is unfortunate, because pay-at-risk, when incorporated into any new wave program, can be a powerful tool for engendering organizational change. Most of the resistance stems from the fact that it is misunderstood to begin with. Executives should take note that employee pay is always at risk in a free enterprise system. Pay-at-risk implies that employees are *entitled* to competitive pay. Although a competitive pay program is *desirable,* it isn't an *entitlement.* In the final analysis, the economic success of a business determines what it can pay people and how many people it can afford to pay.

To be successful, the most powerful new wave programs require a high degree of *employee control* over their work output. If employees do not perceive themselves to be adequately in control of their output, they will place little trust and confidence in the new pay program. Providing a considerable degree of employee control over output in effect empowers employees, a factor that tends both to promote and to reinforce organizational change. In fact, giving employees considerable control over their work output does more to create change than the pay formula associated with the program.

Finally, the more powerful new wave programs, such as gain sharing and team incentives, are group centered, not individual centered. The group's performance is measured and individuals are rewarded on the basis of the group's performance, not his or her own. So use of the group as the basis for rewards is far more important than the formula used to calculate them when it comes to creating and reinforcing organizational change.

When pay is made more variable, ideally putting some amount at risk, and employees are empowered and encouraged to work as groups or teams, the elements for creating a *shared-fate environment* will be in operation. In that case, the new wave program will contribute to promoting and reinforcing organizational change.

SYNOPSIS OF PROGRAMS

Most executives have a general understanding of new wave programs. So I will focus on their potential impact and the organizational requirements necessary for success.

Variable pay and pay-at-risk are not treated as separate, identifiable programs. Each of the programs to be reviewed, by definition, provides a variable pay component. Also, pay-at-risk can be introduced in all cases by reducing (or freezing) the fixed salary component, thereby enlarging the variable component. For example, as in Du Pont's case, the fixed component was set 6 percent below its previous level, and the program allowed employees to exceed their previous fixed wage by 6 percent.

The programs are categorized as follows:

- *Short-term, performance-based, employee-controlled:*
  - Gain sharing.
  - Team incentives.
- *Other short-term plans:*
  - Inclusive employee bonuses.
  - Profit sharing.
  - Skill-based pay.
- *Long-term ownership-based:*
  - Inclusive stock options.
  - Stock purchase plans.
  - Full ESOPs.

Figure 32–1 depicts the salient characteristics of each of these plans. Risk refers to the potential for problems, or the unintended consequences of a program. Degree of difficulty refers to the difficulty in designing and implementing a program. Employee control refers to the degree of control required for the program to succeed. Group-centered refers to the required emphasis on group performance and reward, as opposed to an individual focus.

Reward refers not to potential, but to the reward typically associated with these programs, as a percentage of base pay: Low is defined as up to 10 percent of base pay, moderate 10 to 20 percent, and high as more than 20 percent.

Short-Term/Performance-Based/Employee-Controlled

Two types of programs fall into this category: gain sharing and team or small-group incentives. These are short-term programs in the sense that they pay off in the short term, such as on a weekly, monthly, or quarterly basis. The payoffs always are based on some tangible measure of performance and occasionally on more than one measure.

The successful programs allow for a high degree of employee control over their work output. Well-designed programs involve employees in setting a performance standard and encourage them to devise more effective work methods for achieving their goals. The most effective programs feature self-directed work groups, operating with minimal supervisory direction. In brief, employees are empowered to pursue their work objectives and achieve their rewards.

These programs are also group centered—that is, the group's output is the unit of performance measurement. The emphasis on employee control and the group or team is the primary catalyst for organizational change. The actual financial reward is clearly a secondary reinforcer of change. Inherent in these programs is a highly participative form of management.

FIGURE 32-1

Synopsis of New Compensation Programs

Programs	Potential Outcomes		Organizational Requirements				
	Organization Change	*Motivational Impact*	*Risk*	*Reward*	*Difficulty*	*Employee Control*	*Group Centered*
Gain sharing	H*	M	M	L–M	H	H	H
Team incentives	M*	M–H	M	L–M	M–H	H	H
Employee bonus/inclusive	L*	L–M	M	L–M	M	L–M	L
Profit sharing	L	L	L	L–M	L	L	L
Skill-based pay	L	L	L	L	M–H	L	L
Stock options/inclusive	L	L	L	L–M	M	L	L
Stock purchase plan	L	L	L	L–M	L	L	L
ESOP/full	H	M–H	H	L–H	H	H	H

* L = Low; M = Moderate; H = High.

Gain sharing is not a program, but rather a general descriptor for a variety of programs, such as the Rucker Plan, Improshare, and the Scanlon Plan.[6] The group that shares the gain usually consists of all employees at a plant or company location. Much attention and concern have been devoted to determining historical base periods and formulas for computing the gain.

Team or small-group incentive plans apply the principles of gain sharing but at the department or group level. If gain sharing can be thought of as a macro plan, the team works off a micro plan. Advocates of these plans correctly argue that they create a clearer link between group performance and reward than the larger-scale gain-sharing programs.[7] Their motivational potential therefore is probably higher than the broader gain-sharing schemes.

However, from an organizational change perspective, team incentives may have limited effects. Such programs often are narrow in organizational scope and few have been extended throughout an organization.

In approaching these programs, executives should not underestimate the difficulties involved in implementing them. They promote and reinforce organizational change because they require such change to be effective. Executives must not view them simply as incentive pay programs, and, as a result, focus primarily on payout formulas. Rather, the emphasis must be on changes in culture and management practices to create an environment where employees are sufficiently empowered to make the pay programs work. This is the really difficult task to be accomplished, and it is especially difficult in the larger-scale gain-sharing programs that cover all or large segments of a company.

Other Short-Term Plans

Bonus plans are hardly new, but those that include all employees, or at least all salaried employees, are recent innovations. These plans are not conceptually difficult, but the enormity of implementing them is extremely difficult. There are considerable difficulties in implementing a bonus plan for the top 100 people in a company. When the program is extended to hundreds, even thousands of employees, the difficulties are magnified severalfold.

Each employee bonus plan has an individual focus that requires measuring the performance of a large number of employees against preset objectives. This of course means extending an effective performance-planning process throughout the organization and, in turn, pursuing a major communications and educational effort. In the author's judgment, few organizations have the management capability and organizational discipline to carry off this feat.

The virtue of inclusive employee bonus plans is that they attempt to increase the variable portion of worker pay and link the individual's efforts to organizational goals.

The drawbacks, aside from the difficulty of achieving the purposes, are numerous. Essentially, they are individually focused plans that seldom, if ever, attempt to increase employee control. They are inherently expensive plans and hard to pull off.

Thus, they are moderately risky undertakings. In all but the most successful efforts, their potential for promoting and reinforcing organizational change is low.

Informed executives need little introduction to profit-sharing plans. Many exponents of new wave or alternative compensation would rightfully exclude profit sharing from their list of programs. Their potential for facilitating organizational change or motivating employees is relatively low. However, the difficulty involved in designing and implementing them is relatively low, as is their risk to the organization. In effect, they represent low-risk, low-impact efforts.

Nevertheless, they can be symbolically important in that they link the company's financial performance to an employee reward, however tenuous the linkage.[8] So to some degree they can contribute to the development of a shared-fate environment.

Skill-based pay's major advantage is that it presents an alternative to conventional and outmoded salary administration programs. Pay increases are determined by employees' acquisition of new and needed skills rather than by annual changes in the CPI. A second major advantage is that these increases facilitate the development of a skilled work force, which can be a rare and prized asset in U.S. industry. Because skill-based pay can enhance an organization's human capital, it warrants inclusion on the list of alternative pay programs. Skill-based pay may be particularly valuable to companies that face continuous and rapid change in their production operations.

Although not without its uses, skill-based pay probably has little effect on organizational change. It is an individually focused program, with little need to alter culture or most management practices. Its greatest defect, however, is that skill-based pay bears no relationship to individual, group, or organizational performance. Individuals are rewarded for enhancing their job skills, not for increasing work output. The author has experienced situations in which people were paid for rapidly increasing their skills, but the organization's performance was quite poor. In fact, in these situations, employees were so myopically focused on skill attainment that they were oblivious to actual work performance.

A discussion of skill-based methodology goes well beyond the purpose of this chapter. Suffice it to say, skill-based pay is among the most time-consuming and difficult programs to design and implement.[9] Again, these programs have some useful applications, but they are far from being the most effective vehicles for facilitating organizational change.

Long-Term Ownership-Based Programs

Whereas stock options are hardly new, programs that grant options to all or most employees are both new and still rare. Although stock options are a major tool for changing behavior in the executive suite and have enriched many executives, they are less potent when applied to all employees.

In theory, executives are perceived to influence the price of shares, but this link is ephemeral for most employees. Also, the size of the grants to each employee in an inclusive program is relatively small, and dollar increases in the price of shares, if any, are unlikely to represent a significant percentage of base pay.

The value of inclusive stock option plans is that they tie some employee rewards to the long-term success of the enterprise. This could contribute to creating a shared-fate environment. There is not enough history of these plans to read any firm conclusions about their long-term effect. However, it is likely to be minimal. In addition to the reasons already noted, most employees who exercise options are probably going to sell their shares immediately or soon after receiving them. Unlike the more affluent executives, they simply cannot afford to hold the stock, and their need for cash is greater. Thus, stock option plans, however intended, are probably going to have little long-term effect.

The use of inclusive stock option plans will have little influence on organization change or employee motivation. They are best viewed as one element of an overall employee pay strategy, more in the form of a benefit than a promoter or reinforcer of change.

Many of the same issues apply to stock purchase plans. In fact, most companies tend to consider such plans to be part of the benefits package, not direct pay. There is a history with these plans, and it shows that most companies have encountered difficulties in getting employees to hold their shares. These plans probably are more symbolically important, providing a sense of ownership and, hence, a shared fate, than they are as proactive tools for facilitating organizational change.

ESOPs are a form of corporate ownership, not a pay plan. The intention was to make employees significant owners of American business and industry, that is, capitalists as opposed to simply workers.[10] For a variety of reasons this has not happened on even a minor scale. Despite the limited success of the ESOP concept, it has unusual potential for creating organizational change and, therefore, merits attention.

It is essential to distinguish between the limited and the full ESOP. Many companies have experimented with limited ESOPs that put, for example, something like 5 percent of common shares in a plan owned by employees. This amounts to little more than a cleverly financed stock purchase plan and has little consequence for promoting organizational change.

Defining a full ESOP is more difficult. At the extreme it refers to a situation in which employees hold all of the equity in a corporation. At a minimum, it refers to situations in which employees, through an ESOP, hold a controlling, or at least significant, percentage of the corporation's outstanding shares, probably 30 percent or more. With this ownership position comes some control or influence over corporate governance. It is the full ESOP that has a significant potential for both promoting and reinforcing organizational change.

ESOP employees have two sources of income: the income of their labor, and the income of their capital, as realized short-term through dividends and long-term through stock appreciation. The greater the percentage of equity held by employees, the larger the dividends and, therefore, the greater the proportion of the variable pay component to the fixed wage or salary component. The motivational consequences of this are potentially enormous, depending on profits and dividend policy.

The full ESOP does more than any other program to create a shared-fate environment. If the company fails, employees lose not only their jobs but also their equity, which probably was partially financed with their retirement income funds. As any small business owner well knows, this is the real world. However, few corporate employees are fully acquainted with this stark reality. In effect, the full ESOP creates a high-risk, high-reward culture.

The problem of course is that it is extremely difficult to establish a full ESOP. Few corporate executives or their boards would even consider doing so. The relatively few that do exist came about as the only alternatives to survive a financial crisis.

Managing in a full ESOP environment can be extraordinarily difficult. The workers own the company, yet they are also employees with jobs to perform and policies to adhere to. Getting the role of employee/owner straight is no small task, as the CEO is ultimately accountable to his own employees. A full ESOP demands a high degree of corporate democracy and, theory aside, this will not lend itself to a smooth, efficient operation.

In summary, full ESOPs are powerful vehicles for change, but, given the problems associated with them, are unlikely to become prevalent forms of corporate ownership.

THESE PROGRAMS AREN'T MUTUALLY EXCLUSIVE

The issue is not choosing one program over another—for example, an inclusive stock option plan instead of team incentives. A company can utilize both programs. The issue is choosing the most suitable program or mix of programs that will best promote and reinforce organizational change. This requires executives to think strategically about pay and to consider the costs carefully.[11]

These programs are not the answers to the many problems confronting U.S. businesses. But when properly understood and thoughtfully implemented, they nevertheless can help to facilitate constructive organizational change.

NOTES

1. For a review of Herzberg's theory see *The Motivation to Work* (New York: John Wiley, 1959); and *Work and the Nature of Man* (Cleveland, OH: World Publishing, 1966).
2. There are of course notable exceptions, in particular, Edward E. Lawler, who has made significant contributions to our understanding of pay and its relationship to organization effectiveness. For example, see his *Pay and Organization Development* (Reading, MA: Addison-Wesley, 1981).
3. See F. Sanfilippo; G. A. Wiegman; and E. J. Giblin, "A Compensation Strategy for the 1990s," *The Human Resource Professional*, Fall 1991, pp. 47–51.
4. For an elaboration on the limitations of merit pay programs see E. J. Giblin, G. A. Wiegman, and F. Sanfilippo, "Bringing Pay Up to Date," *Personnel*, November 1990, pp. 17–18.

5. J. E. Santora, "DuPont Returns to the Drawing Board," *Personnel Journal,* February 1991, pp. 34–36.

6. For a comprehensive introduction to gain-sharing programs see B. Graham-Moore and T. Ross, *Productivity Gainsharing* (Englewood Cliffs, NJ: Prentice-Hall, 1988).

7. For a succinct introduction to these plans see J. E. Nickel and S. O'Neal, "Small-Group Incentives: Gain Sharing in the Microcosm," *Compensation and Benefits Review,* March–April 1990, pp. 23–29.

8. E. E. Lawler, *Strategic Pay* (San Francisco: Jossey-Bass, 1990), pp. 123–126.

9. For a worthwhile overview of skill-based plans see J. Kanin-Lovers and A. Porter, "The Ten Commandments of Skill-Based Pay," *Journal of Compensation and Benefits,* March–April 1991, pp. 44–47.

10. An introduction to the ESOP concept can be found in L. O. Kelso and P. Hetter, *Two-Factor Theory: The Economics of Reality* (New York: Alfred A. Knopf, 1967).

11. Lawler, *Strategic Pay,* pp. 13–36.

Chapter Thirty-Three

A Nimble Compensation System for Managing Change

Martin G. Wolf

BACKGROUND

The nimble CEO must use reward systems to manage change effectively. Properly managed, compensation is a change lever that can assist in the change process. Improperly managed, compensation is a change barrier that increases the organization's resistance to change. *Reward,* one of the key processes that senior executives must align with strategy, operations, and culture, communicates the company's value system and serves as a measure of an employee's performance.

Current experience suggests that compensation systems are not responding appropriately to the various types of change triggers (environmental, strategic, operational, and cultural). As a result, they have become a *barrier to,* rather than a *facilitator of,* change. The following are specific problems of current compensation systems:

- They are not sufficiently based on what is affordable.
- They do not achieve the desired emphasis on pay for performance.
- They do not properly reflect changing organization structures (such as flattening, downsizing, and restructuring).
- They do not respond quickly enough to changing job roles and careers.
- They are not credible because they do not reflect employee worth.
- They create needless employee anxiety about the effects of change.

Organizations grappling with a rapidly changing, highly competitive business environment need a reengineered compensation system that reinforces the change process. Such a compensation system should include the following measures:

- Transfer a portion of fixed cost to variable cost (the affordability issue).
- Directly reward quality and customer service achievements and other aspects of good performance.

- Reinforce organizational strategy with the communication value of money.
- Increase work-force flexibility and facilitate change.
- Minimize the disruption caused by change.
- Recognize the value of each individual employee to the organization.

The remainder of this chapter describes a change-oriented system that focuses on using compensation to promote *organizational effectiveness* and makes it easier to move people around without undue anxiety about pay or loss of status. This new system differs from traditional compensation systems in that it incorporates these features:

- It moves from the concept of jobs as relatively permanent entities to the concept of non-permanent assignments. This is an especially critical element in the change process because it allows people to be assigned to posts where they can be most effective.
- Abandons traditional concepts of job evaluation based on the complexity of the task, independent of the competence of the individual holding the job.
- Creates an individual valuation system that recognizes the true value of each employee.
- Changes from an exclusive focus on the present task situation to a recognition of the historical contribution of individuals.
- Directly recognizes special individual skills, competencies, and market premiums.
- Eliminates salary ranges.

PAR—P(ERFORMANCE) A(SSIGNMENT LEVEL) R(ÉSUMÉ VALUE)

Although **PAR** is designed as a complete compensation system, it is essentially modular. Each **PAR** component can be used in conjunction with more traditional compensation approaches, if desired.

P*(erformance)*   This element is designed to separate true pay for performance from pay for continuance in the organization (keeping the "warm body" warm). It addresses the objectives of affordability, reward for achievement, and reinforcement of strategy.

A*(ssignment Level)*   This element is designed to separate the true value to the organization of the employee (based on his or her contribution history) from the measured worth of the tasks performed at a particular moment. This element redefines the traditional concept of internal equity and pays people for their true asset value. It addresses the objectives of increasing work force flexibility and minimizing change disruption.

R(*ésumé Value*)   This element is designed to separate the true market value of the person (based on pay market premiums and individual track records) from the measured relative internal worth of the organization's assignment levels. It addresses the objective of recognizing the individual's value.

P(erformance)

The concept is as appealing and as American as apple pie, but throughout the 1980s, pay for performance did not work. Many reasons have been offered for this failure, but the bottom line appears to be inadequate pay differentials between the different levels of performance.

The entitlement mentality (employees who feel entitled to an annual raise to keep up with inflation) resulted in using most of the "merit budget" as a general pay increase. Very little was left to truly reward merit, and the amount of pay actually earmarked for increased performance was inadequate to reinforce the improvements, let alone motivate them.

The typical practice was to grant periodic merit increases that permanently increased the individual's base salary level. These merit increases actually had two components, of which true merit (pay for performance) was usually the smaller. The larger component was pay for continuance—the portion of the increase that represents the upward movement of wages and salaries in the larger economy. Because this component represented the minimum amount given to anyone who remained with the organization, the pay increase differential between average and outstanding performance was insignificant.

Even in the rare cases where performance was rewarded in a meaningful fashion, the successful behaviors that were reinforced often lingered long after they had been observed. Because increases are almost always granted as a percentage of current pay, the true merit portion of every past increase is compounded continuously by both portions of each new merit increase. As with compound interest on an investment, good performance early on can provide an annuity in later years!

After a few years of large salary increases for top performance, an employee could coast and the annual cost-of-living increases for average performance would compound the high salary previously attained. Another employee lower in the salary range might turn in top performance and thus receive a noticeably larger percentage increase as a reward. However, because the larger percentage was applied to a lower base pay, the actual dollar increase might well be greater for the employee who was coasting than for the new star.

Past efforts to separate pay for performance from pay for continuance have foundered because so little money was available for performance per se. The only viable way to break this dilemma is to make performance-related pay an annual item that must be re-earned each year rather than a perennial feature that gets added into base pay and remains there forever.

If the performance-related component does not become a permanent part of pay, then its size can be increased each year to reflect the amount from the previous year that did not become permanent. The Performance component can be allowed to accumulate in this fashion until it reaches the desired size. The desired final size will vary with job level, the higher paid positions having larger Performance components than lower paid positions.

The logic behind this size differential is twofold. First, higher paid individuals can tolerate a larger variation in compensation because they have proportionately more discretionary income. Second, higher-level positions can have a greater effect on organizational results and thus a greater potential variation in performance.

A(ssignment Level)

The problem with the traditional approach.   Compensation in the traditional organization is determined by some type of job evaluation system. All job evaluation systems, formal or informal, are based on three elements: what you know, what you do, and (to a degree) what you have to put up with environmentally. These three elements are the basis on which employers pay their people. In turn, they often are divided into four potentially measurable factors: skill, effort, responsibility, and working conditions.

In small organizations, the job evaluation process is typically an informal hierarchy of pay. In larger organizations, a more formal approach to position evaluation is employed. This may range from simple market pricing to complex computerized job evaluation programs.

Each evaluated job level carries its own pay level, typically a range rather than a single rate. When the employee changes positions in the organization, he or she is assigned to the pay range that goes with the new job. If the new range is higher than the previous one, a promotional increase is frequently given. The employee is also rewarded in the future with larger or more frequent raises than in the old job. If the new range is lower than the old, the employee's pay is rarely reduced, but the person will receive smaller or less frequent raises in the future.

In organizations where job levels are not public knowledge, it is a common water cooler sport to analyze employee movements and decide if a person was promoted, moved laterally, or demoted (in other words, whether that person's salary range went up, stayed the same, or went down as a result of the job change). Those who are perceived as having moved to a position with a lower salary range tend to be viewed as having failed (been demoted), and those who move to positions with a higher salary are seen as having succeeded (been promoted).

Although change in salary range associated with a change of position is merely a source of gossip to others, it is a matter of great concern to the person who is moved because it directly affects his or her livelihood and standing with fellow employees.

Indeed, when being moved to a new position, an employee's first question is usually about the job's salary level and not its assigned tasks. Employees tend to resist movement to a position that has a lower salary range, even if the salary is kept constant (or even increased slightly as an inducement to accept the change). Employees move eagerly to positions with higher salary ranges, but they expect salary increases to accompany the shifts.

Traditional job evaluation assumes that jobs exist on their own as discrete, relatively permanent entities. Thus, the value of the *position* to the organization is measured independent of the person who is occupying it at any moment. This value translates into a salary range for the *position*. The pay of the *person* in the position then is determined through a separate process that calculates that *person's* value to the organization (the individual's position within the salary range established for the *position*). The valuation of the person typically includes both historical elements (such as tenure and past performance) and current elements (such as market pressures and present performance). The relative weights of these elements vary from organization to organization, but most organizations weigh all of them to some degree.

However, in almost all circumstances, the value of the position sets the upper and lower pay limits. Exceptions are sometimes made regarding the salary minimum for the position, but the salary of a person holding the position rarely is allowed to exceed the position maximum. The salary range for the *position* is the primary determining factor, not the merits of the particular *person* who holds the position.

New approaches to pay. The pressure of virtually continuous structural change requires major cultural change for most organizations. The organization's culture must not only accept frequent change, but encourage it. This stands in contrast to the culture of most traditional organizations, where change is viewed as negative and is resisted. Resistance to change, moreover, is reinforced by the job evaluation process because employees fear that the change may negatively affect the measured worth of their jobs. However, some variations in the assignment/evaluation process are starting to develop.

The emergence of flexible manufacturing on the shop floor has created a demand for greater flexibility in the hourly work force. Employees must be willing to change jobs frequently and to perform much broader ranges of tasks. A number of new approaches have been developed to deal with the compensation problems that arose from these new types of jobs.

One new approach is "broad banding," which collapses many job levels into relatively few, but creates wider pay ranges at each level. Thus, a broader array of jobs have the same level and pay range. This permits freer movement of employees between jobs without any negative impact on their pay levels. In essence, broad banding represents a partial abandonment of pay for the specific content of the job and an increased emphasis on the characteristics of the person holding the job as the determinant of actual pay.

Another new approach is knowledge-based pay (KN Pay), a variation on the professional hierarchy theme. In KN Pay, shop employees are paid more as they master various new tasks and expand their skills. They are paid for their ability to contribute to the organization through the tasks they have learned, including tasks that they *may* be assigned to perform when the manufacturing process is reconfigured. KN Pay is pay for standby ability, for potential or periodic task performance, rather than for tasks currently or continually performed. Compared with traditional pay methods, knowledge-based pay depends more on the person's skills and abilities and less on what he or she is doing at a particular time.

Because modern organizations face the need for continuous adaptation to a changing world, organization structure tends to be much more dynamic than it was in traditional organizations. Jobs are less permanent, and a change *of* job (or at least a significant change *in* the job) has become a regular occurrence. As a result, it is best to think not of jobs but of fulfilling Assignments. Each employee is assigned a constellation of tasks that change regularly. Sometimes the role changes are gradual, but often the changes are frequent and major in scope. The constellation of tasks at any point in time constitutes that employee's Assignment.

Toward a new definition of internal equity. Because of the frequency of Assignment changes, today's organizations must focus on the value to the organization of the person, largely independent of the constellation of tasks that the person is performing at the moment (the evaluated level of the current Assignment). Instead, value to the organization is related largely to the level of the Assignments that the person has actually performed in the past and to the level of the Assignments that the person is capable of performing. This constitutes a new definition of internal equity: paying people equitably for what they can do and for what they have contributed, *not* for what they may be doing at the moment.

Although this concept may sound revolutionary, it really is not new. Evaluation of the capabilities of the person, rather than of the exact nature of his or her current position, has existed in professional hierarchies in science and engineering for many years. Scientists or engineers of very different experience levels typically are assigned to the same project in much the same capacity. The differences in what they do may be largely invisible to an observer on any given day, yet clear differences in the professional competence of each team member exist. These differences are reflected subtly in the degrees of technical direction that they are given and in the freedom they are granted to pursue new avenues suggested by their findings. They also are reflected directly in their salaries.

A scientist or engineer may work as part of a team on a single aspect of a project for years, growing professionally, assuming an increasingly significant role, and receiving greater compensation. Alternatively, a scientist or engineer may work on a number of projects in the course of a single year, some that are less challenging, others that use every bit of his or her expertise. Pay levels depend on the professional competence established over time through past performance, not on the difficulty of the current role.

A similar system is used with program managers (PMs) in the aerospace industry. A PM may wind up a large, very complex program at a time when only a much smaller, simpler program is available. Although the PM will be assigned to the lower level program, his or her pay level will be based on proven personal competence and historically demonstrated value to the organization, not on the difficulty of the current project.

If pay is to be based more on the person's value to the organization and less on a measure of the current position, an effective, consistent, and reasonably objective system for determining each person's value to the organization must be developed. Without such a system, basing compensation levels on the person rather than the job will open the door to increased favoritism and place the organization at increased risk of violating equal opportunity requirements. Indeed, it was because of the difficulties associated with person-based approaches that job evaluation programs originally were developed.

The organization of the 1990s requires an *individual valuation system,* not a job evaluation system. Job evaluation in the traditional sense is no longer relevant if the concept of a job is replaced by a series of assignments. Although the basic compensable elements of what you know and what you do are not changed, how you go about measuring these elements does change.

The organization must take the following steps:

- Identify those aspects of competence and performance that it wants to use as compensable factors.
- Establish their relative weights to reflect the organization's value system.
- Develop a consistent method of measuring the degree to which an individual possesses each of these aspects.
- Document the measurement approach and teach appropriate persons how to apply it properly.

A number of trade-offs regarding the valuing of individuals must be made. These should reflect the organization's unique value system. Consider the following examples.

- Two individuals, A and B, are of equal value to the organization in terms of past and present contributions. However, A is in a discipline for which there is a significant pay market premium, and B is not. Thus, A could command a much higher salary elsewhere than B could.

How should the organization compensate A as compared with B?

- Individuals C and D have performed at the same level on identical Assignments for the past two years. C is felt to have significant potential to move to Assignments of significantly greater scope, but D is believed to be unlikely to progress.

How should the organization compensate C as compared with D? What if D has a 20-year history of success whereas C has only been around for three years?

Determining Assignment level. **PAR** evaluates the individual, not the job. This is accomplished by separating the level of a particular Assignment from the Assignment level of the person in that Assignment. The level of a particular Assignment (an evaluation of the job) is called the Organization Assignment Level (OAL). Each employee has his/her own Assignment level or Personal Assignment Level (PAL).

Step 1: Determine the OAL   Because an Assignment is identical to a job except for its implied permanence, the relative level of Assignments (their OALs) can be measured via conventional job measurement technology. Because Assignments, by definition, change frequently, the measurement approach chosen must be both flexible (to accommodate myriad possible combinations of tasks into Assignments) and easy to use (because it will be employed often as new Assignments are created). Given these criteria, measurements based on Assignment-to-Assignment comparisons—rather than comparisons of an Assignment against a rigid set of definitions that quickly becomes outmoded—are preferred.

Step 2: Weigh the various past and present Assignments held by each individual to determine his or her Personal Assignment Level   This process must be developed by each organization to reflect its values. Remember that the PAL must not be driven solely, or even primarily, by the OAL of the current Assignment. It is intended to be largely independent of the present Assignment's OAL and should reflect the historical level of that person's Assignments.

A number of issues must be considered:

- Is the PAL the highest OAL at which the person has performed successfully in the past? If so, for how long must the person have performed at that level before it is used to determine the PAL?

- Is the PAL simply the average of the OALs at which the person has performed successfully in the past? If so, is greater emphasis given to the OAL of the most recent past Assignments than to those in the more distant past?

- How far into the past does the evaluator go in developing the average?

- What weight, if any, should be given to the OAL of the current Assignment?

The answer to questions such as these must be developed to reflect each organization's value system.

The following example illustrates how the PAL might be developed. Mary Smith has been with ABC Corporation for the 10 years since she got her MBA. For the past three months, Mary has been in a Level 7 Division Controller's role trying to identify the reasons for falling profits in small, newly acquired Division C. Her recent Assignments prior to the present one are as follows:

Title	Level	Months
Division A Controller	8	14
Assistant Corporate Controller	9	9
Division A Controller	8	10
Assistant Corporate Controller	9	6
Division B Controller	10	9
Assistant Corporate Controller	9	4

ABC develops Personal Assignment levels by averaging the highest OALs Mary has held over any 36 of the last 60 months. From the table above, these 36 months are composed of 9 months at Level 10, 19 months at Level 9, and 8 months at Level 8. The computation, shown below, is performed by multiplying the number of months in each level by the number of the level, adding the results, and dividing the sum by 36.

Level	Months	Level × Months
10	9	90
9	19	171
8	8	64
	36	325
PAL = 325 divided by 36 = 9.03		

Based on her history, her PAL is 9. Her current OAL is 7, but that has no impact on her PAL because she has more than 36 months at higher OALs.

R(ésumé Value)

Résumé Value—the going rate for an individual because of his or her unique background—is a concept that is quite evident in the hiring office but notably absent in traditional pay programs. Résumé Value in the hiring office is expressed by greater interest in certain employment candidates and by higher salary offers to some individuals than to others with equal years of experience. However, the greater market attractiveness of certain background characteristics is formally ignored once the person is hired.

Résumé Value is a joint function of pay market premium and of growth potential. For example, the special labor market for attorneys is a pay market premium factor. However, the pay market premium for a new law graduate varies significantly between a Harvard Law School graduate and a graduate of Widener University's night law program.

However, Résumé Value also is affected by growth potential, which is a reflection of past educational and vocational achievements. Class ranking and Law Review membership affect the going price for new graduates of any particular law school. These past educational achievements are valued as predictors of future potential. However, the pay differential between the Harvard and Widener law school graduates could well be reversed after ten years if the Widener graduate displays greater competence on the job.

Determining Résumé Value. The pay market premium component of Résumé Value comes from traditional salary survey data and simply increases the person's pay. It reflects the differences in the going rate for jobs of similar experience, educational requirements, and difficulty level in the various functional specialties. For example, in the electronics industry, a noticeable premium is paid for plant managers who hold electrical or electronic engineering degrees.

The process for measuring the growth potential component must be developed by each organization to reflect its values. Each organization must decide how it wishes to weigh educational and vocational achievements (beyond their aspects that are part of pay market premium) and the role of potential. These values then should be translated into a scale for determining the amount of pay to be awarded for any particular combination of educational/vocational achievements and potential.

Each individual must be assessed using these criteria to determine the amount of pay to be awarded them for the growth potential component. This award is added to the pay market premium (if any) to determine the individual's Résumé Value.

IMPLEMENTING PAR

As was noted earlier, PAR is essentially modular, and any of the various PAR components can be used in conjunction with more traditional compensation approaches.

Option 1

The non-permanent Performance component of pay can be added to a traditional pay program without using the Assignment or the Résumé Value aspects of PAR. One would phase in the annual Performance award by restricting the upward movement of the salary ranges for several years to separate the pay-for-continuance component from the pay-for-performance component. Likewise, the movement of individuals through the salary range would be slowed and equalized because the pay-for-performance component was treated as a separate item.

If an organization adopts the Performance component of the **PAR** system, then the broad salary ranges associated with traditional compensation systems are not needed. Because the pay-for-performance component is treated as a separate item, only pay for continuance remains as part of base salary. Because the effects of wage inflation in the broader economy will be dealt with by raising the pay structure, the only function of a salary *range* is to reward tenure. Thus, organizations need salary ranges broad enough to permit the degree of tenure rewards they wish to grant. Because the tenure awards are just that, and are totally unrelated to performance, they should be of a uniform percentage size and should be granted on a fixed schedule, much like the schedules used for government employees.

For organizations that truly believe in pay for performance, a salary *rate* will suffice for each OAL.

Implementation of option 1. Whether moving to limited ranges or to single rates, the organization can phase in the new approach by lifting existing range minimums each year to reflect the effects of wage inflation in the economy, while holding existing range maximums constant to effectively narrow the range. Over time, the degree of spread will reach the desired point, whether a narrow range or a single rate. At that point, the range maximums would increase each year in line with the new minimums.

Option 2

Organizations can adopt the PAL (Personal Assignment Level) approach without going to the nonpermanent Performance component of pay. PAL can be adopted with or without the concept of Résumé Value.

Implementation of option 2. Adopting PAL without Résumé Value would use existing job levels and their associated salary ranges. Each individual simply would be assigned to one of the existing salary ranges based on personal job history rather than the level of the job currently being performed.

Adopting PAL with Résumé Value also would use existing job levels and their associated salary ranges. Each individual again would be assigned to an existing salary range based on personal job history rather than the level of the current job, and his or her targeted position in the range would be affected by Résumé Value. Those below targeted positions in range would be brought up to this level, and those already above the targeted level would have future salary growth slowed until they fell back to the desired position in the new range.

Option 3

Both the Performance and Résumé Value aspects of **PAR** can be adopted with salary rates or with traditional salary ranges.

This policy can greatly simplify the organization's pay structure. Although it is common practice to have multiple salary structures to reflect industry, discipline, and geographic pay premiums, a single rate/range structure will suffice. Because the Performance aspect is considered separately, if pay premiums are necessary, they can simply be added to the rate/range structure.

Implementation of option 3.   If a single rate is used for each PAL/job level, premium rates can be added for each level to reflect the needed industry, discipline, and geographic pay premiums. If a range with periodic fixed steps for tenure (as described above) is used, then extra steps can be added at each PAL/job level to reflect the needed industry, discipline, and geographic pay premiums.

IN CONCLUSION

Existing approaches to compensation have been widely criticized in recent years, often justifiably. The response to this criticism has been the creation of a broad variety of new approaches attempting to tie compensation more closely to performance or to make pay less a fixed cost and more a variable cost (such as gain sharing or lump sum bonuses in lieu of salary increases). The most promising approaches support the change management process and reward those who are most effective in advancing it. Recasting jobs as assignments is a potentially important technique because it maximizes the flexibility of the individual and links both pay and status to the employee's ability to shift quickly at times of change.

Chapter Thirty-Four

Using Executive Compensation to Promote Change

Johannes M. Pennings

C orporations experience many discontinuities in their markets, customers, technologies, and governmental regulations. These discontinuities differ only with respect to their degree of change in the markets and suddenness with which they erupt. Airline deregulation, the microelectronic sweep, and the substitution of personal computers for mainframes are examples of radical change. Any firm must have the capacity to weather such discontinuities so that a new strategy and structure will match the conditions of a new stage in its corporate life. The firm's ability to change, or to restructure itself, dictates its likelihood of survival; yet restructuring implies a destruction of old methods, procedures, technologies, and skills.

Any restructuring attempt has to start with the assumption that organizations are locked into a set of routines and that they face major hurdles when undertaking strategic transformations. Compared with new ventures, mature corporations are saddled with external commitments to suppliers, customers, and others; and they cherish the unique skills that they have accumulated. These attachments to supply lines, markets, and technologies may evolve into a trap from which it is difficult to escape. When markets change, existing technologies become obsolete, and current product offerings face shrinking demands, organizations have little choice when contemplating change. They must change.

However, change-driven organizations have access to a number of levers to overcome their inertia. These levers include succession, training and development programs, outplacement and selection of personnel, implementation of a new measurement system, and the adoption of aggressive compensation practices. In this chapter, we argue that the compensation system in general, and the executive pay system in particular, can be significant forces in redirecting an organization's strategic thrust by the way they impact on how executives focus their motivational efforts. The efficacy of pay systems to effectuate change is contingent upon the use of other levers, particularly the measurement system that informs the firm about its strategic performance and whose timeliness and accuracy define the appropriate criteria by which compensation decisions are made and implemented.

From a change management perspective, executive compensation must be particularly sensitive to changes in the business situation. When a change trigger forces a paradigm shift to a new business situation the performance management system must be adjusted to reflect the new measures. These measures are the primary area of communication between the executive staff, the board, and the employees. Executive compensation is part of the continual alignment of the performance management system along with the measured requirements of the customer base, competitor positioning, and internal delivery capabilities.

COMPENSATION AND CHANGE

There has been a great deal of controversy about the connection between the executive pay of a firm and its strategic performance. In the wake of the wave of corporate restructuring in the 1980s, there are many cases in which executive compensation has been used as an incentive to senior management to execute a successful strategic turnaround. Growth through acquisition, or aggressive investment in new businesses, markets, and countries, or maintaining a certain performance momentum is no longer sufficient. Rather, executives are pushed to diminish their firm's diversity and streamline income streams. Growth or upsizing often is replaced by downsizing. Mergers and acquisitions are "out" while retrenchment and return to core competencies are "in."

What is interesting is that pay systems increasingly are used as incentives to executives to change the firm's posture, rather than simply maintain a continued trend of growth and a sustained return on investment.

For example, in 1991 Westinghouse Electric aggressively restructured its executive compensation plan to induce its senior management to carve out a new and more specific business focus designed to put the firm back on track. In prior years, Westinghouse committed major blunders, participating in the mergers and acquisition (M&A) craze without considering whether acquisitions unrelated to the core business were appropriate. Earnings and market value plummeted. If Westinghouse executives fail to refocus, they will receive meager levels of pay, at least by U.S. standards.

IBM, which had been reluctant to induce behavior by financial incentives, has begun to institute modest changes in executive compensation to endow the firm with a more inventive and venturesome orientation. Traditionally, the giant computer manufacturer relied on loyalty and conformity to corporate standards as proxies for desirable behavior. IBM too has declined precipitously. The efforts in debureaucratizing the firm include incentive systems that reward entrepreneurial behavior rather than corporate conformity.

These recent initiatives are striking in view of the controversy that surrounds executive pay. Criticism about overpayment of top executives has abounded, particularly in the face of less than outstanding results at their firms. Numerous academic researchers (e.g., Murphy, 1983) have countered such criticism through findings on a link between pay and performance. Yet there remains a great deal of skepticism about the feasibility of tying compensation to performance. This skepticism becomes even stronger if the focus is on strategic performance. There are many complex issues in the debate, such as what constitutes executive compensation and strategic performance, and how to construe their connection. This chapter will address some of these issues.

The overwhelming proportion of U.S. corporations have executive compensation systems, or "plans." Usually, the plan covers a comparatively small number of executives, although in some cases the number exceeds 50 persons. The underlying assumption is that these top managers have a disproportionate influence on corporate performance and have the leverage to direct their firm's strategic destiny. Many of these plans have been devised by compensation consulting firms and are geared toward the maintenance of a firm's growth momentum.

Whereas each firm's system might have its own unique attributes, there is also increased agreement among corporations as to the manner in which these systems are designed. The mechanical features and the formal attributes for making compensation decisions should be distinguished from the use of such systems, particularly when the systems are devised to transform the firm and propel it in a new and different direction. The chapter first will review some of the underpinnings of executive compensation. Subsequently, it will explore the relationship between executive pay and organizational change.

CONCEPTUAL ISSUES IN EXECUTIVE COMPENSATION*

Linking executive pay to restructuring is surprisingly difficult since the terms are not easy to define. Executive pay includes myriad elements, some of which defy attempts to assign them to a specific time period. For example, the pay associated with stock options can be measured at the time they are granted, at the time they are exercised, at the time the exercised options are sold, or by the stock or cash dividends associated with the stock options at the time they were exercised but not yet sold. Similar problems exist in the interpretation of deferred compensation, pension, and "golden parachutes," which provide executives with generous cash payments in the event of forced resignation because of change in control of their company. Even more difficult to interpret are perquisites whose cash value may be small but whose symbolism is highly meaningful.

Compensation thus is only one of a variety of incentives. Power, status, and achievement rival compensation in their relevance for executives. In European and Pacific Basin cultures, such nonpecuniary benefits may even exceed pay in their

---

*The following section draws heavily on a chapter written by the author in *The Compensation Handbook*, edited by Milton Rock and Lance Berger (New York: McGraw-Hill, 1991).

importance to top executives (Pennings, 1993). Furthermore, one should look not only at the level of compensation but also the profile. The profile represents the relative size of base salary, bonuses, long-term incentive compensation, stock options, and the cash value of perks.

MEASUREMENT OF PERFORMANCE AND CHANGE

Performance in general, and strategic performance in particular, are even more difficult to delineate. Firms resort to financial, short-term operational, and accounting indicators, such as return on investment or return on equity, in choosing the criteria for decisions on executive compensation. When trying to encourage strategic change, firms might stretch such indicators over a multiyear period, the assumption being that extending the time frame makes such performance measures strategic or long-term in nature. The multiyear period clearly substitutes accounting performance measures for capital market measures, and shifts executives' attention from short-term to long-term time horizons. But whether such pay bases deserve the label strategic is not quite evident.

Examples of such long-term pay systems are those that link the cost of capital to return on equity over a five-year period—or the so-called par line. Executives are given some long-term bonus payments, "phantom stock," or "performing shares" if returns exceed the cost of capital. However, such financially connected systems tend to blur the meaning of performance, and they can be challenged as to their strategic relevance because the essence of strategy may reach beyond the time frame used in the formula.

The issue becomes even fuzzier and more complicated when the act of tying pay to performance pertains to the marginal contribution attributable to the CEO or any other high executive. Economists consider the marginal productivity of labor to be equivalent to compensation; the higher an executive's marginal productivity, the greater his or her pay.

The link between pay and strategic change can be examined in two distinct ways. Compensation plans might emanate from a firm's intent to bring about change, as for example in the Westinghouse case. But pay systems may also be key levers through which strategic change is accomplished. Linking pay to strategic change can therefore be broken down into two issues:

> What is the meaning of executive compensation as derived from, or part of, the firm's quest for strategic change?
>
> What role does compensation play in the implementation of strategic change?

For example, the adoption of stock option plans attached to milestones of strategic performance can be construed as part of the firm's strategy to delineate its trajectory in the future. These plans can also trigger initiatives to sell off some of the firm's undesirable assets, including those obtained in ill-advised acquisitions.

I view strategic change broadly. Strategy formulation entails the long-term decisions about markets, products, customer segments, technology, and human resources. Strategy represents an effort to match corporate resources with environmental opportunities. The strategic choice (Child, 1972) to operate in a given market with a given technology and other resources is relatively enduring. For example, committing vast resources to a new technology, establishing a tradition of lifetime employment with promotions from within, expanding to overseas markets—all of these represent significant decisions with profound strategic implications that are mirrored in decisions about executive pay. Compensation practices are part and parcel of the strategic posture, whereas strategic change might be communicated by alterations in the executive compensation plans. Stock prices are known to have changed as a result of publicized alterations in pay systems, presumably because investors consider such news germane to the future success of the firm.

Strategy implementation represents a set of decisions not only to preserve ongoing strategic commitments but also to succeed in turning a firm's strategic trajectory around. The reorganization of a firm's design, changes in culture and human resources, and the use of compensation as a lever of strategic change are elements of strategic turnaround. Of course they also can function as vehicles for preserving the existing strategic plans. The point is that executive compensation systems can have profound strategic consequences, regardless of whether those practices emerged from a given strategic posture. The implication is that executive pay may be the result of a given strategy, or it may be the cause of a strategy.

To grasp this paradox better, consider the contribution of Alfred Chandler. In his classic 1962 monograph *Strategy and Structure,* Chandler advocated the argument that strategic changes—such as the move from single product to multiproduct offerings—necessitated changes in organization structure, planning processes, and staffing. In short, "structure follows strategy." In the absence of such a realignment, the firm's strategic turnaround falters.

Chandler's thesis is not without critics. Hall and Saias (1980) suggested that it is the change in structure, personnel, planning, and other organizational practices that enables a firm to change its strategy, that is, "strategy follows structure." Both views might have kernels of truth, in that the firm's strategic posture sets the stage for various decisions about people, structure, and planning. Yet the results of those decisions often take on their own momentum and have their own consequences.

A similar argument can be developed on the role of executive compensation and strategic change. Compensation practices might trigger certain strategic behaviors by those who are governed under a certain compensation system. But the same systems may mirror strategic decisions that are integral parts of the grand strategic design. Separating cause and effect may be tenuous. But we will review these issues further. On one hand, we shall explore questions on the design of executive reward systems, particularly how the designs may reflect a strategic frame of mind. On the other, we shall review the strategic implications or consequences of executive compensation. In the first case, one might say that executive pay emerges as part and parcel of the intended or formulated strategy, whereas the consequences of pay can be construed as elements of the strategy as it is realized or implemented.

STRATEGIC CHANGE AS IMPETUS FOR EXECUTIVE COMPENSATION

The strategic posture of the firm and the types of markets in which it has chosen to compete are crucial in shaping the level and profile of executive compensation. The pay profile is also a function of the degree of the firm's strategic diversification and the competitive conditions in its industry. Compensation practices vary widely depending on whether the firm competes in a discretionary or a constrained industry, and on whether the firm is proactive or reactive in executing strategy.

Firms in discretionary industries with proactive postures usually stress variable and contingent pay arrangements, such as bonuses and long-term incentive compensation. By contrast, more passive firms in constrained industries tend to stress fixed and noncontingent pay such as base salary (Pennings and Bussard, 1989). Ironically, even so-called variable forms of pay, such as bonuses and profit sharing, may be set in such a way that they become fixed features of executive pay policy. In 1982 *Fortune* cited a firm that promised bonuses if ROE exceeded 6 percent, even though it was accustomed to returns of better than 11 percent! The implications are that these bonuses were not at risk and that accepting them as variable would be deceptive. Such executive pay plans have little relevance for organizational change. Instead, they perpetuate a firm's inertia and disinclination to change.

PAY, CHANGE, AND DISCRETION TO CHANGE

A discretionary industry is one in which a competitor enjoys a great deal of latitude in crafting its own strategy. Firms operating in a discretionary industry should have the ability to measure and anticipate market developments. Thus, market research and geopolitical forecasts enable agile firms to tune in to strategically important trends and to take anticipatory actions. Moreover, they may enjoy some leverage in shaping consumer demands or diffusing product innovations.

Commodity markets players and public utility firms usually have little market discretion, whereas firms in financial services, cosmetics, and entertainment operate in relatively free markets. Within free markets, strategically aggressive firms are expected to adopt compensation practices with high variations in levels of pay and differentiations in the profile of pay. Indeed, it has been determined that pay levels or pay profiles vary considerably among firms that are in discretionary industries and have proactive postures (Pennings and Bussard, 1989).

Diversified firms have the potential to customize a specific executive's compensation package to the market to which he or she has been assigned. This fact lies at the heart of so-called strategic reward maps that have been drawn by strategic compensation consultants, such as Booz Allen (Brindisi, 1984) and the Boston Consulting Group. The strategic product matrix of the firm is mapped onto the compensation plan. Its fixed and variable pay components dovetail with the strategic imperatives of the various product markets. They propose to design the compensation profile in such a way as to reflect the riskiness and time horizon of the different marketplaces, together with the corresponding strategic intent of the firm.

For example, Booz Allen distinguishes between the risk posture (ratio of contingent pay to salary) and the time focus (ratio of long-term to short-term variable compensation). As dichotomies, they furnish a two-by-two matrix that matches the strategic mandates of the various divisions. A cash cow division (large market share, low growth) requires a package with a low-risk posture and short-time horizon; the bulk of its executive pay could consist of a salary. The evidence to date suggests, however, that firms are reluctant to differentiate compensation practices strongly by divisions and prefer instead to adopt uniform systems.

Executives in discretionary industries face an easier challenge in changing their firms, so pay systems that are designed to change the firm are likely to have a greater impact on these businesses. However, organizations are also saddled with self-made inertia. As businesses become better at what they do, more consistent and reliable in what they produce, and more accountable for what they have accomplished, they also become more attached to the skills that underpin these accomplishments. This attachment can be a major obstacle for change and might require more drastic changes in key features of the executive compensation plan. Benchmarked peer firms, which are more willing to alter traditions and accumulated strategic skills, should provide prototypes for needed changes in compensation plans. Examples of change-resistant versus change-adaptive firms include IBM vis-à-vis Intel and Microsoft, and Campbell Soup vis-à-vis Heinz and ConAgra.

The globalization of markets implies that they become more discretionary and that benchmarking should involve firms from different countries. General Motors' peer organizations are no longer only Ford and Chrysler in the United States, but major Japanese and European car manufacturers as well.

COMPENSATION NORMS IN INDUSTRIES AND EXECUTIVE LABOR MARKETS

A relevant part of a firm's strategy for compensation centers on the recruitment and retention of members. Firms prefer to conform to industry norms of compensation, but, as with strategy in general, human resources strategies can also be compared on their reactivity. It is likely that conformity to compensation norms is stronger for firms that resort to a great deal of external recruitment of executive talent. A strategy of bolstering an *internal labor market,* that is, promoting from within, might render a firm somewhat immune to such norms.

The norms are key ingredients in strategic choices about human resources and executive labor markets. Compensation consultants have a great impact in promoting and institutionalizing certain compensation plans. They solidify existing practices or disseminate novel ones, thereby setting certain trends. There are both industry norms and compensation norms for various societies. Compensation innovations proliferate, but, as in the world of fashion, the compensation consulting industry has its own designers of pay systems. The dissemination of these systems reflects the eagerness of companies and their boards to stay competitive. For example, the adoption of long-term incentive compensation plans by American corporations reveals a certain degree of faddishness (Larcker, 1983). Organization theorists would argue that such imitations are induced less by the desire to create an optimum incentive for strategic behavior than by pressures to conform, to acquire legitimacy, and to convey the illusion of sound management. Sophisticated compensation plans, disseminated in 10-K or proxy statements, confer public credibility and preserve competitiveness in attracting and retaining high-level executives.

For CEOs, these plans show how well the firm is in tune with the marketplace for executive talent. Numerous executive compensation surveys have contributed to the specification of the price of management labor—both the level and the proportion that are fixed versus those that are variable. They permit firms in certain industries to set pay ranges with relatively precise bounds for executives. But a great amount of research remains to be done in this area. For executives as a labor pool, there are issues such as who is in it and who is not, especially if the pool coincides with a firm's industry or its strategic group. Executive search firms, together with compensation consultants, may assist firms in developing their human resources strategies, but they may blur the boundaries between industries. Also, many firms are reluctant to go to the external labor market (Dalton and Kessner, 1984) and prefer to bolster internal succession. General Electric has a unique succession system, consisting of slates of contenders for any of some 2,000 vacancies that might occur, enabling the firm to pick from a set of diverse individuals, all groomed within the GE culture. GE considers executive staffing too important to be left to headhunters! GE is most likely to assemble an **internal** labor market. But other firms tend to be saddled with job-hoppers and require extensive help from executive recruitment firms. They are less stable and tend to be more receptive to executive compensation systems as instruments of change. At the present time we do not know to what extent internal versus external labor markets affect the level or profile of executive compensation. As suggested before, when the firm represents a well-established internal labor market and its executives have high quitting barriers since they have few opportunities outside the firm, compensation may be modest or below the industry norm. Yet the compensation is likely to exceed a level that would be required to retain executives.

EXECUTIVE PAY AND STRATEGIC CHANGE

It is interesting to consider the change implications of the level and the profile of executive compensation. After all, executive compensation can be paraphrased as "strategic reward systems." Top executives in general and the CEO in particular are governed by a reward system that is usually segregated from the general compensation systems affecting other employees. The reasons for establishing a separate compensation system are numerous. Presumably executives have a distinctive capacity to bring about strategic change. Furthermore, such reward systems are often linked to long-term performance criteria such as the spread between return on equity and the cost of capital over a five-year period. Although such criteria are financial and reflect the vicissitudes of the market, many firms view them as strategic in that the behaviors of senior executives might be influenced by such preconditions.

There has been a lot of research on pay as an incentive for job performance, but virtually all of it has focused on lower-level employees. Thus we do not know whether executive motivation is different from that of other occupational groups. Nor do we know much about the motivational effectiveness of executive compensation systems.

AGENCY THEORY

In examining the issue, it may be helpful to highlight the agency theory (Jensen and Meckling, 1976). According to agency theorists, executives are controlled by a *contract* drawn up between them and the board of directors (representing shareholders). The contract can pertain to behaviors (e.g., implementation of strategic budgets) or to performance (e.g., maintaining returns on assets or increasing earnings per share). Such contracts are fraught with difficulties. For example, senior executives may have knowledge that the board lacks. Agency problems thus can be alleviated by establishing better information systems.

Carrying the agency theory to compensation, the board agrees to compensate executives through contingent rewards systems. These contracts eliminate the need for highly sophisticated monitoring devices, but they also result in the sharing of risks between shareholders and executives. The interests of shareholders and executives may not always be congruent. Executives do not enjoy the shareholders' flexibility in diversifying their risks; and when executives hold large amounts of stock, or their pay profile shows them to be heavily saddled with risk, they may be tempted to shun risky investment decisions that may be in the best interests of the shareholders.

Jensen and Meckling (1976) have indicated that senior executives, including the CEO, often avoid risk because they attempt to preserve their status and tenure in the company. By modifying the pay profile, these authors believe, risk-taking behavior can be encouraged. In contrast, the level of pay may be dysfunctional in motivating certain behaviors or results. Although the evidence to date is scant, there appears to be support for that view (Rapoport, 1984; McGuire and Schneeweis, 1985; and Larcker, 1983). Rapoport (1984) showed, for example, a direct relationship between the magnitude of long-term incentive compensation and the amount of R&D expenditures. The profile of executive compensation appears to foster specific strategic decisions. Under certain conditions, the findings suggest, it is possible to evoke comparatively desirable types of decisions. One should be alert for dysfunctional or strategically undesirable behaviors as well.

The research by Healey (1985) is noteworthy here. He discovered that executives tinkered with their information and control systems to inflate the size of their bonus payments. By refashioning the way financial results are reported, they focused their attention on the management of appearance rather than the management of performance. This research also highlighted a major example of agency problems, that is, the asymmetry of information between the CEO as the agent and the board or the stockholders as the principal, which the CEO may exploit for his or her own advantage.

DISCUSSION

As was noted earlier, much of the debate on executive compensation has focused on the firm's ability to stay its course. A long-term strategy defines the upward trend in financial and/or market-based indicators of performance. Financial benchmarks include return on equity, return on sales, return on investment capital, and net cash flow; and they might be applied to performance of the total company, a particular group, a division, or a strategic business unit. Market-based indicators include the five-year average, the trend of earnings per share, or the ratio of book value to market value, among others, which can be applied only to companywide performance. In other words, they cannot easily be disaggregated into organizational subunits unless the firm resorts to accounting measures such as ratios of R&D spending to assets, or new product development costs to assets, or softer measures such as the value of the amount of new management talent that is nurtured.

However, if compensation is considered as a lever of corporate restructuring, it should upset the status quo. The change-minded firm needs a set of milestones by which it and its CEO can be tracked. And with the agency theory, it is important to recognize that executives have informational superiority regarding the demands for change and the manner in which change is implemented. The choice of CEO, his or her previous track record, and his or her capacity for change become important foundations for selection. The choice of an adequate CEO, coupled with a well-designed compensation and control system, will enhance the likelihood that the restructuring will succeed and alleviate some of the agency problems. Consider a few applications.

ORGANIZATIONAL LIFE CYCLES

Corporations undergo certain transitions. It could be argued that they resemble living organisms with distinctive phases in their history. For example, any successful start-up will eventually grow beyond an entrepreneurial stage and require a CEO with a more formal, analytical, and even mechanistic management style than the founder who gave birth to the firm. The replacement of Steve Jobs by John Scully at Apple

Computer is a key example. Firms that downsize require a still different type of CEO with skills to right the changed company and renew its growth. The pay system that is associated with each mode, or instituted to ease the transition into a new stage, is likely to be different. The difference is accentuated by the measurement system that is required for the different stages. The downsizing firm should not employ entrepreneurial and "upsizing" criteria of performance. Thus, different types of people are necessary for managing change in different stages, and they are likely to respond to different measures of performance and related pay systems.

INTERNATIONAL DIFFERENCES

Restructuring is not limited to the United States. Non-American corporations like Deutsche Bank, Philips Electronics, and Victors have announced plans to restructure their operations. It should be noted, however, that executive pay holds different meanings in different countries. In some, pay is a complex element with symbolic, motivational, and social implications. A European CEO is less likely to be affected by a change in his or her compensation package than an American counterpart because European companies do not have a high variable pay component. Stock options, performance shares, and long-term incentive compensation systems might not have the same effects in France or Japan as in the United States. We need to ascertain the conditions under which a pay system will work in order to accomplish the changes necessary to restabilize an organization that is hit by market discontinuities. It is also important to understand the individual who must live with the compensation system.

Some executives may prefer deferred compensation as protection against unemployment, whereas others go for risky stock options. Many may even prefer nonfinancial rewards, such as time for family, sabbaticals, and a variety of other perks, compared with wealth-generating forms of compensation. Their tax situations may be important considerations in their choices. And when the firm is a multinational corporation, there is probably an even greater need to customize executive pay systems. Ideally, the executive compensation system should dovetail with the motivational makeup of the executive if it is to be most efficient.

Efficiency of executive compensation systems is but one issue. The reward system should also yield the kind of organizational change that is strategically desirable. Agency theory spells out the conditions under which advantageous change is most likely to occur. Stock options and stock appreciation rights, for example, may diminish risk-taking behavior and promote a temptation to hold the status quo. Other long-term incentive compensation tools such as phantom stocks and performance units may be too complex and unwieldy and, therefore, fail to provide incentives for executives to deliver the changes that are in the best interests of the shareholders. Such plans require thorough communication and coaching so that they are meaningful and appear significant. Indeed, communicating the goals of the pay plans is the major challenge to current executive compensation consulting and research. If we succeed in coming up with good answers, we may be able to design more effective systems that combine the preferences of individual executives with the strategic needs of his or her firm, especially when major change is required.

CONCLUSION

It is almost a truism to state that the only constant is change. Viable organizations must have the capacity to manage change, and executive compensation can be an important tool for steering, adjusting, and accelerating organizational responses. Since every organization is saddled with some degree of inertia, overcoming it is crucial to the execution of value-creating change. Pay systems can induce CEOs and other executives to make decisions that are consistent with the mandates of change. A compatible pay system, therefore, is one of the key levers that any change management program should include when restructuring of a firm is inevitable or desirable.

REFERENCES

Brindisi, L. "Creating Shareholder Value: A New Mission for Executive Compensation." Article in Booz Allen newsletter. New York: Booz Allen, 1984.

Chandler, A. *Strategy and Structure*. Cambridge, MA: MIT Press, 1962.

Child, J. "Organizational Structure, Environment and Performance: The Role of Strategic Choice." *Sociology* 6 (1972), pp. 1–22.

Dalton, D. R.; and I. F. Kesner. "Organizational Performance as an Antecedent of Inside/Outside Chief Executive Succession: An Empirical Assessment." *Academy of Management Journal* 28 (1984) pp. 749–62.

Fortune. "The Madness of Executive Compensation." *Fortune* 106 (12 July 1982), pp. 42–52.

Hall, D. J.; and M. A. Saias. "Strategy Follows Structure." *Strategic Management Journal* 1 (1980), pp. 149–63.

Healey, P. M. "The Effect of Bonus Schemes on Accounting Decisions." *Journal of Accounting and Economics* 3 (1985), pp. 85–107.

Jensen, M. C.; and W. H. Meckling. "Theory of the Firm: Managerial Behavior, Agency Costs, and Ownership Structure." *Journal of Financial Economics* 3 (1976), pp. 305–60.

Larcker, D. "The Association between Performance Plan Adoption and Corporate Capital Investment." *Journal of Accounting and Economics* 5 (1983), pp. 3–30.

March, J. G. "Notes on Ambiguity and Executive Compensation." *Scandinavian Journal of Management Studies,* August 1984, pp. 53–64.

McGuire, J. B.; and Th. Schneeweis. *Executive Compensation and Corporate Strategy*. Paper presented at the Strategic Management Society, Barcelona, Spain, 1985.

Murphy, K. "Corporate Performance and Managerial Remuneration: An Empirical Analysis," *Journal of Accounting and Economics* 7 (1985), pp. 11–42.

Pennings, J. M. "Executive Compensation Systems: Pay Follows Strategy or Strategy Follows Pay?" In *The Compensation Handbook*. Ed. M. Rock and L. Berger. New York: McGraw-Hill, 1991.

Pennings, J.M. "Strategic Reward Systems: A Cross National Comparison," *Journal of Management Studies* 23 (March 1993).

Pennings, J. M.; and D. T. Bussard. "Strategy, Control and Executive Compensation: Fitting the Incentive Plan to the Company," *Topics in Total Compensation* 1 (1989), pp. 101–112.

Rapoport, A. "Executive Incentives versus Corporate Growth," *Harvard Business Review* 56 (1978), pp. 81–88.

Rock, M.; and L. Berger. *The Compensation Handbook*. New York: McGraw-Hill, 1991.

Singh, H.; and F. Harianto. "Management-Board Relationships, Takeover Risk, and the Adoption of Golden Parachutes," *Academy of Management Journal* 32 (1989) pp. 7–24.

THE CHANGE MANAGERS

Leonard Abramson

Leonard Abramson has created a highly successful growth company and shaped an industry that is based on the measurement of behavior. In the case of the healthcare industry, the behavior is linked with the quality of the healthcare services provided by doctors and institutions. Through establishment of medical quality standards for healthcare providers, people are better able to make value-driven choices. Standards also foster a cost-conscious industry.

Although Abramson is an intuitive manager, his approach to alignment encompasses the successful principles of growth management. His charismatic style and high energy level are blended with his conviction that an executive must show continual vigilance, be close to the market place, and foster the highest level of fiscal responsibility. Abramson's style, energy, and value system have guided the rapid growth of his organization. He firmly believes that the cultural traits he demands from both himself and the rest of the people in the U.S. Healthcare organization have been the major drivers in the firm's breakneck expansion. And, not surprisingly, he expects them to lead U.S. Healthcare to its next generation of growth.

Continuing the company's growth is the firm's strongest change challenge, Abramson believes, and the characteristics he stresses add up to adaptiveness, which represents the major influence on the company's structure and organization. With adaptiveness in mind, Abramson believes that restrictive management processes (which he calls artifacts) such as organization charts, titles, memos, and meetings within a business day must be eliminated. Abramson exclaims, "It's gotten to the point where even the secretaries have meetings!"

Since growth requires decisiveness and speed, executives should interact directly with each other rather than through memos. According to Abramson, "Memos are signs of insecurity and mistrust. People write them to cover themselves. Furthermore, organization charts and titles create the illusion of authority; authority can only be earned by recognized accomplishments. Executives should not behave like they are in a box on a chart."

Abramson leaves no stone unturned in embedding these principles of nimbleness not only within the organization but also in the healthcare market at large. He supports his ideas and his power of persuasion with unassailable measurement systems that can keep him and other top executives cued in to any developing problems that could turn into change triggers with the potential clout to destabilize the company.

Even while operating a company without walls, Abramson makes sure that all key elements of alignment are in place. Attracting a corps of bright and hungry executive talents to U.S. Healthcare is key to Abramson's growth plan. The compensation program, therefore, is heavily equity oriented because, as Abramson puts it, "The only way people can truly be rich is if they are owners."

A growth company demands risk, so Abramson feels that he needs to take a chance on using less experienced people, giving them a chance both to succeed and to learn from their failures. This conviction leads him to conduct the "star search." This process is used to move younger people quickly through the organization. These people have technical competency and reflect the desired culture as well. In addition to promoting people who reflect the desired culture, U.S. Healthcare carefully uses the recruitment "gatekeeper" to ensure cultural continuity. The culture that Abramson wants to retain is entrepreneurial and risk taking. The success of U.S. Healthcare is found not only on the bottom line but also with the stability engendered by low turnover and high morale. Abramson believes that the best human resources for U.S.

Healthcare will come less from elite schools than from solid institutions drawing from working-class populations. These people will be both bright enough and hungry enough to power the company's growth.

People who work at U.S. Healthcare must have a passion to lead the business. Abramson believes that leadership or management skills are inborn, so U.S. Healthcare doesn't try to make everyone a leader or manager, but rather identifies those who display these skills and reinforces them through promotion, development, and training. These prospective leaders are self-motivated, but their intensity is enhanced by company reinforcement. Abramson believes that a true results-oriented and accomplished entrepreneur will always rise to the top. He states, "If you take away all of their current businesses, they would surface successfully again!"

On a daily basis, Abramson practices his belief in high CEO visibility by moving comfortably through all levels of the organization, directly interacting with people, and taking a hands-on approach in dealing with customers and vendors. This takes up much of his business day, and he considers it time well invested.

Continual feedback is a priceless benefit of the constant face-to-face communications that link the CEO with managers, employees, and external stakeholders. It enables Abramson to catch developing problems and potential change triggers on the spot and act decisively, usually through formation of a multifunctional team to devise a quick counterattack. It is these multifunctional teams that ensure that the company is able to respond continually and competitively to customers' requirements, thereby guaranteeing company growth.

Jeffrey Boetticher

Jeffrey Boetticher is the antithesis of the imperial CEO. The leader of Black Box Corporation, a manufacturer of connectivity products for the computer industry, stresses the empowerment of middle- and lower-level managers. The idea is to push decision making down the ranks as close to the market and customer base as possible. Flexibility and agility are premier qualities in Boetticher's approach toward what it takes to survive in his company's fast-moving, highly competitive industry, which demands almost constant change from its leading players.

Boetticher's nimble style paid dividends when he was confronted with an extraordinary change challenge immediately after taking the helm at Black Box, where he replaced the highly regarded CEO, E.R. (Gene) Yost, whose legacy was of spectacular and sustained performance. The challenge facing Boetticher was that, despite 13 straight years of increased sales and earnings during Yost's watch, Black Box was tiring. Its market was eroding suddenly under pressure from the nationwide recession, and Black Box was unable to respond because its internal structures were not responsively aligned with its markets. Even though the organizational structure would have run counter to Boetticher's managerial predilections in the most normal times, he had to move very carefully to streamline it. The system was, after all, reflective of the way the enormously popular Yost operated, and a radical shake-up—no matter how badly needed—risked morale problems.

Boetticher ultimately accomplished his goals by weaving the key principles of alignment into the sorely needed change program. Key elements included strong communications throughout the organization, use of innovative compensation techniques as incentives and yardsticks for changing employee behavior, and, ultimately, "down-the-line" empowerment.

The new Black Box CEO was the epitome of deliberate speed. He began by defining his own role in the process, a two-part function that called for him to manage the leadership transition and devise a new operating strategy to counter the market threats at the same time. He then had to communicate to all employees a clear-cut, well-integrated action plan that identified the change triggers taking place in the marketplace, explained how they were destabilizing the company, laid out the steps being taken to fight back, and emphasized how employees were to take part.

A believer that "the only thing that changes behavior is measurement," Boetticher not only recognized that other innovations were needed to follow up on the communications but also quickly installed the necessary support systems grouped around a new way of paying out rewards. The compensation system actually became a form of measurement itself with bonuses tightly linked to performance standards set following a strategic organization study ordered by Boetticher. In line with Boetticher's ideas about getting decisions and empowered people closest to the marketplace, Black Box moved incentive compensation from a focus on overall corporate success to the accomplishments of departments and teams in meeting goals and objectives that could better be controlled by the people themselves.

Improved customer service was targeted as one of the primary goals of the Boetticher-led approach to doing business. The warehouse fulfillment team bore much of the weight in this effort, extending the hours for taking orders and getting shipments out the same day with 99.4 percent accuracy. "Those employees earned 140 percent of their bonus and nothing else suffered as a result," Boetticher said.

In the final analysis Boetticher restructured his organization around processes and markets. This enabled the company to respond quickly and efficiently to customer requirements. This empowered organization was now ready to take on the competition.

Gary Fernandes

To manage change you must build bridges to the future. When General Motors acquired Electronic Data Systems (EDS) and founder H. Ross Perot left his management role with the company, the new organization was faced with the dual challenge of additional limitations on self-control and the visible loss in the market of its charismatic leader. At this juncture EDS' senior management dedicated itself to building a bridge to the future.

Gary Fernandes is a charismatic and elegant spokesperson for the change management process at EDS. His ability to visualize and graphically communicate complex concepts is remarkable. Although a product of the EDS system, the system that Fernandes currently represents is change. The largest personal change he faced was the shift to a broad integrative management role, which was necessary for reconciling the various forces of change within the organization. This meant that he could no longer focus on a single aspect of the business, but rather had to be attuned to the way in which the whole business was synchronized—the essence of change management.

Fernandes believes that the two greatest change triggers are success and failure. In the case of EDS, sustaining success was the greatest challenge. He states, "You have to reinvent yourself while you're going forward." The danger is always the narcotic effect of success. The railroads had great success but failed to reinvent themselves as transportation companies and move into automobiles and airplanes. IBM ignored the decline of their mainframe business and did not promote the PC and its networking to mainframes. The narcotic effect of success put these companies into the "zone of self-deception." In Fernandes' view, success, regardless of how exhilarating and rewarding it might be, contains the seeds of failure because it threatens to lull the organization into a smug, self-satisfied state buttressed by the false presumption that the lush days will last forever.

The current trends toward consensual leadership and team building must account for the necessity to have change agents or leaders who can help the company make the quantum leap. Fernandes believes, "Only an individual can see around corners. Only an individual can initiate a vision," but since execution requires high levels of cooperation, only a team can ensure effective implementation.

But companies, for example, must protect their change agents since "the nail that stands out frequently gets hammered." EDS' managers often have offered to take on unpleasant tasks, subjugating personal needs to those of the company. Fernandes believes that the willingness by change agents to accept these difficult assignments is the primary reason for EDS' capability to grow at a rapid pace. These homegrown change agents and managers have sufficient trust in the company to take personal and career risks.

Fernandes is a student of business history. He searches for answers to the question of sustaining growth over many generations of managers. In the past, EDS has been pulled along by its market growth. Its greatest strength has been its management's ability to comprehend and respond to its customer needs. Now in order to continue this process the company must build its own unique "bridge to the future." This means the institutionalization of customer responsiveness through a strong consultative orientation and the consensual development of market plans by business, industry, and geographic groups. In addition, the company is now measuring itself by growth in earnings as much as by sales growth and its new shared accountabilities for the market plan (common goals and measurements) will be rewarded through a new compensation system. The principles of alignment were observed, and EDS is highly likely to get its desired behavior changes (measurement + rewards = behavior change).

Another vehicle utilized by EDS to accomplish change was the creation of a new specialized consulting unit. This unit both services customers and drives the principles of client consulting to other business units. It serves a classic change agent function. The consulting unit will seize upon the need for continued customer vigilance and champion its cause until it has been fully embraced by the organization.

Fernandes believes that real change only happens in response to crisis. Since crisis can be internally or externally induced, the management of crisis can be a real tool of the change manager, particularly if it is used in advance of a real crisis. Fernandes believes that you either wait for the environment or create your own crisis.

All companies need a Jiminy Cricket (a change agent) on their shoulder to get people moving. What a company does not need is a Chicken Little who falsely claims that tragedy is imminent. Management must be vigilant since continual crisis generation will both create skepticism and burn out the organization.

No system can depend on a single individual or group of individuals to sustain change nor will processes all by themselves institutionalize change. Therefore, the solution is to combine the two. What does this mean in practical terms? In the case of EDS, it meant the use of the Gatekeeper process to select the type of hungry individuals who would both sustain growth and bring others like themselves into the company.

EDS, like Leonard Abramson's U.S. Healthcare, selected new employees from working-class backgrounds who had attended less-prestigious colleges, and who had a passion for success at all costs—they sought people who did not have the safety net of privilege. Both companies have established "The Culture of Hunger." EDS found that these employees gave the company the trust, loyalty, and energy it needed to fuel its growth. In addition, EDS sustained its change by utilizing another Gatekeeper extensively. Through internal promotion and transfer processes, EDS moved its most proficient change agents and managers around the company to create and manage crises. Eventually changes were forced to occur.

Like other powerful growth organizations, EDS' management shares the common vision of being the biggest and the best. EDS also believes that its management should not be isolated from its market and, therefore, its executives have a hands-on orientation when it comes to customer marketing and satisfaction. This serves the company well because it enables key decision makers to respond to market triggers more quickly.

In the past, EDS has been propelled by market demand reinforced by its own responsiveness. The company must now more carefully respond to a second change trigger—competition. To address this issue, EDS' management has dedicated itself to functional efficiencies, which means truly getting its alignment synchronized for competitive advantage. EDS' new credo is "get it right."

Another facilitator of change at EDS has been the continuous absorption of other companies. It has been a challenge well-met. The ongoing infusion of new cultures has been a constructive crisis leading to useful change, innovation, and invigoration.

EDS management has resolved that the company will have control of its own destiny, but this destiny must be driven by performance. Since all successful change requires a visionary, EDS' change will be well served by Gary Fernandes.

Paul Grunder

During the middle of the 1970s the corn wet milling industry began to undergo major structural changes that had the potential to affect the long-term survival of the Corn Products Company (CPC). The company had long been a leader in this industry, but it was slow to respond to a new competitive dynamic. An external agent was needed to create the dynamic changes required of this slumbering giant. Much like similar crises at Certainteed and AIRCO (described later), CPC International senior executives knew that a change agent was the only way to propel the company back to the forefront of the industry. Paul Grunder was selected to assume this very challenging role.

In both philosophy and style Grunder reflects the traits needed to set the pace for effective change in the most difficult situations. That is why he was tapped not once, but several times, to head an organization transformation. The most noteworthy and challenging was the redirection of CPC International's corn wet milling business at a point in the 1970s when the company was trapped among adverse market forces that threatened its survival.

True to the role as change agent, Grunder was sent by CPC to S.B. Penick Company, a pharmaceutical and specialty chemical subsidiary of CPC, to realign its businesses with its unique market requirements. Within two years the company had made key structural changes and was beginning to operate more smoothly. Simultaneously the corn wet milling business underwent a downturn, and a series of change triggers began to destabilize the Corn Products Company. Specifically, these changes involved the consolidation of customers in the paper, beverage, corrugator, and textile industry; the outsourcing of technology that had been previously owned on a proprietary basis by the corn wet millers; and increased competition from Archer-Daniels-Midland and Cargill.

All of this spelled trouble for Corn Products, which was still aligned to the old market situation that revolved around multiple customers, traditional competitors, and heavy technology investment. Paul Grunder was brought back from Penick to initiate the Corn Products rescue operation. This would not be an easy task because the culture was deeply rooted in the old, slow-moving corn wet milling philosophies and methods. Grunder would not have an easy road in front of him. President John F. Kennedy once said, "We didn't go to the moon because it was easy, but because it was hard." This was the type of philosophy that Grunder brought to his new assignment. Like other change agents, he was intuitively aware of the wisdom of the statement by EDS' Gary Fernandes, "The nail that stands out frequently gets hammered." Change agents in many ways embark on Kamikaze-like missions. He was ready for a tough flight.

Although Paul Grunder was a change agent, he had the additional skills necessary to be a change manager. Once his vision of restoring competitive levels had been articulated and communicated, he began the process of delivering on that vision. He already knew that the change triggers had forced a destabilization of the company and most likely moved it from an earn to a harvest mode. This shift would necessitate great changes in alignment and organizational behavior.

Like other senior executives in crisis modes, Grunder began to search for and select additional change agents and managers to place in key positions. This new cadre of committed, action-oriented people began to shape a new culture; they actively reinforced change-ready people and discouraged change resisters—those who thought it was business as usual. They made visible gestures to show that the executives understood the gravity of the issues such as eschewing bonuses, flying coach class, sharing secretaries, and closely managing their travel and entertainment expenses. Most of all, both Grunder and his managers worked hard at building a reservoir of trust. This was essential since rewards would come much later.

If the new alignment was actually to take place it was necessary to demonstrate and communicate to all employees that change was necessary. Grunder had to get Corn Products through the "zone of denial." People had to be convinced that this was not an overreaction to a business cycle change, for which no significant action was really required. Grunder cleverly relied on the mainstay change driver *Measurement* to create the desired behavior change. He and his new team communicated data that showed that Corn Products was no longer competitive within its industry.

Once broad acceptance of the crisis situation was prevalent, Grunder took the next step of maximizing employee involvement in the change process. He asked each of his managers to perform detailed analyses of competitors' performances and to develop a plan to bridge the gap between Corn Products processes and competitor processes. To ensure that these plans were not developed in isolation, Grunder created task forces to integrate action across all functions. He wanted to create "the tie breaking edge." Much like Wayne Smith at Airco, Grunder knew that competitive performance in a commodity business springs from execution. The task forces created white papers or change plans that they were empowered to implement. This empowerment fostered high levels of commitment to results and to change.

The "Thursday" letter was initiated to inform people regularly of what was going on. It also became an important management tool for sharing ideas that were working well in the implementation of change. Grunder's change principles are reflected in the acronym SOM—selection, organization, motivation. Change will be driven if the right people are selected, organized properly, and rewarded for self-motivated behavior. By applying these principles scrupulously Grunder was able to set the stage for a stronger future for Corn Products.

One of the important implementation lessons he learned was that the change process is actually facilitated by breaking down larger units into smaller units. This enabled decisions to be made closer to the marketplace. Another important lesson was that pricing in a commodity business is best handled outside of the sales force, where a more independent business management function can balance all cost decisions with market factors to determine product pricing. The pricing decision was at the core of making this business more profitable.

Ultimately Grunder drove the business toward achieving two criteria. The first was making the business competitive with industry leaders on a cost basis, and the second was achieving the same return on assets as the consumer division within CPC (Best Foods). The latter goal was necessary for the Corn Products unit to compete for the internal funds that would enable it to grow. Grunder believes, "If you don't get the right level of performance you won't get the right level of investment."

Paul Grunder got Corn Products moving again. The generation of change managers who he originally charged with making the transition to the dynamics of the new corn wet milling industry continued to grow the company effectively. A star graduate of the first class of business managers is the Chief Executive Officer of CPC International. Perhaps the most powerful legacy of the change agent is the transfer of the change mantle to like-minded individuals.

James L. "Rocky" Johnson

Rocky Johnson grew up in a telephone company. It is ironic that the product of a regulatory environment became one of its change managers when the AT&T break-up ushered in the era of competition in telecommunications.

When Johnson took over the reins as CEO of GTE, he inherited an assortment of unrelated businesses, each having a unique set of business characteristics and market effectiveness. The required move to a more competitive environment heightened the need for a full assessment of the overall market alignment of both the telecommunications and the noncommunications businesses.

Several years earlier the company had come to recognize that market conditions and investment requirements would force it to move out of its businesses in switching and transmission. Now the company began an extensive benchmarking program, called the Best Program, to establish the basis upon which the remaining part of the company could be reengineered. Clearly the change trigger of deregulation caused a major reexamination of alignment to market. The Best Program also set standards of expectation, thereby enabling people to adjust their organizational behavior with that of the most competitive practices in the industry.

Two salient factors emerged from this introspective process. The first focused on where growth would come from and the second on the mission of the organization. The conclusions reached were that growth opportunities were greatest in telecommunications (the company's core business) and that the greatest threat was in not responding to this challenge. Furthermore, noncommunications-related businesses would divert human, capital, and financial resources from meeting telecommunications' goals.

The solution, as clearly outlined in Professor Chandler's chapter, was to go back to basics. The company would devote its efforts to areas where it had the greatest competency. The mission of the organization, therefore, was to become a full line service provider of telecommunications services. From this mission came a key goal, which was to create a "seamless service" to customers. This meant that the company had to recognize and respond effectively to the rapid confluence of the wireless and wireline services. To be a viable force in telecommunications, the company had to offer both types of service.

To begin the mission reengineering process, GTE sold the remaining 50 percent of its interest in U.S. Sprint to United Telecom. This sale plus the divestment of the Lighting Products Group would enable the company to focus its efforts on building its communications services operations. GTE initiated this process by acquiring cellular companies.

In addition to entering into the wireless market, GTE began to recognize that its realignment should have a greater overseas focus. The company had prior experience in Canada and Latin America and determined that Third World countries were an area of growth potential. This became another area of concentration.

Before all of this could take place, however, the larger issue of cost effectiveness in telephone operations had to be addressed. The organization had a history of self-measurement clearly rooted in its plant manufacturing processes. The organization's challenge was to increase the quality of its services and simultaneously reduce its costs. Another measurement-based system called the *Winning Connection,* which set standards comparable to that of the best Bell operating units, was used to mold GTE operational behavior, and it yielded successful results.

The alignment process at GTE would not be complete without attacking the organization structure and adjusting its culture. The prior organization structure was created to handle a multidivisional, diverse collection of medium- to large-size businesses. The new structure was aimed at reducing cost and increasing communications between components of the organization. GTE now had fewer diverse businesses, and it consolidated the key telephone operations functions in one location. The consolidated and streamlined telephone operation unit further accelerated the reengineering effort.

Perhaps the greatest threat addressed by the change program at GTE was the need to move from a utility mind-set to one of a competitive orientation. To attack this dimension GTE regularly surveyed its employees to test their knowledge and satisfaction with existing programs as well as to test their readiness to respond to new initiatives. The results of these surveys helped the company structure its change program by identifying new employee requirements and adapting the programs to meet new needs.

Survey feedback was critical in the alignment, but a program called the *Power of 1* was most effective in communicating the company's near-crisis-level need to reduce its cost position. Employees were given the message that their long-term survival depended on a cost reduction strategy. Although certain individuals might lose or be forced to change jobs and careers, the vast majority of employees would benefit from the strategy. The crisis value of external data proved again to be an effective way to drive change, and it marshalled the support of the employees.

Strong change processes require strong change managers. Rocky Johnson believes future successful change managers will have high levels of interpersonal skills, strong logistical capabilities (ability to manage the alignment process), the capacity to take decisive action and prioritize needs, a demonstrated record of successful change, sufficient flexibility to let their people make mistakes, and the strength to convince people that change is needed.

Consistent with Johnson's beliefs, a survey of employees convinced GTE's executives that multidivisional and multifunctional management training was and would continue to be an important process for building a cadre of leaders. The company, therefore, proceeded to establish a centralized training facility to bring managers from all over the world to receive consistent company instruction in core competencies, values, beliefs, and teamwork. According to Rocky Johnson, "To create a culture of competitiveness you must continuously drive these core processes through teamwork." This is the most essential ingredient in achieving full alignment.

Donald Meads

Don Meads is a stickler for business ethics. Meads firmly believes that the well-run business rests on a strong ethical foundation and that true alignment of the organization cannot be accomplished if ethical principles are not in place.

Meads learned just how formidable his tenets were when he was handed the unenviable task of turning around the troubled building materials maker Certainteed Corp. in the mid-1970s. He helped lead them through a daunting restructuring that turned out to take a lot more time than first envisioned. Business ethics was not new to Meads when he was asked to take the helm at Certainteed. He had been an international business executive with an impeccable reputation gained largely as the CEO of International Basic Economy Corporation, a Rockefeller Family International concern. While on the international scene, he had bribes for business favors dangled in front of him, but he never gave in to temptation. For example, a local religious organization in Latin America offered to guarantee delivery of equipment to a nearby International Basic Economy Corporation installation for a $10,000 contribution, but was emphatically told the company did not make payoffs.

What made the job at Certainteed so difficult was not only that the organization was on the brink of financial disaster but also that it had a dysfunctional management. The company almost sank because it had lost a large sum of money in real estate development, which was an effort to integrate vertically forward from its building materials operations. Although the real estate unit and a related real estate investment trust were divested in the mid-1970s as a result of a combination of recession and surging interest rates, there also were serious questions about the capability of the real estate management to implement strategy. There were management difficulties in the main company as well.

Meads had to attack on several fronts at the same time and serve several constituencies. Radical surgery was performed immediately in excising the real estate development unit. This move was to stop cash hemorrhaging and convince creditors the firm was serious. Negotiating with bankers finally eased the financial pressures by leading to settlements on both the main company's debt and the debt of the beleaguered REIT.

Fortunately the main businesses—fiberglass insulation, roofing materials, PVC pipe—were healthy and prospered nicely after the recession slowed down. At the same time, Certainteed brought on stream, with superior results, an expensive plant in Texas that produced fiberglass reinforcements for a wide range of plastic products, such as auto parts. This was a quick contributor to results.

Meads got Certainteed back into the black and back on track within a year. He credits his adherence to strong ethics with playing a key role. While personally consumed in putting out the financial fires, Meads infused surviving managers with an ethical fire that matched his efforts to restore fiscal integrity. While he was shoring up the finances, his team was concentrating on operations. It was a deftly played simultaneous linkage that helped bring the company through and drove home the concept of "survivorship" throughout the company. Survivorship became both a value and a rallying point.

Although the Certainteed case was an extreme example, Meads says the successful reorganization proved that adherence to ethical principles is an important qualitative asset in an organization. But ethics are no less important for maintaining balance in the nontroubled company. Meads points out that "management by values" is essential in any organization stabilization program and that no change plan can be rewardingly implemented without a level of trust that starts at the top.

Joseph Neubauer

What is the best training ground for a change-driven CEO? In the view of ARA's Joseph Neubauer, it is working in executive positions in many different environments and preferably in a variety of staff and line jobs. The way Neubauer sees it, the diversity of skills and experiences and the seasoning of different contexts are essential to having the pervasive grasp and the quickness of mind to make the speedy decisions required to execute change management. In fact, Neubauer puts a premium on the rapid response, claiming that many future decisions must be made on experience-based judgments rather than long, detailed studies that may delay a nimble change process.

But Neubauer, who led a major overhaul of his diversified service company after joining it following a series of high-level posts at other organizations, points to other qualities that will be critical. "The new breed CEO," he states, will be characterized by a high-energy level, a passion for the job, and a willingness to touch base with all levels of the company consistently and easily." Moving about without the aid of intermediaries creates trust through consistent behavior, allows on-the-scene detection of disharmony and problems, and helps assemble the unfiltered information needed for major decisions.

In fact, Neubauer believes the CEO, much in the style of General George Patton, will be leading the charge in the future organization rather than its systems. However, much of this effort will be directed toward rallying the entire organization behind him or her by creating an air of collegiality. "That CEO," he said, "will help stabilize the organization in times of rapid change by clearly communicating mission and values from top to bottom; stressing a limited agenda of three to four items at a time, and having them change infrequently; and getting people to buy into his or her vision."

Neubauer put these managerial characteristics to work en masse when he directed ARA's transformation from a widely diversified collection of service companies managed almost separately by entrepreneurs to a more focused company centered on common themes. Financial systems were initially installed as linchpins. Improved feedback processes were installed to help the CEO better plan and control key activities, and the yardstick for performance measurement was significantly changed to return on assets from return on sales. Continuing the alignment theme, Neubauer moved to influence organizational behavior by forcing some elements of corporate cost into the operating units and then building his strategic measures into compensation decisions.

Finally, Neubauer initiated a study to examine the company's information flow so he could better understand the company's structure. Neubauer also developed companywide mission and values statements and set up more formal strategic and human resource planning to create a concept of a "family" with shared values.

Although Neubauer sees the CEO as having a critical position in managing the company—especially amid great change—he is also a firm advocate of empowering lower-level employees who can make more effective decisions because they are closer to the market. He further believes that the CEO should have frequent contact with customers, vendors, and employees. This combination of involvements, including the idea of "CEO selective intervention" to help people throughout the company reach important decisions, constitutes a widespread web for quickly recognizing change triggers from many directions.

Neubauer says that there must be a compact between employees and the company. The company must be a "good place to work," including high standards, fair and adequate compensation, business growth, and equitable treatment for all. The employee must perform in accordance with expectations. The CEO's contribution to the company includes a demonstration of integrity and honesty, ability to motivate people to share, and a constant show of respect for all. To do so, the CEO must also act decisively, stay continually informed, and act with consistency.

Stanley W. Silverman

To Stanley W. Silverman, an organization rewards its shareholders by creating value for its customers. Successful executives of the 1990s must create a culture that focuses on customer satisfaction so that the organization is able to meet or exceed the needs of the customer more effectively than its competition.

"An organization must respond to the business environment and competitive situation it faces," states Silverman. This was the key principle when Silverman's PQ Corporation reorganized in 1987. In this case, PQ acted as its own change trigger by responding to the changing global business environment in which it operated. Over the past 20 years, PQ has expanded from a North American–based commodity chemical company with $30 million in sales to a diversified, complex global organization operating in 17 countries, with revenues at the $400 million level.

PQ did the job by paying attention to principles of alignment and ensuring that operations, structure, culture, and reward systems were meshing with each other. PQ initially determined that overall it would remain in an "earn" (moderate growth) mode but change was needed to sustain that basic position because the company was running into forces such as globalized markets, more intensified competition, and changing customer requirements.

Structure was an early priority because of the pressure to change from an amalgam of small independent regional units into a worldwide integrated network. Three global businesses were established to cover markets, facilitate technology transfer, and emphasize synergy. Once structure was handled, PQ focused on its core principles. A statement encompassing mission, vision, and guiding values was drafted. The arduous process that led to developing this product ultimately succeeded because it was accomplished in a participative environment that helped encourage employee buy-in.

Interestingly, one of the most prized values that emerged was the philosophy of continuous quality improvement (CQI), which provided a rallying point during the change period, a goal for the revamped organization, a basis for measurement against competitors, and a business system pegged to customer satisfaction. This central value was later placed at the heart of the PQ compensation system and utilized as a motivator to change behavior.

During one of PQ's management retreats, the decision was made to form a multifunctional task force to develop a new performance appraisal system, which later was renamed the performance improvement system. This system is based on managers obtaining input from an employee's subordinates, peers, and internal customers that is then shared with the employee to help the individual become a more effective contributor and team member.

PQ emphasizes participative efforts in fostering other important dimensions of change. Meetings are multilevel, with people from the shop floor gathering with managers from different functions to reach change decisions. In a number of PQ's business units, plant operators are given discretionary authority in making capital investment decisions on projects which they feel will improve the operation of their plant. Moreover, individuals are given sufficient room to adapt techniques to their individual business situations, provided they adhere to such elements of the core culture as CQI, employee empowerment, and customer satisfaction.

Executives must lead the change process, according to Silverman. "Managers must also be leaders," he says, "and must articulate a vision throughout the work force; serve as a consistent role model for values; understand the strengths and weaknesses of the organization as well as the movements within the external market; maintain patience during the change process; and encourage managers to include all employees in the decision-making process."

Constant communication with employees, customers, and suppliers is critical both to understanding internal and external environments and to ensuring that the organization is in alignment. The right set of core values is critical to ensuring alignment. These core values include establishment of joint goals between manager and subordinate, dedication to the CQI philosophy, open communication among organization levels, and commitment to employee empowerment and customer satisfaction. But perhaps the most significant core value is placing corporate results ahead of individual and unit results. He states, "Stockholders are focused on maximizing corporate results, not those of individual operating units." The challenge is to maintain the perennial balancing act between corporate focus and individual initiative. Silverman thinks PQ has successfully walked the tightrope by aligning the company with the market, by establishing a strong culture, and then by aligning the internal parts. These successes have been achieved by paying for results and continuous improvement, by encouraging people from different functions and levels to form teams to improve the business process, and by empowering all employees to operate at the limits of their authority.

PQ Corp.'s move to change was driven by the changing business environment in which it operated. It evolved from a small, provincial U.S.-based company to a global powerhouse in 20 years. PQ was a virtual model of alignment in refitting the ship. The structural reorganization was keyed to deemphasizing independent strategic business units and creating three global businesses that were highly related and would maximize technology transfer among themselves. The culture was geared toward a participative, highly communicative mode that maximized commitment to PQ as a group. Compensation was harmonized with these other tenets to reward those who met their goals, exceeded customer needs, and were committed to the philosophy of continuous quality improvement.

Wayne Smith

Wayne Smith, Group Vice President of the UK–based BOC Group and head of Airco, its U.S. gases business, is the consummate adaptive change manager. As a prisoner of war in North Vietnam for 5½ years he learned to survive under the most adverse conditions. Many years later the spirit and endurance he needed to overcome this earlier hardship have been applied to setting the leadership standards necessary to drive Airco to be the best in its industry.

This change manager has much more than the enthusiasm of a leader; he has the organizing skill of a manager. Smith knew, because of his experience in Airco's commodity-driven business, that execution is the only real means of differentiation. However, execution without a vision has no energy to sustain itself. He decided, therefore, to mobilize his entire company to align itself with its customers. The vehicle he used was Total Quality Management.

Before reaching out to a Total Quality Management program Smith carefully applied the alignment process described in this book. He began by meeting with his managers to redefine the mission of the company and to identify past and future change triggers. His management team then began to examine the issues and implications of the change triggers and to formulate flexible action plans. An integral part of the new mission was a new focus on customer satisfaction on the part of every employee. The change driver was the measurement of employees in terms of how well they satisfied their customer's requirements.

It was apparent from the new mission and the derivative strategies that Airco's organization structure had to be realigned. Again, Airco focused on organizing to meet its customers' requirements. It dismantled its bulky network of strategic business units (SBUs) in favor of centralizing key functions, which is appropriate for an earn or harvest company—particularly one in a commodities industry. This constructive and simplified approach made it easier to focus attention on customer needs and to avoid the internal divisiveness characteristic of SBU competition.

One of Airco's immediate major challenges involved reconciling the compounding effects of assimilating 23 separate acquisitions during a declining economy while introducing a new mission and strategy into Airco's core business. Smith is a nimble manager, but he knew that he could surmount this obstacle only if he got everyone moving in lock step. If everyone marched in formation there was a greater chance of accomplishing the new mission.

The key to success would be in Airco's ability to execute its plans better than its competitors. Execution was defined more broadly than the efficient management of the value chain. It included the concept of value added. In some cases the process of solving customer problems meant helping them to use Airco's products more efficiently. Whereas the short-term effect of successfully helping to solve customers' problems could well have been to reduce Airco's market share, Smith was confident in his strategy and believed that his overall growth goal would be met by building customer confidence and attracting new business.

A bonafide winner, Smith next had to transfer this aura to the organization. To do this, he created a vision at the "Princeton Meeting." He and his managers built a five-year plan based on an environmental scan of change triggers and their impact on Airco's business. They reached a consensus on the prioritization of key issues.

The process forced them to discuss areas previously considered out-of-bounds for discussion. They set their sights on being more profitable than the industry average and on being recognized in the financial community as providing superior returns. To develop action plans, they identified (much like GTE) the success factors that characterized the best practices of their competitors. A conceptual breakthrough occurred when they decided that, to implement their plan, they must pay people to improve work, not just to work. This required the creation of a culture of performance, a culture that was easy to instill because fear and insecurity over the company's troublesome prospects served as strange allies of management in priming people for change.

What were these actual triggers of change?

- Customer servicing complaints.
- Weak competitive performance within the industry.
- A need for a culture better aligned with its market.

The TQM process was designed to align the company with its market by specifically addressing these issues. It created a set of self-directed techniques that reinforced the identification and solution of customer-driven issues throughout all levels and all functions of the company. The process is paying major dividends in satisfying the change triggers that were destabilizing the company.

Corporate values, strategies, and individual job requirements became integral parts of performance appraisal and selection processes. Special computerized management systems are being built to share the results of good ideas throughout the organization. One of the most creative behavior modification tools developed was survey feedback collected from superiors, peers, and subordinates. The surveys rated incumbents along key dimensions deemed to be critical to the company's success. Each employee could, therefore, adjust his or her behavior based on such feedback in line with the company's expectations.

Airco is striving to be a model of alignment driven by an executive who enjoys a history of the highest degree of success in braving adverse conditions.

Index

Other excellent resources available from Irwin Professional Publishing...

The Living Organization
Transforming Teams into Workplace Communities
John Nirenberg
Co-published with Pfeiffer & Co.
(300 pages)

Shows managers the next step after teams—a blueprint for transforming today's organizations from a management versus labor struggle into productive, cooperative, workplace communities.
ISBN 1-55623-943-2

A Manager's Guide to Globalization
Six Keys to Success in a Changing World
Stephen H. Rhinesmith
Co-published with the American Society for Training and Development
(240 pages)

Helps you understand and develop the keys to management success in an increasingly challenging international market. You'll discover how to develop a global competitiveness, manage complexity and organizational adaptability, lead multicultural teams, and enhance personal and organizational learning.
ISBN 1-55623-904-1

Power Vision
How to Unlock the Six Dimensions of Executive Potential
George W. Watts
(206 pages)

Shows how managers can exceed their career and life goals by viewing themselves honestly, capitalizing on their strengths, and overcoming their weaknesses. Also tells how to become a more effective manager who makes profitable and positive contributions to the company.
ISBN 1-55623-808-8

Available at fine bookstores and libraries everywhere.